The rough
YUGOS

=The=
rough
guides

Other available *Rough Guides* include:
**KENYA, TUNISIA, SPAIN, PORTUGAL, FRANCE,
GREECE, CRETE, YUGOSLAVIA, EASTERN EUROPE, CHINA,
MEXICO, PERU, PARIS, AMSTERDAM, NEW YORK,
SCANDINAVIA, BRITTANY & NORMANDY**
and
HALF THE EARTH: WOMEN'S EXPERIENCES OF TRAVEL
(with Pandora Press)
Forthcoming:
WEST AFRICA, BRAZIL, ITALY and **GERMANY**

Series Editor
MARK ELLINGHAM

The rough guide to
YUGOSLAVIA

Researched by
**MARTIN DUNFORD, JACK HOLLAND
AND JOHN MCGHIE**
Written and edited by
**MARTIN DUNFORD AND
JACK HOLLAND**

HARRAP
COLUMBUS
Rough
Guide

First published in 1985 and reprinted in 1986 and 1987 by
Routledge & Kegan Paul Ltd.

Reprinted in 1989
by Harrap Columbus Ltd,
19-23 Ludgate Hill,
London EC4M 7PD

Set in Linotron Helvetica and Sabon
by Input Typesetting Ltd, London
and printed in Great Britain
by The Guernsey Press Co. Ltd,
Guernsey, Channel Islands.

British Library Cataloguing in Publication Data
Dunford, Martin
    The rough guide to Yugoslavia
    1. Yugoslavia, 1981-
    I. Title. II. Holland, Jack 1959-. III. McGhie
    John. IV. Series
    914.97′0424

ISBN 0-7471-0095-0

Thanks to Eve and Chris, Igor and Milena, Ivo
Armenko (YTO London), Jasminka Stanojčić
(Tourist Ass. of Serbia), Marc Dubin, Mira, John
Hodgson, Sloboda Štetić and John Horton.

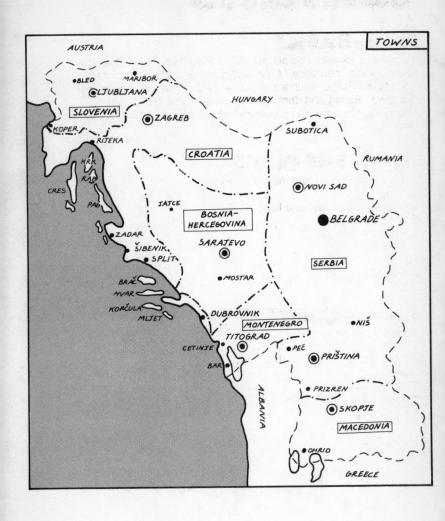

CONTENTS

This book is dedicated to the continuation of a free, non-aligned and socialist Yugoslavia

Part one
BASICS

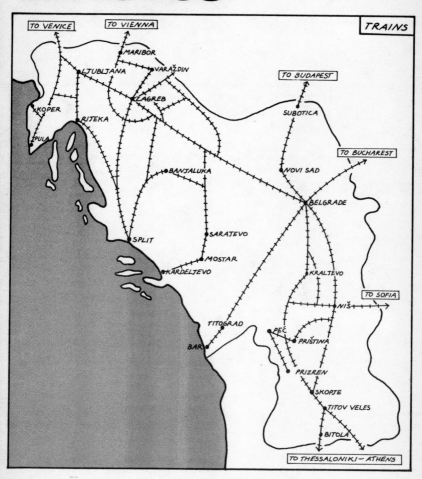

YUGOSLAVIA: WHERE TO GO AND WHEN

Most people think of Yugoslavia as one country; no Yugoslav ever does. Dominated by the Turks for 500 years, plundered by the Venetians for almost as long, Yugoslavia today sports a mixture of cultures and religions that were only welded into a working federation of south Slav republics by the experience of the last war. It's a poor country: agriculture sometimes seems stuck in the last century, wages are among the lowest in Europe and budget post-war rebuilding hasn't always been a success. But despite this, some fearsome economic problems and escalating inflation, each of the republics retains its identity and most people remain firmly loyal to the Yugoslav ideal.

Backpackers rarely spare Yugoslavia a second glance as they hurry down to Greece and 80 per cent of those who do holiday here are swallowed up by a handful of coastal resorts, making for a popular impression of the country that's far from the truth. Rather, the keyword is variety: the **Adriatic coast** is one of the most beautiful anywhere, and long enough to make avoiding touristed patches easy; targets include **Zadar, Split, Trogir** and relatively unexplored islands like **Rab** and **Korčula**; and once you've separated the town from its holidaymakers, **Dubrovnik** provides a just highspot. A few miles inland things change radically, and the influence of Turkey is clearly apparent. **Bosnia**, with **Sarajevo** as its focus, merges gently into the sweeping hills of **Serbia** and a clutch of medieval monasteries that lead ultimately to **Belgrade**, the capital, a drab city where many arrive but few want to stay. The rest of the country veers from the well-oiled formality of the north to **Kosovo's** restless Albanian community and the baking heat of **Macedonia**: really, the list is endless — see the **Chapter introductions** for more details.

None of this need prove expensive though. Generally things come cheaper south of a line drawn between Dubrovnik and Belgrade. With a careful eye on your **budget** you can get by on £6–£8 a day; for around £10–£12 a day you live very well. **Rooms** go for £4–£8 for a double and anywhere with even vague pretensions to tourism will have a stock. Still cheaper are the rooms in student halls, available in high season and an excellent way of finding above-average accommodation. Discovering Yugoslav **food** is possible without breaking the bank — a basic filling meal costs about £2 with wine, beer or heady spirits as cheap accompaniment. **Transport** is also inexpensive: buses are the way to travel, with routes forming a cobweb between villages and towns and ticket prices low — 1p for each kilometre is a fair allowance.

The **climate** follows two patterns: Mediterranean on the coast — warm summers, mild winters — and Continental inland — hot summers, cold winters. Come to the coast in July or August and you'll find almost everywhere full of tourists; arrive in May, early or late September and you lose almost all the crowds, just a little of the heat, and avoid

Average temperatures

	Jan.	Apr.	May	Jun.	Jul.	Aug.	Sept.	Oct.
Belgrade	0	9.5	17.8	20.5	22.7	22.8	18.9	13.3
Bled	0.3	6.7	17.2	21	23.3	23	21.7	16
Budva	8.6	13.9	17.4	21.7	23.9	24	21.1	17.2
Dubrovnik	8.3	13.4	17.8	22.2	25.6	25	22.3	17.8
Hvar	8.4	13.9	18.3	22.8	25	25	22.5	18.3
Ljubljana	1	9.2	14.3	17.5	19.5	18.5	14.4	9.7
Opatija	5.5	10	16.7	21.2	23.8	24	20.6	15
Sarajevo	−1.6	9.6	14.7	18	19.2	17.8	13.4	8.8
Split	7.5	12.8	18.9	23.9	26.7	26.1	22.8	16.7

Remember that these are average temperatures — midday figures are considerably higher.
To convert to Fahrenheit: as a quick reference 10°C = 50°F; 15°C = 59°F; 20°C = 68°F; 25°C = 77°F.

high season prices. The interior, particularly Bosnia-Hercogovina and Macedonia, can swelter in summer – you need to start your travels early to avoid the midday meltdown. But from late autumn onwards the mountain ranges of Montenegro and Serbia become impassable; in the north the skiing season starts from November on. Roughly speaking, it's warmer the further south you go – check the climate table for details.

GETTING THERE

By air

JAT – Yugoslav airlines – fly daily from London to Zagreb, Ljubljana and Belgrade, in season to Pula, Split and Dubrovnik, and there are regular internal flights linking all of Yugoslavia's major airports; in addition JAT lay on summer-season services from Manchester/Birmingham to Pula/Dubrovnik. **Scheduled returns** start at around £250 (for an Apex fare), though out of season it's possible to get seats a lot cheaper; further information from JAT, 201 Regent Street, London W1 (01 734 6252). For some reason cheap **charter flights** are hard to come by: scour the pages of the London magazines *LAM* and *Time Out,* or the Sunday newspapers, and you may be lucky. The *Yugoslav Travel Club* (98A Garratt Lane, London SW17; 01 767 3528) or *Pan Adriatic Travel* (11 Lower John Street, London W1: 01 439 1916) regularly offer bargain flights to all the regional capitals and coastal cities, with average prices currently hovering around £150 return. A further option, and a viable one, is to take a cheap **charter to NE Italy** (Venice, Verona, Trieste) and pick up a train from there – Italian trains are unbelievably cheap and travelling time from Venice to, say, Ljubljana is just six hours.

Package tours, especially if you book at the last minute, can work out good value if you're after a straight no-nonsense rest and don't mind being tied to one city. Just be sure to avoid the really nastily built-up stretches in Istria, one or two of the islands (notably Krk and Hvar) and the resorts around Dubrovnik. *Pan Adriatic* (address above) and *Yugotours* (both 150 Regent Street, London W1; 01 734 7321) between them offer a complete range, which as well as straight sun-and-sea breaks includes mountain/spa holidays, monastery tours, wine and gourmet splurges and plenty more; bear in mind that Yugotours give a 30 per cent discount on late bookings. Package holidays do mean you're committed to a 2/3 week stay, but if you want to stop on it's sometimes possible – if a little naughty – to sell the return half of your ticket.

From the USA *Pan-Am* fly daily in summer from New York and/ or Chicago to Belgrade and Dubrovnik; standard APEX fares start at around $860 return. **Canadians** can take the frequent direct summer services to Belgrade from Toronto for an APEX return price of Canadian $1500. From **Australia**, there are two flights a week between Sydney and Belgrade; an excursion ticket – valid for a year and the only one available – costs a little in excess of Australian $2000. All of these, however, are scheduled fares, and it's possible to pick up cheap charters for a great deal less, providing you're not too choosy about where you fly to – Athens, Venice, Istanbul are credible alternatives. Hunt through the travel pages of the Sunday newspapers and you may strike lucky.

By rail

Those under 26 have two choices: either invest in an **Inter-Rail** pass (currently stable at £115), which entitles the holder to a month's free travel on all European trains and half-price reductions in Britain and on Sealink services; or, for about the same price, buy a **Transalpino** ticket to Belgrade or any other large Yugoslav city and take it from there. Inter-Rail (on sale at BR stations) is a good idea if you're planning a grand tour, but you won't get to use it much in Yugoslavia – railways there are just about the slowest and most frustrating way of getting around. Transalpino tickets are valid for two months and you can stop off on the way – available from most travel agents or their main London office at 71/75 Buckingham Palace Road, SW1 (01 834 6283). **Ordinary returns**, if you're 26 or over, come considerably more expensive; London-Belgrade is presently about £170 return and rising.

By coach

The cheapest and probably the most uncomfortable way of getting to Yugoslavia is by **long-distance coach**. A number of companies – *Olympic* is one (01 837 9141) but again the pages of *LAM* and *Time Out* are the best source of bargains – offer high season daily departures, theoretically taking around 36 hours to Zagreb, 40–odd to Belgrade, at a cost of about £35 one-way. One thing is important: most are Greek cowboy operators, hurtling down the central Yugoslav highway en route to Athens. The Yugoslav authorities don't allow their own nationals to travel on these buses and don't sanction them stopping, so you should be prepared for being surreptitiously dumped several miles outside the city of your choice; this is likely to happen even if you've been told otherwise beforehand. Other than that it's not as horrendous a journey as you might think; certainly at around half the journey time it's considerably less wearing than the notorious Greek run, and plentiful supplies of food and drink and/or German currency can make it almost enjoyable.

By Adriatic ferry

Yugoslavia is well connected to Italy and Greece by a series of regular *ferries* – a painless if relatively expensive way to arrive in the country. Yugoslavia's national line, *Jadrolinija,* operates a main coastal service (calling at all major ports) that extends to **Corfu** and **Igoumenitsa** roughly three times weekly in summer – deck-passenger fares work out between £16–£25 depending on where you decide to get off. Major peak season links with Italy include **Venice** to **Split** once a week (15 hours; £30); **Rimini** to **Zadar** once a week (12 hours; £20); **Ancona** to **Split** (10 hours; £25); **Pescara** to **Split** 5 times a week (8 hours; £25); **Bari** to **Dubrovnik** 4 times a week (9 hours; £25). Remember that there are other permutations on this, and just about all the important Yugoslav and Italian ports are connected one way or another. Pick up an *Adriatica* ferries leaflet for times, rates and frequencies – and see the **Travel Details** listings at the end of each coastal chapter.

By Car – driving or hitching

Either way, **driving** isn't the most relaxing way of getting to Yugoslavia. It's a long haul, and unless you take it easy you're likely to need a couple of days to recover when you arrive. There are **three possible routes**, and the one you take will really depend on what you want to see on the way. Probably the least direct is down through France to Lyon, and across northern Italy. More obvious – and periodically more spectacular – are the German autoroutes, over the Alps and east from there; or through Germany to Munich, and south via Austria into Slovenia. For each of these routes allow a minimum of 30 hours (London-Ljubljana). A slower, more expensive, but infinitely more luxurious approach is possible using the Adriatic ferries (see above.)

Those **hitching** have the same three options, but don't forget that lifts in France can be hopelessly infrequent – a better bet are the trucks doing the Germany-Greece run. If you do have problems, be content with reaching Italy and, if your budget will allow, taking a train the rest of the way. Italian trains come cheap: Ventimiglia to Rijeka – a 24-hour journey – costs marginally over £15.

RED TAPE AND VISAS

British, Irish and Dutch citizens need only a full passport to enter Yugoslavia: with a British Visitor's Passport you'll be given a tourist pass on arrival (this is valid for 90 days and can't be extended). If you hold a US, Canadian, New Zealand or Australian passport you'll need a **visa**, from either a Yugoslav embassy or consulate. It is possible to get one at the border but this takes time, costs money and is officially discouraged. If you're unlucky enough to hold a South African passport you can't come into the country at all.

On entry you're given a stamp that entitles you to a stay of 90 days; usually the date stamp on these is illegible and if you leave with a recently expired visa no one's going to kick up a fuss. If you do need an **extension** the choice is between hopping over the border for a fresh stamp or facing the bureaucracy of the local *Obstinski Sup*, who'll expect good reasons for wanting to prolong your visit; find them by asking at your accommodation or the local *milicija*. Arrive by train and an official may take your passport and disappear. Don't panic: you'll get it back later, stamped with the visa. While in the country you're required to carry your passport at all times – see p. 8.

HEALTH AND INSURANCE

There are no **innoculations** required for travel in Yugoslavia, but an up-to-date typhoid booster is a good idea, especially if you're heading for out-of-the-way places where food preparations aren't going to be over-careful. Along these lines, diarrhoea is likely to be the most immediate and unavoidable problem, so stock up on *Diocalm* or get a prescription for *Lomotil* before you leave.

Minor complaints can be solved at the chemist or *Apoteka* (in Croatian *Ljekarna*), where you'll also find other essentials and often someone who speaks English. In larger towns there's usually a **24–hour Apoteka** – see our listings. For serious medical attention phone 94 for the ambulance service; outpatient and casualty wards are found in most **hospitals** or *Bolnica*, signposted by a white H on a blue background. The local Turist Biro will put you on to English-speaking doctors. On production of a passport British citizens get **free medical care** automatically in health centres and hospitals, along with free emergency treatment, though you have to pay a small amount for any drugs or medicines supplied. Citizens of most other countries have to pay for both treatment and medicines, something that makes it a good idea to take out some form of **medical insurance** before you leave. This is also worth considering if you're British: policies are available from travel agents or insurance brokers (the latter are often cheaper) at about £12 a month, and not only cover health costs but also loss, theft or damage to your gear. You'll need receipts for any medicines you buy, and if you have anything stolen an official statement from the nearest police station. Usually this is straightforward, but out in the wilds you may find the local *milicija* unable or unwilling to comprehend your request: if so wait and register your loss in the nearest large town.

CASH AND COMMUNICATIONS

Yugoslav **currency** is *dinars,* and comes in notes of 10, 20, 50, 100, 500, and 1000 din, with coins of 1, 2, 5 and 10 din and fiddly little things called *para*: 100 para = 1 din. The currency was pepped up a few years ago by introducing the 'new' dinar (often seen abbreviated to **ND**) but you occasionally still hear prices in old dinar, easily recognisable by the string of noughts on the end – divide by 100 to get the new dinar figure.

Currently you're only allowed to buy 1500 din outside Yugoslavia. All British banks will supply this, but you may have to order a week or two in advance. Exchange rates are slightly worse in Yugoslavia, so you gain by taking more than your legal allowance. It's also prohibited to take more than 1500 in dinars out of the country; don't save them to spend at airports or frontiers when you leave – duty-free shops only take Sterling, US dollars, Deutschmarks and other strong currencies. If you're coming from Greece it's worth knowing that 1000 drachma notes aren't exchangeable anywhere in Yugoslavia.

You may be offered **black market rates** for your hard cash. Whether you take advantage of this is really up to you but it's worth bearing three things in mind: first, it's strictly illegal; second you'll have to change a lot of cash before it becomes worthwhile taking the risk; third, assume that anyone who approaches you (rather than vice versa) is out to fleece you – a cynical but realistic rule when it comes to money.

Best way of carrying the bulk of your money is in **Travellers' Cheques**, available from any British bank whether or not you have an account, and cashable in almost all Yugoslav banks, tourist offices, post offices and most major stores. Even on a Sunday you should always be able to find somewhere to change money, and don't worry about getting ripped off – exchange rates are standard across the country. Most banks will accept **Eurocheque** cards with your chequebook or (for some British banks) a Eurochequebook. You get the same rate as Travellers' Cheques but commission charges vary. When you cash these or Travellers' Cheques you may be offered **Dinar Cheques**, for which you're given a 10 per cent bonus; though theoretically welcomed in shops, restaurants, etc, the scheme has proved unpopular, and many proprietors are reticent about taking them. Where they're most useful is in paying larger bills (e.g. at a hotel or for an expensive purchase where it's clearly stated they'll be accepted). Don't hang on to your used ones either – they're notoriously difficult to re-exchange.

Credit cards like *Amex*, *Diners* and *Visa* can also be used to get cash, but only in major banks (*Jugobanka* is one) and larger cities – there don't seem to be any hard and fast rules on this, so don't depend on your card. In the north and on the coast cards are readily accepted in larger shops, stores and more upmarket restaurants.

Main **post offices** (*pošta*) are open 0700–1900 Monday to Saturday with occasional Sunday hours in larger cities. Most kiosks sell stamps (*marka*) too – more convenient and you avoid lengthy queuing. Every post office has a **poste restante** desk; to claim your mail produce your passport and a small fee. To send a letter to Yugoslavia poste restante, address the envelope 'Poste Restante, Pošta', followed by the name of the town.

Post offices are also the best places to make **phone calls**: queue at the relevant desk, state the number you want and either take the call or dial it from a booth. International phone boxes vary in design but usually take 2, 5, and 10 din coins; only whole unused coins are returned, and there's no cheap rate. To dial a number first use the international code then the STD (area) code omitting the initial O. Some main international codes: **Britain** 99 44; **Irish Republic** 99 353; **Australia** only through operator (901); **United States and Canada** 99 1. **Internal calls** seem to be dogged with problems – 15 minutes' repeated dialling is not uncommon.
See "Inflation", p.17

INFORMATION AND MAPS

We've printed plans of all the major Yugoslav cities and just about anywhere else you're likely to need one. To supplement these pick up a reasonably detailed map of the country from the **Yugoslav Tourist Office** – along with their country-wide lists of campsites, private rooms and hotels, ferry time-tables and glossy leaflets on every region of Yugoslavia. Major branches include:

GREAT BRITAIN AND IRELAND 143 Regent Street, London W1 (01 734 5243).
USA AND CANADA 630 Fifth Avenue, New York NY 10020 (757 2801).
HOLLAND Vijzelstraat 4, Amsterdam (220 484).
SWEDEN Slojdgatan 10, Box 7004, 10386 Stockholm 40 (101 993).
DENMARK Trommesalen 2, 1614 Copenhagen V (116 300)

In Yugoslavia itself, most places of any size have some kind of office where you can pick up information and in most cases town plans; these tend to be organised locally and trade under a variety of titles – **Turist Biro** is the most common. Addresses are listed in the guide. **Travel agents** are also thick on the ground – useful for changing money and buying train, bus or *Inex Adria* plane tickets. *Putnik*, *Kompas* and *Atlas* are three of the biggest, but names change regionally.

One thing you'll probably want to get before leaving is a large-scale **road map** of the country: *Michelin* produce the best value and most widely available one; alternatives include those by *Kummerley and Frey* or *Hallwag* – though both are considerably more expensive. If you're keeping to the coast *The Yugoslav Coast* series of five booklets (published by the Yugoslav Lexicographical Institute and only available in Yugoslavia) are a good buy, with detailed maps, excellent town plans and lots of in-depth – if rather dated – information on every town, village and monument bar none. For **hikers and climbers** the only region mapped in any sort of detail is the Julian Alps: two 1:50,000 walking maps cover the east and west alps and for real enthusiasts, there are 1:20,000 charts of the Triglav and Bohinj districts. If you're doing any serious climbing/walking in the area Robin Collomb's *Alpine Guide* should prove indispensable – published by West Col at £5.25. Almost everything listed here can be readily obtained from *Stanfords* (12–14 Long Acre, London WC2; 01 836 1321) or *McCarta Ltd* (122 Kings Cross Road, London WC1; 01 278 8278).

POLICE, TROUBLE AND SEXUAL HARASSMENT

Known as **Milicija**, МИЛИЦИА , Yugoslav police are generally easygoing and helpful. Stations are signposted and **92** is the universal emergency number.

Since tourism took off on the coast Yugoslavia has lost much of its false image as a dour land where the police wait to pounce on erring visitors. A few points should be followed though. Don't take photos of military camps or installations (usually indicated by a no-photography symbol), railway stations or bridges – if you're caught you may lose your film, possibly your camera, and go through all the attendant hassles. Carry your **passport** at all times – checking your entry visa often gives a bored cop something to do. At all official accommodation your passport is exchanged for a daily *potvrda*, a date-stamped card that should be carried until you get your passport back, and then held on to until you leave the country. Really, it's usually the case that the police are being no more than mildly inquisitive if they stop you; be polite and friendly and ructions won't arise. If you do find yourself in trouble, wait till you can explain things to someone in English – a few ill-chosen words in a foreign language can cause a lot of misunderstanding. **Consulates** vary in the amount of help they can offer – all the British consulate will do is repatriate you, and only then very begrudgingly; they'll never – repeat never – give you any cash if you've run out or been ripped off. You'll find addresses in our town listings.

Women travelling alone can expect to bump into familiar southern Mediterranean machismo almost everywhere – usually nothing too sinister but irritating enough at the best of times. Attitudes vary from the package-holiday mentality of the Adriatic resorts, where all women travellers on their own are automatically regarded as 'available', to the Islamic and more backward regions inland where woman as peasant chattel is still the accepted order of things. A suitably firm response should be enough to cope with most situations.

GETTING AROUND

Buses and trains
Most people get around by **bus**: it's absurdly cheap and a comprehensive system of services takes you just about everywhere you may conceivably want to go. Yugoslavia's workers' collective system has spawned numerous bus companies, each of which decides its own routes. Sometimes this means duplication and occasionally confusion, but buses generally leave on time, undaunted by distance or natural barriers, and at rates everyone can afford. Keep in mind that prices can vary, and journeys cost proportionately less in the poorer east of the country than in Slovenia and on the coast. You can normally pay on the bus but not always, so wherever possible buy a ticket in advance – and book a seat; use the phrase *ima reservati?* to do so. Always remember too, which company you're travelling with – your ticket won't be valid for any other. On top of the price of your ticket there's usually a small charge for stashing your gear in the hold.

Trains, on the other hand, are most definitely not the way to travel: aside from the north-west the system is scant (and it's getting more so) and other than on really major routes can be excruciatingly slow, stopping and starting every few minutes, waiting hours in dead-end stations for no obvious reason. Fares don't differ greatly from buses, and if anything a train-ride will cost you slightly more. Given the nature of the country, however, any train journeys you do make are likely to be some of the most spectacular you ever will – certainly you have plenty of time to admire the views. One jaunt not to be missed is the **Belgrade-Bar line**, a feat of engineering of which the Yugoslavs are especially proud, linking coast and capital by way of some of the most wild and enchanting mountain scenery the country has to offer. Rail timings and routes are listed in *Vozni Red*, the nationwide train timetable – the purchase of which should provoke stares of amused disbelief. Always buy tickets in advance, preferably from an authorised travel agent – the queues tend to be shorter than at stations.

Driving and hitching
Driving in Yugoslavia gives obvious advantages, but you need to keep your wits about you. Though there's been a vast improvement in recent years, motorways are only just adequate and lesser roads can be poorly surfaced, often breaking up into tracks when you make a side turn. This can make driving a dodgy business: the **Adriatic Highway** (*Jadranska Magistrala*), the main coastal route, is littered with wrecks, and overtaking seems to be done with little concern for personal safety or regard for what's heading the other way. In the countryside, wandering farm animals and inattentive horses and carts create problems all of their own.

As far as documentation goes you'll need to carry **registration** (which must be in your own name), **driving licence** (international driving licences aren't officially required for Yugoslavia, but are for many neighbouring countries) and an international **green card** of insurance, available from your insurance agent for a small fee. Rules of the road include driving on the right and speed limits of 120kph on motorways, 100kph on other roads, 80 or 60kph in towns; speeding **fines** must be paid on the spot. Though I've yet to see any Yugoslav driver wearing one, **seatbelts** are compulsory for driver and front seat passenger; kids under 12 and drunks must sit in the back; drunks sitting behind the wheel face a steep fine and/or imprisonment. A warning triangle should always be carried and if you pass an **accident** you're legally required to stop and offer assistance. Petrol coupons known as *Bons* are needed for **fuel**: buy them at home from the YTO or on the border and get a 10 per cent discount – otherwise they're available from Turist Biros, some hotels and the Yugoslav motoring organisation **AMSJ**, but *never* from filling stations. Remember that you *have to* pay for coupons in foreign currency; unused coupons can be cashed at the border. It's also worth noting that stations aren't as frequent as elsewhere in western Europe – remember to fill up if you're heading into the wilds. Should you break down the national **SPI** organisation will tow you away and arrange repairs, though it doesn't come cheap – nationwide phone **987**.

Car hire is expensive – prices start at around £300 a week – but you can cut costs considerably by organising things before you leave. Book a car with *Pan Adriatic Travel* (address on p. 4) and you'll pay less than half that. Those renting by the day will find city hire firms in our listings.

By European standards **taxis** are an inexpensive way of getting around town, especially if you're in a group. Make sure the driver starts the meter straight away or you'll face overcharging.

Hitching, just about anywhere in the country, is dire: only on out-of-the-way rural roads is there any chance of lifts, and then they'll just be short local hops. Long lifts are out – Yugoslavs tend to regard foreign hitchhikers with a certain amount of suspicion – and the main coast road is so jam-packed with holiday traffic throughout the season as to not make it worth the bother. Anyway, given the prices of buses and trains it shouldn't be necessary to hitch too often.

Ferries
Jadrolinja, the main Yugoslav ferry operator, is inexpensive, punctual and extremely comprehensive. Just about every inhabited island is connected by some kind of regular ferry, and there's a main coastal service which cruises up and down the coast from **Rijeka** to **Bar** throughout the summer season, calling at most of the major ports and islands –

Dubrovnik, Korčula, Split, Zadar and Rab among them. This runs almost daily in season, dropping to twice a week in the winter months; about half the ferries go on to **Corfu** and **Igoumenitsa** in Greece. You're allowed **stopovers** of up to a week provided you have your ticket validated when you leave the boat. It's worth remembering, though, that this is much the most expensive way of doing the coast, and if money's an issue you'd be better off using the local island ferries (which tend to be cheaper) and covering longer distances by bus. Local island ferry times are listed in the back of *Vozni Red* (the national rail timetable); timetables for the main coastal ferry and international services are free from tourist offices. Tickets are sold from the Jadrolinija offices on every quayside shortly before departure – though for local services it's nearly always possible to buy them on board. On journeys of any length I'd advise taking food and drink, as what you get on board is pricey and frequently inedible. For frequencies and journey-times again see the Travel Details section at the end of the coastal chapters.

Flights

JAT and a domestic operator, **Inex Adria**, between them link Yugoslavia's major cities in a broad network of domestic flights – surprisingly cheap, extremely reliable, and in a country where bus and train travel can be so wearingly slow, a really positive alternative; often the price of a flight can work out little more than the price of a standard rail fare. Planes are best for long strides from the coast up to Belgrade or Zagreb, or for getting to the north from the south of the country quickly: Dubrovnik to Belgrade, for example, works out at just £15 at present, which for a journey that would take the best part of a day and a night by bus and cost around half as much, isn't at all bad. If you do consider taking a plane make sure of your seat well in advance – low fares mean high demand, and many flights are booked solid in high season. Schedules are available from *JAT* offices, which you can find in most large towns. *Inex Adria* offer a less extensive choice of destinations, but often undercut *JAT* prices; tickets and times from travel agents.

SLEEPING

Finding a **bed** for the night isn't always as cheap as you might imagine: for all kinds of accommodation two rates are levelled – one for Yugoslavs, another for foreigners – and foreigners' (*stranci*) prices can be several times what the natives pay. For easy reference the Yugoslav tourist board produce annual foreigners' price lists for hotels, private rooms and campsites nationwide – prices are always quoted in dollars or deutschmarks and, while in the main correct, shouldn't be taken too literally. One point to remember: for each night's accommodation you'll be given a coupon. Keep it: if you get stopped by the police it's your only proof you're not sleeping rough or in unlicensed rooms – both illegal.

Yugoslav **hotels** are classifed A to D; prices are strictly controlled and must be displayed clearly in your room, so there's little chance of getting fleeced. While you can forget the top two categories, C/D hotels work out quite reasonably, costing around £10–£12 a night for a double room; facilities will be basic – with a shared bathroom and infrequent supplies of hot water – but standards are generally kept well above the acceptable minimum.

Private rooms (*sobe*) are a cheaper, more intimate option: well organised and reliable, they set you back around £4–£8 for a double (single rooms are hard to come by and can cost almost as much) though it's as well to realise they can disappear at an alarming rate in season. Plentiful on the coast and in the touristed areas of Serbia, Montenegro and Macedonia, they're normally available from the local tourist office, though it's often wiser to try and hunt them down independently (some houses display signs) – that way you avoid tourist office surcharges which on the coast can be up to 30 per cent extra for a stay of less than four nights. Failing that, people sometimes tout rooms at bus stations: if offered a bed like this it's often a good idea to take it, just as long as you firmly ascertain the price (bargain strenuously) and location beforehand. Tourist offices also deal in apartments, which can work out slightly cheaper if there's a group of you – a four-person apartment goes for, very roughly, £16 a night.

Youth Hostels (*FSJ Doms*) do exist in Yugoslavia – in larger cities, seaside resorts and more popular places inland – but they're nearly always full in season, and unless you book in advance there's little chance of a bed. To use them you technically need a YHA card (available from the *YHA Shop*, 14 Southampton Street, London WC1; age 16–21 £3, 21 and over £5), though most places seem ready to waive that rule and let you in for a few extra dinars. Prices vary quite a lot, from £2 a head in Zagreb to over £4 in Belgrade, and curfews are common and strictly observed – you'll rarely be let in after midnight. A cheap and excellent alternative are the **Studentski Doms**, student dormitories that let out beds to travellers in July and August for between £2 and £3 pp. It's a service largely laid on for young Yugoslavs, and the people who run it sometimes find it hard to get their heads round the idea of foreigners using it – why aren't they staying in the best hotels? –

but persevere, it's one of the best bargains going. There are Studentski Doms in most university cities, principally Skopje, Sarajevo, Split, Zagreb and Ljubljana.

Campsites (*autocamps*) keep to the coast and the mountainous areas of Slovenia and tend to be huge hyper affairs, with space for thousands of trailers, masses of facilities, shops and minigolf. Smaller, less regimented sites do exist but they're few and far between, and most of the inland republics don't have many of any description; for a comprehensive list see the YTO *Camping* booklet. Again prices vary, but they're rarely excessive and those on foot shouldn't find themselves paying more than about £2 a head all-in; if you've a car or motorbike, or you're pulling a caravan, add about £1 to that. **Camping rough** is illegal and the police don't take too kindly to those they catch in the act; tentative suggestions are indicated in the guide, but all things considered it's not worth taking the risk unless you have to.

EATING AND DRINKING

Yugoslav **food** tends to the cheap and filling, with a distinctive variety of dishes that is one of the country's most enduring hangovers from its complex and divided past. There are plenty of national dishes – kebabs and goulash are well-known examples – but it's a cuisine spiced everywhere with regional variation: in Slovenia and northern Croatia the Austrian influence prevails in starchy main courses and strudels; the Vojvodina sports a clear Hungarian strain; and in Serbia, Bosnia and Macedonia menus are tinged with Turkish dishes. Dalmatia and Istria remain firmly fishy – squid is cheap and delicious all the way down the coast – with plentiful pasta pointing to the long-standing Italian connection. Again prices vary from region to region: north of an invisible line between Dubrovnik and Belgrade things are likely to be more expensive; south – in Serbia and Macedonia – food gets markedly cheaper. Either way, even on the breadline you should be able to afford to eat in all but the really classy or heavily touristed restaurants.

Foremost among Yugoslav **snacks** is the *burek*, a greasy Turkish-style pastry on which the nation starts the day: sold at street kiosks in the mornings, it comes most commonly with cheese (*sa sirom*) and sporadically with meat (*sa mesom*) or apple (*sa jabukam*). Other fast foods include the ubiquitous *ćevapčići* – little wads of spiced minced meat served in groups of ten with copious sticks of spring onion, *pljeskavica* (beefburger basically) and *ražnjići* (shish kebab). All three are available from street stalls but you'll find them equally on restaurant menus country-wide. If you've a burning preference for things greasy buy your own bread and cheese/meat from the supermarket or, failing that, get the delicatessen counter to make you up a sandwich – they normally oblige.

Sit-down eating comes more expensive – though not much. Cheapest places to do it are a *Krčma* (a small snack-bar) or, more usually, an *Express Restaurant*, self-service and often with much the same food as far chintzier places at a fraction of the price. One word of advice: don't be put off by the dried-up look of most of the dishes laid out for display – just ask for a fresh plateful, the quality's usually pretty good. More common is the *Gostiona* or simple *Restoran*, where you can get a straight two-course meal for a little over £2 with wine. Regular starters include *Pršut* (Dalmatian smoked ham), delicious but expensive, a rich array of different broths, and *Čorba*, a thick soup imported from Turkey many moons ago and now found mainly in the eastern reaches of the country – with bread, a meal in itself. Meat dishes predominate on the main course, beef, pork and veal mainly, garnished with incendiary peppers and tomato/onion sauces. Whatever you choose, it'll invariably come with a handful of chips; to which you can add a couple of side salads for all to dig in. **Vegetarians** are going to have a hard time: other than a number of aubergine/pepper based dishes from Bosnia there's precious little to tempt the palate – vegetarian restaurants as such don't exist at all and the dubious delights of Yugoslav pizzas form the only alternative.

For sweeter teeth there's Yugoslav ice cream, which enjoys a popularity

Basics

Hleb (Serb), *Kruh* (Croat)	Bread	*Voće*	Fruit
Puter/Maslac	Butter	*Jogurt*	Yogurt
Sir	Cheese	*Šećer*	Sugar
Meso	Meat	*So*	Salt
Riba	Fish	*Biber*	Pepper
Jaje	Eggs	*Ulje*	Oil
Povrće	Vegetables	*Sirće*	Vinegar

Soups and starters

Juha	Soup (broth)	*Pašteta*	Pâté
Čorba	Thick soup	*Riblja čorba*	Fish soup
Boršč	Borshch (Beetroot soup)	*Juha od povrća*	Vegetable soup
		Pileća juha	Chicken soup
Govedja juha sa jajem	Beef soup with egg	*Burek*	Cheese pastry
		Pršut	Smoked ham

Meat and poultry

Govedjina	Beef	*Teletina*	Veal
Svinjetina	Pork	*Piletina*	Chicken
Šunka	Ham	*Jagnjetina*	Lamb
Ovčetina	Mutton	*Slanina*	Bacon
Kobasice	Sausages	*Džigerica*	Liver
Ćufte	Meatballs	*Gulaš*	Goulash
Ćulbastija	Grilled veal or pork with pepper and onions		
Ćevapčići	Spiced minced meat rolls		
Pljeskavica	Beefburger		
Ražnjići	Shish kebab		
Musaka	Layers of minced meat and aubergine		
Djuveč	Lamb or pork casserole with rice and tomatoes		
Punjene Paprike	Peppers stuffed with minced meat and tomato		
Sarma	Cabbage leaves stuffed with minced meat and rice		
Mučkalice	Steak in a rich pepper sauce		
Pasticada	Beef with dumplings		

Fish

Barbun	Red mullet	*Skampi*	Scampi
Lignji	Squid	*Pastrmka*	Trout
Zubatac	Bream	*Bakalar*	Cod
Sardela	Sardines	*Skuša*	Mackerel
Tunj	Tuna	*Skoljka*	Mussels

here on a par with Italy – every street corner has its *Slastičarnica* (ice cream parlours that also sell soft drinks, *burek*, cakes, yogurt, etc) dolloping out a kaleidoscopic range of flavours; a *kugla* is a scoop, *kornet* a cone. Cakes and pastries too are serious stuff for your average Yugoslav: they differ quite considerably from region to region – *strudels* to the north, Turkish *baklava* in the east, *palačinken* or crèpes just about nationwide – but all enjoy a characteristic Balkan sweetness and richness. **Coffee** comes Turkish inland, expresso or capucino on the coast; **tea** is normally served straight (with milk is '*sa mleko*', with lemon '*sa limun*') and though rarely more than a teabag dunked in hot water, can be very good.

Yugoslav wines are consistently good and ridiculously cheap, drunk by the *dva deci* (2/10 litre), if you're just tasting, *pola litra* (½) or *litro* (1/1) – ask for a *flaša* if you want a bottle. Local plonk (*domače vino*) costs around £1 in a restaurant, less if bought from a supermarket, and in Slovenia, Croatia and parts of northern Serbia – the more established wine-growing areas – it's rare you get anything undrinkable. Of

---

Vegetables

(Prženi) Krompir	(Fried) Potatoes	*Beli Luk*	Garlic
Pomfrit	Chips	*Gljive/Šampinjons*	Mushrooms
Kupus	Cabbage	*Krastavac*	Gherkins
Kukuruz	Corn on the Cob	*Pasulj*	Beans
Paprike	Green peppers	*Grašak*	Peas
Paradajz	Tomatoes	*Salata*	Salad
Pirinač/Riza	Rice	*Zelena salata*	Green salad
Luk	Onion	*Mešana salata*	Mixed salad

Terms

Doručak	Breakfast	*Kuvano*	Boiled
Ručak	Lunch	*Na rostilju*	Grilled
Večera	Dinner	*Peceno*	Roast
Przeno	Fried	*Vruće/Hladno*	Hot/Cold

Cheese, desserts, fruit

Kajmak	Curd cheese	*Gibanica*	Rich fruit cake
Vlasić	Mild sheep's cheese from Bosnia	*Narandza*	Oranges
		Limun	Lemon
Paški Sir	Hard strong cheese from Pag	*Breskve*	Peaches
		Kruške	Pears
Baklava	Turkish pastry with syrup	*Šljive*	Plums
		Ananas	Pineapple
Palačinken	Crèpes	*Grožđje*	Grapes
Strudla	Strudel	*Dinja*	Melon
Sladoled	Ice cream	*Kompot*	Stewed fruit

Drinks

(Mineralni) Voda	(Mineral) Water	*Vino*	Wine
Mleko	Milk	*Crno Vino*	Red wine
Kafa	Coffee	*Bijelo Vino*	White wine
Turska Kava	Turkish coffee	*Slatko*	Sweet
Čaj	Tea	*Oporo*	Dry
Voćni Sok	Fruit Juice	*Spricer*	White wine with soda/mineral water
Rakija	Spirits		
Pivo	Beer	*Živeli*	Cheers!

worldwide and Sainsbury's fame are the Slovenian *Rizlings* – *Laski* (delicate, verging on the sweet) and *Renski* – drier, less fruity and, in my opinion, much the better of the two. Dalmatian wines range from crisp dry whites – *Kastelet, Grk, Pošip* – to dark, heady reds like *Dingač* (from the Pelješac peninsula) and *Plavac* from Primosten; *Prošek* is a sweet dessert wine, best, they say, from Rab, but really almost universal. Istrian wines are excellent too – try *Semion*, a bone-dry white, or *Teran*, a light, fresh red. A popular drink is *Spricer*, wine with soda or fizzy mineral water – delicious and refreshing in the heat of the day; you can buy it by the glass or simply ask for a jug of water with your wine.

Drinking is mainly done in a *Kafana*, unpretentious places that serve both soft and alchoholic drinks; more upmarket is a bar or *konoba* – dimly-lit young peoples' haunts, more expensive, with loud music and standing room only.

Beer comes by the half litre bottle; when you ask for it make it clear you want the local brew (*domače*), otherwise you may find yourself paying over the odds for imported Scandinavian brands; really, the Yugoslav stuff is just as good – light, thirst-quenching and deceptively strong. Early morning your fellow-drinkers may be starting the day on a down-in-one dose of strong **spirit** (*rakija*) – common practice just about everywhere. There's a strikingly complete array: best known is *Šljivovica*, a sharp clear brandy made from plums; *Prepečenica* is a double-strength version. *Vinjak* is the blanket term for locally-produced French-style cognac, generally a little more expensive and smoother than Šljivovica but varying greatly from brand to brand – *Rubin* and *Slovin* are my favourites but there are cheaper, rougher varieties. Well known too is *Maraskino* – from Zadar – a velvety smooth, very sweet cherry liqueur; alright if you like that kind of thing. *Mastika* is widely drunk, distilled from mastic resin and a flavoursome dash of firewater not unlike Greek ouzo; and finally *Lozavača*, a mind-frying spirit they drink on the coast instead of Šljivovica. All of these are worryingly cheap: very broadly £1 a bottle from the supermarket, 20p a glass in a bar; home-distilled stuff on market stalls comes even cheaper – that's if you're adventurous enough to try it.

FESTIVALS, MUSIC AND DANCE

Yugoslavia has some excellent **festivals**, usually in the summer and often centred around the more beautiful towns and buildings. Most important of these is the **Dubrovnik Festival** running from 10 July to 25 August, a first-rate series of concerts ballet and drama played against a backdrop of historical settings.

Ohrid's Summer Festival is not nearly so prestigious, but still worth catching between 12 July and 20 August – concerts are held in the old churches and the *Balkan Festival of Folk Music and Dance* finds a venue in Ohrid's fortress. **Struga**, nearby, hosts a **Poetry Festival** at the end of August – an event usually attended by poets of international repute. Also worth looking out for: **Zagreb's** great **Folklore Festival** in late July, another international event; **Ljubljana's Jazz Festival** in mid-June; **Zadar's** concerts in St Donat's Church and **Sibenik's** concerts in the Cathedral, both in July and August; and, from mid-July to mid-August, **Split's Summer Festival**, a mixed bag of music, opera, ballet and folklore happenings.

In addition to these, there are a host of other **events**, including some specifically tourist-geared, and designed to slot into holiday packages, 'Peasant' weddings are most common, mass ceremonies in full costume – you come across them in **Plitvice** in the last week of May, **Ljubljana** in late June, **Bohinj** in mid-July and, or more seriously, at **Galičnik** in the second week of July. Ancient customs and ceremonies abound: each Thursday between May and September in **Korčula** the *Moreška* sword dances take place, lively and colourful dance theatre from the C16th. **Sinj's** *Alka*, a furious joust-like competition, takes place on 15 August, and **Ptuj's** *Kurenti Processions*, weird ceremonies dating from pre-Christian times, take to the streets in late February-early March. Exact times and venues can be found in local tourist offices.

Most of the country's grassroots

musical tradition has been sacrificed to cassettes of Michael Jackson and Frankie, but folk singing and dancing continues in pockets in all regions. Whenever you chance upon a wedding or saints' day celebration there's bound to be much festivity; even the performances put on by the tourist board are much less formal – and much more enjoyable – than you might imagine. Until this century the majority of Yugoslavia's peoples were illiterate. History was handed down in the oral tradition through songs of great exploits: the battle of Kosovo and the doings of folk heroes were recounted in epic poems, often thousands of verses long, memorised by troubadours known as **Guslari** from the single-stringed *gusla* on which they accompanied themselves. Though originally found everywhere, today you're only likely to hear spontaneous performances in the remoter villages of Serbia, Montenegro and Macedonia. Contemporary traditional music echoes the influence of Turkey, especially in the south: fast-running codas on wind instruments, notes rising in quarter tones. In Bosnia-Hercegovina old Turkish songs of unrequited love (supposedly sung in walled gardens by young girls eager to attract lovers) called **Sevdalinka** are frequent, and, if you can find the uncommercialised variety, hauntingly beautiful. Listen too for rousing **Partisan songs**, often delivered by ex-fighters at the end of a boozy night's reminiscing.

Dancing provided easy entertainment in previous centuries, and though supplanted by TV and disco it's been part of the folk idiom for so long that it's quick to resurface at any celebration. The **kolo** (*oro* in Macedonia) is almost the national dance: simply a linking of hands and moving slowly in a line or circle, it has myriad permutations and complexities, and though often accompanied by Turkish-style music, the leader of the *kolo* clenches his right fist behind his back – symbol of secret defiance against Turkish rule. In each region, practically in each village, the *kolo* developed along individual lines, often for a specific purpose: for as well as celebration the *kolo* was danced to ward off evil spirits, to bring fertility to a newly-married couple, to bless the sowing of a spring crop or celebrate the harvest.

The best place to find music and dance nearest the original is **Macedonia**: Macedonians seem to burst into song at the slightest excuse, and dancing is an inevitable accompaniment to an evening's drinking. Express any interest and you'll be dragged in: before you fall over remember that, for the Macedonians, to dance well is a sign of honour.

CHURCHES, MOSQUES AND MUSEUMS

Yugoslavia's mixture of Orthodox, Catholic and Muslim faiths provides a good variety of places of worship to explore; and while freedom of religious belief is guaranteed by law, each of the faiths has experienced a waning of worship – today it's mostly the old who fill the churches and mosques.

The ancient **Serbian-Orthodox** churches and monasteries especially have lost much of their monastic function and are open to visitors – though you'll find that the tradition of building them in the most beautiful and ancient places has left many inaccessible today. In the medieval church elaborate **frescoes** formed an aid to worship, depicting biblical stories and fierce portraits of patron saints. You'll find an in-depth account of churches and their art in the Contexts section (see p. 230) and indi-vidual monasteries are described throughout the guide.

Catholic churches keep to Slovenia and Croatia. Built during the Venetian occupation, those on the coast follow trends then current in Italy – scaled-down Romanesque and Gothic churches are one of the delights of the Adriatic, and everywhere you go Venetian-Gothic campanili dominate the skyline. Slovenia's churches went up when the Baroque style was in full swing – hence the churches dotted around the north don't pull any decorative punches.

Turkish domination of the Balkans means that **mosques** are clustered around the country, though you'll find the greatest concentrations in Bosnia, Kosovo and Macedonia. The basic layout of a mosque is a carpet-covered square with a *mihrab* cut into the eastern end facing Mecca; from this niche the *imam* or priest leads the congregation in prayer, the women grouped behind the men on a balcony or behind a low balustrade. Occasionally you'll hear the *muezzin* singing the *ezan* or call to prayer from a minaret, though these days it's more usually relayed by loudspeaker. The Islamic faith prohibits reproduction of the human form, with the result that the richest mosques are covered in passages from the Koran and non-figurative decoration of tiles and ornamented plaster. Normally it's only this and the size that distinguishes one mosque from the next. Visitors are allowed in major mosques but expected to observe certain proprieties: shoes should be removed before entering, women cover their heads, and you'll often be asked to leave a small donation.

Yugoslavia's **museums** all too often go for collections of quantity rather than quality, and exclusively Serbo-Croat labelling doesn't help matters. Generally speaking you'll find three main types: a **Narodni Musej** or national museum refers to an archaeological/ethnographic collection gathered from around the republic; each republic usually has several such museums. A **Gradski (Mestni) Musej** or town museum gives an account of a town's history through artefacts, fine art and photos. **Liberation Museums** proliferate in almost every town and village, each relating the history of the last war with reference to that particular area. They vary greatly in quality, layout and accessibility but you should certainly see at least one – the

best are in Belgrade and Sarajevo. Designed as much for didactic impact as historical record – you often pass crocodiles of schoolkids gawping at photos of Nazi atrocities – they are meant as a constant reminder of Partisan sacrifices in the war years.

After the war Yugoslavia laid heavy emphasis on the social function of art, initially giving rise to dreary and poorly executed themes of Socialist Realism. Subsequent artists have expanded these techniques to encompass more liberal and experimental styles, but much of what you find in modern galleries tends to be heavily derivative. Modern and Contemporary collections are normally housed in separate galleries: sadly most of these too are unremarkable, watered-down imitations of what was going on elsewhere in Europe at the time. To find something you enjoy you'll need to be very selective. **Naïve art**, however, has become a peculiarly Yugoslav development, formally encouraged by the state and the country's major post-war movement. You'll see work by Generalić and Kovačić, the best-known of the artists, scattered around the galleries, and at its best in Zagreb.

Opening times of museums and galleries vary greatly, but as a rough rule close on Mondays, sometimes Sundays, and open 0900/1000–1200/1300, and a couple or more afternoons 1600/1700–1800/1900. Ticket costs are negligible, but can often be halved by flashing a valid ISIC card. Full opening hours for each museum are detailed in the guide.

OTHER THINGS

CAMPING GAS Cartouches for the smallest camping stoves are nigh impossible to find anywhere in Yugoslavia. Bring your own supply or a large-cylinder stove.

CIGARETTES Turkish-type tobaccos grown in Macedonia and Serbia make for some flavoursome cigarettes. My favourites were the red *Drina*, and *57*, a little stronger, are also popular.

CONTACTS *British-Yugoslav Society*, 121 Marsham Street, London SW1 (01 828 2762). Triannual journal, short courses in Serbo-Croat, lectures and access to cheap flights and holidays. Annual membership £7.

CONTRACEPTIVES Heathen-looking condoms are sold in kiosks, less openly so in Catholic areas. The Pill is available without prescription from most chemists.
EMERGENCIES Countrywide, the numbers to phone for Police and Ambulance are respectively 92 and 94. The breakdown number for the Yugoslav motoring organisation (AMSJ) is 987.

FILMS Domestic colour films are poor quality, imported ones expensive, so stock up before you leave. Bear in mind that you're only officially allowed to import 5 colour films.

GAY LIFE No real 'scene' as such, and the fact that homosexuality is illegal in all but two of the republics – Slovenia and Croatia – means that places to make contacts are few and usually outdoors. What gay life there is predominates in Ljubljana and the more cosmopolitan coastal resorts – Rab and Poreč among them.

LAUNDRY Launderettes don't exist, and you're confined to utilising your landlady's sink or washing machine (in private rooms) or getting it done in your hotel – an expensive business.

MEDIA British and American **newspapers** are easier to find than they were but still only tend to appear in larger coastal resorts and, infrequently, the northern capitals. For the record *Borba* is the party voice, on sale nationwide and supplemented by the Cyrillic ПОЛИТИКА and myriad regional newspapers – *Delo* in Slovenia, *Slobodna Dalmacija* on the coast, *Rilindja* in Kosovo are just a few. *Yugoslav Life* is the sole English-language organ, published monthly by the national news agency and unspeakably dull. For **radio**, you can pick up the *BBC World Service* on 13–49m short wave throughout the day; *Radio Yugoslavia* broadcast daily news in English at 1530, 1830, 2000 and 2215 – short wave 31.9, 41.44 and 49.18m. The regional capitals also put out regular English-language bulletins, most of which are listed in the guide.

NATURISM A Big Thing in Yugoslavia, and long officially encouraged in an attempt to open up the country to the West and dispel all myths of socialist puritanism. Every resort has its official naturist beach – denoted by the initials FKK – and stripping off in secluded places is rarely frowned upon. The biggest naturist campsite is at Vrsar in Istria; others are scattered up and down the entire coast.

PUBLIC HOLIDAYS Almost all shops, offices and banks, along with many museums, are closed nationwide on the following days: 2 January; 1 and 2 May; 4 July (Partisan Day); 29 and 30 November (Republic Day). Each of the republics celebrates the Day of its Uprising in 1941 with a holiday: Serbia 7 July; Montenegro 13 July; Slovenia 22 July; Croatia and Bosnia-Hercegovina 22 July; Macedonia 2 August and 11 October.

RAZORS Time was when you could pay your hotel bills in Yugoslavia with a few packets of Gillette razorblades: even today the domestic brands are pretty useless and twin bladers a rarity – best bring your own. As an alternative, getting a shave at a barber's isn't expensive and is wonderfully luxurious.

SHOPS AND OPENING HOURS Big city stores and supermarkets have taken to western ways by opening 0800–2000 (*Non-Stop* they proclaim), Saturdays 0800–1500. In smaller places and as you head south shops tend to follow the tradition of early morning and late afternoon hours – roughly 0700–1200 and 1700–2000. Markets kick off at around 0530, banking hours are 0700–1900, Saturdays 0700–1300 but can vary locally; post offices open 0700–1900 Monday-Saturday with varying Sunday hours in big cities.

SKIING Yugoslavia's ski resorts offer all the amenities of neighbouring Austria and Italy at a fraction of the cost. The major resorts lie in the north-west around Kranjska Gora, and in the Olympic left-overs at Sarajevo; here and just about everywhere the local tourist biro will hire out equipment and sell bargain 'Season Tickets' for ski-lifts, etc.

TAMPAX Only sporadically available from chemists and large city department stores, so it's a good idea to bring supplies.

TIME One hour ahead of GMT and BST.

INFLATION ALERT!

Bear in mind that when this book was researched prices were relatively stable in Yugoslavia, since when inflation has soared to somewhere in excess of 200 per cent. We've tried to avoid quoting prices wherever possible; if you do see a price, treat it as past history.

A GLOSSARY OF TERMS

APSE Semi-circular recess at the altar end of a church.

BAN One-time military governor of Slavonia, Croatia and parts of Hungary.

BASILICA Church with nave, aisles and clerestory, based on Roman-style building.

BEG Minor official in the Ottoman empire.

BEZISTAN Turkish covered market.

BORA Chill, intense north-easterly wind that blows across the north Adriatic coast.

BYZANTINE EMPIRE Ruled much of the southern part of Yugoslavia from Byzantium (Istanbul) from the 7th to 12th centuries.

ČARŠIJA Bazaar.

CESTA Northern word for a street.

ČETNIKS Military group led by Mihailović in WW2; initially fighting against Axis powers, they expended most of their later energies on the Partisans, tacitly supported by German and Italian troops.

CIBORIUM Canopy fixed over an altar; often decorated.

CLERESTORY Arcade of windows in the upper storey of a church.

DECUMANUS Central street of a Roman town or garrison.

DZAMIJA Mosque.

EXONARTHEX Short porch before the narthex of a church.

EZAN Islamic call to prayer, sung by the *muezzin* from a minaret.

GRAD Name given to central part of a town: e.g. *Stari Grad* – Old Town, *Donji Grad* – Lower Town, *Gornji Grad* – Upper Town.

HAMMAM Turkish baths, today often converted into galleries, restaurants, etc.

HAN Hostelry, usually small, once used by travellers on trade routes.

ICONOSTASIS Decorated screen in Orthodox church containing tiers of icons that separates sanctuary from nave and priest from congregation during Eucharist.

IMAM Approximate Islamic equivalent of a Christian Priest (Islam has no clergy).

JANISSARY Soldier of the Sultan's personal guard, often taken from Christian family as a child and brought up as Muslim. In the later years of the Ottoman empire they became a dangerous religious/military autonomous power.

KARST Name given to typical scenery of a limestone region: landscape is generally bare, with disappearing rivers, gorges, caverns, etc.

KOLO 'Walking dance', often performed at weddings and celebrations.

KONAK Turkish-style villa.

KORSO Often the main social event of a town, the *Korso* generally happens early in the evening: crowds of people stroll between two roughly fixed points, meeting and chatting in a casual procession that can involve most of the town. The further south you go, the better attended the *Korso*.

KUĆA House.

LOGGIA Covered area on the side of a building, often arcaded.

LUKA Harbour.

MIHRAB Niche in the wall of a mosque indicating the direction of Mecca and prayer.

MINBAR Pulpit from which imam delivers 'lesson' at Friday prayers.

MINARET Slim tower attached to mosque from which *muezzin* gives *ezan* – the call to prayer.

MUEZZIN Singer who delivers call to prayer.

NAOS Innermost part of an Orthodox church, lying below the central cupola and in front of the iconostasis.

NARTHEX Entrance hall of Orthodox church, often decorated with frescoes on secular subjects.

OBALA Broad street, normally facing sea.

OTTOMAN EMPIRE Turkish empire which ruled most of Yugoslavia (except Slovenia and the coast) from the 14th to 19th centuries.

PARTISANS Guerilla groups instrumental in liberating Yugoslavia from Axis powers in WW2. Led by Josip Broz Tito, their Communist organisation founded the post-war Socialist Federation of Yugoslavia.

PASHA High-ranking official of the Ottoman empire.

PATRIARCHATE Controlling office of a see of the Orthodox church.

PERISTYLE Colonnade surrounding a court or building.

PUT Road.

PUTTI Small sculpted cherubim used as decoration in a church.

RAYAH Subject class of Ottoman colonies.

ŠETALIŠTE Boulevard.

STOLNICA Cathedral.

SVET Saint, such as Sveti Stefan – Saint Stephen. Abbreviated Sv.

TRG or POLJANA Square; *Trg Bratsva i Jedinstva* – Square of Brotherhood and Unity.

TURBE Small mausoleum of a Turkish dignitary, usually found near a mosque.

ULICA Street, often named after Partisan hero, such as Ul. Ive Lola Ribar.

USKOKS Piratical group that terrorised the northern Adriatic in the late 16th century.

USTAŠE Croatian Fascist group led by Ante Pavelić; during WW2 they fought alongside Italians, committing many atrocities against the civilian Serb population.

VIZIER Below the Sultan, the most important official in the Ottoman empire.

Part two
THE GUIDE

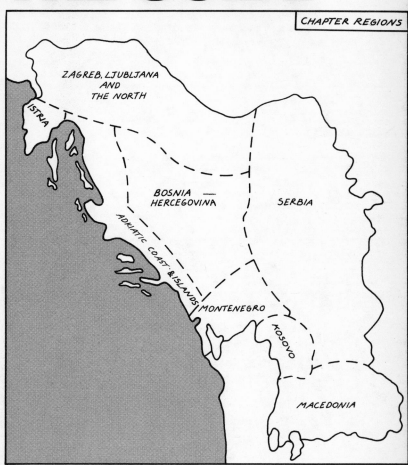

ISTRIA

ZAGREB, LJUBLJANA
AND
THE NORTH

BOSNIA —
HERCEGOVINA

SERBIA

ADRIATIC COAST & ISLANDS

MONTENEGRO

KOSOVO

MACEDONIA

Chapter one
LJUBLJANA, ZAGREB AND THE NORTH

Arriving by road or rail, **the North** – a serviceable label for the stretch of land that takes in most of Slovenia and the top of Croatia – is the first most people see of Yugoslavia. Initially **Slovenia** doesn't seem that different from north Italy or Austria – yet historically and culturally the Slovenes are a people apart. While much of the rest of the country was under Turkish control, what's now Slovenia was a feudal state administered by Austrian and German overlords, eventually becoming part of the Austro-Hungarian empire. The Slovenes absorbed the culture of their captors but transmitted a strong sense of regional identity through the Slovene language, which was (and is) rather different from Serbo-Croat. Economically and industrially the North is streets ahead of the rest of the country, with higher wages, lower unemployment and a more westernised lifestyle. That they're rich uncle to the other republics leads to disgruntled complaints from Slovenes in particular that their taxes are channelled into development programmes for poorer areas like Kosovo, but by and large things progress smoothly and efficiently here: shops are well stocked, tourist facilities are excellent, and buying a bus ticket isn't the ugly scrap often experienced elsewhere. The political scene is the most liberal in the country and, on a more superficial level, the North is the most 'civilised' part of Yugoslavia – and hence a useful introduction to the country as a whole.

The landscape is as varied as it is beautiful: along the Austrian border the **Julian Alps** provide stunning mountain scenery and skiing at a fraction of Austrian or Swiss prices; further south is the brittle Karst, dry limestone land riddled with spectacular caves like those at **Postojna**. Slovenia's capital **Ljubljana** is best of the cities, a vital, youthful place cluttered with Baroque and Habsburg building, followed closely by **Zagreb**, the urbane capital of Croatia with a bristling nightlife and an explorable old centre. Between runs a broad corridor of lush hills dunked in the plain, dotted with white-walled farmhouses and acres of vineyards – industry remaining thankfully and carefully hidden away.

LJUBLJANA

LJUBLJANA curls under its castle-topped hill, an old centre marooned

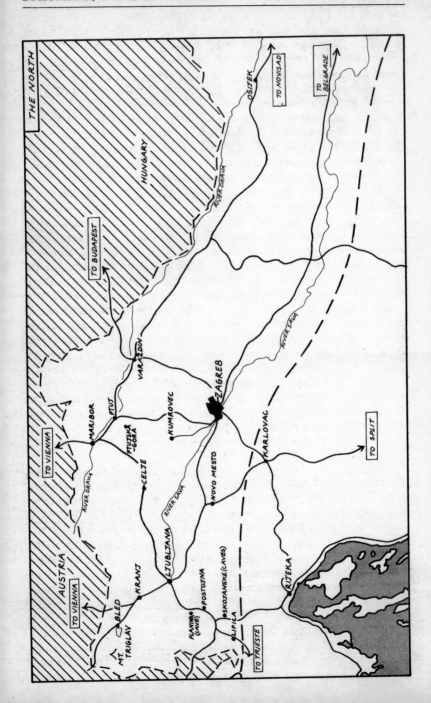

in the shapeless modernity that stretches out across the plain. It's most people's favourite place in the North, which in a way is odd: Ptuj is prettier, Maribor is equally old, Zagreb has finer museums and churches. Where Ljubljana tops them is in its vitality, its self-conscious air of being the growing capital of a rich and industrious republic. At first glance it seems Austrian, a few strands of Vienna pulled out of place, typically exuberant and refined; but really Ljubljana is Slovenian through and through, outside influences absorbed and tinkered with over the years. What follows is an account of the centre, but that is only part of the picture; first and foremost Ljubljana is a place to meet people, to get involved in the nightlife; the buildings just provide the backdrop.

Getting about and somewhere to stay

Everywhere you're likely to want to be in Ljubljana's compact centre is within walking distance of **Prešernov Trg**, though to reach it from the bus/train station it's worth taking bus 2 or 9 – pay on board or buy a token (*jettoni*) from most kiosks. Both these buses stop near the **Tourist Information Centre** (**TIC**) at Titova Cesta 11 (0800–2100, Sundays 0800–1200, 1700–2000) who supply glossy leaflets, a useful *Calendar of Events* and, discouragingly out of the centre, **private rooms**. Much better to take advantage of the **Student Centre** where rooms are cheap, excellent and available from 15 June to 15 September, possibly longer. The venue for these rooms has shifted over recent years but seems to have settled at 27 April 31 (bus 14) – ask first at the TIC. At such cheap prices it's hardly worth struggling out to the **campsite** at Titova 260a (end of no.8 bus route). Arrive out of the summer period and it's worth checking the **Zvezni Student Centre** at Kardeljeva Ploščad 27 for rooms – out of town but open all year; get the TIC to phone first.

The Centre

Prešernov Trg is the hub around which everything revolves, and over-looking all, the **Fransciscan Church** blushes a sandy red to the uninterested square. In its tired-feeling interior the old wall paintings look like faded photographs, and even Francesco Robba's *high altar* seems a little weary. Robba was one of several Italians brought in to remodel the city in its heyday: Ljubljana lay between Austria and Italy on one side, the Middle East on the other; traders passed through and stopped off and Ljubljana got rich. So rich that by the 18th century it could afford to indulge itself in Baroque excesses: across the *tromostovje* (triple bridge) a **fountain**, also by Robba, symbolises the meeting of rivers Sava, Krka and Ljubljanica (he stole the idea from a Bernini in Rome) and the whole stretch down from Prešernov Trg west of the river is decaying Baroque. East of the river, most of the houses are ramshackle medieval, occasionally slicked up as boutiques and stores but mainly high, dark and crumbling, memories of an earlier, less fanciful past.

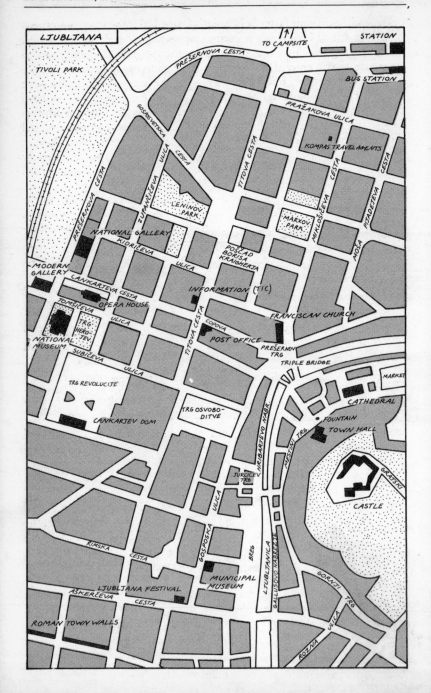

LJUBLJANA

TIVOLI PARK

STATION

TO CAMPSITE

BUS STATION

PREŠERNOVA CESTA

PRAŽAKOVA ULICA

KOMPAS TRAVEL AGENTS

GOSASVETSKA

ŽUPANČIČEVA ULICA

ULICA CESTA

TITOVA CESTA

MIKLOŠIČEVA CESTA

PRAŽAKOVA CESTA

PILADEŽEVA

MOŠA PIJADE

LENINOV PARK

MARXOV PARK

PREŠERNOVA CESTA

NATIONAL GALLERY

KIDRIČEVA

POSLAD BORISA KRAIGHERJA

ULICA

MODERN GALLERY

CANKARJEVA CESTA

INFORMATION (TIC)

FRANCISCAN CHURCH

TOMŠIČEVA

OPERA HOUSE

TITOVA CESTA

ČOPOVA

TRG HERO-JEV

ULICA

POST OFFICE

PREŠERNOV TRG

NATIONAL MUSEUM

SUBIČEVA

ULICA

TRIPLE BRIDGE

MARKET

TRG REVOLUCIJE

CATHEDRAL

FOUNTAIN

TOWN HALL

TRG OSVOBO-DITVE

HRIBARJEVO NABR.

MESTNI TRG

CANKARJEV DOM

GRAJSKI

CASTLE

JURIČIČEV TRG

GOSPOSKA ULICA

RIMSKA

CESTA

BREG

LJUBLJANICA

GALLUSOVO NABREŽJE

GORNJI TRG

LJUBLJANA FESTIVAL

MUNICIPAL MUSEUM

AŠKERČEVA

CESTA

ROMAN TOWN WALLS

ROZNA ULICA

Depending on your tastes **St Nikolas's Cathedral** is the most sumptuous or overblown of Ljubljana's Baroque statements, all whimsical grandeur and elaborate embellishment, its size more than anything inducing hushed reverence as you enter. Doubtless the other churches in town were once nearly as impressive, but most have gone the way of the Fransciscan church; Baroque buildings are particularly sad when they fall on hard times. Behind the Cathedral you can't fail to miss the **General Market** (daily, not Sundays), a brash free-for-all as everyone competes to sell their particular produce. Lining the river side the herb sellers have a bewildering Macbethian selection – stock up on what you can identify as prices are minimal. As a sort of unofficial adjunct, old women sell poisonous-looking medicinal mushrooms. Purchase at your peril.

Opposite the market Studenska winds up the wooded hillside to the **castle**, visible from everywhere in town and currently being restored to the glory it had when protecting the town's defensive position in earlier times – what's left today dates mainly from a C16th rebuilding. Climb the clocktower (0800–1900) for a wide and superlative view of the old town crowded below, the urban sprawl of high-rises beyond and the Kamniski Alps to the north. Best time to be here is towards sunset, when the haze across the plains burns red and golden, suffusing the town in luxurious light.

After peaking in the 18th century Ljubljana remained the important centre of Napoleon's Illyrian Provinces, but later under Austrian control all attempts at making the town a cultural and political capital of Slovenia were repressed, leaving it with an enforced provincialism that took years to wear off. Another legacy was the sedate neo-Classical mansions the Austrians built: three out of the town's four main **museums** are housed in buildings of this period, and to be honest that's the best thing about them. Listen to the tourist office and you'd think each was a meeting of the British Museum and the Louvre; don't be fooled. In a roughly descending order of mediocrity the *Municipal Museum* at Gospoka 15 (Tuesdays and Thursdays 0900–1200 and 1600–1800, Sundays 0900–1200) has dull furniture and duller statuary; the *National Museum*, Trg Herojev 1 (daily 0900–1300 and 1600–1900 Wednesdays and Fridays; closed Mondays) is notable only for its extravagant staircase; the *National Gallery*, Cankarjeva 20 (daily 1000–1800, Sundays 1000–1300, closed Mondays) has a collection of unknown paintings from the 18th and 19th centuries, and the *Modern Gallery*, Cankarjeva 15 (times as Narodna Gallerija) 20th century Slovenian art, uniformly duff save for paintings by the Kralj brothers. The museums lie between the old town and park, a spacious area spliced by the wide strip of Titova Cesta, Ljubljana's main street and a useful landmark when exploring.

Evenings

Ljubljana has a nightlife second to none in Yugoslavia: on a summer's evening the cafés around Prešernov Trg spill out on to the streets with the hectic atmosphere of a mass open-air bar: In fact there *is* an outdoor bar, at the top of Hribarjevo Nabrežje – a great place to get into conversation with the locals or just hang out. For more restrained outdoor drinking try the *café* on Juričičev Trg: nearby (take a right of Juričičev Trg) *Café Rosa* is very much home to Ljubljana's smart set – quiet, relaxed and intimate: recommended. At the other end of the scale *Pod Lipice* on Rimska Cesta can be boisterous, perhaps because it's rather out of the way. The *Evropa Café* on the junction of Titova Cesta and Gospovetska is indecently plush and palatial, like a C19th ballroom; *Pri Vitezu*, Breg 20, is good for an early evening drink, and the *Holiday Inn Bar*, Miklosičeva 3, for late nights and diehards. Finally, and best of the lot for my money, the *outdoor café* at Titova 4 draws a broad mixture of Ljubljana's youth in a convivial setting, and you can eat here – try the spiced beans. Two **venues** to be checked out are the *Ljubljana Festival*, Trg Francoske Revolucije 2, a permanent outdoor stage often with gigs by home-grown new wave bands (look out too for flyposters announcing gigs at student halls) and the *Cankarjev Dom*, Trg Revolucije 2 (beneath the digital clock), assorted entertainment in a futuristic culture centre.

Good **restaurants** too: the *Pizza Place* at Copova 14 must serve up the cheapest food in town – tasty pizzas for next to nothing. *Emona* at Cankarjeva Cesta 2 has a wider choice, though not nearly so good or so cheap. The *Evropa Café* (see above) also does pizzas and omelettes, etc. More upmarket, but not wildly more expensive, *Maček* at Cankerjevo Nabrežje 15 has fish specialities (*Operna Klet* on Zupančičeva Ul., near the Opera House, is similar and a bit more expensive), and *Union Klet*, Miklosičeva 1, a good selection of wines and interesting menu of meats.

Ljubljana listings

American Centre Cankarjeva Cesta 11 US newspapers and mags, 'What's On' listings, etc. Monday-Friday 0900–1600, Sunday 1000–1300.

Books Good selection of English books, maps and tourist bumf at the store next to the bus stop before Titova Cesta joins Subičeva.

Calendar of Events A leaflet put out by the TIC with full details of what's on each month. Useful and free.

Car Hire *Kompas-Hertz*, Miklosičeva 11. *Integral*, Titova Cesta 38.

First Aid Zaloška 25. Telephone 94.

Flea Market Gallusova Nabrežje, Saturday mornings. Lively market with vast selection of local junk and the odd bargain.

JAT Miklosičeva 34. The JAT coach from the bus station takes the best part of an hour to reach the airport at Vrdnik.

Kompas   Miklosičeva 11, for speedy issue of internal and international train and coach tickets. English-speaking and helpful.

NME   and occasional English **newspapers** from the supermarket on Trg Revolucije.

Police   Prešernova 18. Telephone 92.

Post Office and Telephones Titova Cesta 8. Monday-Friday 0800–2000, Saturday 0800–1400. 24–hour service at Cigaletova 15.

Radio Ljubljana   VHF broadcasts in English every day except Sunday – tourist news 0935, weather 0635, news 2215 and 0130. 88.5, 96.5, 100.1 MHZ.

Slovenian Alpine Association   Dvoržakova 9. Useful maps and info if you're heading up into the Alps.

AROUND LJUBLJANA: THE POSTOJNA CAVES AND LIPICA

Emphatically not to be missed while you're in Ljubljana is a visit to the **POSTOJNA CAVES** – easily managed either as a day trip or en route to Koper or Opatija. Regular buses link Lubljana with Postojna, and when in town signs direct you to the caves and their suitably cavernous entrance. Tours run every half hour in the season (last tours: May-September 1800, April and October 1700, November-March 1300 week-days, 1500 Saturdays and Sundays; dress warmly) and once inside a railway whizzes you helter-skelter through 2km of preliminary systems before the guided tour starts. It's little use trying to describe the vast and fantastic jungles of rock formations; the point is to see them for yourself – breathtaking stuff. Postojna's caves are about 4 million years old and provide a chilly home for *Proteus anguineus*, a weird creature that looks like a cross between a bloated sperm and a prawn. Actually it's a sort of salamander; one of whose odd capabilities is to give birth to live young in temperatures above 15° C but lay eggs if it's colder. They live their 70–year lives down here in total darkness and hence are blind – and very confused at being put on display to inquisitive tourists. Discovered in 1818, Postojna's 18km system wasn't explored for years, and large sections are still uncharted: when in the war Italian occupying forces used the entrance caves as a fuel dump they didn't have a map of the system; the local Partisans, however, did, and worked their way through a side passage to blow up the stores – you can still see the walls blackened by explosion.

Caves abound in the limestone Karst around Postojna. A 7km bus trip away the PLANINA CAVE is little visited and provides a good contrast – fewer rock formations but dramatic arched river passages. To the south west the SKOJANSKE SYSTEM is reckoned to be the most spectacular of the lot though little advertised; I didn't make it, but if you're into neve-testing expeditions in semi-darkness, this could be just the place.

The other site you're steered to near Postojna, the **PREDJAMSKI GRAD CASTLE**, is 9km out and only reachable with your own transport or by an organised trip – I tried bumming a lift with the tourist coaches from Postojna but it wasn't on; you might be luckier. Pushed up high against a cave entrance the C16th castle is a damp and melancholy sort of place, unimproved by a lacklustre collection of odds and ends from this and an earlier castle that stood nearby. The previous castle was the home of one Erasmus, a brigand knight of the C15th who spent his days waylaying the merchant caravans that passed through the region. Sheriff of Nottingham to his Robin Hood was the Governor of Trieste, who laid exasperated siege to the castle for over a year. Secure in his defensive position and supplied by a secret passage to the outside world, Erasmus taunted the governor by tossing fresh cherries and the occasional roast ox over the wall to show he was far from beaten. Such hubris couldn't go unnoticed, and Erasmus finally met with one of the more ignominious deaths on record: he was blown to bits by a cannon ball while sitting on the castle loo.

A less spectacular alternative to the cave stop-off is **LIPICA**, near the Italian border; buses run from Divača or, if you're reading this on the coast, tourist coaches ply the route. Very much the 'oasis in the barren Karst', as it's always described, Lipica gave its name to the horses you associate with the Spanish Riding School of Vienna – **Lippizaners**. The Austrian Archduke Charles established the stud farm here in 1580, and it's been breeding the graceful white horses ever since. Though the school is nothing so grand as that at Vienna, tours are given round the stud (0830–1700, on the half hour in the morning, hour in the afternoon) and twice a day the horses give the elegant displays for which they're famous (Monday-Friday 1100 and 1430; Saturday and Sunday 1500).

BLED AND BOHINJ

At the tail end of the Julian Alps and in easy reach from Ljubljana, the **mountain lakes** of BLED and BOHINJ are Slovenia's number one tourist pull. And for good reason: all the delights and trappings of their Austrian and Italian neighbours are here but at affordable prices. Tour operators have been quick to include the lakes in their brochures, and while Bled, surrounded by Olympian mountains and busily oozing charm, lives up to expectations it's also chock-full with English and German tourists, which can't help but reduce the attraction. Bohinj, in contrast, is less-visited, more beautiful and cheaper – if you want to explore the imposing and exhilarating mountains around Mt Triglav, Yugoslavia's highest peak, this is the place to head for.

There's no denying that **BLED** has all the right ingredients – a placid mirror lake with romantic island, a fairy-tale castle high on a bluff, and a backdrop of snow-tipped mountains. As such it's worth a day of anyone's time, and one advantage of the tourist trade is that everything is well packaged. The **Tourist Office** (keep to the road down from the bus station and you'll see a sign) fall over themselves to supply info: a free *Bled Information* booklet has every practical detail you need from bike hire to acupuncture facilities, and their *Alpine Guide* gives comprehensive hiking routes for the whole area including Triglav (though to attempt this you need the help of mountain guides). Accommodation options are their private **rooms** (expensive and surcharged for stays under 3 days) or the **Youth Hostel** (cheap, and cheaper still with YHA card). For the Youth Hostel head straight up Grayska from the station, past the farmyards and small shrine till you reach the Hostel at No. 17 – dormitory accommodation and a strict 10.30 curfew/lockout. The nearest **campsite** is sheltered at the western end of the lake amid the pines; catch a bus towards Bohinj and get off at Kidričeva street. There is nowhere cheap to **eat** in Bled – try the *Gostolina* at the bottom of Grayska, or hit the supermarkets.

Even if you don't stay there it's a good idea to observe the Youth Hostel's curfew: rise early while the hotels are still sleeping and Bled is all yours, and at its most atmospheric. A path just behind the Youth Hostel runs up to **Bled Castle** (0800–2000 daily) which at a closer look turns out to be a picturesque restaurant with a fine view and very ordinary museum. Ignac Novak, one of Bled's more enterprising sons, was castillian here in the C18th; his great plan was to drain the lake and use the residual clay as raw material for a brick factory he intended to build on the shore. With an astute eye to tourism even then, the council turned him down.

During the day there's a constant relay of boats ferrying tourists back and forth to Bled's **Island**. With an early start (hire a boat from below the Grand Hotel) you can beat them to it. Crowning the island is a natty Baroque-decorated church, last in a line on a spot that's long held religious significance for the people around the lake: under the present building are remains of early graves and (below the north chapel) a very early pre-Roman temple. As soon as the tourist boats start up the peace of the island is wrecked by over-amplified disco noise from a restaurant – so get here early.

Buses run hourly from Bled to Bohinj through the **Sava Bohinjka valley**, dense, verdant and often laden with mist and low cloud. Along its sides are dotted *kolozecs*, wooden frames for drying hay and wheat, and found all over Slovenia: on the damp alpine ground crops don't dry well – hanging them onto a *kolozec* lets the sharp winds do the work. Around Bohinj the double *kolozec* with workroom above and high-pitched roof is usual; further northwest they become much more decorative, with patterned animals and figures cut into the weatherboards; near Lujbljana long ranks of single *kolozecs* are common.

In appearance and character **BOHINJ** is utterly different from Bled: the lake crooks a narrow finger under the wild mountains, woods slope gently down to the water enclosing it in secretive tranquillity and a stillness hangs over all – in comparison to Bled it feels almost uninhabited. First bus stop by the lake puts you down opposite the **Tourist Office** (Monday-Friday 0700–1800, July and August daily 0700–2000) who have rooms at roughly half the Bled price, along with apartments and bike hire. Pride of place at this end of the lake goes to the **Church of St John** (daily July and August 0900–1200, 1500–1800) a solid-looking structure whose nave and frescoes date back to the C14th, but once you've seen this and sorted out a room there's no reason to hang about. Most accommodation is at the western end of the lake; in between are the campsite and cable car at the foot of **Mt Vogel**. If the Alps look dramatic from the lakeside, from Vogel's summit they're breathtaking. As the cable car briskly climbs the 3500–feet slopes – not for fainthearts this – the panorama is gradually revealed, with Triglav the crest of a line of pale red mountains, more like a clenched claw than the three-headed god after which it's named. The cable car runs every half hour from 0730–1800. Finally, the ideal time to be around is the end of September when the return of the cattle from the higher alpine pastures is celebrated in the mass booze-up called the *Krajvi Bal* – cow dance.

A note on skiing
Bled is a good centre for exploring the ski resorts of the region: best of the lot, though furthest away, **KRANJSKA GORA**, is one of Yugoslavia's main centres, with a good supply of private rooms, four chair lifts, twelve ski-tows and excellent skiing from December to mid-March. Alternatives include **PLANICA**, to the west, with fine cross-country courses, or, between Bled and Bohinj, **BOHINJ BISTRICA**, which forms the base for the 'Kobla' resort – a good beginners' course and medium incline, all well organised. The **MT VOGEL** resort, reached from the foot of lake Bohinj, too has good ski-tows and easy slopes amid spectacular scenery – its season usually stretches from November to early May.

EASTERN SLOVENIA: MARIBOR, PTUJ AND BEYOND

It's difficult to find anything complimentary to say about **MARIBOR**. The trucks that thunder through on the quick route down from Austria make it a place of noise and dirt, and to me it was an unfriendly, unwelcoming town I was glad to see the back of. A **Franciscan Church** hogs most of the centre, one of two uninteresting churches (the other is the lumpish Cathedral, featureless outside, Baroque in) with the **Town Hall** in between. This now houses the **City Museum** (tours on the hour: Tuesday-Saturday 0900–1200/1500–1800; Sundays 1000, 1100, 1200), really the only conceivable point of interest – a large collection with a little of everything, including costumes used in the *Korenti* dances of Ptuj (of which more later), and one of the most inept ceiling paintings in Europe. If you need to stay, the **Tourist Office** on Grayski Trg (next door to cinema; Monday-Saturday 0800–1930) doles out private rooms, away from the centre but dirt cheap, plus details of skiing facilities in the nearby Mariborsko Pohorje. For a free map of town, ask at the tourist office left of the bus station. Nightlife is pretty dead: 'In Maribor', someone told me, 'we drink all day and watch TV at night. It is very depressing.' I think he was right.

25km down the road and an easy local bus ride away, **PTUJ** is the antidote to all this. Usually billed as the oldest town in Slovenia, it's about the most attractive as well, rising up from the Drava valley in a flutter of red roofs and topped by a friendly-looking castle. But the best thing is its streets, scaled-down mansions standing shoulder to shoulder on scaled-down boulevards, medieval crumbling next to Baroque extravagances. Out of the windows hang plants and the locals; watching the world go by is a major occupation here.

The town doesn't have a centre as such, but if it did it'd be the Trg Mladinski Brigad, with an Austrian-style town hall at one end, and, **Priory Church** (open mornings only) at the other. Begun in the C12th this is mainly Gothic, though splashed with Baroque; there's a fine carved choir of 1446. Nearby, its rather unambitious **tower** started life in the C16th as a belltower, became city watchtower in the C17th and was retired in the 18th, being given an onion bulb spire for decoration. Roman tombstones have been imbedded in its lower reaches, but a more noticeable leftover of Roman times is the **Tablet** that stands below like an oversize tooth: a funeral monument to a Roman mayor, it's just possible to make out its carvings of Orpheus entertaining assembled fauna. Right at the other end of the street the **Archaeological Museum** (15 April–1 December, closed Mondays, 1000–1300) lives in what was once a Dominican Monastery, a mustardy building gutted in the C18 and now hung with spidery decoration – worth a look though for the carvings and statuary around likeably dishevelled cloisters.

A path opposite the monastery winds up to the **Castle** (15 April–1 December, closed Mondays; hourly guided tours 0900 to 1500 – you have to tag along with a group). There's been a castle of sorts here for as long as there's been a town, since Ptuj was the only bridging point across the Drava for miles around and held the defences against the tribes of the north. Here the Romans maintained a large base and the fleeing

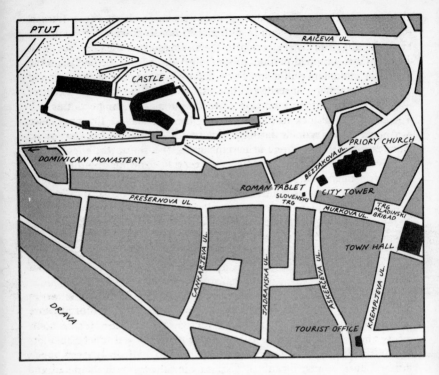

Slavs fought off the Hungarians in the C6th migrations. An agglomeration of styles from the C14th to the 18th the castle was home to a succession of noble families who made it rich in the town. Last of these were the Herbensteins who lived here until 1945: of Austro-Scottish descent, they'd welcomed the Nazi invaders in 1941, and only their wealth and influence rescued them from just desserts at the end of the war. Their portraits hang on the walls of the museum the castle now holds, a collection mixed in theme and quality: first floor has period rooms, the usual stuff with original tapestries and wallpaper; on the second are some excellent pieces of *medieval carving* – St George unconcernedly killing a rather homely dragon, SS Barbara and Catherine delicately and exquisitely crafted. There's also armour, furniture and, if you're interested, a collection of worn-out musical instruments.

At Shrovetide (late February/early March) Ptuj is venue to one of the oldest and most unusual customs in Yugoslavia. The **Kurenti processions** are a sort of fertility rite and celebration of the dead confused together: participants wear sinister masks of sheepskin and feathers with a coloured beak for a nose and white beads for teeth, possibly representing ancestral spirits – have a look at a picture and you'll see that there is something deeply and primitively frightening about them. So dressed, the Kurenti move in hopping procession from house to house, scaring off evil spirits with the din from cowbells tied to their costumes and leading the devil before them, wrapped in a net to symbolize his capture. Behind them the *Orači* or ploughers pull a small wooden plough, scattering sand around to show the sowing of seed, and housewives smash clay pots at their feet – possibly the leftovers of a sacrifice tradition – in the hope this will bring health and luck to the household. Lent rituals like this were once widespread in Europe's farming communities; perhaps because of its oddness the Kurenti is one of few to survive this far north.

Private rooms in Ptuj aren't cheap or central – and for about the same price you might just as well stay at the *Hotel Poetovio*, at the end of Trstenjakova. If this is full the **Tourist Office** at Trg Svobode 4 (Monday-Friday 0800–1500, Saturday 0800–1300) will put you on to the rooms. For **food** you fare better: in ascending order *Zlatorog* at Bezjakoca 10 is cheap and ordinary, the *Evropa Gostolina* on Trg Mladinski Brigad varied and boozy, and the *fish restaurant* at the river end of Cankarjeva best of all. The brassy *Café Gloria* at Presernova 20 is the noisy hangout of Ptuj's youth.

12 km southeast of Ptuj the village of **PTUJSKA GORA** is worth visiting if you're into things Gothic. Its pocket-sized **Church of St Mary** was built around 1415, and though altered over the years retains some of its fine original carvings, most likeable of which is a relief above the high altar showing the *Virgin as Protectress of the World*. Seven angels lift her cloak to reveal ranks of figures, each drawn with the detail and attention of a portrait; which is what they were, depicting the assembled families of the Counts of Celje.

The rolling hills east of Ptuj form Slovenia's extensive **vineyard region**, centred around two small towns that give their name to the local white wines: *Ljutomer* and *Jeruzalem*. Ljutomer Rizling is well known in Britain as party plonk, but some of the wines made here are in a much higher league: as a rule of thumb go for the bottles with a numbered circular black label, indication of a sort of Slovenian *appelation controlé*. *Šipon* and *Haložan* are among the best, but my favourite is *Renski Rizling* – smooth, dry and not too fruity.

First impressions of **VARAŽDIN** suggest another Maribor, and though it's a great deal better there's not that much to see. The centre is dotted with provincial-Baroque houses of the C17th and 18th, and the castle is a quaint relation of that at Ptuj; it too contains a museum, though not as good. Across the road from the castle the cemetery doubles as an elaborate town park, modelled somewhat strangely on the gardens of Versailles.

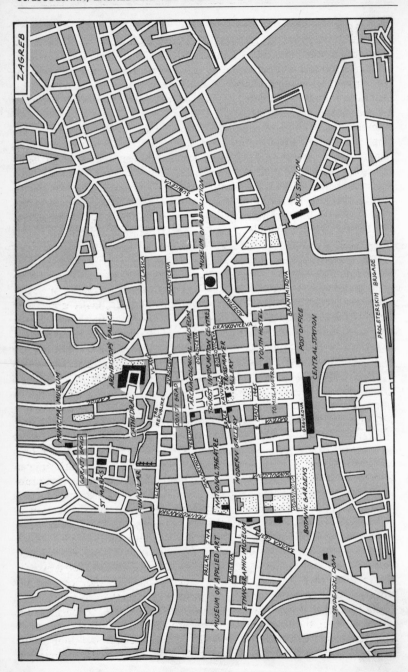

ZAGREB

If you're coming from the south, **ZAGREB**, Yugoslavia's second city, will make you feel you're back in central Europe. Like Ljubljana, Austria, not Turkey, left its mark here, and where Belgrade has a trodden-on eastern feel, Zagreb's buildings are grand, peach-coloured monuments to the decadence and self-esteem of the Hapsburgs, its people urbane and cosmopolitan, tripping through the streets with an assured, cultured air. Once a hotbed of Croat nationalism and capital of the wartime puppet state of Pavelić, it's now widely regarded as the cultural and artistic heart of Yugoslavia, and though all Serb-Croat differences have long since been resolved, there's a Croat disdain of Belgrade that still persists; you can't help but get the impression that Zagreb considers itself a cut above the rest. Two days here are well spent: in fact, a handful of good museums, side trips to the nearby hills, and an above-average nightlife should keep you well occupied for at least that.

Getting around and finding a place to stay

Zagreb's centre splits neatly into two disparate parts: the upper town, **Gornji Grad**, a quiet enclave from which the city originally grew, and the lower town, **Donji Grad**, the latter-day modern centre, bustling with trams and shoppers. The **railway station** is centrally placed on Tomislava Trg, and the **bus station** ten minutes' walk or two minutes' tram ride away, on the corner of Branimirova. Zagreb sprawls, but there's nothing apart from accommodation to take you out of the compact city centre. Tram and bus tickets cost a flat fare and last 1½ hours. The **Tourist Information Centre** (Monday-Friday 0800–2000, Saturday/Sunday 0900–1800), on Zrinjski Trg, has no accommodation but does a cheap map, more detailed than the one we've printed, and *What's On* pamphlets to the city. **Room-wise**, the situation is bleak: the dozen or so rooms at *Generalturist* (Zrinjski Trg) and *Croatiaturist* (Trg Tomislava) can disappear quickly at any time of year, and doubles in even the more run-down **hotels** – the *Sport* or the *Siget* – may well break your budget. A much better bet is the **Youth Hostel** five minutes from the station at Petrinjska 17: cheap, very cheerful and open all year round; for breakfast use the *burek* joint around the corner. If the Youth Hostel's full – which is rarely – the **Studentski Centar**, at Savska Cesta 25, lets out student dorms in July and August – enquire in the office next to the hairdresser's. For **campers**, there's *campsite Mladost* on the banks of the Sava: tram 4 from the railway station or tram 14 from Trg Republike.

Cheap **eating** poses few problems, and self-service restaurants are dotted all over the town centre. Here's three: *Mosor*, on the corner of Trg Republike, *Turist*, at Masarykova 7, and *Sljeme*, next door to the Youth Hostel on Petrinjska. Best of the rest are *Splendid Express* on

Strossmayer Trg, an excellent *Pizzeria* in the upper town at Kamenita 2a, and – remember this is unprecedented in Yugoslavia – *Medulić*, a restaurant with a vegetarian menu, at Medulićeva 2. The area for **drinking** is Tkalčićeva, where there are a number of convivial bars with music – try *Stara Tkalča*; or *Gostionica Badanj*, a crowded, divey cellar bar, opposite the Cathedral.

Donji Grad

The lower town fans south from Trg Republike, the city's busy core, flanked by cafés, hotels and department stores and hectic with the whizz of trams and hurrying pedestrians. From here a series of squares form a shady, green backbone to the city, interrupted by statuesque Austrian pavilions as far as the downbeat hustle of the railway station. On Zrinjski Trg is the **Archaeological Museum** (Monday-Friday 0830–1330, Monday, Wednesday, Friday 1630–1930, Sunday 1000–1300), which has a good prehistoric section – fragments from the so-called 'Krapina Man', found in northern Croatia – some early Croatian finds, and what ranks as Yugoslavia's largest selection of Egyptian antiquities, with a set of mummies, sarcophagi and tomb inscriptions.

Facing Zrinjski Trg, the **Strossmayer Gallery** was closed when I was here, with it's collection scattered all over the city. It's meant to be open by now, but if not you should be able to see at least some of the paintings in Zagreb's other galleries. By Yugoslav standards it's pretty good, instigated by Bishop Strossmayer's donation in 1867, from which it has since grown severalfold. As well as canvases by Goya, El Greco and a number of Venetians – Carpaccio, the Bellinis and Veronese – it takes in a small group of Dutch and Flemish works, notably the bawdy scenes of David Teniers and Van Ostade and the more refined studies of Nicholas Maes – one of Rembrandt's later pupils. Strossmayer himself is in many ways a Croatian hero: an accomplished linguist, art connoisseur, horse-breeder and raconteur, and founder of Zagreb university, he led Croat resistance to the tyranny of Austria-Hungary and fought for the ultimate union of Croats and Serbs in a Yugoslav state – not a belief dear to many Croat hearts at the time. Mestrović's **statue** of him behind the museum has all the sculptor's familiar motifs – long bony fingers and a gown spread tightly over akimbo knees – and it's one of his more successful works. A fierce patriot himself, Mestrović must have honoured Strossmayer highly, carving his likeness into the blend of firmness and humanism for which the Bishop was known.

Across the road is the **Modern Gallery** (Tuesday-Sunday 1000–1300/1700–2000), housing a vast collection of late C19th and C20th Croatian art produced by names that, apart from Mestrović, mean little or nothing to most visitors. While worth the paltry entrance fee (you may see something you like) it's unlikely to prove of much interest to non-devotees of modern Croatian art. Slightly more interesting are the **Museum of Applied Arts**, in a long gabled building on Maršala Tita Trg (Tuesday-Sunday 1000–1300, Tuesday/Thursday 1700–2000) and the **Ethnographic Museum** (Tuesday/Wednesday/Thursday 0900–1300, 1700–2000, Friday/Saturday/Sunday 0900–1300), just a few steps away in Mažuranicév Trg. The applied arts collection includes the furniture and accessories of periods from the Renaissance to the present day – an impressive display – while the ethnographic museum sports a down-at-heel heap of artefacts brought back from the South Pacific, Asia and Africa by obscure but intrepid Yugoslav explorers, and a colourful assortment of costumes from every corner of Croatia.

Behind Trg Republike soar the filigree spires of the **Cathedral**, ringed by the ivy-cloaked turrets of the Archbishop's Palace – 'a sumptuous Kremlin' fancied Arthur Evans before its decimation by earthquake in 1880. After the disaster it was rebuilt with an enthusiastic reversion to Gothic forms, leaving a high bare church with little to keep you for long. From here, Kaptol curves north round the mottled brown roofs of the upper town, most ancient and atmospheric part of Zagreb.

Gornji Grad

Modern Zagreb grew out of two adjacent medieval settlements, the religious community of Kaptol, and Gradec on the hill above – a royal Hungarian city charterd by King Bela IV after he fled here from the Tartars in 1242. Gradec is roughly the present upper town, a leafy, tranquil backwater of tiny streets, small squares and Baroque palaces high above the grey urban spread of modern Zagreb. To reach it take one of the streets that scurry up behind Trg Republike or for a miserly fee, climb onto the sporadic *funicular* a little way down Ilica.

Radićev Trg is centre of Gornji Grad and, historically, of Zagreb: a restrained golden-brown square around the **Church of St Mark**, whose coloured tiled roof shows the coats of arms of the constituent parts of Croatia to the sky and – it would seem from opening any book on Zagreb – thousands of enterprising photographers. Named after the martyred leader of the Croat peasant party and in many ways the symbolic heart of Croatia, it's said that it only fell once, and then to the Tartars, who everything succumbed to sooner or later. It also saw the quite ruthless put-down of the C16th peasants' revolt, whose leader, Matija Gubec, in a mock ceremony arranged by the Austrian authorities and after the vilest tortures imaginable, was seated in a throne here and crowned with a band of white-hot steel. St Mark's is small, homely and Gothic, originally C14th but like the Cathedral since ravaged by earthquake and fire and modified with C19th skin, Baroque bell-tower and 1930s interior decorations. The frescoes are typically Slav: huge, musclebound figures caught in dramatic mid-gesture; Mestrović's crucifix is more sensitive, merging more responsively with the rest of the church.

The best way to appreciate the upper town is to wander aimlessly, drinking in its peace and enjoying the views over Zagreb and the plains beyond. Brief stops are, however, worth making at the **Town Museum**, at Opatička 20 (Tuesday-Friday 0900–1300, Thursday 1600–1900, Sunday 1000–1300), which tells the tale of Zagreb's development from medieval times to the early C20th with the help of paintings and lumber from the city's wealthier households, and the **Gallery of Primitive Art**, Cirolometodska 3, with – if you can find it open – what is generally considered the world's finest exhibition of naive painting. Other than an extremely shabby **Croatian Historical Museum**, assembled in one of the more crumbly of the upper town's Baroque mansions, the one remaining thing to see is the **Mestrović Atelier** Mletačka 8 (Tuesday-Saturday 1000–1300/ 1700–1900, Sunday 1000–1300), housed in the artist's former home and studio, and with an intimacy that the Mestrović gallery in Split lacks. On display are sketches, photographs, memorabilia from exhibitions worldwide and small-scale studies for his more familiar public creations: there's a miniature of his *Grgur Ninski* (the giant version is in Split), studies for the *Crucifixion* in St Mark's and some quite lovely female statuettes – all in all a fine museum, and one you don't have to be a Mestrović fan to enjoy.

Things
American Centre Zrinjski Trg 13 (Monday-Saturday 1100–1630). Library, newspapers, reading room.

British Council Ilica 12/1 (Monday-Friday 0730–1430). Library, newspapers, reading room.

Car hire *Avis* (Hotel Intercontinetal, Krsnjavoga 1), *Hertz* (Krsnjavoga 13), *Unis* (Gajeva 29a).

Consulates Britain (Ilica 12; tel. 445 522), Netherlands (Proleterskih Brigada 72; tel. 537 282), USA (Brace Kavuriaca 2; tel. 444 800).

Emergencies Hospital (Djordićeva 26), 94; Police tel. 92

Folk-Lore Festival Held at the end of July, performances of ethnic music and dance from the world over. Venues include the Lisinski concert hall and outdoor stages all over town.

JAT Zrinjski Trg 17. Buses leave from behind the Hotel Esplanade every 20 minutes.

Market *Dolac*, on a tiered square behind Trg Republike. Every day, but at its vibrant best on Friday and Saturday.

Post offices Two large central offices: one at Jurisičeva 13, the other next to the railway station at Branimirova 4 with 24–hour telephone booths.

Plitvice Lakes Information Office Trg Tomislava 19.

Radio Zagreb   English-language broadcasts every day except Saturday. VHF 90.5, 98.1, 99.7 MHz.

Sljeme   One of the more popular excursions from Zagreb is the 20–minute cable-car (*žičara*) ride to the wooded peak of Sljeme, 1035m up, on the northern fringes of the city. Not much to see but good walking and wonderful views over Zagreb and the Zagorje mountains beyond. Take tram 14 to the end, then tram 15 and it's a 10–minute walk through the tunnel and up the valley.

NORTH OF ZAGREB: THE ZAGORJE

Spread roughly between Zagreb and Maribor, the **Zagorje** is an area that deserves two over-used adjectives – delightful and charming. Minature wooded hills are crowned with the castles they seem designed for, streams tumble through lush ground sprinkled with vineyards. A landscape of chocolate-box enchantment, it's also a place of pilgrimage for at **KUMROVEC**, right at the centre of the region, is the birthplace of Josip Broz – **Tito**. Born in 1892 he was the seventh son of a Slovenian mother and Croat father, who after rising from the deep poverty of his childhood by working as a metalworker, became an officer in the Austrian army (Croatia then being part of Austria-Hungary). In 1915 he was captured by the Russians, and joined the Red Army two years later, beginning his involvement with Communism. It's a pity that none of this, or his later achievements, are recounted in the tiny museum that's now part of the simple peasant **House** in which he was born. Along with lifelike recreations of 1890s rooms, the museum has only the usual photos and mementos. I went expecting more, but then again celebrations of the man, his life and works are near-ubiquitous in this country: perhaps Kumrovec is admirable for its restraint.

If you're heading north to Ptuj, Maribor or Austria, Kumrovec is a stop-off manageable by bus; other towns in the Zagorje are only usefully reached with your own wheels. **BELEC** near Zlatar in the Ivančiče hills has a couple of impressive churches: one medieval, alongside the ruins of a C13th castle, the other, deceptively ordinary from the outside, holding a fantastic riot of frothy Baroque furniture and ornament which (and it's easy to believe this) was commissioned by a local countess after she'd had a nightmarish vision.

There are over a hundred **castles** in the Zagorje region, enduring evidence of its long feudal past. Many are now museums or hotels, but perhaps the most-visited is **TRACOŠČAN**. Really it's a bit of a fake – the original was much cut about in the C19th to provide what you see today – but its mock-Norman posture and lakeside setting go down well with admirers of the pretty-pretty. 10km east of the main Zagreb-Ptuj road, it's worth the detour if you're passing.

SOUTH AND EAST OF ZAGREB: KARLOVAC, DELNICE AND THE PLAINS OF SLAVONIA

Less than an hour's ride **south of Zagreb** is **KARLOVAC**, a spacious industrial town whose name crowns a fair percentage of the nation's beer bottles. Within wide boulevards it harbours a small old centre but, frankly, I'd push straight on to the coast if that's where you're heading. Soon the grim flats ruck into a spectacular landscape of green, dimpled river valleys and wooded hillsides, cascades of slender evergreens thrust high to catch the light. **DELNICE**, the region's main ski resort, sits at a height of well over 2000 feet, where mountains spread irregularly distant, serrated with cloaks of shaggy pines. Soon after, and gradually – almost imperceptibly – soft green scenery shifts to the stark grey barrenness of Karst, and before long Rijeka and the Adriatic Coast lie below you.

East from Zagreb the *autoput* cuts through the harrowingly dull plains of **Slavonia**, strongest contender for the most unceasingly tedious of all Yugoslav regions. Quite unfairly, it's this area more than any other that has given Yugoslavia a bad name among the backpacking cognoscenti: as Greek-bound travellers watch vistas of flat, chequered farmland fade drearily into the distance they not surprisingly feel in no hurry to come back. **SLAVONSKI BROD** (Bosanski Brod is its other half, across the Sava in Bosnia) lies mid-way between Zagreb and Belgrade, a potential stop-over if the journey becomes too soporific but otherwise to be avoided. **DJAKOVO**, just north-east, was the episcopal seat of Bishop Strossmayer and is now the home of a prodigious neo-Gothic Cathedral; **OSIJEK**, towards the Hungarian border, is an Austrian-Style garden city famous, apparently, for its matches. Why Nagel's guide gives it six pages I wasn't able to find out.

TRAVEL DETAILS

Buses

From Ljubljana to Zagreb (hourly; 2¾hours); Belgrade (four a day; 10hrs); Bled (half hourly; 1½hrs); Maribor (hourly; 3¾hrs); Ptuj (4; 4hrs); Postojna (hourly; 1¾hrs); Rijeka (4; 2¾hrs); Opatija (3; 3hrs); Koper (hourly; 2hrs)

From Maribor to Ptuj (hourly; 45min)

From Zagreb to Bled (3 daily; 4½hrs); Belgrade (hourly; 7hrs); Dubrovnik (3; 12hrs); Maribor (hourly; 3hrs); Plitvice (half hourly; 3hrs); Rijeka (hourly; 4hrs); Sarajevo (4; 8hrs); Split (3; 9hrs); Zadar (hourly; 5hrs).

Trains

From Ljubljana to Zagreb (hourly; 2hrs); Trieste (3 daily; 4hrs); Maribor (hourly 3hrs); Postojna (hourly; 1hr); Rijeka (4; 2hrs)

From Zagreb to Belgrade (hourly; 6hrs); Rijeka (4; 4hrs); Sarajevo (1; 8½hrs); Kardeljevo (1; 11hrs); Split (8; 7hrs)

International trains

From Ljubljana to Munich (7 daily; 8hrs); Salzburg (6; 6hrs); Venice (2; 6hrs)

From Zagreb to Venice (2 daily; 9hrs); Vienna (3; 7½hrs); Budapest (2; 7½hrs).

Chapter two

ISTRIA

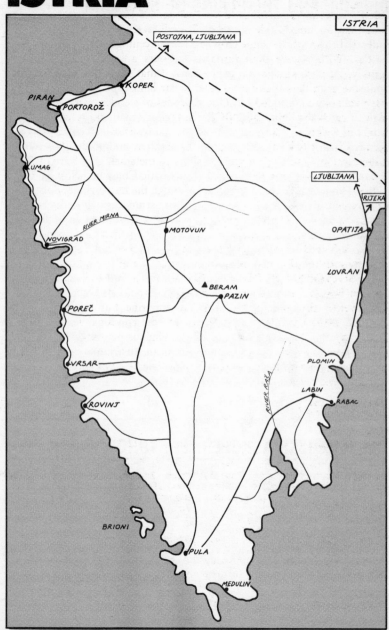

Istria is Yugoslavia at its most developed. Many of the towns here were tourist resorts well back into the last century and in recent years their proximity to northern Europe has proved tempting ground for exploitation. The coast, particularly the western side, is infested with autocamps and hotels; the beaches (concrete mainly) tend to be bloated with people, and finding a room can be nigh impossible unless you book well in advance. The police here take a fairly strong line with those sleeping rough.

All of which may sound horrendous, as Istria at its worst can be. But through all the crowds, concrete and autocamps, it has managed to retain a charm and identity that make parts at least well worth exploring. Development has on the whole been kept clear of the beautiful Venetian towns and even at the coast it's possible to get away from the real gluts of people. The Karst interior with its villages pitched high in the mountains is still amazingly unexplored, and where Benidorm and co. had nothing much to start with, Istria can draw on a rich historical legacy.

The basis of this is Italian – from the 400 years of Venetian rule that preceded the region's incorporation into the Austro-Hungarian empire, and eventually into the Yugoslav federation. There's still a sizeable Italian minority here, and Italian is very much the second language. And along the coast diminutive Venetian towns like **Piran** and **Rovinj**, with their cobbled piazzas, shuttered houses and back alleys laden with laundry, are almost overwhelmingly pretty. **Koper** too is worth a look and, more port than resort, makes a good base from which to explore northern Istria. By the same token **Pula**, with its Roman amphitheatre, is a rewarding place to spend a few days: rooms there are cheap and relatively easy to come by and most of Istria's more interesting spots only a short bus ride away. During the summer a ferry runs five times weekly (twice weekly out of season), linking all the main Istrian towns with each other and with Trieste.

SLOVENE ISTRIA: KOPER, PORTOROŽ, PIRAN

The subject of bitter post-war wrangles between the Italians and Yugoslavs, Istria's northern coast didn't technically become part of Yugoslavia until 1954. Until then it had been divided by the Allies into two zones: 'Zone A' (Trieste and around) which came under a temporary Anglo-American administration, and 'Zone B' (Koper, Piran, Umag and Novigrad), which for the time being was kept under Yugoslav control. In a compromise designed to appease both parties 'Zone A' was eventually handed over to the Italians (principally to keep it from falling into Soviet clutches) and 'Zone B' became formally part of Slovenia – a move that, rather than appease, actually incurred the disgust of both sides: Tito had always regarded Trieste as a legitimately Slav city and the Italians found it hard to renounce their misplaced historical claims on Istria as a whole. Nowadays the northern coast is probably the most Italianate part of the region: there's a steady flow of traffic over the no-longer sensitive border, Italian is widely spoken and all road signs are in Italian as well as Slovene.

Arriving from Italy, **KOPER** (Italian Capodistria) is the first large town you reach, from the main road a disappointing spectacle of mauve-maroon tower blocks, cranes and industrial estates. Don't be fooled by this: within its off-putting surge of development Koper is a tottery old Venetian town, crowded on to a former island in a dense lattice of narrow streets. The **bus** and **train stations** are next to each other, 20 minutes' walk from the centre or a short ride on one of the frequent yellow buses. These drop you just outside the old city: there only residents are allowed to drive and most people seem to get around on bicycles.

All of Koper's paved streets and alleys converge on **Titov Trg**, fulcrum of the old city, flanked by a Venetian Loggia and Koper's most enduring symbol, the **Praetor's Palace**, which with its battlements, balconies, busts and coats of arms is like the backdrop for a particularly wild opera. The **Cathedral**, on the same square, is clearly the product of two architectural eras, a large church with a façade that's a meeting of C15th Venetian Gothic and the Renaissance styles of a hundred years later. Inside, there are two paintings by Carpaccio (said to be a native of the town), easily recognisable in each transept, and on the high altar the carved marble sarcophagus of St Nazarius an obscure saint who for equally obscure reasons is patron of the town. Follow Kidričeva west from the square and you reach the **Civic Museum**, which when I was in Koper had been closed for six months and was uncertain as to when it would reopen; its collection of Venetian paintings is reputedly excellent.

There's not much else to see in Koper but it makes a good base for seeing the rest of Slovene Istria – no beaches and a busy working harbour have kept it relatively untouristed – and for nipping over the border, 10 km away, to Italy: to-ing and fro-ing between the two countries is almost constant – the Italians come here for cheap goods, the Yugoslavs hop across for classier clothes and consumer items – and buses to Trieste (pay in lire for the return journey) are almost hourly. **Private rooms** are plentifully available through an office at the station or at Koper's **Turist Biro** in town (Ukmarjev Trg 7; daily 0700–2000). The nearest **campsite** is in IZOLA, a ten-minute bus ride away in the Piran direction. I wouldn't **swim** anywhere here – the water is muggy and polluted and doesn't really clear up until you get near Piran; there *are* beaches at ANKARAN, near the Italian border, but you're still well within range of Koper's cranes and tankers and even nearer the more perilous excretions of Trieste.

Ten minutes south down the coast lies **IZOLA**, a pretty, red-roofed, belfried town, though like Koper still hugged tight by industry and port facilities. Soon after, the road veers north onto a long tapering peninsula that projects like a dormant lizard's tail into the Adriatic and you pass through **PORTOROŽ** ('Port of Roses'), a sprawling resort that by the end of the last century was already well known for its mild climate and the health-inducing properties of its salty mud baths. Maladied middle-aged Austrians flocked here by the thousand to be smothered with murky balm dredged up from the nearby salt pans: up went the Palace Hotel, in came the opportunists and so began Portorož. After the last war the transition from health to package resort wasn't hard to make, and Portorož is now one of the ugliest, most developed stretches of coast in all Yugoslavia, a horrible ghetto of bars, chalets, hotels and autocamps, where 'having fun' has become meaningless because there's literally nothing else to do.

Best hurry on to **PIRAN**, which lies away from it all on the narrowing tip of the peninsula. Sure, there are tourists here too – thronging the main square, milling around the souvenir-stacked harbour, packing the ranks of restaurants – but few actually stay, and there are sparse echoes of Portorož's money-spinning complexes in the midst of the town's close web of arched alleys and little squares. **Tartinijev Trg** – named after the violinist and composer, born in a house on this square and remembered by a central bronze statue – is one of the loveliest squares on the coast, fringed by a mix of Venetian palaces and a portentous Austrian town hall. The red-painted corner palace bears the inscription 'lassa pur dir' ('Let them talk'), which legend explains away as a retort to nosey towns-people who didn't approve of the owner's more dubious romantic liaisons. It now houses the **Turist Biro** (Monday-Saturday 0800–1200/1700–2000, Sunday 0900–1200), where **rooms** can be in desperately short supply in season; the cheapest **hotel** is the C Category *Sidro* across the square. Scores of **restaurants** here and on the seafront serve up tempting arrays of seafood: best is the *self-service* place, which does the same dishes as the others but for half the price.

Further homage to Tartini is paid in the **Maritime Museum** on the left side of the harbour (Tuesday-Saturday 0900–1800), along with a display on Piran's salt industry – you'd be surprised how interesting this is – and a scatter of paintings that includes naive ex-votive works by Piran sailors and an amazingly bad portrait of the local authorities by Tintoretto.

Behind the town stagger remains of what in its day must have been a formidable set of **fortifications**, perforated with the same fairy-tale 'V's as the palace at Koper. You can walk most of the way along, round as far as the great barn-like Baroque church that crowns a commanding spot high on a ridge above the town. The campanile is visible from just about everywhere in Piran, and may seem irritatingly familiar – it's a replica of St Mark's in the square at Venice. A few dinars gets you a view of the broad swing of the Italian coastline – the marshy flats of Venetia, hazily distant – and behind, green Istria, enclosing the town with clumps of soldierly cypresses.

THE WEST COAST: TOWARDS PULA

Soon after Piran begins the worst part of the coast: in itself beautiful enough, with fields of rich red Istrian soil and pinewoods sloping gently down to the sea, but with development at its most intense. Packages fill most of the hotels, autocamps blot out the seaside in between and rooms are snapped up so far in advance as to make beds on the offchance a joke. **SAVUDRIJA**, on the western tip of Istria, is one of the better places, still relatively unaffected, with pleasant beaches, two acceptable **campsites** (one nudist) and dense pinewoods – good territory for sleeping rough. A few kilometres south lie evidence of Roman expansion in the ancient settlement of Sipar, submerged but within easy snorkelling range.

UMAG is rather less idyllic, a small town almost entirely given over to a holiday business that sprouts mercilessly out on each side in a profusion of concrete lidos, holiday chalets, and autocamps. Places to stay are at a premium and if you want a space on the 'beaches' you have to squeeze in with the others. **NOVIGRAD** is larger but otherwise more of the same, a decaying Istrian fishing port that was rescued from obscurity with the coming of the tourist trade and is now, only too obviously, flourishing.

After Novigrad the coast degenerates still further into the most extensive chain of tourist reservations in the country: complex follows complex without let-up as far as the Limski Kanal. To hear an Istrian talk about this stretch of coast would put a Texan to shame. It boasts a record number of visitors, the biggest hotel in the country, the largest nudist camp in Europe, the most verdant vineyards and olive plantations – the list is endless. *Adriatikturist* in Poreč have details on all kinds of accommodation, but although there's space for 35,000 people most beds are taken well in advance and your chances of getting one on spec are pretty remote.

This seems a shame as **POREČ** itself is quite a pretty little place, set on a small promontory and cut into an ordered mesh of streets that dates from its time as a Roman encampment. The ancient *Decumanus* still runs straight as a die through the centre and the Roman forum, **Marafor Trg**, is littered with the untidy remains of temples to Mars and Neptune – at least those parts of them that haven't found their way to the local museum, housed in a Baroque palace on the main street.

More impressive – and Poreč's star turn – is the C6th **Basilica of Euphrasius**, centred in a crowded complex of buildings down a side-turn off Ljubljanska. This is actually the culmination of a number of earlier churches, remains of which are still evident. The first, the Oratory of St Maur (who is said to have lived in a house on this site), is in scattered pieces on the north side of the basilica, a secret place of worship dating from a time when Christianity was still a clandestine religion – fragments of mosaic show the sign of the fish, symbol of underground Christians at the time. The mosaic floor of a later, rather less secretive, church has been carefully revealed through gaps in the existing basilica floor. Bishop Euphrasius built the present complex a century later in 543, ostentatiously combining his palace with a baptistery, atrium and mosaic-adorned **basilica**.

The **mosaics** have a Byzantine solemnity quite different from the earlier geometric designs, studded with semi-precious gems, encrusted with mother-of-pearl and interrupted everywhere with Euphrasius's monogram – he was a notoriously arrogant man. Mosaics were the common form of decoration at the time: these are almost exactly contemporary with those at Ravenna in Italy and are generally reckoned to compare quite well. Certainly they're in pristine condition and, confined to the apse, form an exotic climax to what is otherwise a rather bare interior: the Virgin sits enthroned with Child in the centre – a position which up to then had always been reserved for the figure of Christ Pantocrator – flanked by St Maur, a worldly-looking Euphrasius holding a model of his church and next to him his brother – clearly the bishop believed in keeping things in the family. Underneath are scenes of the *Annunciation* and *Visitation*, the latter surprisingly realistic, with the imaginative invention of a doltish eavesdropping servant.

Once you've studied the mosaics and the C13th ciborium in front of them, glanced at the scant treasury and fought your way through the people swarming to snap the church, there's not a great deal else to see, either here or in Poreč as a whole, which I tired of very quickly. Tourist figures make dry reading, but Poreč's are astronomical: it recently overtook Opatija as Yugoslavia's top resort and the numbers arriving here continue to soar, something that is clearly manifest in Poreč today. Things are more expensive, the locals more rude, the streets are jammed with people and it's one of the few places in Yugoslavia you can buy the *NME*...

After Poreč the tourist settlements continue, grim, purpose-built modern resorts stuffed with tennis courts and swimming pools. There's nowhere to stay even if you wanted to, and to be certain of getting cheap accommodation, you'll need to head some way downcoast to PULA. From there it's easy enough to double back to any places of interest.

One of the more fashionable of these is **VRSAR**, a tidy fishing village set high above a sheltered harbour, once the summer residence of the Poreč bishops and now best known as the location of one of the world's largest nudist colonies. There's a Bishops' Castle here, and a Romanesque church, but any such sights are overwhelmed in summer-time by the naked enthusiasts from the camp, half a mile down the coast at KOVERSADA. Started in 1960, this is the oldest naturist resort on the Adriatic, a self-contained mini-city where 15,000 people can go without clothes for 24 hours a day.

The **Limski Kanal**, end of the Poreč tourist-spread, cuts a deep fjord into the red-earthed Istrian mainland, thick woods sheer on either side and the sea clear turquoise below. The sense of relief and escape is unmistakeable. In Roman times it marked the boundary between the Pula and Poreč regions – *Lim* means border or limit – and later it became a favourite shelter of the Neretva pirates who used it as a base from which to wage war on the Venetians. More recently it was used as a location for a film about Vikings – the weather's more reliable here than in Norway. You can sample the oysters and mussels cultivated all the way along (a much-lauded local delicacy) in a restaurant at the head of the fjord.

There are few more pleasant towns in Istria than **ROVINJ**. Delicately poised between medieval port and modern tourist resort, it has managed to preserve its character by restricting serious development to well outside the town centre. Its harbour is a likeable mix of fishing boats and swanky yachts, its quaysides a blend of sunshaded café tables and the thick orange of fishermen's nets. Spacious Venetian houses and elegant piazzas lend an overridingly Italian air, and the festive mood the tourists bring – notwithstanding a nickname like 'the Montmartre of Istria' – marks Rovinj out sharply from its neighbours up the coast.

Were it not for the hotels that tentacle out on either side, it would be more accurate to describe Rovinj as a village: it only takes a few minutes to walk from end to end. The 'Montmartre' tag stems from its painters, who have gravitated here since 1954 and every year in early August hold an open-air exhibition of their work. A Baroque gabled arch leads off M. Tita Trg to **Grisia Ulica**, lined with galleries and ateliers and climbing steeply through a clutter of streets to the **Cathedral** (Daily 1000–1200/1600–1900), which dominates the town from the summit of Rovinj's stumpy peninsula. An C18th Baroque church, this is justly more famous for the tremendous views from the top of the campanile than for any particular beauty.

Beaches around town are on the whole pretty grotty. For better swimming take a 15 minute boat ride to the tiny **Crveni Otok** (Red Island), one of seven little islands off the coast around Rovinji five minutes from where the boat docks, and well signposted, is a beach reserved for nudists. Accommodation is marginally less hopeless than Poreč: *Kompas* and *Generalturist* in the harbour have a limited number of private **rooms** but these disappear rapidly in summer. Best and nearest of several **campsites** is *Polari*, 3km down the coast in the direction of Pula – taxi boats go there or you can follow the seaside path.

Not long out of Rovinj Istria's junky developments begin to thin out, and the landscape flattens into scrubby moorland pasture. Offshore lie the snaky forms of the **BRIONI ISLANDS** – Veli Brijun, Mali Brijun and their fragmented archipelago, closed to the public at present but once a fashionable resort and summer residence of Tito, where he would entertain foreign statesmen and conduct high-level discussions. Veli Brijun was open to organised tours when I was around and may even be open to independent travellers by now (if so, ferries are likely to leave from FAŽANA), but the rest, including Tito's house on Vanga, remain firmly shut to all but visiting foreign politicians.

PULA

'Pola is a queer old place', said James Joyce at the turn of the century and even now it's difficult to disagree. In his day **PULA** – or Pola as it was then – was chief port of the Austro-Hungarian empire. Today its strategic location at the head of the Adriatic has made it Yugoslavia's most important naval base: cranes ring the harbour and throngs of sailors crowd the streets, giving it a rough working air that is refreshing after the contrivances of Istria's tourist complexes and twee seaside towns. But at the same time Pula belongs to a quite different era, one in which huge tankers and modern warships really have no place. For what distinguishes the town, and forms its main attraction, is the enormous legacy of the Romans.

Legend has Pula founded by the Colchians, who, according to the Argonauts legend, fled here in search of the Golden Fleece; the name stems from the Greek word *polai* meaning 'the pursued'. The **Romans** put the city squarely on the map when they arrived in 177 BC, transforming it into an important commercial centre which, over the next hundred years, and particularly during the Augustan period, was endowed with all the imperial trimmings appropriate to its rising status. Most dominant of these is the **Amphitheatre** (Daily 0800–2000) just north of the centre, a great grey elliptical skein of connecting arches, silhouetted against the skyline from wherever you stand in the city. Built towards the end of the 1st century BC, measurements of 132 by 105 by 32 metres make it the sixth largest in the world, with space for over 23,000 spectators. Only a small part of the seating remains anything like intact, and the interior tiers and galleries were long ago quarried by local people who used the soft limestone to build their houses, but the outer shell is nigh on complete. Actually, we're lucky so much does survive: the Venetians, once planned to dismantle the whole lot and reassemble it piece by piece on the Lido, until dissuaded by the arguments of one of their more enlightened senators. His gallant stand is remembered by a plaque on one of the towers, up which a slightly hair-raising climb gives a good sense of the enormity of the structure and a view of Pula's industrious harbour. You can also explore some of the cavernous rooms underneath – like those exposed under the Coliseum – which would have been used for keeping wild animals and Christians before they met their death.

They're now given over to piles of crusty amphora, reconstructed olive presses and other lacklustre exhibits. The arena itself has been put to good advantage and is used to stage the **Yugoslav film festival**, held every year in the last week of July.

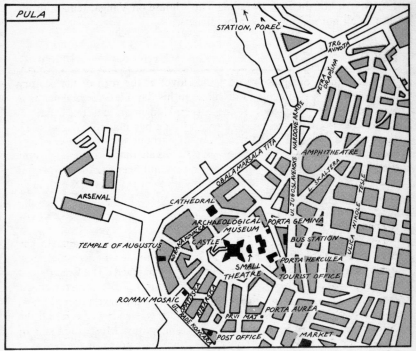

PULA

STATION, POREČ

TRG AVNOTA

PETRA DRAPŠINA

UI. JUGOSLAVENSKE NARODNE ARMIJE

AMPHITHEATRE

OBALA MARŠALA TITA

L. ŠKALTERA

ULICA NIKOLE TESLE

ARSENAL

CATHEDRAL

ARCHAEOLOGICAL MUSEUM

PORTA GEMINA

KANA KOVAČIČA

CASTLE

BUS STATION

TEMPLE OF AUGUSTUS

SMALL THEATRE

PORTA HERCULEA

TOURIST OFFICE

ROMAN MOSAIC

UI. RADE KONČARA

PORTA AUREA

PRVI MAJ

POST OFFICE

MARKET

Central Pula circles a pyramidal hill, scaled by secluded streets and topped with a star-shaped Venetian fortress. Whichever way you walk, if you stay on the main streets and keep the hill on the same side you'll end up where you started. **Prvomajska** is the axis along which most things happen, running from the **Porta Aurea**, a triumphal arch erected in 30 BC by a local family of nobles, to **Trg Republike**, the ancient Roman forum, where stands the slim **Temple of Augustus**, built between 2 BC and 14 AD to celebrate the cult of the Emperor. Inside is a permanent exhibition of the best of Pula's Roman finds including a lovely set of athletic figurines and tiny sculptures, the sculpted torso of a Roman centurion found in the amphitheatre and a beautifully realised figure of a slave kneeling at the sandalled feet (more or less all that's left) of his master. Next door stood a twin temple to Diana of which only the back end remains – easy to miss and ingeniously incorporated into Pula's Gothic-Renaissance town hall.

On the east side of the hill, hiding in the trees behind the Porta Gemina, is the **Archaeological Museum** (Daily 0900–1900) where the rest of Pula's more transportable Roman relics have finished up: pillars, capitals and deformed togaed statues mingled haphazardly with ceramics, jewellery and trinkets from all over Istria. Behind the museum a well-disguised path leads past the remains of a smaller **Roman theatre** and round the right-hand side of the **fort**, whose mossy overgrown bastions are now the home of Pula's *Revolution Museum*. Just below is the **Cathedral** (Daily 0700–1200/1600–1800), a broad, simple and very spacious basilica that's a real hotchpotch of periods and styles, the Romanesque outcome of a C16th basilica built on the foundations of a Roman temple and restored in the C15th with a dignified Renaissance façade. To cap it all the high altar is a plain marble Roman sarcophagus said to contain the remains of the C11th Magyar king Solomon. I was too confused to find out why. . . .

One of Pula's Roman treasures that isn't in any museum is a C2nd floor **mosaic**, discovered in the backyard of a house on Prvomajska, now restored and on permanent display behind a metal grill. Most is non-figurative – geometric flower-patterns and meanders – but a central panel shows the punishment of Dirce, depicted at the moment of her travail being tied to the horns of a bull by the twins Amphion and Zethus, tough customers, avenging their mother Antiope whom Dirce had wronged.

Some practical points

Pula isn't particularly beautiful but you do need a full day here to see everything, and it's a good base from which to explore other parts of Istria; unless you come during the July film festival **accommodation** is cheaper and easier to come by than almost anywhere else. *Arenaturist* – a few seconds from the bus station on Trg Bratstva i Jedinstva – have **rooms**, the nearest **campsite** is *Stoja*, 3km south (bus 1) and there's a **Youth Hostel** at Verudela (Bus 4). People don't visit Pula as a resort but if you're really desperate for a swim there are rocky **beaches** fringed with hotels and the like at VERUDELA and MEDULIN (where there's a large naturist campsite) further down the coast. Back in town **restaurants** are few and far between – the *Narodni* on Prvomajska is central and cheap. What nightlife there is centres on the *Jadran Kavana*, Trg Bratstva i Jedinstva.

Pula is one of the few Istrian towns with a **rail** link – the station is a 15–minute walk north from the centre; the **bus station** is more centrally placed on Ulica JNA and most local buses leave from Trg Bratstva i Jedinstva. Pula's **airport** is 6km east of the city: JAT buses leave the bus station one hour before departures. **Ferries** link Pula with Venice once a week – currently Fridays – and there's an almost daily service running down to Lošinj and Zadar.

INLAND ISTRIA

The contrast between inland Istria and the coast could hardly be greater, and you don't need to travel for long before the olive groves and vineyards have given way to an interior that is harsh and unprepossessing, scarred by the wind and dominated completely by grey Karst mountains that soak up water as soon as it falls. It's a region well served by hardship, but somehow the Istrians have continued to eke a living out of this unyielding landscape, perching their towns and villages high on hillsides alongside life-giving valleys.

If you only see one of these it should be **MOTOVUN**, an unwieldy clump of houses straddling a green wooded hill. Stout ramparts surround the old nucleus of the town, affording fantastic views over the Mirna valley and countryside which produces some of the finest Istrian wines – *Teran* and *Malvasija* are among the better known. Inevitably the town gets crowded – it's a favourite with day-excursionists from the nearby resorts – but the place has a genuine medieval charm, and its main square, fronted by a Renaissance church, a tranquil nobility unequalled in Istria. If you want to stay, **rooms** are available but much sought-after, and you'd be well advised to turn up early in the day.

If Motovun's roots are Venetian, those of **BERAM**, an unspoilt hilltop village a few kilometres south, are quite definitely Slav, with some of the most exciting native art of the whole region. Half a mile north of the village is the chapel of **Sv Marija na Škrilinah** (Our Lady of the Rocks), a diminutive Gothic church with a set of **frescoes** dating from 1474 and painted by a local artist who signed himself Vincent of Kastav (he is known to have also painted the frescoes at Hrvrastolje, near Koper). Of countless well-executed biblical scenes two large frescoes stand out. As well as showing a marvellous equestrian pageant, the splendidly rich *Adoration of the Kings* reveals a wealth of fine detail – distant ships, mountains, churches and wildlife – that strongly resembles early Flemish painting. Similarly, the *Dance of Death* stands out in macabre clarity against a blood-red background on the west wall: skeletons clasp scythes and blow trumpets in a clarion call to the grave, weaving in and out of a Chaucerian procession of citizens and notaries led by the Pope and with a rich merchant bringing up the rear, greedily clinging to his possessions and indicating the money on the table he would so dearly love to buy himself out with.

PAZIN, a few twists in the road south of Beram, has little in the way of art treasures but its dramatic setting is worth any number of pictures, dominated by a brooding grey castle which sits on steep cliffs plunging 250 feet down to the Fojba river. The castle, originally C9th but rebuilt and restructured many times since, literally overhangs the gorge below, where a huge round abyss sucks water into an underground torrent that resurfaces 30 kilometres away in the Limski Kanal. This chasm was supposed to have prompted Dante's description of the gateway to Hell in his *Inferno*, and it inspired Jules Verne to propel one of his characters – Matthias Sandorf – over the side of the castle and into the pit. In the book, Sandorf manages to swim along the subterranean river until he reaches the coast – a feat destined, I suspect, to remain forever in the realms of fiction.

Pazin has had a turbulent history, occupying the important junction in the centre of Istria which marked the frontier between the Venetian coast and Austrian hinterland. It changed hands several times but in the main was ruled by a group of semi-independent local counts. Apart from spectacular scenery and the castle, which now houses an **Ethnographic Museum**, there's very little of note in the town itself; the museum, however (Daily 1000–1300/1600–1800) is worth a visit, with a fine collection of traditional Istrian costumes and handicrafts.

ISTRIA'S EAST COAST

From Pula the main road cuts off Istria's most unfathomed corner: apart from MEDULIN there are no resorts and few towns or villages; roads are bad and public transport worse. But if you're looking for more deserted spots and have transport, this part of the coast is unbelievably unspoilt and the beaches, if you can find them, delightful.

Beyond here, the first town of any size is **LABIN**, about 5 kilometres inland, on a hill which has been so extensively and carelessly mined that its houses are now considered unsafe and the population has been resettled in the ugly and functional appendage of PODLABIN, down the hill. Old Labin is now almost deserted, a ghost town whose cracked façades and rubble-strewn streets offer a unique and undisturbed chance to appreciate one of these Istrian hilltop settlements at their silent best. The view from the town walls is superb: sea mist tends to shroud the gulf during the hot part of the day but when it lifts the mountainous shape of Cres appears, and beyond that Krk and the sinister distant shoreline.

Buses run roughly every hour to **RABAC** on the coast, an awful fledgling hyper-resort beginning to rival Poreč in magnitude and only slightly trailing in the number of tourists it attracts. A hulking row of modern hotels runs across the bay, fronted by a large and noisy campsite and an even noisier beach: this, plus the difficulty in finding anywhere remotely cheap to stay, make Rabac worth missing out entirely.

The road from Labin to Opatija passes through some of the most beautiful coastal scenery in the country, as yet largely undeveloped, Istria's green rim dropping steep and sheer into the sea and spawning few viable places to stop. At some points steps have been carved out of the cliff-face; at others a winding donkey track is the only route down, but for the most part the sea is simply inaccessible. **PLOMIN** is typical of the local villages: ancient and windswept, most of its people have been sucked into the tourist trade on more lucrative parts of the coast and many of its old stone houses are boarded up and empty. Far below, the sea lashes the rocks and the grey outline of Cres looms out of the mist, reachable by regular car ferry from BRESTOVA, a couple of miles further on.

Brestova onwards, Istria's seaside industry begins to reappear. **MOŠĆENIČKA DRAGA** is an oversized holiday camp in a small cove, with a pebble beach that's packed throughout the season. **MEDVEJA** is much the same, brimming with rock lobsters looking over to the hazy pink of industrial Rijeka. **LOVRAN** is just as popular but more elegant, with palatial Austrian villas and grandiose follies, and curly balustrades green with clinging espaliers.

After Lovran there's no break until **OPATIJA**, oldest established and still one of the most popular Yugoslav resorts. A town in the best tradition of seaside magnificence, and pretty in an overpowering Austro-Hungarian sort of way, it boasts little more than a handful of concrete beaches packed closely with sunbathing bodies. Tourist maps mark only hotels – great elegant pleasure palaces from the C19th that grace Opatija's main street or hide in shady parks, rearing up magnificently where you least expect them. A Rijeka businessman built the first villa here in 1844, and after a visit by the trend-setting wife of the Austrian Emperor the town was promoted as a handy health resort for aristocratic Austrians (ironic now when you think of filthy old Rijeka just a few miles down the coast). Today it's much more parvenu, an expensive garden-city whose nostalgic turn-of-the-century opulence attracts a fair-sized chunk of Istria's plenteous tourist fodder. In restaurants and bars there's a good chance of getting stung if you stick to the main drag, and **rooms** – available from *Kvarner Express* or *Generalturist* – work out extremely pricey in high season. Better to head on instead for Rijeka and access to lovelier and far more untamed stretches of Yugoslavia's coast.

TRAVEL DETAILS

Buses

From Koper to Ljubljana (hourly; 2hrs); Poreč (hourly; 2hrs); Rijeka (4; 2hrs); Trieste (hourly; 1hr); Rovinj (4; 2½hrs); Piran (4 an hour; 45min).

From Poreč to Opatija (8 daily; 4hrs); Pazin (9; 1hr); Rijeka (8; 4hrs); Pula (hourly; 1½hrs).

From Pula to Split (3 daily; 10hrs); Pazin (4; 2hrs); Zagreb (hourly; 6hrs); Rijeka (hourly; 2½ hrs); Vrsar (5; 1½hrs).

A ferry runs from Trieste to Pula 4 times a week in high season, twice a week in low season; stops include Poreč, Piran and Koper.

Chapter three
THE ADRIATIC COAST AND ISLANDS

The **Adriatic coast** is Yugoslavia's greatest pull, and deservedly so. For centuries this region was ruled by Venice, spawning towns, churches and an architecture that wouldn't look out of place on the other side of the water. All along, well-preserved medieval towns sit on tiny islands or jut into the sea on slim peninsulas, beneath a grizzled Karst landscape that drops sheer into some of the clearest – and cleanest – water anywhere. There are the usual holiday hangouts, and tourism has mushroomed in recent years, but the crowds are rarely difficult to avoid: the abundant Adriatic archipelago can swallow up any number of sightseeing hordes, and on the mainland tourist settlements have kept well away from the main towns.

You're likely to start your travels from **Rijeka** or **Split**, largely industrial ports and jumping-off points for the islands and other towns up and down the coast; though Split itself is worth an extended visit for the prodigious remains of **Diocletian's Palace**. Regular **ferries** ply the coastal route between Rijeka and Bar (in Montenegro), calling at all the principal towns and islands, and supplemented by a comprehensive network of local boats as well as long-distance buses. If you're making a thorough exploration your itinerary should include the coast from **Zadar to Split** (by far the most interesting stretch), **Dubrovnik** – touristed out, some say, but still unmissable – and a fair sprinkling of **islands** – **Hvar, Korčula** and **Rab** are among the most beautiful and most popular; others like **Pag** and **Mljet** offer haunts still well estranged from the beaten tourist track.

Things are more expensive than in the interior of the country but you can still live very cheaply, even in the larger tourist centres. Ferries don't cost much, rooms are plentiful and, for the most part, affordable, the food is good, with an abundance of fish, and Dalmatian wines are among Yugoslavia's best – crisp, dry and dirt cheap.

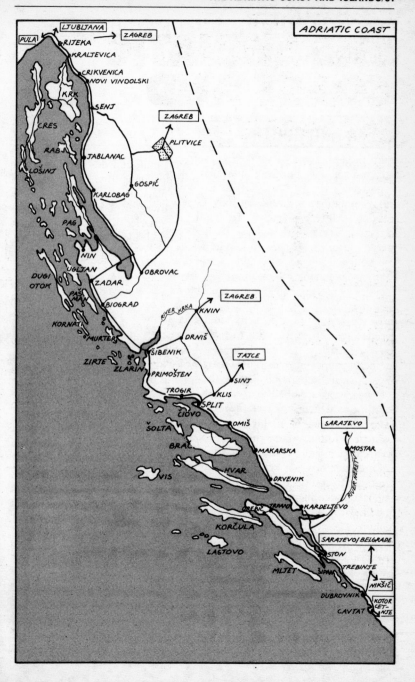

THE KVARNER GULF AND ISLANDS

RIJEKA AND SOUTH

From the sea, rows of hooked cumbrous cranes and rusty sea-stained tankers front the soaraway apartment blocks that make up the bulk of Yugoslavia's largest port, **RIJEKA:** a down-to-earth, unpretentious city and the major transit-point for Italy, Greece and the whole of the Adriatic seaboard. More backpackers trudge the streets here than anywhere else in the country and, though it's by no means beautiful and not worth a special journey, if you do end up in Rijeka it's worth dumping your bags (24–hour left luggage at the bus station) and spending the wait between connections having a look around.

History has dealt Rijeka some cruel blows, and if it seems a little mixed-up (others have called it characterless) that's because it's yet another of those Balkan cities whose national identity was only assured a few decades ago. From the 15th to the 18th century it remained firmly and solely Austrian, after which time it became the prey of a number of competing super-powers. The Treaty of London of 1915 promised it as reward to the Italians for joining the war on the Allied side and though this was soon annulled at Versailles, it gave the Italians a taste for a coastline to which they were never entitled – the Italian population here has always been negligible. In 1919 the renegade Italian soldier-poet Gabriele d'Annunzio marched into Rijeka with several thousand men and occupied the city; he was eventually forced to leave – but only after a peace conference that left Rijeka split in two by a new and bitter Italian-Yugoslav frontier.

The last war united Rijeka with Tito's Yugoslavia, a war-damaged city that had to be partially rebuilt – though much of the solid Austrian building does remain. **Korzo Narodne Revolucije** runs the length of the centre and is the focus of a vigorous *korso* and a pulsing city life. Left under the clock tower is what they hopefully call the *Stari Grad* (Old Town): an area of bombed-out squares, peeling plaster and shiny black-glass department stores. The **Church of Sv Vid** – a domed Baroque church modelled on Santa Maria della Salute in Venice – has a curious story attached to it. In 1296 a man was losing at cards outside an earlier church and ran inside, flinging stones at the crucifix, which began to bleed. He was swallowed up whole by the ground beneath him – that is, except for his hand. The 'miraculous cross' stands behind glass on the high altar:

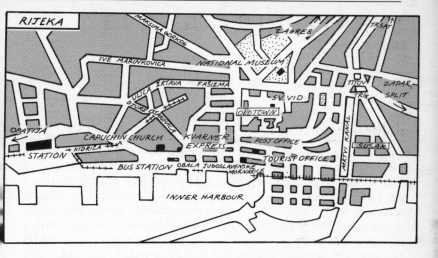

until recently a commemorative bronze hand used to dangle from it, and the stone (at any rate, *a* stone) fills a gash in the side of Christ.

Not far from Sv Vid – the other side of the old town – is the **History and Maritime Museum** (Tuesday-Saturday 0900–1300), housed in a marvellously over-the-top C19th building where d'Annunzio installed himself for his short period of power. In huge, echoing stucco'd rooms are costumes, weaponry and a lot of C18th and 19th furniture – most tarnished and faded, some astonishingly kitschy. Nothing of great note but worth an hour of anyone's time.

If you cross the thick pea-soup channel of the Riječina – which once marked the Italian border – and climb the steps off Titov Trg (bus 1 is an alternative) you come eventually to **TRSAT** where, the angels have it, the House of the Virgin Mary and Joseph rested for 3½ years on its miraculous way from the infidel in Nazareth to safer climes in Loreto in Italy. The Baroque **Church of Our Lady** stands on the site, and feels a very holy place: a shrine and place of pilgrimage for women who climb the hill from Rijeka every morning to worship. **Trsat Castle** is further up, an ivied hotchpotch of turrets and towers, walkways and parapets, that looks backwards up the great grey tear in the mountains behind, and forward over Rijeka, which lies under a dim yellowish haze of industrial smog. Beyond slinks the island of Cres and, to the right, the sheer mountain wall of the Istrian peninsula. While parts of the castle date back to the Romans, this was originally a stronghold of the Frankopans – a family of Croatian aristocrats from Krk who, on and off, and with the say-so of Austria and Venice, ruled this northern part of the Dalmatian coast for several hundred years. After their demise an Austrian general took the place over, constructing a Doric temple that served as his family's mausoleum. Now, the only thing to admire is the view; for the rest, the castle serves as a seasonal restaurant and open-air theatre.

Ferries, food and accommodation
Ferries leave from the quay around the corner from the bus station – the *Jadrolinija* office is opposite. Connections to Cres and Lošinj once daily; to Corfu and Igoumenitsa roughly three times a week; and to points all down the coast between six and seven times a week in summer. Since you're only likely to come to Rijeka to catch a boat there's little point in staying the night, but if you do get stuck the *Kvarner Express* office (Monday-Friday 0730–2000, Saturday 0800–1700) on Trg Togliatti has a stock of private **rooms**. Cheapest **hotel** in town is the *Kontinental*, or there's a **campsite**, about 8km out on the Opatija road (bus 32 from R. Končara). For maps and general information, go to the **Information Centre** on Trg Republike (open every day). There are a couple of self-service **restaurants** around, one on Trg Republike, one on the seafront, so cheap eating is no problem; with a little more money try *Tri Palme*, on the front in Ivana Zajca.

HEADING SOUTH

Rijeka's industry stretches way, way down the coast to the deep inlet of Bakar, normally pervaded by the rich, pungent smell of sulphur from the oil refinery whose flame dashes strident yellow across to the orange pipelines opposite. **BAKAR** the town seems to have had a raw deal of it: though undeniably a pretty place, nestled haphazardly at the far end of the bay, it's been well stifled and doesn't invite a closer look. Further round the bay fishermen watch for shoals of tuna from high outstretched ladders; tuna is a speciality here, eaten with a sparkling local wine called *Bakarska Voda*. Then **KRALJEVICA**, whose tiny old centre and castles have long since been hemmed in by the splurge of Rijeka's port suburbs. The shipyards here once employed the young Tito as a metalworker (he was dismissed for organising a successful strike) and they now bear his name. The castles – **Stari Grad** and **Novi Grad** – were the work of the Frankopan and Zrinjski families respectively, families of Croatian nobility who, in the 1660s, after many years of indirect Austro-Hungarian rule, allied themselves against the Austrians and were executed for their trouble. Nearby, UVALA SCOTT is a bay where the lesser-known brother of Walter Scott is supposed to have retired and quietly corresponded with Byron. How true this is, I wasn't able to find out.

CRES AND LOŠINJ

CRES and LOŠINJ – really one island separated by an artificial channel

– were known for a long time as the *Absyrtides*, the place where Jason and his Argonauts fled with the Golden Fleece and Medea killed her brother Absyrtus as he pursued her. Of the two, Lošinj is smaller and greener, while Cres (pronounced 'Tsress') is the longest and one of the barest of all the islands on this coast: a green-grey hunk of land spotted only with buttons of gorse and hardy figs and olives, and criss-crossed by stark white dry-stone walls.

CRES TOWN is a tiny oasis amongst all this, grouped around a small harbour, watched over by streaky grey hills of Karst and still relatively undisturbed by tourism. It has the crumpled look of so many of the towns on this coast: tiny alleys lead nowhere; miniscule courtyards shelter through arches, where a green abundance burgeons over the rails of balconies and mauve and pink sprout from cracks in walls. Apart from a small **museum** (piles of encrusted Roman amphorae and coins, manuscripts and sculpture from Venetian and Austrian days) and the **Cathedral** with its C15th Renaissance portal, there's not much to see, but if you want to stay, the **Turist Biro** (Daily 0700–1300/1400–2100) has **rooms** and will provide you with a map. There's also a **campsite** on the north edge of town – about 15 minutes' walk by the sea – and you can either **swim** from there or take a boat to the next bay along, where the beaches are better and emptier. Boats leave (early) from the Turist biro pier or can be hired by the hour or day from the shed below Hotel Kimen.

Around eight buses a day ply the route south to VELI LOSINJ. Not far out of Cres Town you pass **Lake Vrana**, an emerald-green ellipse of fresh water that supplies both Cres and Lošinj. But for this lake, both islands would be utterly dry. Before long you reach the furthest tip of Cres and **OSOR**, oldest settlement on either island and a once prosperous city whose fortunes were checked by a series of sackings and the virulent spread of infection. Abbé Fortis, writing in the C18th, described it as no more than 'a corpse of a city . . . where there are perhaps more empty and ruined houses than inhabitants', and T.G. Jackson paints a depressing picture of decayed houses and people eaten away by malaria and disease. Now, huddled at the point where the bridge leads over to Lošinj, it's a bit of a gem: Mestrović figures line narrow streets which converge on a main square that – if you're here on a hot summer's afternoon – breathes a peace which seems almost undisturbable. There are rooms (ask around in the village), a couple of restaurants, and a beautifully situated campsite, which is smaller, cheaper and – if you do want peace – altogether a better option than the one at Cres. And there are plenty of places to swim. . . .

LOŠINJ is a slim sliver of land hanging limply from the side of Cres: smaller, more popular, and with a thick woolly tree cover that comes as a relief after the obdurate greyness of its neighbour. The island's main centre is **MALI LOŠINJ**, larger and more developed than Cres, with its yachting marina and newly finished bungalows creeping over the wooded prongs that shelter the town. Unlike Cres, Lošinj has been in the tourist business for some time and since the C19th and the decline of its ship-building industry, it has needed its visitors to survive.

It hasn't however been over-exploited. Mali Lošinj remains a colourful, flowery sort of place: slim cypresses nose their way through tiers of peachy cream and orange houses, which drip blood-purple bougainvillea and sport rhythmic splutters of spiky green palms. The harbour has a tarnished, colonial feel, with its shuttered Austrian palaces lining a busy waterfront behind rows of potted cacti and sub-tropical plants. Most of the hotels have been kept well out of the way on the Čikat peninsula, together with an enormous campsite and all the trappings of a well-entrenched tourist industry, including the island's most crowded beaches. If you're **camping**, special buses leave the harbour for Čikat about a dozen times daily (they're actually for hotel workers but no one seems to mind you using them), or it's a 15–minute walk. The *Istra*, on the seafront, is the cheapest **hotel**, and the **Turist Biro** (Daily 0700–2200) nearby has plenteous **private rooms**.

Again, once you've clambered around among the stepped alleys and winding streets of Mali Lošinj, taken a look at the Baroque church of Sv Marija on the hill and the anti-Uskok castle (what's left of it) behind that, there's not much else to do apart from swim and eat. There's a reasonably priced *gostiona* just off the main drag – behind where the painters do their stuff – or, cheaper still, a *snack-bar* which sells ready-to-eat meals on the corner of Trg Moše Pijade. For **swimming** follow the coastal path to Veli Lošinj, along which there are a number of quiet spots on the rocks, and where you can take all your clothes off, should you want to avoid the populous FKK cove on Čikat. **VELI LOŠINJ** itself is a 5–kilometre walk: despite the name ('Veli' means 'big'; 'Mali' means 'little'), a smaller, quieter version of its sister, strung tightly around a tiny natural harbour and dominated by the hangar-like Baroque church of Sv Antun, and a crenellated Venetian tower that peers roundly over the waterside houses. If you want to stay, the **Turist Biro** has **rooms**, and there's a **campsite**.

Once you're this far down the Cres-Lošinj strip of land, **island-hopping** becomes problematic as there are no regular ferry connections with any of the other major Kvarner islands. You can, however, avoid going all the way back to Rijeka by taking one of the twice-weekly excursions to Rab. These are run by the Turist Biro, save a lot of time and hassle, and work out only slightly more expensive than the boat and bus.

KRK

Although technically under Venice from 1115, **KRK** was officially the home of the Frankopans, a family of Croat nobles who ruled parts of the Kvarner Gulf under the auspices of the Venetians and somehow – through luck, diplomacy and shrewd judgment – managed to maintain a fair semblance of independence for around 300 years. The last Frankopan count to hold any real power was Ivan who, in the late C15th made Venice his heir as a ploy to ward off his over-ambitious brothers and went poaching new estates on the mainland. When finally ejected back to his island, he went mad, upped the taxes, looted the churches and his armies raped, murdered and tortured the people. In 1480 the Venetians had no choice but to intervene, taking the poor deranged man away and absorbing Krk properly into the Most Serene Republic – which is how it stayed until the very late C18th.

Now it's one of the most popular of all the Adriatic islands – a result more of its convenient location, I suspect, than for any intrinsic attractions. A number of Yugoslavs warned me about Krk: 'You won't like it,' they said, 'it's crowded, industrial. . . .' And while much of that can be put down to inter-island rivalry – which remains strong every-where – in essence it holds true. Krk is more developed touristically than many places on the coast and, with its forbidding industrial and commercial installations, often seems little more than an extension of Rijeka's infrastructure on the mainland. Crossing over on the bridge from Kraljevica offers an uninviting prospect of broad white drums of oil pipes, gantrys and smoking chimneys mingling with a scrubby, desolate landscape: all in all, not a pretty sight.

Things pick up as you head south: **OMIŠALJ** is the first stop of any size and not unpleasant, although I'd recommend you push on further to escape the emissions of the omnipresent industry. **KRK TOWN** – the island's main centre – is in the full throes of rapid expansion, spreading perniciously over the nearby hills in formless abandon. The nucleus of all this is a small walled city: quaint enough, but with an atmosphere long spoiled by an excess of tacky souvenir shops, filigree parlours and the like. Thin cobbled streets make valiant attempts to climb away from it all, but never quite escape. **Trg M.Tita** is the main square, just inside the walls. Here you'll find the **Turist Biro** (Daily 0800–2200), which has maps (at a price) and **rooms**. Follow the road that winds right, take the second right and you're at the Romanesque **Cathedral** (Daily 0800–1300/1600–1900) – not to be confused with the attached Church of St Quirinus (which sports the onion-dome campanile). There's not much to the Cathedral, but the **Bishop's Residence** – incorporated into the town walls – has a collection of C16th and 17th Italian paintings, sporadically open for business these days (try asking in the Cathedral). Next door, the solid Frankopan fortifications are embellished with the Lion of St Mark – symbol of Venetian sovereignty; the oldest parts date back to 1191.

Hotels to the left of town and a **campsite** to the right (do a left before the football pitch) ensure that the **beaches** (rocks) remain well-populated throughout the season. You should be able to find somewhere to stretch out on the campsite side, but don't expect anything too secluded.

PUNAT, a few miles down the coast, isn't much of an alternative, with a concrete beach normally packed with people from the adjacent campsite. The town itself is sleepy, set on an almost closed bay where the sea dreams tranquilly like a mill-pond, but it's had all the trappings of tourism dumped onto it – souvenirs, a fun-fair, a massive mega-marina just to the right of town. If for any reason you do find yourself here take a taxi boat across the bay to the **Franciscan Monastery** on the islet of KOŠULJE (the more of you in the boat, the cheaper it is – fix the price beforehand), which has a chapel with a lovely wooden ceiling, a polyptych by Santa Croce and a large and dignified *Last Judgment* by Ughetti. The adjoining **museum** (0900–1200/1500–1900) has an interesting mish-mash of stuff with no particular connections: an international selection of banknotes and coins up to a century old, a genealogy of Israel from Adam and Eve to Christ, some ancient typewriters and gramophones.

Further south is some of Krk's best scenery, where the road to Baška passes through a deep, spurred river valley and grey, furrowed peaks tower high above before slipping luxuriantly into a dark blanket of pines. **BAŠKA** is set in a wide bay ringed by stark mountains: a compact old town whose real attraction is its mile-long stretch of pebble beach, hard under the wild-west heights of the Karst. It was in Baška that a tablet was found bearing the oldest known text of **Glagolitic script**. This was one of the oldest Slav alphabets – C9th, some say – and has had a symbolic importance for Croat nationalists ever since the battles with Rome to use it in a specifically Slav liturgy. The original stone is now in Zagreb, but most places on Krk seem to have sprouted copies.

The ferry journey to RAB is a still, ghostly trip through the gossamer sheen of the Adriatic, past the island of GRGUR, where a giant 'Tito' and star carved painstakingly out of the rock reminds you where you are. A little way beyond lies GOLI, an obstinate hummock of mottled rock that was used as an island-gaol for Stalinists and those opposed to Tito after the war.

RAB

RAB is the smallest, most written about, and possibly the most frequently visited of all the Kvarner islands. Much of it rises to a stony grey spine that supports little more than a few goats, but the rest is lush and green, with a sharply indented coast and some good – if crowded – beaches and coves. The real pull is **RAB TOWN**, which comes with the sort of recommendations that could easily lead to disappointment but here rarely

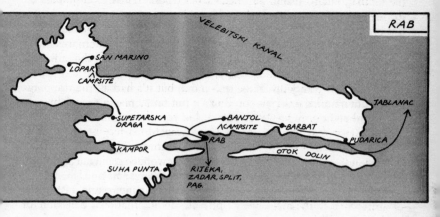

do. Certainly, Rab's beauty can take your breath away. Squeezed onto a slender ridge of land, with its four Romanesque campanili – the city's trademark – spaced evenly along the peninsular, it presents two faces to the sea: one a bright, buzzing waterfront, noisy with chatter and the whirr of outboards; the other a dreaming medieval city, grey and ochre, broken up with gurgles of prickly green palm, huddles of leaning junipers and sprigs of olivey cacti pushing their way between the city's balconied palaces. Within, it's a close-knit maze of narrow, curvy streets, stepped passages and miniature courtyards where trees spring out abandoned of palaces. Somehow, all of Rab's shapes and colours seem just about right.

The main street, **Ive Lole Ribar,** runs the length of the city, culminating in a small piazza mostly taken up by a Venetian Loggia and, tucked away in the corner, the tiny Gothic church of St Nicholas. The Venetians held sway here for something like 600 years, keeping the island poor and independent in a number of ways: by restricting the supply of salt (which was needed for preserving fish), destroying vast expanses of trees, and insisting that all Dalmatian goods were sold in Venice at fixed prices. In addition, tributes were extracted by the Turks and the island ravaged by plague, leaving the green tip of Rab's peninsula derelict and abandoned to this day. After the Venetians left the Austrians took over, and things didn't begin to improve until the formation of Yugoslavia earlier this century.

At the far end of the street the Renaissance **Dominis-Nemir Palace** was the birthplace in 1560 of Mark Anthony de Dominis, scholar, priest and sometime Archbishop of Split – until his conversion to Protestantism and move to England where he became Dean of Windsor and Vicar of West Ilsley in Berkshire. While there he wrote his ten volume *De Republica*

Ecclesiastica – a vicious attack on the Catholic church – and then headed back to Rome to repent and explain his conduct. There, imprisoned, he died, and his body was burnt as a heretic – an ignominious end for a man whose scientific and philosophical work was later to influence figures as diverse as Newton, Goethe and Descartes. Opposite, the remains of the Nemira Palace are now the *Restaurant Grand*, where bands pump out loud easy listening throughout most summer evenings.

Follow any street up from here and you're on **Rade Končara**, which runs along the highest point on Rab's jut of land. Spaced along it are most of the **churches**. **Sv Justina** is attached to the onion-capped campanile: a small Renaissance church that's been turned into a museum of sacred art, with an assortment of manuscripts, Baroque sculpture, stonework and robes. Amid this look out for a *polyptych* by Paolo Veneziano (mid-C14th), a *Death of Joseph* dubiously ascribed to Titian, and the fragment of tombstone by the door – gaze at this long enough and a seemingly worn and incomprehensible script melts into a figure of the Madonna and Child. Further down the street, the Church of **Sv Andrija** sports campanile no.2 and, a little way beyond, stands the largest and most beautiful campanile of them all: C12th, perfectly symmetrical, and with a bell whose peel was made mellow – legend tells – by gold and silver dropped into the casting pot by Rab's wealthier citizens.

A few steps away is the **Cathedral of Sv Marija**, a principally C12th Romanesque church that is a marvellous amalgam of distinct, elegant parts. The west front is striped pale grey and pink, a series of scuffed and hollowed blind arches, cut by a Renaissance doorway that supports a savage *pietà* of 1414. Inside, the walls are crumbly honey and grey with, here and there, flecks of the same agate-coloured marble. Three aisles look towards a high choir flanked by rich, almost gaudily carved stalls and, dominating all, a light, delicate ciborium in grey cipollino marble. The plaited slabs above the arches date back to the 8th and 9th centuries; the rest is contemporary with the church.

The Cathedral also harbours the head of St Christopher: a powerful relic responsible – so they say – for dispatching Hungarian, Croat and even Norman would-be invaders, though it didn't prevent submission to the Venetians in 1115. Look at the map-picture over the doorway as you go out – Rab, watched over by Christ and Mary: throughout the years that followed, and the atrocities of marauding pirates and Turks, Rab remained a civilised Christian enclave in barbarous seas. 'The community who built this cathedral was so civilised,' wrote Rebecca West, 'that it could conceive a God who would be pleased not by the howlings of His worshippers and the beating of their breasts, but by their gaiety, by their accomplishment, by their restraint and dignity.'

You need at least a couple of days to get the feel of Rab and the rest of the island. It can get crowded, especially in July and August, but not disastrously so, and you should normally be able to pick up a **room** either from the touts at the bus station or at the **Turist Biro** (Daily 0700–1200), housed in the Gothic-Renaissance palace on Maršala Tita Trg. The cheapest **hotel** is the *Beograd* – just around the corner – and the closest **campsite** about a mile from the old city in the resort suburb of Banjol; simply follow the sea path south around a couple of headlands, or take a **boat** from the taxi rank on M.Tita Trg (the more people there are the cheaper it is). I did most of my **eating** in the *Restaurant Park*, in Trg Heroja, and much of my **drinking** in the *Buffet Alligator* – up a side street opposite the Restaurant Grand – where a good proportion of Rab's youth flock to watch old 'Top of the Pops' videos.

The nearest **beaches** are in the coves towards and around the Padova campsite – sandy but very crowded. Far better to wade across to the little offshore island, quieter and more relaxed. Official **naturist facilities** are the other side of Rab town, round the point of the next bay – again, a taxi-boat ride from M.Tita Trg.

KAMPOR – a ten minute bus ride from Rab town (roughly six a day) – has a large sandy beach little used by anyone except locals and the handful of people who fill the few private rooms there. On the way you pass the darkened shells of buildings that survive from an Italian wartime concentration camp where over a two-month period nearly 5000 Yugoslavs died, starved of food and drink by corrupt Italian officials. A memorial complex not far from the beach remembers it all with despressingly long lines of marked graves – one for each four people that died – and a symbolic mosaic that depicts the war, the suffering, and ultimate Partisan victory. Like Istria, this part of Yugoslavia had a hard time of it during the war: Mussolini embraced Italy's long and misfounded historic claims to this stretch of coast, intending to create a separate Italianate state run on Fascist lines. Slavs who dissented paid the price.

LOPAR, where the ferry arrives from Krk, is just a handful of houses spread around a muddy bay. Around eight buses a day leave for Rab town, but as they don't always connect with the ferries you may have a bit of a wait. If you do, the sandy beach isn't particularly picturesque, but it is empty. A far longer, prettier, and more exploited stretch of beach exists just the other side of town at the tent-bungalow township of San Marino.

Those **island-hopping** by car and wanting to go on to PAG have no choice but to return to the mainland – to JABLANAC – and take a ferry from there. On foot you can either take the twice-weekly ferry to NOVALJA or pick up the daily boat to LUN – it leaves at noon. Bear in mind that buses from Lun to Pag Town are infrequent and you may have to hitch.

PAG

From the mainland **PAG** looks uninvitingly desolate, a snowy pumice-stone that seems as if it could barely support any form of life. Only 9000 people live here, looking after three times as many sheep, who scour the stony slopes in search of the odd blade of grass; Pag, at its greenest, only sprouts a few olives and some stumpy stick-like shrubs. Hot afternoons always seem hotter here than anywhere else: nothing stirs, seemingly nothing grows, the air hangs still and sultry and all around is arid, quasi-desert.

Which is not to say it doesn't have its attractions. **PAG TOWN**, the island's capital, retains a tight grid of narrow medieval streets that were the design of one Juraj Dalmatinac in 1443, after wrangles between Venice, Hungary and nearby Zadar left the old city of Pag – about 2 kilometres south of today's town – virtually a ruin. He laid out the town to a rectangular plan around a central square – **Trg Bratstva i Jedinstva** – and designed the Gothic-Renaissance Rector's Palace, now a café and department store. The lovely C15th **Parish Church** is also his work, a building that's a strange mixture of Gothic and early Renaissance styles, with vaulted wooden aisles and a flat stucco ceiling, divided by round-arched Gothic-Renaissance arcading. The red marble Baroque altars are adorned with examples of the delicate local lace, a craft that remains refreshingly unexploited – only made in Pag Town and sold by women in the dark, full-skirted local costume. The rewards and the drawbacks of blanket tourism seem to have passed Pag by – there are no souvenir shops, and the wearing of the traditional dress is completely authentic. So too, *Paški Sir* – the local cheese and the island's other speciality – is still largely the preserve of the people who live here. It's a hard cheese, quite salty, quite delicious. The salt – they say – is a result of the sea, which washes and taints the whole low island with its spray: the sheep eat the grass, and produce milk that gives the cheese its distinctive flavour. Pag is a salty kind of place all round: the precious stuff is the island's main industry – witness the salt pans behind the town – and even the tap water tastes slightly brackish.

If you want to stay, the *Hotel Jadran* near the ferry terminal is cheap, or the **Turist Biro** (Daily 0800–2100) by the bridge has a supply of inexpensive private rooms; plus there's a small **campsite**. The island is fairly well blessed with **beaches**, and a pebble beach skirts the strip of land that bridges Pag to the other side of the bay. When I was there it wasn't oppressively crowded, but if you're in search of seclusion, or just somewhere to sleep, there are plenty of short, relatively deserted stretches along the eastern side of the bay, within easy walking distance of the town.

Around six buses a day make the short trip down to **NOVALJA** –

Pag's major resort and haven of most of the tourists who come here. There's a large **campsite** (part nudist), a number of hotels and again a plentiful stock of private **rooms,** For itself, the town isn't all that memorable: it first grew up as the harbour of Kissa (today Caska), which was the island's first notable community, settled by the Romans in the 1st century AD. There are bits and pieces from those years laying around, but for the most part Pag remains almost totally unexplored archaeologically.

CRIKVENICA, NOVI . . . AND THE PLITVICE LAKES

CRIKVENICA (pronounced 'Tsrikvenitsa') is first, last and unashamedly a seaside resort – and it has been for nigh on a century. Between the wars it was one of the more modish playgrounds of some of the ritzier Yugoslavs, but now it's irretrievably package-tour country, spreading itself lazily along the sea for several miles in a mess of hotels, promenades and ping pong. Personally, I'd only come here to take one of the plenteous ferries to KRK.

From Crikvenica you can walk the few kilometres along the seafront to **SELCE**, more caravan-bungalow site than small village, or beyond to **NOVI VINODOLSKI** (Novi for short). A straggly resort-town cut in half by the main road, one part is gardeny, Sidcupesque suburbia while the rest – the small old quarter – is piled up on the hill above a scrappy harbour. There's no beach to speak of, and nothing to see but for the minute remains of a Frankopan castle and a small town museum – and when I was in Novi even that seemed closed for lack of interest.

The **PLITVICE LAKES** are one of Yugoslavia's greatest tourist attractions: in summer the road here is a continuous line of German, Austrian and Italian cars with boats and campers attached, and the whole park has been groomed to be as efficient and orderly as possible; buses put you down at carefully numbered walk-ways, boats leave regularly from marked points. None of this lessens the beauty: the 16 lakes that tumble into each other amid the forests have a minor key majesty, the same unspectacular loveliness as an ornamental garden. You need a couple of days to see the whole system, and even if you're not into walking, exploring the lakes seems almost effortless.

The odd thing about Plitvice's lakes is their limestone. Usually water eats away at limestone rock forming potholes and caverns – the Karst you find bordering the coast. But here the reverse happens. Minerals in the water are picked up by plants in the lakes and turned into stone, shaping coral-like patterns beneath the water. Starting out, it's best to do as the tourists and take the bus for the southern system that starts below lake Prošćan. Wooded paths follow the succession of lake and waterfall; streams burst out of rocks; brilliant dragonflies hover everywhere; the lake waters shimmer blue and green. The second system heads towards Slap Plitvice falls, a high wall of water and the thing that comes closest to the description 'dramatic'.

To **get here** from the coast is easy – plentiful buses from Senj and Zadar, good connections too from Zagreb. To **leave** can be tricky: notionally buses pull up at the stops here, but if the bus is full, or the driver doesn't like the size of your pack, they just drive past. This is quite likely to happen to you at weekends, and short of standing in the middle of the road there's little you can do. Near the southern bus stop the **Tourist Office** (0700–2000 daily) sells entrance tickets and points you to **hotels**, cheapest of which is the nearby *Bellevue*, with a few rooms at about the same price you pay for private accommodation; to check there are vacancies phone the hotel – 048 76344. Other useful facilities include **bike hire**, a cheap **supermarket** and a **campsite** at the northern entrance – you have to ask to be dropped off here as it's not a usual stop.

SENJ – AND SOUTH TO DALMATIA

'May God preserve us from the hands of Senj.' So runs a popular Yugoslav saying, inspired by a band of pirates known as the **Uskoks** who in 1537 made **SENJ** their home and terrorised the waters round about for almost a century. Refugees from the Turks, they at first only harassed Turkish shipping, but after the Venetians disowned them it soon became apparent that no one was safe. Uskok exploits were legendary: they used to taste the blood of their enemies as a pledge of brotherhood and stories of them eating a man's heart and dipping their bread in his blood abound. Adventurers and indolent aristocrats flocked here from all over Europe to join in the capery, and for some time the entire town was wholly devoted to robbery, piracy and murder. After a time, however, the Uskoks asked to be transported inland and given the chance to live by other means. Each time their pleas were ignored: it suited Venice and Austria to leave them be, as a convenient worry to Turkish ships and a source of cut-price trinkets for their ladies at home. Only after the Uskok War of 1615–17 – supposedly over Uskok atrocities – did they deal with the problem: many Uskoks were hanged, some beheaded, and the rest were transported to a meagre existence inland – as they had requested all along.

Today Senj is much less notorious, a quiet little town only busy with people changing buses for the Plitvice lakes. Extensive war damage has never been properly repaired, and it can only be a matter of time before the town flakes away to nothing: its streets are piled with rubble, its façades the epitome of peely decay, plaster breaking off in jagged chunks to reveal bricks and grainy timbers. The only reminder of the Uskoks is the **Nehaj Fortress** (literally 'fear not' or 'heedless'), sturdily safeguarding the town from a rubbly peak to the left of the harbour. Constructed in

1558 from materials obtained from churches and monasteries destroyed by the Turks, this was the creation of one General Lenković, an Uskok commander who clearly wanted the sort of stronghold that was perfect for throwing debauched banquets and pouring boiling oil on those rash enough to attempt capture. Certainly when you're up here the logic behind the name becomes clear – you can see so much it's easy to feel safe. These days there's not much in the castle itself: just a few photographs, a couple of cannons and a small lapidarium (Daily 0900–1500).

Finally the **Bora**. The saying goes that 'it is born in Senj, married in Rijeka, and it dies in Trieste', which doesn't explain much about a wind which, when it's at its strongest, can overturn cars, capsize boats and lift you off your feet. A cold, dry north-easterly, it billows across the central European plain and gets bottled up behind the Adriatic mountains, escaping through the passes at places like Senj and, further south, Omiš. When it's blowing, take care.

Continuing south, **JABLANAC** is the ferryport for Rab and Pag; if you're not going to either of those islands I wouldn't bother to stop. **KARLOBAG** too serves Pag with frequent ferries but is really nothing more than a dilapidated clutter of houses beneath the veiney Karst. From here there's little to detain you before Zadar – about 80 kilometres further south. Inland are vast stretches of bare, rugged Karst mountains, grey parched limestone as far as you can see, speckled with green and the occasional oasis of grass and trees. This is the land of the *Ličani*, traditionally fierce warriors hardened by life here and somehow managing to squeeze a living out of these sullen slopes. Soon you reach the end of the purely Croatian part of the coast and cross the slender green of the Maslenica canal into Dalmatia proper. The Velebit mountains fade into the distance behind and the ground levels into the fertile flats of the **Ravni Kotari** and, eventually, ZADAR.

DALMATIA – THE NORTH

ZADAR

ZADAR, ancient capital of Dalmatia, is a large town with a small historic centre crowded on to a tapered thumb of land that juts north into the Adriatic. Pretty comprehensively destroyed in the last war by Allied bombs, it lacks the museumy, preserved quality of so many of the towns on this coast, and is really much the better for it – a pleasant, thoughtless muddle of different architectures and styles, where lone Corinthian columns stand alongside rectangular 1950s blocks, and Romanesque churches compete for space with glassy café-bars. Zadar was part of Italy until 1947, and though fast diminishing, you'll find the influence still strong – Italian is widely spoken, particularly amongst the older people, and the place has much of the vibrancy of an Italian coastal town.

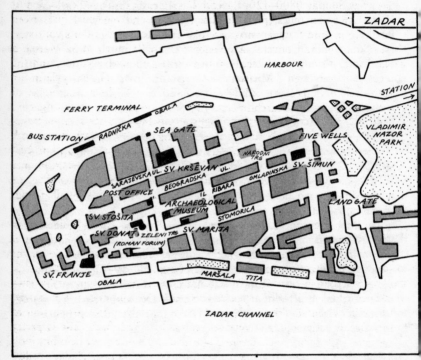

Most of Zadar's older buildings escaped the worst of the bombing, and today's centre retains a medieval network of narrow streets barred to motor traffic. **Zeleni Trg** is the best place to start your explorations: most things of interest are grouped around here and nothing is more than 5 minutes' saunter away. It's a messy square, flooded with café tables; part waste ground, part car park, part decimated Roman Forum which these days is little more than a grassy litter of stone, a few free-standing columns and hastily dumped sarcophagi. Much of the forum found its way to the lumpish C9th **Church of Sv Donat** (Daily 0700–2000), built atop the Roman pavement by St Donat himself – an Irishman who may have been bishop here for a time. A hulking, triple-apsed drum of stone, it's externally not unlike San Vitale of Ravenna, and some maintain it was modelled on Charlemagne's Palatinate Chapel in Aachen, though any comparisons with either of those buildings are soon dispelled by the bare barn-like interior. Past purposes have included shop, military store and museum, though for the moment it lies empty, used only occasionally for summer concerts.

In complete contrast is the streamlined modern **Archaeological Museum** opposite (Tuesday-Friday 0730–1200/1800–2030, Saturday/Sunday 0800–1200), which has a neatly displayed collection of Zadar's Roman relics, pre-Christian, Roman and medieval finds from nearby Nin, and fragments of sculpture from most of Zadar's churches. Next door is the Convent and much renovated **Church of Sv Marija**, a Renaissance-fronted, white, clean mix of just about everything, and the recently converted **Museum of Sacral Art** (Tuesday-Saturday 0900–1200/1800–2000, Sunday 0930–1200), a positive storehouse of the pick of Zadar's church treasures and very much the pride of the city. Exhibits vary enormously but highspots include an early six-painting *polyptych* by Carpaccio, a large C15th gang of *Apostles* carved in wood, a soft, resonant *St Jerome* by Palma the Younger and, among arm and skull reliquaries too numerous to mention, some very beautiful and diverse iconic representations of the *Madonna and Child*. Altogether, it's a fabulous museum, subtly arranged, beautifully lit, and just small enough to be manageable.

Looking back across the square, the **Campanile** was only finished in the last century, by the English writer and architect T.G. Jackson; if you've been to Rab you may find it familiar – he modelled it on the Cathedral bell tower there. Behind is the **Cathedral of Sv Stošija** (St Anastasia), a perfect – if late – example of the Romanesque style, with an arcaded west front that echoes Pisa and the churches of Lombardy. Inside is high and capacious, with a nave greedily out of proportion to the narrow aisles hidden away on each side. The lofty arcade is pretty enough, with pillars picked out in red marble, but it can't help but look a little lost in the broad expanses of flat, grey stone. Zadar's other Romanesque church, **Sv Krševan** (St Christopher), is again more impressive outside than in (the key is fairly elusive anyway) with a west front similar to the Cathedral's and a superb colonnaded east end of three apses – all exactingly proportioned.

Walk south and you're on **Narodni Trg**: focus of most daily action and home of the tourist office and a small **Ethnographic Museum** (Monday-Friday 0900–1400, Sunday 0900–1200) – ethnic costumes and faded photographs of moustachioed young bucks. Left from here is the Baroque **Church of Sv Simun**, whose very thorough restoration should be nearing completion by now. If you can get in, take a look at the silver-gilt *coffin reliquary* of the saint, held on the high altar by two Baroque angels cast in bronze from captured Turkish cannons. It's an extravagant work of art, executed in 1380 by a Milanese silversmith for the Hungarian

Queen Elisabeth out of 250 kilos of silver. The story goes that Elisabeth so wanted a piece of the Saint's body that she broke off a finger and hid it in her bosom, sending herself quite mad until she could replace it; a mixture of awe and horror prompted her to commission the reliquary. The lid shows the bearded saint in high relief and, on the front, two panels dramatise the legendary discovery of the body in a monastery on the outskirts of Zadar and the triumphant entry into the city of the Hungarian King Lodowick (Elisabeth's husband) after a year-and-a-half-long siege by the Venetians; the centre panel is a rough copy of Giotto's fresco of *The Presentation in the Temple* in Padua. One last thing: if the church is still closed, you should be able to see the coffin in the church of Sv Marija, in Zeleni Trg.

Zadar's last notable building is the monastic **Church of Sv Franje**, founded by St Francis himself when he visited Zadar in 1219 and said to be the oldest Gothic church in Dalmatia; actually it's a fairly dull renovation with a flat C18th roof. The **treasury** is what you come here for, though you may have to agitate to get it opened. Inside are C13th and 14th choral manuscripts, a delicate *Virgin and Child* from the C15th and a remarkable C12th wooden crucifix, the work of a local artist.

A few details

Detailed maps and information are available at the *Sunturist* office (Monday-Friday 0700–1400/1600–2100, Saturday 0700–2100, Sunday 0730–1300/1800–2100) on Narodni Trg. So too are **rooms**, though if you should find they've all gone you can always try the *Liburnija* office around the corner. Those with a little more money should go to the *Hotel Zagreb* on Obala M.Tita; those with less should take bus no. 5 through the Albanian-speaking suburb of Arbanasi to **campsite Punta Bajlo;** those with no money at all can try **sleeping rough** in the rampart park overlooking the delightful old harbour – the police are wise to this but it's worth a try. There's an official **Youth Hostel** in the suburb of Borik on the north side of town: bus nos 5 or 8 will take you there – and to another **campsite** just beyond.

Aim to spend at least a couple of days in Zadar. The town itself is worth it, and there's an abundance of **islands** within easy striking distance. A dozen boats a day make the half-hour trip to UGLJAN, and there are less frequent connections to countless smaller and more deserted hunks of land beyond – Iz, Rava, Dugi Otok (Long Island), Sestrunj, Molat, Silba and Olib, to name just a few. There are daily **summer connections** too (except Fridays) to LOŠINJ and PULA, and from there a weekly link to VENICE. Three ferries a month link Zadar with ANCONA; one a week with RIMINI; three a month with TRIESTE. Nearer home, VIR is connected to the mainland by bridge and around nine buses a day go there; and about a dozen buses a day head out to NIN, an interesting and curious place in itself, and with a good sandy beach.

NIN

NIN is probably more exclusively Croatian than anywhere on this stretch of coast. Initially settled by the Romans as Aenona, it was for centuries one of the residences of the early Croat kings and served as the major see of their bishops. It was here that maverick Zadrians would flee the savage imperialism of Venice; here that Grgur Ninski obdurately defended the heretic Glagolitic liturgy against the hegemony of Rome; and here too that a combination of epidemic malaria and Venetian sabotage forced a thriving city into quiet decay. By the time T.G. Jackson got here in 1887 Nin was no more than a large village whose inhabitants were so wan and unwholesome from malaria that his guides wouldn't let him stay there overnight.

Nin is built on a small island and connected to the mainland by two tiny bridges. Apart from the banishment of malaria, it can't have changed much since Jackson's day: scatterings of Roman ruins, solitary arches and mossy, crumbling walls all testify to some sort of past, though there's little left now but a blowy desolation and a fine, little-used stretch of duney beach. A bitty **Temple to Diana** figures among some scanty Roman remains, and there's a small **Archaeological Museum** with a few trinkets from the Roman and Croatian eras; most of the major finds have found their way to Zadar, Split or Zagreb.

Home to a family of swallows, the small cruciform church of **Sv Kriz**, just off the main street, is the oldest intact church in the country, with an inscription on the lintel referring to Župan (Count) Godežav dated AD 800. Get the key from the museum. From the Zadar bus you'll have noticed another tiny church cowed under some slender Scots pines, **Sv Nikola**, an C11th three-apsed church built on an ancient burial mound and fortified by the Turks. Like Sv Kriz there's nothing much here but the site is impressive, looking over the blustery lowlands to the time-ravaged shape of Nin and the silver-grey ridge of the Velebit mountains, wonderfully unreal in the distance.

UGLJAN AND PAŠMAN

UGLJAN is nearest and most developed of the scatter of islands that fill the seas off Zadar, and it's long been connected to its closest neighbour, PAŠMAN, by a road bridge. About six buses a day ply the route between the two islands, neither of which have made great concessions to the business of tourism. First and foremost they're places to relax, sunbathe and escape the coastal crowds.

The Zadar ferry drops you at **PREKO** (literally 'across' from Zadar), Ugljan's largest village, which has a Turist Biro and a good stock of rooms. Buses to most other destinations normally meet the ferries: you can take a bus down to **UGLJAN VILLAGE**, which passes the island's only **campsite** or, a little further on, to **MULINE**, which has a good sandy beach. In Preko the locals swim from the harbour or from a thickly vegetated islet in the bay – Galovac – where there's a Franciscan monastery that in the days of the Austrian occupation churned out valuable Croat propaganda on its printing press. Overlooking the town – and deceptively close – is the C10th **Fortress of Sv Mihovil**, quite a step away through the central valley and up the ridge on the far side of the island. The view is worth it if the fort isn't: fine panoramas of Zadar, Nin *et al.* in one direction; in the other, Iz, Dugi Otok and, on a clear day, Ancona and the Italian coast. Preko runs gently into **KALI**, which crowns a small hillock about a mile down the coast. More immediately picturesque than Preko, it's also firmly and solely committed to the local fishing industry, and you'll find little to do beyond wandering its pinched, slopy streets.

Down towards Ugljan's southern tip is **KUKLJICA**, another small fishing hamlet set in a wide green bay. In season it's normally full of Czechs, who block-book the bungalow-complex on the pined prong, but in spite of that things rarely seem too disturbed: there are usually rooms available from the Turist Biro by the church and there's a good, shallow strip of beach (concreted for sunbathing and seldom overbearingly crowded) just 15 minutes' walk on the western edge of the island; if you want solitude follow the rough path on the right to the nudist beach, a little way along.

PAŠMAN is a lengthy string of balding low hummocks, not as green as Ugljan and much less visited. Whereas on Ugljan there are signs of an incipient tourist industry, Pašman has yet to get started, which isn't all to its good – the island can at times seem a bit bleak. **TKON**, the main village, is where the Biograd ferry stops – a dusty, beleagured sort of place with nothing to recommend it apart from some good secluded beaches just south of town. The Turist Biro has a small supply of rooms and there's a **naturist campsite** a couple of kilometres outside the village. If you want to keep your clothes on you can use the orthodox camp 6 km away in **PAŠMAN VILLAGE**, which again has good beaches and little else besides. The island's best beach is a sandy affair at ZDRELAC, not far from the Ugljan bridge, but Pašman's enforced diet of beach-lounging isn't going to be to everyone's taste.

SOUTH TO ŠIBENIK

BIOGRAD is another former city of Croat kings, long since fallen on hard times. For years it vied with Zadar and Nin for prominence on this coast, holding on to power until Good Friday 1126 when the Venetians razed it to its foundations, plunging it into a decline from which it never really recovered. The people here still commemorate the fateful day with a special Mass, and by tradition a Black Knight is supposed to emerge from the waves to save the last Croat queen. Today it's a popular resort, a shabby sort of fun-palace fronted by a marina and some modern hotels. The local museum has one or two interesting finds from offshore wrecks, but otherwise there's little to tempt you off the Šibenik road; that is, unless you're going to Pašman, which is linked to Biograd by ten or so daily ferries.

The Turks got as far as **VRANA**, and there's evidence of it today in the shape of a ruined *han* which, in its prime, was the largest in Europe. The *Morlaachi* – a wild people who used to inhabit this part of the coast – got the blame for the ruins: indeed, according to Abbé Fortis they had a reputation (misfounded, says he) for being 'fierce, unreasonable, void of humanity and capable of any crime' so they can hardly have been surprised. Today, Vrana is a small, rather ordinary village, nestled timidly at the top end of the lake of the same name.

Soon after the lake a road sweeps off right for **MURTER**, which lies flat and close against the mainland – a dull, bare island, but with useful access to the **KORNATI ISLES**, which scatter like frosty pebbles just west of here. Most of the people on Murter own land there, and if you're into 'Robinson Crusoe'-style holidays on uninhabited islands – this is what the tourist office actually calls them – they'll arrange one. Only for stalwart outdoor types, all you get is a spartan fisherman's hut and a few essentials necessary to survive.

ŠIBENIK

ŠIBENIK is a prosperous-looking place with the brash, workaday air of a busy port, a long thin city slung along the wide crack of the Krka estuary. Its outskirts seem none too enticing, but they lead into a small explorable centre grouped around a dignified Gothic-Renaissance Cathedral. This, together with a fair smattering of nearby islands and trips upriver to the Krka Falls, make it worth spending at least a day or two looking around.

When I was last in Šibenik the **Tourist Office** had been in more or less continual disarray for about a year. They should have found a home by now – probably in Trg Republike – but if they haven't, *Dalmacijaturist*, also in Trg Republike, should be able to help with **rooms** and sell you a detailed map. There's a **Youth Hostel** east of the centre in Put Lugusa (follow JNA until it becomes Rade Končara and do a right) and a cheapish central **hotel**, the C category *Jadran*, on the seafront. The nearest **campsite** is 8 km away in the *Solaris* mega-complex, for which ten buses a day leave the marketplace; or there's a much more attractive but less accessible site out near the Krka falls – in July and August buses run direct, other times it's a bus to Skradin and a 3–km walk. Don't – unless you've booked – turn up in the latter part of June, when the whole town is taken up with a UNICEF International Children's Festival. If you're happy to camp, though, it's an exciting time: events – many in English – play throughout the day, and in the evening the city's streets and squares are turned over to all manner of street theatre, music and mime.

In the C16th Šibenik was a recognised centre of culture and the arts, and the **Cathedral of Sv Jakov** is a good reminder of those years, the product of a long-running saga that stirred the imaginations and emptied the pockets of the townspeople. The inadequacy of the existing building and a keep-up-with-the-Joneses attitude to the neighbouring city of Trogir led to plans being drawn up for a new cathedral in 1402 but war, lack of funds and disputes over the site delayed the start of work until 1431. Over the next ten years the Gothic lower storey went up, but scandals and general slacking led the Šibenik nobles to dismiss the initial team of masons and take on, at great expense, one of rather better repute, Juraj Dalmatinac (George the Dalmatian), who brought lighter, more floral elements to the building. To the original straight basilica plan he added a transept, and he enlarged and raised the choir, topping it with an octagonal cupola of extraordinary light and beauty. Things went well, but exploitation by Venice, two outbreaks of plague and a catastrophic fire led to frequent stoppages. Juraj died in 1473 and a new mason from Florence took over, signing a contract that forced him to follow Juraj's design while adding a clear Renaissance strain of his own: he is known to have been responsible for the whole of the west front.

Entry is by the *North Door*, framed by arches braided with leaves, fruit and swirling arabesques. Two lions roar companionably at each other, supporting the pious, remorseful and rather crudely carved figures of Adam and Eve. Inside is a harmonious blend of Gothic and Renaissance forms, your eyes drawn towards the sanctuary by the sheer space and light of the east end, which jets in through plentiful windows to illuminate the soft grey Dalmatian stone. Under the southern apse is Juraj's master-piece, the *Baptistery*, a womb-like cubby-hole of decorated Gothic carving, sculpted to his plans by later masons. Four scallop-shell niches rise from each side to form a rich, vaulted roof, beneath which cherubim scamper playfully, upholding the red marble font. It's a delightful piece of work, an incidental but fitting conclusion to the Cathedral as a whole.

Around the outside of the three apses Juraj carved a unique *frieze* of 71 stone heads, showing a vivid cross-section of his society: the story is that they are portraits of those who refused to contribute to the cost of the Cathedral. Certainly you can't help feeling you're looking at real people, some of whom Juraj obviously found ridiculous, some he seems to have actively disliked. On the north apse, beneath two angels with a scroll, he inscribed his claim to the work: 'these apses have been made by Juraj the Dalmatian, son of Maté.'

The rest of the medieval city clings to the side of the hill in a steep tangle of alleys, steps and arches. Zagrebačka and 12 Kolovoza 1941 form the backbone, cutting across from the open modern square of Poljana M. Tita to Trg Republike, beyond which the oldest parts heap up behind the **castle of Sv Ana** – nearest and most accessible of Sibenik's impressive fortifications. Opposite the cathedral is a C16th Loggia and, next door, the Rector's Palace, which now fulfills the function of **Town Museum** (Tuesday-Friday 1200–1300/1900–2100, Saturday/Sunday 1000–1200) with a display of local archaeological finds from Neolithic to early medieval times; regrettably, lack of any foreign language info makes it difficult to appreciate. On the corner the tiny church of **Sv Barbara** has a modest collection of ecclesiastical items, best of which is a small C15th polyptych by Blaz Jurjav of Trogir, one of the most accomplished of Dalmatian Renaissance artists.

AROUND ŠIBENIK: THE ISLANDS AND THE KRKA FALLS

Most of the **islands** off Šibenik are pretty easy to reach: about half a dozen boats a day run to Zlarin, four or five to Prvić and around three to Kaprije, Zirje and Obonjan. **ZLARIN** is the most popular, twenty minutes through the thin chink in the rock opposite the port, down a short fortified gorge and out through scattered remnants of Venetian sea defences. It has just one village, seamed around a deep bay and once renowned for its naval expertise. Women still sporadically wear the local costume and one small workshop is the only reminder of a coral industry long since dead. There are some grubby **beaches** near the village, better ones if you're prepared to walk, and a C category **hotel** and a **Turist Biro** offering **rooms** make it a feasible alternative to staying in Sibenik. Its sister island, PRVIĆ, has rooms on offer too.

Further out, **OBONJAN** and **KAKAN** are known collectively as the *Otoci Mladosti* or 'Islands of Youth', Obonjan for its role as holiday centre of the Yugoslav scouts, and Kakan for its function as 'seventh continent – a centre for the world's children'. Otherwise both are wholly uninhabited. KAPRIJE and ZIRJE I didn't get to, but they're both said to be very quiet, with accommodation difficult to come by. Heading back towards the mainland, **KRAPANJ** is smallest of the populated Adriatic islands, best known to outsiders for its sponge divers and with a monastic museum collection of corals, sponges and other underwater goodies. Back on the mainland and south, **PRIMOŠTEN** grows vines lauded by the United Nations as a supreme example of man's achievment, since conditions here are just about as unfavourable as you can possibly get. The result is *Babić*, a potent and expensive red. Primošten itself is a small town on what was originally an island linked to the mainland by a bridge – a pleasant enough place, with most of its growing tourist clutter kept well out of the way on the peninsula next door.

Few visitors to Šibenik miss the **KRKA FALLS** (Slapovi Krke), a little way inland where the river has narrowed into a green fertile valley. Four buses a day go there direct during July and August; at other times take the Skradin bus – the driver will tell you the stop – and walk down a spectacular 4–km road or a stony short cut to the river. Once you're there everything's laid on: restaurants, cafés, souvenir shops – and a lot of tourists. While not especially high, the falls are impressive as they cascade frothily from level to level, throwing themselves out of the trees through limpid, yielding reeds. You could spend an entire day here, lolling around on the rocks under the tumbling water, sunbathing and paddling in the more docile patches. One thing though: out of July and August check the bus times back – I found myself doing more walking than I had bargained for.

Taxi boats upstream leave from near the coach park; the more of you there are the cheaper it is – they're not keen on taking singles or couples. The boats take you to ROSKI SLAPOVI – some rather less dramatic falls – and the islet of VISOVAC, home of a Franciscan monastery and its valuable library, with some early incunabula and a beautifully illustrated C15th *Aesop's Fables*.

TROGIR

But for the advent of a few cranes across the water, and the sounds of Neil Young drifting over the main square, **TROGIR** can have changed little over the years, and today it's one of the most beautiful towns on this coast, a brown-beige welter of palaces, jutting belfries and shambly streets clustered onto a small island. Sure, it has its visitors, but is by no means overrun, and most are shunted down the coast to package hotels where they tend to remain, only venturing into town for a quick glimpse of the Cathedral or the odd meal. You can see the town in a day and don't need to stay, but it makes a good base for seeing this part of the coast – Split is only a short bus ride away and you can cover most of the major sites there in a day-trip.

Life revolves around Narodni Trg, a creamy-white square flanked by the Cathedral, Communal Palace and Loggia, which spill pools of steps onto its smooth, polished stones. Trogir's fervent Slavness erupted into controversy between world wars when the Venetian Lion of St Mark on the Loggia was defaced – an event that was probably no more than drunken high jinks but none the less provoked angry reactions from

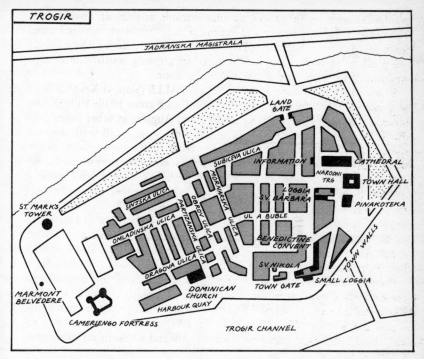

TROGIR

JADRANSKA MAGISTRALA

LAND GATE

SUBICEVA ULICA

INFORMATION

CATHEDRAL

NARODNI TRG

TOWN HALL

LOGGIA SV. BARBARA

MORNARSKA ULICA

PINAKOTEKA

ST. MARK'S TOWER

SINJSKA ULICA

PARTIZANSKA ULICA

OBROV ULICA

UL. A BUBLE

OMLADINSKA ULICA

BENEDICTINE CONVENT

DRAGOVA ULICA

SV. NIKOLA

SMALL LOGGIA

TOWN WALLS

MARMONT BELVEDERE

DOMINICAN CHURCH

TOWN GATE

HARBOUR QUAY

CAMERLENGO FORTRESS

TROGIR CHANNEL

Mussolini and spirited denunciations of 'Yugoslav barbarism' from the League of Nations; attacks that seem odd and rather unfair since Trogir had not belonged to Venice for 140 years, had suffered greatly at her hands and was still to that day coveted by the Italians. Back in tip-top condition, the loggia has since been properly adulterated with a Mestrović relief.

Opposite stands the **Cathedral** (Daily 0900–1200/1500–1900), a squat Romanesque structure begun in roughly 1200 and finished some three centuries later with a soaring Venetian-Gothic campanile. Officially dedicated to Sv Lovro (Lawrence), for the people here it's always been the church of Sv Ivan (John), patron saint of the city and a miracle-working Bishop here in the C11th. Entry is through the sacristy on the far side – on Radovan Trg – but it's worth looking in on the porch to ascend the tower, see the putti-ed Renaissance Baptistery and the *West Portal*. Carved in 1240 by a Slav master named Radovan, this is an astonishing piece of work, a microcosm of the medieval world and mind, with orthodox iconography mingling with profane scenes from ordinary life. Radovan laid claim to the work in an inscription above the door, calling himself 'most excellent in his art' – a boast that seems a lot less arrogant when you see just how excellent he was. His theme was Sin and Redemption, with a gradual movement upwards from the Old Testament figures at the bottom to New Testament scenes on the arches and lunette. Adam and Eve stand with an anxious kind of modesty, either side of a series of receding pillars that sit upon the bent-double backs of down-and-outs from the eastern Mediterranean – probably Turks, Jews and other undesirables. Above is a wierd menagerie of creatures in writhing, bucking confusion, along with scenes of everyday peasant life, laced together with twisted, tendrilled carvings that symbolise the months and seasons.

Inside, the Cathedral is an austere mixture of Romanesque and Gothic, with a dimness and parched stone sobriety highlighted only by the *Chapel of Sv Ivan*, a fine piece of Renaissance crafting, with a carved figure of the saint and putti peeping cheekily from behind half-closed doors. The *Sacristy treasure*, predominantly dull, obscures a handful of interesting objects – a tiny Gothic altar worked in ivory, and a C14th Gothic jug, scaled and moulded into a snake-like form.

Across the square is the tiny abbey church of St John the Baptist, latterly known as the **Pinakoteka** and given over to a display of sacral art from the best of Trogir's churches. It can be difficult to get into, but the key should be available from a nun in the house opposite the entrance; if not, ask at the Cathedral. Its engaging assortment of paintings is well worth the effort, with some sensitive work by Blaz Jurjev and Paolo Veneziano, canvases of *John the Baptist* and *St Jerome* by Gentile Bellini (painted for the Cathedral organ in 1489 as a reminder to Venice that Trogir, too, could afford the best artists) and Nicholas the Florentine's *Pietà*, a monumental tombstone carved for a local family of nobles and with a savage realism comparable to Juraj Dalmatinac, from whom he must have learnt a lot.

Cut through to the **Convent of Sv Nikola** (Daily 0830–1230/1500–1930), which too has a small *treasury*, pride of which is a Greek C3rd *relief of Kairos*, sculpted out of orange marble, a dynamic fragment representing the Greek god of the Fleeting Moment – that favourable instance when all stands at its best. Once past he's impossible to catch, and the back of his head is shaven just to make it more difficult.

Out through the gate and along the quayside – streaky in summer with the masts of foreign yachts – is the **Dominican Church**, a light, high building with another tomb sculpted by Nicholas the Florentine: this one records a woman's lament for her son and husband who died violent deaths in 1469. A *lapidarium* shelters a rich collection of stone fragments around a delightfully luxuriant courtyard; no doubt one of the scarred Lions of St Mark is the controversial one from the Loggia.

Continue past the stoic bulk of the **Kamerlengo Fortress** – now an open-air cinema – to the far end of the island and there, ignominiously planted next to the town football pitch, is Marmont's **Gloriette**, a little stone belvedere where Marshal Marmont, French governor here in the C19th and probably the best colonial ruler the city ever had, would play cards with his fellow officers, until – as a result of Napoleon's staunch anti-Dalmatian policies – he was forced to resign. It's kept here in his honour, on land that in Marmont's day was little more than malarial marsh.

Back in the town centre the **Town Museum** (just off Narodni Trg, Daily 0900–1200/1700–1930) gives a summarial glimpse of Trogir through the ages from Greek times – there's an exquisite Greek relief of a woman working – to the inevitable display on the revolution. Almost next door is the Čipiko Palace, where in 1650 the codex of Petronius' *Satyricon* was found. Now it serves as the **Turist Biro** (Monday-Saturday 0800–2000, Sunday 0800–1400) with maps, info and plentiful private **rooms**. There's a **campsite** on the mainland and another, far nicer, 15–20 minutes' walk away on Čiovo. If everything's full *Motel Trogir*, again on the mainland, does cheap doubles. Budget eating is easy: the *gostiona* on Narodni Trg is good and not expensive, and there's a *pizza restaurant* just inside the main town gate. **Boats** leave for Mali and Veli Drvenik – with Čiovo the nearest islands – every day at 1430; remember, you can't come back the same day. Only local buses use the bus station; those heading north or south zip past quickly and you have to stand in the road to flag them down.

ČIOVO AND THE ROAD TO SPLIT

People do swim off Trogir but to me the water looked murky. ČIOVO is more tempting, though as an island it's neither pretty nor especially interesting. It used to be known as Bua or Boa ('place of snakes') in the mistaken and rather colourful belief that it was the home of a lot of cattle-eating snakes. **SLATINE** is its main resort (ten buses a day) but the beaches there – and on the way – are for the most part dirty and litter-stewn. The other side of the island is a better bet, around the Rozac campsite and further on at **OKRUG**, where the water is clean and the rocks aren't too crowded. Rooms are available in most of the larger villages, but confirm the fact in Trogir before you decide to stay.

From Trogir the coast swings round to Split in a wide curving bay, sheltered from the open sea by Čiovo and Split's inching peninsula. Nobles from hereabouts lined this broad sweep of coast with fortifications against the Turks – thirteen castles in all, of which seven remain – unwittingly giving it the latter-day label of **Riviera of the Seven Castles**, a convenient tag, but one that nowadays doesn't really describe it very well. Rapid and enthusiastic development has obscured the castles, converting them for use as discos, restaurants and the like, and the villages that were spawned by them have long since merged into a spread of seaside pleasure complexes for the workers of Split. **KASTEL ŠTAFILIĆ** is the first, cringing under the thundrous noise of aircraft from nearby Split airport. It runs imperceptibly into **KASTEL NOVI**, where there's a Turist Biro offering cheap **rooms**, and then **STARI**, which has a long stretch of stony beach. Nearer Split, in fact offputtingly near its smoky stacks, is **KASTEL GOMILICA**, which has a **Youth Hostel** and perhaps the best preserved fortress. Soon after, the road becomes edged with hi-tech installations and industrial splurge, and before long you're veering gently round into Split.

SPLIT

By far the largest town in Dalmatia, **SPLIT** has a bustling lack of restraint you won't find anywhere else on the coast. It's a hectic place, full of shouting stall-owners, in-transit travellers and white-suited sailors who give it a vibrant night-on-the-town feel. With a population of well over 200,000, it is also reputedly growing faster than any other Yugoslav city – pollution hangs over its industrial quarters and shells of orange breeze-block litter fast expanding suburbs. But at the heart of all this, hemmed in by sprawling estates and a modern harbour, lies **Diocletian's Palace**, a crumbling old town, and some of the most outstanding classical architecture in the world.

It was, in fact, the palace that gave birth to the town. Before the Roman Emperor Diocletian decided to retire here in 305 Split didn't exist at all, and it was only in the Middle Ages that it began to spread outside the walls. After Diocletian's death in 313 a succession of Roman despots, pretenders and power-seekers set up shop here, squabbling over the declining fortunes and intrigues of the divided empire. These were bloody times, and the palace was never really restored; after the fall of Rome it stayed empty for some time, falling into disrepair until 614 when refugees from nearby Salona fled here from their Slav invaders, moulding themselves a home in what must have been one of the most grandiose squats of all time. They built fortifications, walled up arches, boarded up windows and repelled constant attacks from barbarians. And since then people have always lived here, propping up the place in return for shelter in a neat and long-lasting symbiosis. After the war the authorities planned to restore the Palace to its former grandeur but had to abandon the idea – after they discovered that without the people the whole lot would fall down.

Medieval Split was fought over – like the rest of Dalmatia – by Hungary and Venice, enjoying a period of comparative peace and prosperity under the Venetians. By the time the 20th century arrived Split was a port of some size and, despite fierce fighting during the last war, which left much of it totally gutted, it has picked itself up and grown, a boom-town swelled by migrants from all over the country.

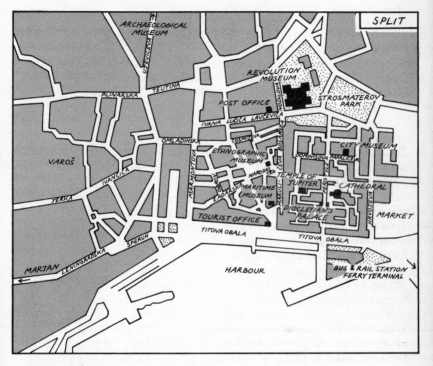

Split – definitives

Split is the major centre for the whole of Dalmatia and it's well connected by bus, train, boat or plane with just about anywhere you care to mention. The **Bus Station**, **Railway Station** and **Ferry terminal** are almost next door to each other, so whichever way you arrive you'll find yourself on **Obala Bratstva i Jedinstva**, five minutes' walk from the centre. Look remotely foreign and you'll be harried by hordes of people offering black-market rooms: if you accept one (and there's no reason why you shouldn't) make sure you know the price and location first – Split's a big place and you may find yourself doing a lot of walking. Otherwise the **Turist Biro** on Titova Obala (Monday-Saturday 0700–2100, Sunday 0800–1200) has a good stock of **private accommodation**, again scattered all over town. The nearest **campsite** is a couple of miles out at the end of the 7 or 17 bus line. Cheapest of all, if you're here between mid-July and late-August, is the **Studentski Dom**: take a 15 or 17 bus from Titova Obala and get off at the M. Gorkog/J.Poduje junction; the Dom is down a well-camouflaged right-turn off Bakotičeva, just past the petrol station.

Of Split's **hotels**, the *Slavija*, just inside the west wall of the palace at Buvinova 3, is the cheapest, with the *Srebna Vrata*, on the other side of the palace, a close second. Those stony broke should slip up to the Marjan Park; though expressly forbidden, it's possible to get your head down if you bury yourself deeply enough in the woods.

There are places to **eat** all over town and few are excessively expensive. *Bastion Express* at Marmontova 9 is probably the cheapest you'll find, but you don't pay a lot extra for the atmosphere of the places on the seafront. The *Srebna Vrata* (hotel) restaurant is good and cheap, and there's an excellent all-day *burek joint* opposite the post office at Ilegalac 15.

Action – as ever – revolves around the *korso*, a histrionic affair that every night packs the blocked-off waterfront to the gills. Hang around here, look lost and someone's bound to come and speak to you. *Luxor*, in the peristyle, is an amiable sort of dive late on in the evening, and there are some spirited small bars in the wanderable Varoš district just west of Trg Republike. The liveliest time to be in Split is during the **summer festival** – every year between July and 15 August – when there are outdoor performances of music, drama and opera all over town – ask at the Turist Biro for details. In the first week of July Split also hosts an annual binge of Dalmatian folk music, normally centred on Trg Republike.

If you can put up with the noise, crowds and entrance fee, *Bačvice* is the main city **beach**, or there are others dotted all over the Marjan peninsula. However, I suspect that once you've seen the water in Split harbour – very nasty – you'll want to get as far away from town as possible before chancing a dip. Try the beaches south of the city, near Omiš, or, better still, take a trip out to one of the **islands**. Apart from Vis and Lastovo, – currently out of bounds to foreigners due to their sensitive military significance – you can get to all of the offshore islands from Split, and there are regular **ferries** too to PESCARA, ANCONA, BAR, CORFU, IGOUMENITSA and countless places up and down the Yugoslav coast (see the 'ferries' listings at the end of this chapter).

Diocletian's Palace and central Split

The best way to see Split is aimlessly, drifting through the cluttered streets, alleyways and sometimes mere cracks of Diocletian's Palace which, with an adjoining medieval addition, make up the nucleus of the town centre. The Palace was begun in AD 295 and finished ten years later when Diocletian, very much the local boy made good, came back to his native Illyria to cure his rheumatism, grow cabbages (tradition says) and escape the cares of an empire that was rotting away at its very foundations. When made Emperor 21 years earlier, he had divided the job into four – the Tetrachy – probably the worst thing he ever did, as the subsequent fight for power shattered his peace until the day he died. Under the terms of the Tetrarchy he had been forced to give his only daughter Valeria in marriage to one of his partners – a cruel uncaring brute by all accounts – who eventually died, leaving her to be passed from successor to successor like a rag doll. Her child was murdered and she was continually mistreated, finally escaping to Syria while Diocletian, daily more involved in the Tetrarchy power struggle and broken by Valeria's fate, poisoned himself in despair.

The original **Palace** was a rough rectangle of luxury apartments for the ex-emperor and a fortified garrison for the imperial guard. It measured about 200 yards north-south and 240 yards east-west with walls between 50 and 70 feet high and around 8 feet thick. On each corner stood a commanding and impenetrable keep – three of which remain – and along each of the land walls four small look-out posts. Clearly, Diocletian liked to make himself secure. The C18th architect Robert Adam came here in 1757, and despite nearly being tried as a spy, produced a set of drawings of the palace that led to the development of the whole Georgian style – the Adam brothers built large chunks of London, Bath and Bristol – and influenced architectual thinking to this day. If you can, get your hands on a copy of Adam's book – it gives a good idea of what the whole thing must have looked like.

It's not too fanciful to assume that Diocletian was a vain man: he built this huge and monumental complex of buildings as testament to his own glory, walling himself up in rooms you could only reach after passing through numerous corridors and ante-chambers. The steps from the peri-style lead up to a **vestibule**, where cringing inferiors would stew before being admitted to the Presence himself. Now domeless, it's still solid and imposing, and it probably had just the sort of demeaning effect that Diocletian wanted. Sadly, little remains of the **imperial apartments**, which took up the whole of the southern half of the palace: nowadays they're either grassy rubble or built-over houses. As the ground sloped south they had to be supported by a vast **catacomb complex** underneath, which until 1956 was undiscovered and filled with several centuries' accumu-lated junk. Now, suffused with damp, parts have been cleared out and laid open to the public (Monday-Saturday 0800–2000, Sunday 0800–1200/1600–1900), giving you a fair idea of what the great man's rooms must have looked like – plan-wise at least. For Diocletian, the palace was both an escape and a prison, and it's not hard to imagine him pacing up and down .hese cold echoing halls, bemoaning the fate of his family and his failure to escape the cares of state. From here it's out into daylight and Split's busy waterfront or back down a corridor lined with chic jewellery stalls to the **Peristyle**, fringed with stately arches and in Diocletian's day the central courtyard of the Palace. Today it serves as main town square, muddled with café tables and the coloured sunshades of market stalls.

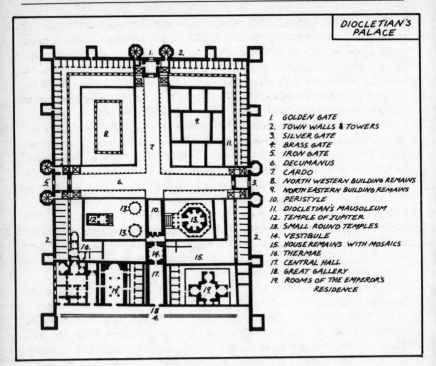

DIOCLETIAN'S PALACE

1. GOLDEN GATE
2. TOWN WALLS & TOWERS
3. SILVER GATE
4. BRASS GATE
5. IRON GATE
6. DECUMANUS
7. CARDO
8. NORTH WESTERN BUILDING REMAINS
9. NORTH EASTERN BUILDING REMAINS
10. PERISTYLE
11. DIOCLETIAN'S MAUSOLEUM
12. TEMPLE OF JUPITER
13. SMALL ROUND TEMPLES
14. VESTIBULE
15. HOUSE REMAINS WITH MOSAICS
16. THERMAE
17. CENTRAL HALL
18. GREAT GALLERY
19. ROOMS OF THE EMPEROR'S RESIDENCE

On the right is the **Cathedral** (Monday-Saturday 0900–1300), the result of much piecemeal inspiration over the years. Formerly just an octagonal domed chamber, and part of Diocletian's original palace, it was almost certainly constructed as Diocletian's Mausoleum. His body is known to have rested here for 170 years until one day it disappeared, no one knows where. Since then it's been sanctified, a choir added, and it has amassed an extensive treasury.

Inside, the dome is scarred black and mysterious, ringed by two series of purely decorative Corinthian columns and with a frieze above which apparently contains portraits of Diocletian and his wife. Carved into the main doors is an inspired C13th comic strip showing 28 *Scenes from the Life of Christ*, scuffed and scraped at the bottom but pristinely preserved further up. The pulpit too is a beautifully proportioned example of Romanesque art, sitting on capitals tangled with snakes, strange beasts and foliage. Best of all though is Juraj Dalmatinac's carving on the Altar of St Anastasius, a crushingly realistic *Flagellation of Christ* in which He is pawed and brutalised by some peculiarly oafish persecutors. Above lies the figure of St Anastasius himself, with the millstone hung around his neck with which Diocletian – arch-persecutor of Christians – had him thrown into the sea. The *choir* can't help but seem a little tacked on to all this, but its latticed stalls include some of the most delicate wood carving I think I've ever seen. Upstairs, the *treasury* sports a dull mélange of reliquaries, handwritten missals and C13th Madonnas, only recently uncovered under later Baroque excesses. And on the way out, a haul up the Campanile is worth the small charge, giving a fine panorama of the roofs and TV aerials of today's Palace, and beyond that, Split's relentless suburbs in front of *papier-mâché* mountains of Karst.

A **Temple of Jupiter** hides on the other side of the Palace peristyle, through a gap in the arched arcade. Though very much a pagan edifice, with a richly coffered ceiling and the figures of Hercules. Apollo and others adorning the eastern portal, it's been used as the Baptistery of the Cathedral for many years, and that's where you have to ask for the key. Later Christian additions include a lean, ascetic *John the Baptist* by Mestrović – a late work, done in 1954 – and, more famously, an C11th *baptismal font* with a relief popularly believed to be a grovelling subject paying homage to a Croatian king. It's one of those pieces whose fame has spread disproportionately, breeding reproductions that you seem to bump into in every corner of Split.

Back at the peristyle, continue north and you come to the grandest and best conserved of the palace gates – the **Zlatna Vrata** or Golden Gate – which was the landward and therefore the most important entrance to the palace. Outside looms another Mestrović figure, Bishop **Grgur Ninski**, an important historical character for the Croats since he fought Rome for the right of his people to use their own language in their liturgy. Incredibly, the mammoth statue used to stand in the peristyle before it was removed by the wartime Italians, probably more for political than aesthetic reasons. It still seems out of place here, and says less about Croatian nationalism than Mestrović's mastery of overstatement, attracting an amused curiosity from passers-by.

The east-west axis of the Palace – the ancient *decumanus* – takes you out through the west gate into Narodni Trg, second social hub of the city and the beginning of the later, medieval part of the centre, a more irregular net of tightly-drawn streets and passages that stretches west as far as Ulica Marmontova. Beyond is Trg Republike and the foot of the steep slope up to the wooded heights of Marjan, where you can escape Split's turmoil and look south over Šolta, Brač and, inky in the distance, the island of Hvar.

Split's museums

Archaeological Museum, Zrinjsko-Frankopanska 25. Ten minutes' walk from the palace. (Tuesday-Saturday 0900–1300/1700–2000, Sunday 1000–1200. It's worth buying the informative booklet). An impressive selection of Illyrian, Greek, medieval and particularly Roman artefacts, including a good ragbag of finds from nearby Salona (those that haven't been looted or left under the ground). Nothing special stands out but it's an enormously comprehensive array, conjuring up a good picture of life for your average Salonan noble: exhibits range from delicate votive figurines to amulets and jewellery embellished with tiny peep-shows of lewd love-making. The courtyard outside is reserved for weightier hunks of stone, again a large proportion of which are Roman: notice the sarcophagus relief of the Calydonian boar hunt – which, in Robert Adam's pictures, stood outside the Baptistery – and another, remarkably preserved, of the Hipploytus and Phaedra myth. Later sarcophagi include the latterly labelled *Good Shepherd*, C4th, with the archetypal Christian motif of the shepherd merged with pagan symbols of Eros and Hades on the end panels. An excellent museum, and one well worth venturing into the north of town to see.

Museum of Croatian Archaeological Monuments, Šetalište Mose Pijade. Fifteen minutes' walk from the city centre or bus 7 or 12. (Tuesday-Saturday 0900–1600, Sunday 1000–1200). Housed in a gleaming new purpose-built edifice with huge open-plan halls and piped organ music, this museum has a similar importance for the Croats as the medieval monasteries do for the Serbs: it illustrates that there was life in Croatia before invader after invader came along and imposed their own cultures. Prize exhibit is an oversize baptismal font from Nin, in perfect nick and with an inscription that identifies it as early C9th. The rest is mainly a guide to early Croat civilisation with jewellery, weapons and fragmentary reconstructions of chancel screens and ciboria from C9th and 10th churches. If it wasn't so beautifully displayed it might not be that interesting, but as it is it works – even for the non-Croat layman.

Mestrović Gallery, Šetalište Mose Pijade 39. Twenty minutes' walk from the city centre or bus 7 or 12 (Daily 1000–1900). This museum has taken over the neo-classical building that Mestrović planned as his home, and redesigned it as a fittingly grand shrine to Yugoslavia's most famous and revered modern artist; even if you're not mad about the man, it's an impressive collection.

Ivan Mestrović came from the small Croatian village of Otavice, near Drniš, and spearheaded the Croat artistic movement of the early C20th. Best known for boldly fashioned bodies curled into elegant poses, his prowess as a sculptor and grasp of the human form are indisputable, and much of his work admirable for its sheer skill. Where he often fails is in the self-consciousness of his work, in the monumentality of his lines, the size of his figures and the universality of his chosen subjects. As well as producing hundreds of Lamentations, Pietàs (one exhibited in New York weighed 5 tons), Last Suppers, etc., his commonest themes are things like Despair, Psyche, Family and Hope, and it's this striving to say everything about something in one piece of sculpture that lets him down. His heads of *Soldiers* and *Heroes* are almost caricatures, the giant *Adam and Eve* ungainly and ridiculous, and he's really much more successful when representing people he knew and met, particularly members of his family. The portraits of his children are refreshingly simple and the bust of his *Mother* both honest and sensitive. On the same floor is a neat portrayal of the Yugoslav painter Bukovac – an austere-looking man – who reciprocates in the same room with a portrait of a young and earnest Mestrović. It's a pity Mestrović's self-portraits couldn't be so dispassionate – looking at them you can't help feeling he took himself just a little too seriously.

City Museum, Papalićeva 5 (Monday-Saturday 0900–1300, Thursday 0900–1700) Housed in the flowery Gothic Papalić Palace, exhibits include city documents, weaponry and fragments of sculpture. Not exactly a must.

For the rest there's a tiny **Maritime Museum** on Trg Preporoda (Monday-Saturday 0900–1200), with a few dusty paintings, severed figureheads and yellowing naval documents that might be worth ten minutes if it's raining outside; an **Ethnographic Museum** (Monday-Saturday 0800–1300/1800–2000, Sunday 1000–1200), housed in the old Gothic town hall on Narodni Trg, which has a shabby collection of Dalmatian costumes, weaponry and folk arts; and a **Revolution Museum** (Monday-Friday 0900–1300/1800–2000, Saturday/Sunday 0900–1200), occupying the old city hospital and, like all such museums, not of much interest to anyone who's not a Yugo-revolution/W.W.II addict.

Odds and sods

Books   You'll find an eclectic selection of second-hand English books at the *Antikvarijat* bookshop in Ban Mladenova, near Trg Republike.

Consulates   British (Titova Obala 10/11; tel. 41464), Dutch (Rooseveltova 19; tel. 522 739).

Emergencies   Hospital, Spinčićieva 1 (tel. 94), Police, Titova Obala 5 (tel. 92).

Ferry tickets   The *Jadrolinija* office is at the ferry terminal.

Food   Best bet are the market and delicatessens at the bottom end of Hrvojeva.

JAT   Titova Obala 9.

Left luggage   24–hour left luggage at the train station.

Local buses   Most city buses leave from Titova Obala or Marmontova. Local bus station for Omiš, Trogir, Seven Castles, etc. a little way down Žrtava Fašizma, 10 minutes' walk from the palace.

Post office   Il Lavcevica 9 (Monday-Friday 0700–2100, Saturday 0700–1400. Telephones open every day).

Rent-a-car   *Hertz / InterRent*, Obala JNA 1.

SALONA, KLIS AND THE ALKA SINJSKA

Leaving Split, bus 1, 10 or one of the half-hourly services to Sinj will take you to **SALONA** (or Solin as it's now called) – in its day the most important Roman settlement on this coast, and since excavated in a series of sites scattered about the industrial outskirts of Split. To see something of this get off the bus on the far side of Solin and follow the coast road to **Manastirine**, a ruin of cemetery and Roman basilica piled high with sarcophagi, where you may be able to find a guide who speaks a kind of broken French. Through an avenue of cypresses is the city proper, a desolate place, still mainly covered by scrub and to be honest not tremendously interesting. The city walls zig-zag round a complex of basilicas towards a late C2nd **amphitheatre**, of which a fairly complete storey is still standing, though it must have looked pretty tame beside the likes of Pula and Nîmes. Just east of here are the remains of another theatre and the ancient forum. From there you can either take the bus back to Split or press on to Klis.

The villas of the wealthier Salonans once stretched as far as **KLIS**, a key strategic point in the defence of Split and since the Middle Ages strengthened by an apparently unassailable fortress high on a jutting crag above the village. The Turks took the fort in 1537, harassing Split with the threat of Islam until the Venetians wrested it back a century later. Today it's remarkably complete – quite a climb from the village that clusters around it – and it seems strange that the normally entrepreneurial Yugoslavs haven't turned it into more of a tourist attraction: the views are dazzling, and it's open every day 0800–1200/1400–1700.

From Klis the road forges through scrubby, rubbly country to **SINJ** where, if you happen to be around on 15 August you can witness the **Alka Sinjska**. This annual event commemorates a day back in 1715 when the people here – heavily outnumbered – wiped the floor with a large portion of the Turkish army. It's actually a sort of medieval joust, but instead of the knights fighting each other they attempt to thread their lances through a series of divided rings dangled from a rope – all at a terrific gallop. The points they score depend on which ring they manage to pierce. It's a riotous, boozy business, involving all the surrounding villages and taking up the whole day in a blaze of colour, costumes and procession, building up to a crescendo when the contest itself takes place. If you're in the area at roughly the right time it's worth a special journey; otherwise don't bother stopping – there's nothing else to see in Sinj.

SOUTHERN DALMATIA: ISLANDS AND COAST

BRAČ AND ŠOLTA

For centuries **BRAČ** has earned a living quarrying its fabled milk-white stone – used by Diocletian for his Palace and in places as diverse as Berlin's Reichstag, the high altar of Liverpool's Catholic Cathedral and even the White House in Washington. There's plenty left and a number of quarries still provide employment for a sizeable chunk of the population. Otherwise Brač remains relatively unexploited: roads are few, none of its villages especially picturesque, and, once you get away from the coast, the rugged interior harsh and unwelcoming. This said, tourism is beginning to take off and **SUPETAR** the island's capital – a simple unpretentious place gathered around a small harbour – now takes on a holiday-camp type atmosphere in summer, very nearly swamped by the young Slavs and older Germans who congregate in the Plaža Hotel complex, monopolising the town's pine-fringed semi-circle of pebble beach. The neo-Byzantine ice cream you can see poking its dome above the cypresses is the Petrinović family **mausoleum**, the work of an obscure Dalmatian sculptor called Rosandić. Mestrovićian in its monumentality, it was built for a rich local family who made their fortune selling British coal to Chile and Chilean nitrates to the Brits. Enterprise indeed.

Rooms and **maps** are available at the **Turist Biro** (Daily 0800–1100/1500–1900) – dead in front of you as you get off the ferry – and there's a **campsite** a mile or so out of town on the Postira road. If you can't stand Supetar's crowds **SUTIVAN**, a few miles down the coast, is smaller and quieter with emptier beaches and a small cache of rooms. Buses there are infrequent but you can hire a bike from the Hotel Plaža beach, or there's a direct ferry from Split once a day. In the opposite direction **POSTIRA** is an agreeable little place, and just 4 kilometres from a good sandy beach at **LOVREČINA**.

About half a dozen buses a day leave for **BOL**, Brač's livelier second town and main resort, where there's a decent but crowded piece of beach and a Dominican monastery with a collection of church art and archaeological finds. **Rooms** are available from the **Turist Biro** – though they're snapped up fast in summer – and there are two small private **campsites**. A better and slightly less populated beach is the one you see on all the tourist posters, the much-eulogised *Zlatni Rat* (Golden Horn), pouting into the sea about a kilometre's walk from town.

Up above, and a good two- to three-hour climb, Brač rises to its greatest natural attraction, **Vidova Gora**, at nearly 800 metres the highest point on the island and a favourite excursion spot for anyone here more than a couple of days: summer evening views over to Hvar and Vis are stunning. From Bol you can island-hop to Jelsa on HVAR – there's at least one boat a day, more in high season.

ŠOLTA is smaller and less developed, separated by a narrow channel just a few hundred metres wide. And like Brač, at just an hour away by boat it's a main contender for day trips from Split. Ferries stop at all the seaside villages – they have to as Šolta's roads are at best poor, at worst non-existent – and if you're not into walking you can best get around the island by sea. Of the three Split-facing villages, only **STOMORSKA** is remotely attractive, with a small beach and pretty harbour; **ROGAC** isn't much more than a few houses and a bar, and **NEČUJAM** is at present just building-site, dumper trucks and diggers noisily depositing the facilities for tomorrow's tourists.

The island was used as a prison for political dissidents in Roman times and during medieval inquisitons as a place to banish heretics. I doubt very much if it's changed recognisably since either era. At the moment it's very much a place to escape to: there are rooms in Nečujam and Stomorska but you may have to hunt for them; and though there's no official campsite, camping out is easy enough. If you do decide to stay make sure you take some provisions as restaurants and bars are few and far between. Frankly, if you want a wild nightlife, I'd stay in Split.

HVAR

Hvar seems to draw more superlatives – and more people – than any other Yugoslav island; people talk of its verdant colour, its perpetually fragrant air and mild climate, and the island's hoteliers have enough faith in the weather to offer a money-back guarantee if the temperature ever drops below zero. And the island is undeniably beautiful – a slim, green slice of land punctured by jaggy inlets and cloaked with hills of spongy lavender – but it's on the brink of a massive commercialisation. Hvar town already sprawls in an unfinished concrete mush over the next few headlands, loud music pounds from fast-multiplying coffee bars, and the July and August air is thick with the guttural tones of English and German. If you're reading this anywhere but Hvar I'd get there now, and thank your stars that Yugoslav tourism is ten years behind Greek.

Above all, don't let my pessimism put you off – so far development has been kept well clear of **HVAR TOWN** and it's easy to escape the crowds. If you're not offered a **room** at the bus station – and you almost certainly will be – the **Turist Biro** (Daily 0700–1200/1500–2300) or various quayside receptions will find you one. The nearest **campsite** is 3 km away, near the ferryport at VIRA, and is connected by regular buses.

You can **swim** from the rocks around the headlands – they're rarely overcrowded away from the hotels – or take a taxi boat to more peaceable spots on the *Pakleni Otoci* ('Islands of Hell'), a string of sleek islets just outside the bay. Nearest, and officially naturist, is JEROLIM; Palmižana cove, on the long squiggle of SV KLIMENT, isn't officially nudist but no one seems to mind you stripping off. Jerolim boasts a small café but to anywhere else you should take your own food and drink. Boats can be hired from one of the cafés in Hvar harbour and work out a good deal if there's enough of you. **Eating** everywhere in Hvar tends to the expensive: best value are the 'tourist menus' laid on by several of the hotels – not the most convivial places to eat but a good bet if you want to hang on to your cash.

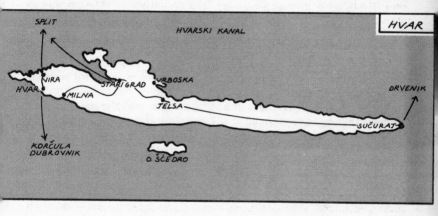

Even by Dalmatian standards, Hvar's history seems pretty rough-and-tumble. Originally a Greek colony, the island has been the temporary property of a motley crew of different rulers – Hungary, Genoa, Bosnia and Dubrovnik all had a go at one time or another – and like the rest of Dalmatia it only achieved a period of relative peace and stability under the Venetians. In 1571 the notorious Algerian corsair Uliz Ali sacked Hvar town on behalf of the Turks, reducing it to a smouldering rubble that had to be rebuilt from scratch. Now its harbour is alive with a constant hum of activity, whether it be the Rijeka ferry lumbering into its latest port of call, hydrofoils buzzing insect-like around the bay, or tiny boat-taxis ferrying people to naked pursuits on the Pakleni islands. The town is carelessly contoured around the bay, grainy-grey and brown with green splashes of palms and pines oozing their way through every crack. A creamy brown piazza cuts its way in, flanked by the long bulk of the Venetian Arsenal and culminating in the skeletal campanile of Hvar's **Cathedral**. This is dull – only the **Bishop's Treasury** is worth a close inspection with a small but fine selection of chalices, reliquaries and embroidery. Look out for a nicely worked C16th *crozier*, carved into a serpent, encrusted with saints and embossed with a figure of the Virgin attended by Moses and an Archangel (Daily 0900–1200/1700–1900).

From here its a long gentle climb past the shell of the Gothic Hektorović Palace and up through the close-knit old town and groves of incensey pines to the C16th **Spanish Fortress** (why 'Spanish' nobody knows), now rather dubiously turned into a bar/disco/restaurant complex. Whether you're into this or not pay the admission charge and walk in, if only for the views over Hvar and the islands beyond. Take a good look at Vis; because of its sensitive military installations, this is the closest you'll get. At the top left end of the harbour you can see the **Franciscan Monastery** (Daily 0900–1200/1600–1800), with a small collection of paintings, mostly obscure Venetian, best a tender *Ecce Homo* by Bassano and an almost life-size *Last Supper*, attributed to Matteo Ingoli. The latter is an accomplished work with the feel of a party in full swing: conversations flow, figures turn and gesticulate, while waiters stand idly by and chat. Take a look too at the monastic church, light and pleasingly simple with some beautifully carved choir stalls and an ornate polyptyched partion.

Hvar's second fiddle is **STARIGRAD**, where the main coastal ferry calls and the Split ferry puts in twice a day during the summer months. Set at the far end of a deep inlet, it's a sleepier place, less developed and less attractive, yet more popular with Yugoslavs. The one local sight is the **summer house and garden** of C16th poet Petar Hektorović, whose greatest work *Fishing and Talks with Fishermen* (!) was the first realistic poem in Croatian literature. He seems to have been very much into fish, since the main feature of his house is a delightful central cloister with a pond healthily stocked with mullet (Daily 1000–1200).

I prefer **JELSA** to Starigrad: it's prettier, with a livelier feel, as yet unmonopolised by big hotels which, as in Hvar, keep a respectful distance in the woods. Rooms are on offer at a waterside **Turist Biro**, there's a **campsite** next door to the Hotel Mina, and plenty of boats and bikes for hire. A short walk or ride along the coast takes you past plentiful empty rocks and pebble coves – or you can head out to the FKK island of ZEČEVO. **VRBOSKA**, 20 minutes' cycle away, is really no more than a village, but its attractions include two churches with Venetian paintings, a tiny fishing museum and a large **naturist campsite**. SUĆURAJ, on the furthest tip of the island, has a couple of sandy beaches and is linked to the mainland by frequent ferries. For the rest, there are numerous deserted coves, all accessible if you have your own transport. Those **hopping to Brač** need to be early risers – the daily boats from Jelsa leave well before dawn.

KORČULA AND THE PELJEŠAC PENINSULA

Like Hvar, **KORČULA** was first settled by the Greeks, who gave it the name *Korkyra Melaina* or Black Corfu for its dark and densely wooded appearance. Even now, after Mljet it's perhaps the greenest of the Adriatic islands and, alongside Krk, Rab and Hvar, undoubtedly one of the most popular. It's biggest problem is water, – which has to be imported from the mainland. Campaigns for water have been current here for decades, and village processions to pray for the stuff are still not uncommon. At the moment they're putting the finishing touches to a long-promised pipeline that will cut Korčula's weighty water bill in half – just as well, as the island's tourists are increasing severalfold each year.

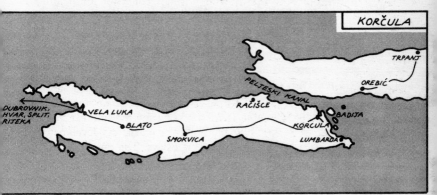

Korčula town

KORČULA TOWN sits on a beetle-shaped hump of land, a medieval walled city ribbed with a series of narrow streets that branch off the spine of the main street like the veins of a leaf; it's a careful plan, designed to reduce the effects of wind. The Venetians arrived here in 1420 and stayed nearly four centuries; the Algerian King Uliz Ali attacked the city in 1571, but it was so stoutly defended by the inhabitants that the frustrated Ali went off in a fit of pique to massacre Hvar, and Korčula lived to fight another day – no thanks to the Venetians, who had fled at the mere sight of the Muslim legions. The fact that Korčula was Venetian for so long enforces the inhabitants' claim that the city was birthplace of **Marco Polo**, and they've opened his house to the public just to prove the point. The story is certainly credible – many Venetian sea captains were drawn from these colonies and it's known for sure that Polo was captured off Korčula by the Genoese, in whose prisons he wrote his *Travels* – but don't go expecting much from his house, which these days is little more than a ruin where you ascend an open tower to look down on the overgrown shell of the rest of the building.

Nearby is the **Cathedral of Sv Marko** (Daily 0700–1200/1600–1900), squeezed into a space between the buildings that roughly passes for a main square – land has always been precious here. Lean back and look at the façade, askew to the rest of the church, with a gorgeous fluted rose window and bizarre cornice frilled with strange beasts. In the centre a matronly creature looks anonymously down with half-closed eyes: no one knows for sure who she is and wild speculations have ranged from the Roman Emperor Diocletian's wife to one of a number of Hungarian Queens, who was supposed to have put up the money to build the church. In through a west door framed by peculiarly promiscuous Adam and Eve is a church that ranks as one of my favourites on this coast. It took 300 years to build and the result is a curious mixture of styles that show a kind of muddled continuity from the Gothic forms of the nave to the Renaissance northern aisle, tacked on some time in the C16th. There's something rather touching about the way it's been squashed into a space quite obviously too small for it: all the proportions seem wrong, yet the effect – while not especially harmonious – is quite lovely. Features include paintings by Tintoretto and Bassano, but the best have been removed to the **Bishop's Treasury** (Monday-Saturday 1000–1200/1600–1800), one of the most beautiful collections of fine and sacral art in the country. A small but exquisite set of paintings takes in a striking *Portrait of a Man* by Carpaccio, a tender, perceptive *Virgin and Child* by Bassano, some Tiepolo studies of hands and a tiny *Madonna* by Dalmatian Renaissance artist Blaz Jurjav of Trogir. Oddities include an ivory statuette of Mary Queen of Scots, whose skirts open to reveal kneeling figures in doublet and hose. How this got here no one was able to tell me.

Opposite, in another Venetian palace, is the **Town Museum** (Monday-Saturday 1000–1200/1600–1800) whose comparatively modest display contains a plaster cast of a C3rd BC Greek tablet from Lumbarda – the earliest evidence of civilisation on Korčula – and a room devoted to the liberation struggle with some faded photos featuring **Fitzroy Maclean**. He stayed here for a short time as head of the Allied mission during the war – he's the skinny cropped one with a beret – and came back after the war, Tito relaxing the restrictive rules on house-purchase for foreigners.

Back down Glavna Ulica, follow the signs to the **Icon Gallery** (Monday-Saturday 0900–1200/1600–1800), housed in the rooms of the All Saints' Brotherhood, where there's a permanent exhibition of Cretan icons pillaged by Korčula sailors in the C17th. An enclosed bridge across the street takes you into the church of the Brotherhood, a Renaissance building with an expressive Baroque Pietà and a ciborium modelled on the one in the Cathedral.

Lastly, try and see the **Moreška**, a traditional folk dance/drama that came to Korčula via Italy from Spain. Its Spanish origins suggest it relates to their conflict with the Moors, but in Dalmatia its rise was most likely

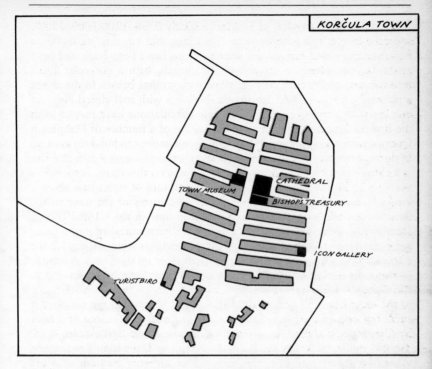

KORČULA TOWN

TOWN MUSEUM

CATHEDRAL

BISHOPS TREASURY

ICON GALLERY

TURISTBIRO

connected with the victory over the Turks at Lepanto in 1571; others have related it to more ancient fertility rites, comparing it to regional English dramas such as the Mumming plays. Whatever its meaning, the Moreška is these days something of a tourist attraction, and its annual performance on 27 July has become a weekly summer event, held every Thursday at 9 p.m. on the open-air stage by the main town gate.

Basically it's the story of a conflict between the Turks (in red) and the Moors (in black) when the heroine, Bula (literally 'veiled woman') is kidnapped by the evil Moorish king and his army. Her Turkish betrothed tries to win her back in a sword fight that is a carefully planned sequence, with clashes taking place inside a constantly shifting circle of dancers. The dance gets gradually more frantic, rising to a climax in which the Black King is forced to surrender while his white adversary unchains Bula and carries her off triumphant. If you want to see the Moreška, tickets are on sale at the Turist Biro – get them early, as in season they disappear fast.

There are a number of ways of **getting to Korčula:** car ferries make the 15–minute trip from Orebić to Dominče, 3 km from Korčula town, hourly; if you're on foot a small boat will take you there direct. The main coastal service (Rijeka-Bar) calls at Korčula roughly four times a week, there's a daily all-year connection between Split and Vela Luka (which is linked by bus to Korčula town), and there are two buses direct from Dubrovnik every day. Once you're here the **Turist Biro** (Monday-Saturday 0700–1930, Sunday 1000–1300) opposite the bus station will find you a **room** – though these can be tight in summer – or there's a **campsite** a mile or so out on the road to Dominče (hourly buses). **Restaurants** in the old town tend to be expensive: of them, *Adio Mare* is the best, least pricey and most atmospheric – housed in a ruin near Marco Polo's house. There's also a good *pizzeria* behind the Hotel Korčula and a couple of grill restaurants outside the town walls near the harbour.

Beaches, islets and inland

Beaches near the town are generally pretty grim, and you'd do better to take a boat out to one of the off-lying small islands. **BADIJA**, the largest and nearest, is an odd mix – part nudist and site of a Franciscan monastery turned water-sports centre; STUPE is the official FKK island; VRNIK is noted for its stone quarries, which have gone into the construction of, among other buildings, Istanbul's Agia Sophia. Korčula's best beaches – and a delicious local wine called *Grk* – are at **LUMBARDA** – hourly buses or an 8–km walk – but they too can get quite crowded.

Ten or so buses a day ply the island-long route between Korčula town and Vela Luka, on a journey that takes about an hour and a quarter. On the way you pass through **BLATO**, the island's largest settlement but with little to see apart from the *Kumpanjina*, another traditional battle-dance, not dissimilar to the Moreška but much less touristy and only performed once a year on 23 April. The origins of this one are known for certain – it celebrates a victory over Saracen pirates – but it's likely that the tradition goes back much further, again to ancient spring and fertility rites. At the far end of the island, **VELA LUKA** is a workaday place, by no means unpleasant but a town to arrive at rather than spend any time in. If you're stuck, there's a **Turist Biro** with rooms.

Just 15 minutes away, on Pelješac, and clearly visible from Korčula, is **OREBIĆ**, once the natural last home for generations of retired mariners. They built palatial mansions set back from the sea behind a luscious foliage of palms, cacti and tropical colour, and sat back and reflected on a lifetime's seafaring, spinning yarns on their comfortable, land-bound balconies. A small **Maritime Museum** on the seafront gives the lowdown. More recently, Orebić, with its stretch of beach about a mile from the harbour, has become something of a resort – there's a campsite nearby, and the Tourist Biro has rooms.

From Orebić the road climbs up into the heights of the **PELJEŠAC PENINSULA**, a slim mountainous finger of land that clings tenuously to the coast at Ston. If you're in a hurry, take the turn-off for **TRPANJ**, an unremarkable little town where six ferries cross daily to KARDELJEVO on the mainland proper, cutting out a long detour. The route south down Pelješac is more interesting though, sweeping and dipping through a woolly landscape striped with the grey of tumbledown terraces and rich green vineyards. Pelješac's vines produce a full-bodied red wine called *Dingač*, a potent heady brew. Half an hour and you're looking down on **TRSTENIK**, a huddle of orange roofs around a glistening blue bay, where you can swim from two small beaches or take a ferry to Mljet. From here onwards tiny villages line the coast: idyllic spots, and often served with small campsites, but only really feasible if you've got your own transport.

At the bottom end of Pelješac is **STON**, known for its salt flats and oyster beds – two towns really, resting on either side of the slim neck that joins the peninsula to the mainland. Once the furthest northern outpost of the Dubrovnik republic, there's not a lot here now – only a frescoed Serbian church a couple of miles outside, high on a hill and hard to reach – and unless you've got bags of time, I'd keep straight on for Dubrovnik.

SOUTH TO DUBROVNIK

Once free of the amorphous straggle of Split the coast down to Kardeljevo sports some of the best beaches in Dalmatia – most are pebble, some actually have sand and all are served by countless campsites. The ex-pirate stronghold of **OMIŠ** is the first town of any size, cowering under the sharp drama of the scenery behind, where the olive-green river Cetina has furrowed a deep gorge, tearing the bone-grey Karst into wierd, angry shapes. The town itself is very ordinary, but it's possible to make trips up the canyon by boat, or if you prefer, to walk, battling against the wind that blows down here, the full force of which can lift you off your feet. Other than this, a **campsite** and an excellent wide **beach**, Omiš seems a beaten place, overshadowed by the landscape, pounded by the wind, and uglified by a vicious spread of indiscriminate new development.

From Omiš the road runs down to Vrujla Bay, a deep indent that signals the start of the so-called '**Makarska Riviera**', a string of resorts that vary from the over-used and exploited to the relatively unknown. **BRELA** has one of the best bits of beach on this part of the coast and a tourist business that's still in its formative stages. It can get crowded but is rarely as packed as **BAŠKA VODA**, a 5–kilometre walk away and much more established. Three kilometres down the coastal footpath **PROMAJNA** (also with a good campsite), and **BRATUŠ**, the next village on, are still fairly unheard of and quiet even in high season.

MAKARSKA is a bright, lively, no-nonsense seaside town, ranged around a broad bay between two stumpy pinewooded peninsulas and backed by the muscley grey Karst of the Biokovo mountains. Its one museum has a psychedelic collection of highly polished seashells but this apart there's nothing to do but swim, drink and eat. Makarska's facilities are well geared to all of these things: the beach is nearly 2 km long, with plenty of space if you're prepared to walk, and you can swim nude on the seaward side of the right-hand promontory. There's a **campsite** at the far end of the beach, two **Youth Hostels** just beyond (though you'll need to book) and the **Turist Biro** (Daily 0700–2200) on the promenade almost always has **rooms** to spare. So long as you avoid the smart places on the seafront most of the grill **restaurants** dotted all over town are pretty standard, and there's a *self-service* restaurant down by the beach. Makarska is also one way of getting to BRAČ: **ferries** leave for Sumartin between four and five times daily in season.

From Makarska the coastal highway follows a slim ribbon of green between titanic grey mountains and the deep azure of the Adriatic. Most of the villages – IGRANE, BRIST, GRADAC – have small beaches, campsites abound and rooms are there for the asking. The slim streak of land offshore is the island of Hvar, reach ble on almost hourly ferries from DRVENIK. Not far past Gradac is **KARDELJEVO** (formerly Ploče) link-town for the interior and a modern functional port. If you arrive by boat, make straight for the bus/train station, if by bus or train, head immediately for the port; luckily they're only two minutes apart. Train connections include all the major Yugoslav cities and Salzburg, Vienna and Munich, and there are frequent ferries to TRPANJ on the Pelješac peninsula, which if you're going to Korčula is much the best route you can take.

Kardeljevo to Dubrovnik is a straight run with no worthwhile stops. **SLANO** may once have been one but it's long since been deflowered for its position in a deep indented bay. The approach to Dubrovnik follows the deep cut of the Dubrava river estuary where the rich idle away their money playing about in boats. Once round you're very soon enmeshed by the cranes and warehouses of GRUŽ, the working harbour of the city they call 'the Pearl of the Adriatic'.

DUBROVNIK

DUBROVNIK bursts in season with an almost constant flow of holiday-makers – package-tourists, backpackers, elderly cruisers on the 'trip of a lifetime' – who throng the streets in intimidating gangs and guided tours in search of the 'pearls', 'gems', and 'jewels' that have littered the pages of guidebooks for years. For all that, no tour of the coast would be complete without it, and it's important you don't get switched off to the place as soon as you arrive. Give Dubrovnik time – at least a couple of days – see it in the early morning before most of the tourists have crept out of their hotels, and the city will gradually start to reveal itself; slowly you begin to see what all the fuss is about.

Libertas, Dubrovnik's motto, which plasters the sides of buses and the city's tourist literature, says quite a lot about its history, for Dubrovnik managed to keep its freedom for several centuries while the rest of this coast suffered under the various yokes of foreign imperialists. Not only is the Venetian Lion of St Mark conspicuous by its absence here, but the symbol of Dubrovnik's independence, St Blaise, fills every conceivable crack and niche in the city. Ragusa, Dubrovnik's name until this century, exploited its favourable position on the Adriatic with a maritime and commercial genius unmatched anywhere else in Europe at the time, and by the turn of the C14th was a successful and self-contained city-state (its galleons gave us our word 'argosy', which means simply 'ship of Ragusa'). While coming under the nominal suzerainty of Venice, and later Hungary, it somehow managed to stave off direct intervention in its business and remain solidly unattached until the early C19th.

A fire at the end of the C13th, plague in the mid–14th, and an earthquake in 1667 which left the city battered to pieces by a tidal wave, are just a few of the disasters that threatened this fragile independence; not to mention the perennial threat of invasion by predatory super-powers that stood by always ready to pounce. Fiercely – and ficklely – Catholic, Dubrovnik enjoyed the passive protection of Spain and the Papacy, and its skilled diplomats fended off the attentions of the Ottoman empire with cunning and pragmatic obsequiousness – and regular payment of enormous tributes. Every year two envoys would visit Constantinople, hand over the cash and stay for a year in fawning acquiescence until someone arrived to relieve them. Meanwhile, Dubrovnik could get on with managing its own affairs, developing a system that, in its Whiggish liberalism, often seems years ahead of its time. By 1417 they had passed a law abolishing the slave-trade, 1432 saw the establishment of a health service and three years later the foundations of a free education plan. Combine this with a town-planning scheme second to none and you're reminded more of the rational humanism of C17th Holland than the imperial despotism that was the normal state of play in the Balkans. This then, was how civilisation could flower in Dalmatia when left alone by foreign exploiters.

The organisation of the **city-state** took the form of a rigid oligarchy. There were three clearly defined classes, nobles, commoners and workers, and marriage or any association between them was severely frowned upon. The nobles called the tune: they organised themselves into a grand Council of all males over the age of 18, which in turn deputed power to an elected Senate that took care of day-to-day business, delegating responsibility to another series of councils who administered the law and the city's purse. No personality was ever allowed to emerge from all this to excercise power himself, and the Rector, a token, almost figure-head leader, was elected for just one month, during which time he could only leave his palace for state occasions. After his month was up he could only stand again after a period of two years.

The old city

Forget the new town and head straight for the old walled heart of Dubrovnik; all motor vehicles are banned from the centre and buses drop you outside the **Pile Gate**. Best way to get your bearings is by making a tour of the city walls (Daily 0900–1930) which still stretch almost all the way round. To us they're picturesque but to the Ragusans they were a life-saver, and one glance at the thickness gives some idea how seriously

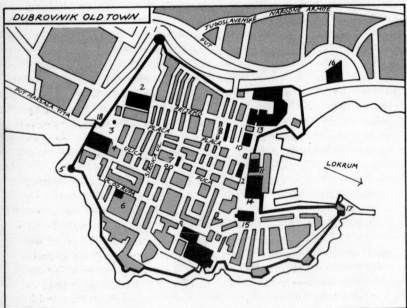

DUBROVNIK OLD TOWN

LOKRUM

1. MINČETA FORTRESS.
2. FRANCISISCAN MONASTERY
3. ONOFRIO'S LARGE FOUNTAIN.
4. ST. CLAIRE'S NUNNERY.
5. BOKAR FORTRESS.
6. RUPE MUSEUM.
7. SERBIAN ORTHODOX CHURCH.
8. SYNAGOGUE.
9. JESUIT CHURCH
10. SPONZA PALACE.

11. CITY HALL
12. SV. VLAHO
13. DOMINICAN MONASTERY.
14. RECTOR'S PALACE.
15. CATHEDRAL
16. REVELIN FORTRESS.
17. ST JOHN'S FORTRESS, MARITIME MUSEUM, AQUARIUM.
18. PILE GATE

they took the defence of their city. Within is a sea of roofs, faded by time into a pastelly patchwork of like colours, punctured now and then by a sculpted dome or tower and laid out with the sort of uniform irregularity that very few cities ever achieve. Just inside the Pile Gate is **Onofrio's Large Fountain,** a bulbous domed object where visitors to this hygiene-conscious city had to wash themselves before they were admitted any further. **Placa** runs dead straight from here, the city's main street, lined with stately blocks (now housing Dubrovnik's considerable tourist trade) and polished slippery by the tramp of thousands of feet. At the far end it broadens into the pigeon-choked **Luža Square,** flanked on all sides by historic buildings and watched over for the moment by a couple of restorative cranes.

On the left is the **Sponza Palace,** once the customs house and mint and a building which grew in storeys as Dubrovnik grew in wealth, its façade an elegant weld of florid Venetian Gothic and quieter Renaissance forms. Open mornings only, and made over to a *revolution museum* and *fine art gallery*, its majestic courtyard gives just the sort of impression of enlightenment the Dubrovnik nobles must have wanted to project. Across the square the Baroque church of **Sv Vlaho** (St Blaise) is in graceful counterpoint to the palace. St Blaise is said to have warned of impending Venetian attack, saving the city and earning himself the title of Dubrovnik's patron saint; his gilded silver figure holds a little maquette of pre-earthquake Dubrovnik on the high altar, though it's difficult to get close enough for a good look.

Beyond Sv Vlaho is the **Rector's Palace,** where the incumbent Rector sat out his term of office in what was, effectively, a prison – he had virtually no power and could only leave with the say-so of the nobles who elected him. He could have spent a month locked in worse places: built in the C15th by a loose partnership of three architects, the palace is a masterpiece of quiet, unpretentious proportion, fringed with a loggia of cherubed pillars. Its atrium is the venue of summer concerts and the rest normally houses the *City Museum*, but when I was there it was in the grip of a large and expensive restoration designed to give a face-lift to the whole city – shortage of funds had dragged it out longer than necessary but it could be over by now. If so, the **Cathedral** will have re-opened too, though, apart from a few Italian paintings – Parmegianino, Palma Giovane, Titian – there's precious little to tempt you there. Dubrovnik's original Cathedral, funded as a votive gift from Richard the Lionheart, was destroyed in the earthquake, and the present structure is an C18th replacement. Far better the **Treasury** across the street (Daily 0900–1200/1400–1800), which has a C12th skull *reliquary of St Blaise*, an exquisite piece in the shape of a gold Byzantine crown, stuck with portraits of saints and frosted with delicate gold and enamel filigree work. Even more eyecatching, though, is a bizarre *Allegory of the Flora and*

Fauna of Dubrovnik, C15th, in the form of a jug and basin festooned with snakes, fish and lizards clambering over thick clumps of seaweed, described by Rebecca West as having 'the infinite elaborateness of eczema'.

From here you can cut through to the small harbour, presided over by the monolithic hulk of the **Fort of St John** (Sv Ivan), which usually houses an *ethnographic and maritime museum* but like so much of the rest of the city could well still be closed for repairs. There's an open collection of folk art – costumes mainly – on the other side of town in the **Rupe Granary** (Daily except Saturday 0900–1300) together with a dull lapidarium of fragments from Dubrovnik buildings. Lastly the **Franciscan Monastery** (Daily 0900–1200/1400–1600), has a *treasury* that includes fine Gothic reliquaries, manuscripts, a late C16th view of Dubrovnik and an *apothecary's shop* which, dated at 1317, lists itself as the oldest in Europe. Most of the time you'll be peering over people's heads – guided tours are thick on the ground in this, one of their favourite stops – but a deliciously cultivated cloister provides something of an escape from it all. In the opposite corner of town, the Gothic-Renaissance cloister of the **Dominican Monastery** (Monday-Saturday 0900–1200/1500–1800) is another retreat, together with a plain Gothic church that has a Titian painting of *Mary Magdalen and St Blaise* – holding the ubiquitous cityscape – and a *St Dominic* by the C19th Croatian artist Bukovac – studies for which you may have seen in his house in Cavtat.

Consuming matters

Dubrovnik has no rail connection and **ferries** arrive in the port-suburb of GRUŽ, a mile or so north of the old city, just beyond the **bus station**. From both it's a 1, 2, 3 or 6 bus ride to the centre. Free **maps**, an in-depth **information booklet** and **private rooms** are available from a booth near the bus station or the **Turist Biro** at the Pile end of Placa (Monday-Saturday 0900–2100, Sunday 0900–1200/1500–1900). You may be offered a place to stay at the bus station but if not, and you want to avoid the tourist office surcharge, take a walk down Jugoslavenske Narodne Armije or around Gruž, where **rooms** are thick on the ground. **Hotels** are expensive across the board: the cheapest you'll find are the C category *Dubravka*, in the old town, or the *Stadion*, behind the bus station. There's a **Youth Hostel** at Oktobarske Revolucije 25, where you really have to book to be sure of a bed, or failing that the **International Youth and Student Centre** at Ivanska 14 (bus 2 or 6). Bus 6 also goes to Dubrovnik's main **campsite**, *Solitudo* – an enormous complex where the tentless can get cabins for around the price of a private room. The penurious can camp – police permitting – in a terraced park overlooking the sea below Maršala Tita.

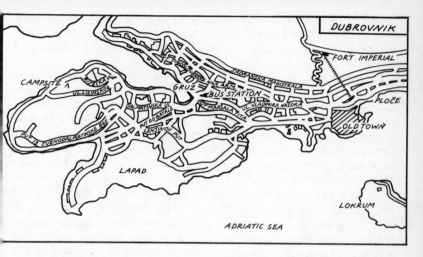

Food and drink are easy to find in the old town: if you're rich Ul. Prijeko is lined with chintzy fish joints; otherwise there's an early morning fruit and veg market on Gunduličeva Poljana, and the same square is surrounded by supermarkets, two self-service restaurants and cheap grills. *Bokčilo* is reasonable, so is *Jug* in Izmedu Polača, and *Krčma Pomet*, across Placa on Zudioska, does downbeat café snacks. The **Summer Festival** (roughly 10 July–25 August) is a good, if crowded, time to be in town, with concerts and performances in most of Dubrovnik's courtyards, squares and bastions – often the only chance to see the inside of them. Seats can be pricey, but it's allowed, if not exactly encouraged, to go in for free once a performance has begun (say, first intermission) if seats are available. Bureaucratic wrangles and budgetary problems have led to some falling-off in quality, but the vibrancy is still there. For a full programme go to the festival office at Od Sigurate 1.

The city **beach** just south of the Ploče Gate is dirty and crowded, and you're better off taking one of the half-hourly boats to the wooded island of LOKRUM in the bay, where there are a number of quieter places to swim – best a sheltered salt lake in the centre of the island. Nudists are confined to a short stretch of wind-buffetted rock on the far side. It's a beautiful island, larger than it looks, and you can get carefreely lost along the shady paths that criss-cross its dense pinewoods. I'd take some food and drink but if you don't there's a self-serve restaurant – along with a small natural history museum – slightly incongruously housed in a Benedictine monastery.

A few facts
Bookshops The bookshop around the corner from the Turist Biro has

a good selection of maps and English books on things Yugoslav.

Cable-Car   Leaves every half-hour between 0900 and 2000 for terrific views from the top of Mount Srd. At a pound a time it's one way of seeing the city, though if money's tight you'd do better to content yourself with a trek around the city walls.

Car-Hire   *InterRent* (Gruska Obala 98), *Hertz* (Aleja IL Ribara 50).

Ferry tickets   *Jadrolinija* are at Gruska Obala 74.

JAT   Pile 7. Airport buses depart from Hotel Petka, by the ferry terminal.

Post office/Telephone   Maršala Tita 16 (Daily 0700–2200).

MLJET AND THE ELAPHITES

MLJET is best reached by car ferry from Trstenik, on Peljesač, but boats also go once daily from Dubrovnik, stopping at all the inhabitied ELAPHITE islands and putting in at most of Mljet's eastern settlements as far as Polače. Times vary from day to day so check first with the Turist Biro in Dubrovnik.

The string of seven islands that crowd the sea as far as the Pelješac peninsular are known as the ELAPHITES or deer islands, a name apparently first coined by Pliny. Of the three that are actually inhabited **KOLOČEP**, just half an hour from Dubrovnik, is the smallest, just one square mile in area and with a population of under 500. Boats dock at **DONJE ČELO**, not much more than a handful of houses grouped around a small bay, two hotels and a few fishermen. Tourist outings from Dubrovnik dump their loads here for 20 minutes to photograph each other with a background of fishing nets, but otherwise things go on largely undisturbed. There's a **sandy beach** in the harbour, a **nudist beach** around the headland, and a **campsite** at **GORNJE ČELO**, the only other settlement.

LOPUD is a littler larger, and enjoyed a certain amount of prosperity in Dubrovnik's balmy days when it was the seat of the Vice-Rector and a favoured watering-hole of the city's nobles. Now its only village, strung around a wide, curving bay, enjoys the fruits of a modest tourist industry, slightly more uptempo than Koločep, with a fair sprinkling of bars, restaurants, a couple of hotels and a pension. There's a small **town museum** with an uninspired collection of junk brought back by centuries of Lopud mariners and some Venetian School paintings in an appalling state of repair. If you want to stay the *Atlas* office on the front will find you a **room**; better though to strike out with tent for remoter parts of the island, which is easily small enough for a really thorough exploration.

ŠIPAN is the largest and probably the quietest island in the Elaphite chain, a ring of hills enclosing a fertile plain thick with vines and olive trees. **ŠIPANSKA LUKA**, the main 'town', is buried at the end of a deep inlet, a ramshackle cluster of houses around a new hotel. There are a few rooms going in summer, and if you're after some real isolation you could do worse than forge into the interior. If not, push on to Mljet which, if not exactly riotous, is at least a great deal prettier.

Though among the most beautiful of all the Adriatic islands, **MLJET** is surprisingly unvisited: there's no one large town and the people that do come here are usually on day-trips and seldom stay. It has fair claim to being the island of Melita, where St Paul ran aground on his way to Italy and was bitten by a viper before he set sail again; Mljet's snakes were once so widespread that a colony of mongooses had to be imported to get rid of them. Now there's a mongoose problem.

POLAČE is the principal ferry port, with the remains of a C14th Roman mansion hard by the harbour. If you can't find a room here someone will be able to tell you where you can. An irregular bus service connects with **BABINO POLJE**, the island's largest village, **GOVEDJARI**, heaped up high on a bluff a little way inland, and **POMONA**, where there's a large hotel which rents out bikes and mopeds, a **tourist booth** that doles out maps and a **campsite** – though camping in the deep woods is perfectly feasible. Tourist hydrofoils put in here, and parties crocodile their way up to Mljet's greatest pull – **Malo** and **Veliko Jezero**, two sea-water lakes surrounded by dense pine forest and with a slim outlet to the sea at SOLINE. On a tiny islet in Veliko Jezero is a C12th Benedictine abbey, now a hotel where the groups from Dubrovnik eat their lunch. Mljet isn't exactly blessed with **beaches** – there are only a couple of sandy coves on the far eastern tip of the island – but the swimming in the lakes is delicious and once the daytrippers have gone you've more or less got the island to yourself. One small point: if you're thinking of taking the daily boat to Dubrovnik from here remember to be up bright and early – it leaves at four every morning.

INLAND AND SOUTH: TREBINJE, CAVTAT AND THE ROAD TO MONTENEGRO

In the search for the 'mysterious east' **TREBINJE**, a Hercegovinan Muslim town 30km inland from Dubrovnik, is about as far as most tourists get – a situation that's unfair to both tourists and town. A short bus ride through blasted moonscapes of forest scorched in recent fires, it sits surrounded by bleak Karstland desolation, a modern town that manages to be almost as drab as the land around. What the tourists come to see, the clumsily fortified **Stari Grad**, doesn't do a lot to redeem things. Turkish houses have been tarted up as cafés and restaurants, and only a few vestiges of the Ottoman tradition remain: the domeless **Osman Pasha Mosque**, built in the 1720s, is still in use though normally closed; find the young *imam*, who'll expect a donation for unlocking the place. Out of the old town signs direct you to the **Begova Kuča** (Bey's House) which turns out to be an unremarkable building whose women's quarters now front a restaurant armed with waitresses in national costume. Since the early days of Dubrovnik tourism Trebinje and its Saturday market have been built up as a money-spinning day trip; if you do want to see oriental towns, save your energy for a deeper exploration of Bosnia and Hercegovina.

Immediately south of Dubrovnik you run into places like **KUPARI** and **MLINI**, not so long ago quiet fishing villages but, bought up by tour operators, now almost wholly package-deal territory. The vast tourist settlement at Kupari is an alternative **campsite** for Dubrovnik, but otherwise there's absolutely no reason to stop.

Further on, and about a mile off the main coastal highway, is **CAVTAT**, the ancient Greek colony of Epidaurus which was evacuated in preference for Dubrovnik after a thorough ransacking by the Slavs in the C7th. Though a pretty enough place, set on a sweet-smelling wooded peninsula, it's these days an expensive resort, with a palm-fringed seafront clogged with people, costly restaurants and gift shops. On a prime spot high above, the **Račić Mausoleum** (Daily 1000–1200/1500–1800) is showpiece of the town, built by Ivan Mestrović for a local family in 1921. As a meditation on the nature of death it's a depressing sort of monument, with the cool, resounding, and ultimately rather empty kind of grandeur typical of Mestrović. Other Cavtat sights include a small and rather ordinary **grotto** and the house of the C19th Croatian painter Bukovac, which has been turned into a **museum** of his work (Tuesday-Saturday 1000–1200/1600–1900, Sunday/Monday 1600–1900). The only **beach** – by the Hotel Albatross – can teem with people in high season, and there are better places to swim on the rocks that knobble Cavtat's jut of land; **FKK facilities** are just the other side of the Croatia Hotel. Ample **accommodation** is available from the **Turist Biro** and there's also a small **campsite**. For **food** it's hard to find anything not exclusively tourist-geared and the *pizzeria* in the harbour is your best bet; drinks tend to be cheaper at the *Inex bar*, on the far side of the bay.

After Cavtat the peace is disturbed at roughly ten-minute intervals by the ear-shattering screech of low-flying aircraft, either taking off or sweeping into Dubrovnik airport at nearby **ČILIPI**. Even so, Čilipi somehow stays a sleepy village until Sunday, when charabancs from Dubrovnik hustle in to catch the ethnic costumes on their way to Mass. From here it's a short ride through a bloomy green and orange landscape spiked with cypresses, to the gardeny resort of HERCEG-NOVI and the republic of Montenegro. . . .

TRAVEL DETAILS

Buses

From Split to Dubrovnik (hourly; 5hrs); Makarska (half hourly; 2hrs); Rijeka (hourly; 8 hrs); Sarajevo (5; 6½hrs); Šibenik (2; 2½hrs); Sarajevo (5; 5hrs); Zagreb (4; 9hrs) Zadar (hourly; 4hrs); Sinj (half hourly; 45mins).

From Rijeka Zagreb (hourly; 4hrs); Belgrade (3; 9hrs); Pula (hourly; 2½hrs); Zadar (8; 4hrs); Split (8; 8hrs); Rab (4; 3hrs); Postojna (4; 3hrs); Senj (10; 2hrs); Cres/Lošinj (6; 4/5hrs); Ljubljana (6; 3hrs); Trieste 3; 3hrs); Koper (4; 2hrs); Krk (3; 1½hrs).

From Zadar to Plitvice (5 daily; 3hrs); Zagreb (4; 5hrs); Split (2; 4hrs); Biograd (hourly; 1hr); Nin (8; 45min); Sibenik (hourly;2hrs); Trogir (hourly; 3hrs).

From Dubrovnik to Zadar (6 daily; 9hrs) Split (1; 5hrs); Orebić/Korčula (2; 4hrs); Kotor (6; 2hrs); Belgrade (3; 14hrs); Trebinje (4; 1hr); Ulcinj (1; 4½hrs).

Trains

Split – Zagreb (8 daily; 7hrs); Kardeljevo – Sarajevo (5; 3hrs)

Ferries

The **main *Jadrolinija* ferry** calls at most of the following places roughly once daily in season: Rijeka-Rab-Zadar-Split-Hvar-Korčula-Dubrovnik-Bar.

Local ferries include: **Rijeka-Cres** (1 daily; 2½hrs): **Brestova-Cres** (Porozina) 12; 15mins): **Rijeka-Lošinj** (1; 6½hrs): **Lošinj-Pula** (1; 3½hrs): **Zadar-Pula** (1; 8hrs): **Crikvenica-Krk** (Silo) (10; ½hr): **Senj-Krk** (Baška) 2; 1hr): **Senj-Rab** (Lopar) 2; 2hrs): **Krk** (Baška) – **Rab** (Lopar) (10; 1hr): **Jablanac-Pag** (Novalja) 6; 1½hrs): **Karlobag-Pag** (6; 1hr): **Zadar-Ugljan** (Preko) 12; ½hr): **Biograd-Pašman** (Tkon) (10; 15mins): **Split-Šolta** (4; 1hr): **Split-Brač** (Supetar) 12; 1hr): **Makarska-Brač** (Sumartin) (5; ½hr): **Split-Hvar** (Staringrad) (3; 2hrs): **Split-Hvar** (Vira) (3; 2hrs): **Drvenik-Hvar** (Sućuraj) (10; 20mins): **Kardeljevo-Trpanj** (6; 1hr): **Orebić-Korčula** (Dominče) (14; 15mins): **Split-Korčula** (V.Luka) (1; 3½hrs): **Rab-Pag** (Novalja) (2weekly; 3hrs): **Dubrovnik-Mljet/Lopud** (1 daily; 3½hrs/1hr).

International ferries

From Rijeka Igoumenitsa (3 weekly; 36hrs).

From Zadar to Trieste (3 times a month; 9hrs); Rimini (once weekly; 8hrs); Ancona (3 times a month; 8hrs).

From Split to Trieste (3 times a month; 11hrs); Venice (weekly; 14hrs); Rimini (weekly; 12hrs); Ancona (2 weekly; 9hrs); Pescara (4 weekly; 7½hrs); Bari (weekly; 18hrs).

From Dubrovnik to Venice (3 times a month; 24hrs); Rimini (weekly; 21hrs); Ancona (weekly; 15hrs); Bari (4 weekly; 8hrs).

Chapter four
MONTENEGRO

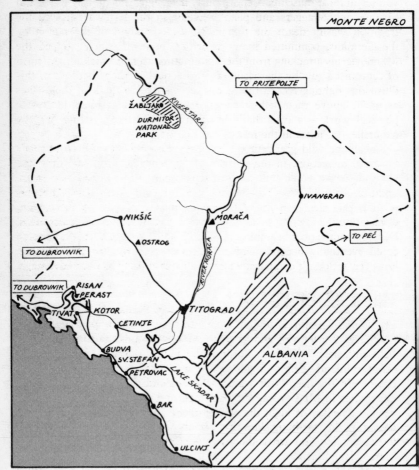

Smallest of the six republics, **Montenegro** packs in some of the most stunning scenery in the country. The scarcely populated interior of vast mountain ranges is harsh and wonderfully rugged; large settlements are few, with only a scattering of alpine-style villages cut off for much of the year and remote even in summer, when the snows of the brutal winters have eventually melted. **Cetinje**, the ancient capital, stands in splendid isolation, as difficult to reach now as it was for the Turks, who never managed to subdue the uncompromising land or people. The Montenegrins have always been a fiercely independent lot, meeting aggression from outside by retreating to the mountains and conducting vicious guerrilla warfare – a warrior cult which accounts for the pictures of fighters you see in most museums – enormously muscular, ridiculously brave and bristling with daggers and pistols. Events in the last war showed the tradition wasn't dead: the Italians, given command of the region by the Germans, committed many atrocities, none of which stopped the Montenegrins attacking from their mountain bases and making any form of centralised rule by the occupiers impractical. Perhaps because of this illustrious fighting record the Montenegrins like to think of themselves as a cut above their fellow countrymen, disdaining things like mere physical work – a trait that's left them the butt of a string of 'lazy Montenegrin' jokes in the rest of the country.

For all the wild grandeur of the interior though, it's **the coast** that's the chief attraction. In the north is the spectacular **Gulf of Kotor** and along the coast you'll find some of the country's finest beaches – clean, often sandy and always with somewhere to escape the throngs. That this is so is due largely to the 1979 earthquake which shook the region, devastating the town of Kotor and leaving medieval **Budva** a ghost town. Development is now beginning to pick up and signs are that Montenegro could eventually become Yugoslavia's second Istria; for the moment, however, it doesn't compare, which is almost entirely to your advantage.

THE GULF OF KOTOR

The **Gulf of Kotor** is undoubtedly the single most impressive coastal feature in Yugoslavia, and in terms of sheer natural beauty is hard to beat anywhere in Europe. Bordered by high mountains, it's more of a series of inland fjords than gulf: green and massive, the mountains sweep down into the deep clear water, while behind the stark Njeguši range culminates in **Mt Lovčen**, 6000feet high and one of the country's most dramatic peaks. At night the waters of the Gulf lie black and profound, mirroring the star-hung skies that rise above the featureless sillouettes of the mountains, and across the water the sound of birds and boat engines carries clear for miles.

With such a perfect harbour it's not surprising that the Gulf's sailors had so important an impact on the maritime history of the Adriatic. In the Dark Ages pirates roamed the shores with impunity, though with the rise of Venice they were restricted to the southern coast and in the C15th finally overcome. Even under Venetian rule, Kotor maintained its reputation, and the skills of its sailors were often utilised – most notably at Lepanto, where navigators from Perast led the victorious Venetian fleet. Later Peter the Great formed the backbone of his navy from sailors from the Gulf, and more recently, in April 1941, Kotor saw the evacuation of the Royalist Yugoslav government, fleeing the occupying Italians in what turned out to be permanent exile.

The 1979 earthquake left most of the Gulf intact, with the city of Kotor taking the worst of the damage, the towns – villages really – that rim the water's edge remain more or less unscathed. Hopping from one to the next is easily done by bus, but rooms in the smaller places are few and fill fast. Coming from the north, HERCEG-NOVI, RISAN or PERAST provide good breaks in the journey before you reach rooms a-plenty in KOTOR.

Strung along a hillside at the entrance to the gulf, **HERCEG-NOVI** is by no means as new as the name suggests. Built from scratch in 1382 by the Bosnian King Tvrtko to give Bosnia access to the sea, its site was of vital strategic value, and was consequently fought over by anyone with aspirations of controlling the Adriatic. In a dizzying succession of rulers the town changed hands a dozen times, though the most lasting impact on what you see today was inevitably provided by the Venetians, Turks and Austrians – a mixed heritage that's left a rag-bag of styles.

It was the Austrians who turned Herceg-Novi into a popular watering hole in the C19th century, and the atmosphere of genteel respectability remains, the mild climate encouraging hoards of German tourists and some of the most abundant vegetation on the coast. Wisteria, bougain-villea, palms and orange groves tumble down the hill, exploding from every inch of available ground and pricking colour against a back-drop of deep, fecund green. This said, Herceg-Novi doesn't have much to detain you: there's no beach as the seafront has been concreted over to provide a sunbathing strip for the hotels, and though you can swim from here it's heavily populated by the hotel crowds. Back in the centre, a Ruritanian-style clock tower, the promising entrance to the **Old Town**, preludes a few medieval Venetian houses in a pretty shabby state, the years of neglect aided by the recent 'quake. This same earthquake also did away with the C16th **Spanish Fort** that overlooked the town – a few crumbling heaps of stone mark a fine vantage point from which to see Herceg-Novi's flora and the entrance to the Gulf beyond.

Herceg-Novi's best buildings don't deign to be in the centre: a 15–minute walk past the Hotel Plaža takes you to **Savina**, a Serbian Orthodox monastery traditionally founded in the C13th by St Sava. Two churches stand side by side in the courtyard, the larger, a cheerful meeting of Byzantine and Baroque, imposing over a simple chapel. This medieval building is now the monastery's **treasury**, piled high with gold and silver ornaments, centrepiece of which is a C13th crystal cross that reputedly belonged to the saint himself.

Getting accommodation is really a matter of luck; **rooms** are few and far between in the high season – try the **Turist Biro** at the bus station or the principal office, *Savina*, on the main street running opposite the central square, and don't expect anything cheap. Alternatively there's an **autocamp** 3km out on the Kotor road.

From Herceg-Novi the bus route avoids the coastal villages, and there's nothing to stop for until **KAMENARI** near the narrow entrance to the Gulf, where a ferry crosses to the faster western route to Kotor. Unless you're in a hurry stick to the coast road, which in a few kilometres swings out into the Gulf proper. **RISAN**, first town of note, is an ancient place founded by the Illyrian tribe and perhaps the home of their queen, Teuta. The Romans later formed a large settlement here, and near the hospital are well-preserved mosaics of the C2nd. Little else remains: Risan was destroyed around the year 1000, possibly by an earthquake or landslide, and the modern town is nothing more than new houses and weekend villas sloping down to the sea. **Rooms** here, however, are in good supply throughout the year – find them via the **Tourist Office** or by following the usual signs.

Two kilometres round the bay sits **PERAST**, one of the loveliest places in Montenegro and under Venetian control for nearly 400 years. The houses that run by the waterside are toytown Venetian Gothic, with a homely grandeur that's the residue of a magnificent past. For getting on for half a millennium Perast was the muscle of Adriatic maritime strength, holding forth against repeated Turkish attacks when the rest of the Gulf had fallen. The sailors of Venice and later Russia came to the nautical school here and learned the skills of Perast's mariners; its cartographers charted the coasts; its navigators steered the Venetian fleet at Lepanto; its engineers designed ports in the Baltic. Eventually earthquakes, political manoeuvring and simple age took away Perast's pre-eminence and left it to a graceful retirement. A **museum** (Daily 0800–1300, closed Sundays) in what was once the palace of the town's leading nautical family keeps a few tokens of naval exploits from later years, but it's not all that memorable. What is is the view of the town, best seen by climbing up the hillside between the decaying houses that are unconcernedly falling back to nature, grass and ivy exploring the front rooms of the C17th. Down on the seafront, captains' houses look confidently out to the entrance of the Gulf, and over the red roofs the mountains ring the tranquil sea. Perast is picturesque in the full sense of the word.

You may need to hunt around on the waterfront for someone to take you to one or both of the **islands** that float like rafts off Perast: guided tours are irregular, and it's easier, if a little more expensive, to hire a small boat. Darkened by cypresses SV DJORDJE has a much-restored Benedictine abbey and little else. Its companion, GOSPA OD SKRPJELA ('Our Lady of the Chisels') is more interesting. To trace its origins you have to choose your legend. In one, a sailor, shipwrecked in the Gulf, clung to a stone here one night, promising that if he survived he'd build a church to the Virgin on the rock. Morning and rescue came, the sailor kept his word and dumped stones until the island rose. The alternative, a little less colourful, is that on 22 July 1452 two sailors found an icon of the Virgin and Child on the rock and took it to Perast; next day it was found that the icon had mysteriously made its way back to the rock, so the Perastians built it an island and fittingly grand church. Though severely battered and rebuilt over the years the church remains, and in the sea-blue and seaweed-green Baroque interior you can still find the miraculous icon, held in a marble altarpiece of great value – for the green Italian marble the Perastians paid an equal weight of silver. The icon was much revered by the Gulf's sailors, and round the walls are 2000 silver ex-voto plaques, promised to the Virgin in moments of peril and given on safe return. And in the small museum next door a room is crammed with gifts from those who survived shipwreck; a treasury of everyday objects, plates, cutlery, even sewing machines. Each year the villagers hold two **celebrations** of the island and its icon, and if you're around these are well worth joining in. On 22 July a great procession – the *fašinada* – sails out to strengthen the island with new boulders, and on 28 August the icon is taken to Perast's church to commemorate a battle with the Turks in which the Virgin appeared in horrific form, scaring off the attackers and saving the day for the Perastians. Much drinking and dancing go on, and marksmen enjoy a game called *gadjanje kokota* – shooting the cock. This involves tying an unfortunate rooster to a piece of wood and floating him out into the bay. The locals then blast away with assorted arms, and when the feathers settle someone is declared the best shot and everyone goes off to get drunk. Tough chaps these Montenegrins.

You can see all of Perast in an hour or so, but you'll probably want to stay longer. Frequent buses ply the Herceg-Novi – Kotor route, making it an easy stop-off, and for **rooms** best bet is track down the **Tourist Office**, whereabouts and opening times of which are erratic. Failing this, follow the few signs for *sobe* or just ask – Perast is a tiny place. The sole place to **eat** is the *Vile Perast Hotel* – not as bad as it sounds and cheaper than you'd think.

KOTOR is an exciting place to arrive at, tucked away at the end of the Gulf with the steep slopes of Mount Lovčen towering vertiginously overhead. And it's an initial promise that on the whole is met – despite earthquake damage to the old centre of town. Most of what's visible was built by the Venetians from the C15th on, though the stout ramparts that zig-zag up the mountainside date from the C9th, a reminder of the town's long-standing importance as a sea port. Until the 1979 quake Kotor in fact rivalled Dubrovnik in the undisturbed preservation of its Venetian palaces and churches – a state of affairs that a frenzy of dumper trucks and builders are now working overtime to restore. At the moment the town resembles nothing so much as a giant building site, and this makes finding your way around nearly impossible: the cramped streets twist and turn, narrow down into tiny piazzas just to double back on themselves – the only solution is to try and keep the mountains behind you, the sea ahead and hope for the best.

In the middle of this labyrinth, the **Cathedral of Sv Tryphon** is about the only building as yet made safe in the patching-up operations. It's a rather austere structure, predominantly Romanesque once you get past a fine front added in the C17th after another in Kotor's long line of earthquakes did away with the original. Just inside is an intricately carved doorway, single survivor of the C9th rotunda on which the later church was built. Its open basilica plan is sparse and light, only the *ciborium* straddling the altar catching the eye, red marble columns supporting a triangular awning crowned with an angel and richly decorated with scenes from the life of St Tryphon. Kotor came to have Tryphon as its patron saint in 890, when a passing merchant ship loaded with relics offered the townspeople a good deal on its most precious object, the head of the saint who'd been put to death 600 years earlier. This bargain was much too good to miss, and Tryphon's head still rests in the cathedral's **treasury**. Closed after the earthquake, this may be permanently reopened by now, and should definitely be seen, not just for the treasures and ornaments but for a superb medieval wooden *crucifix*, as full of the the horror of suffering as anything crafted by the German carvers of the time. The reliquaries sit in their glass cases like so many dolls' limbs dipped in silver, bits of arm and leg of dubious origin gathered over the centuries. Like the ornaments the earlier ones are best – the priest dismissed the C17th and 18th works with a sniffy 'decadent rubbish' when showing me the collection.

Other than the cathedral, Kotor's buildings are out of bounds until restoration is completed. No great shame – much of the pleasure of the town lies in exploring its Italianate streets and, if you have the strength, climbing the old walls to the Fortress of Sv Ivan. I didn't make it, but the views are said to be worth the exhaustion. Like Perast, Kotor is also a handy stop-off and base for exploring the Gulf: **rooms** are cheap and plentiful in the new town; book them from the red **info kiosks** outside the main city gate. The nearest **campsite** is also inexpensive and a walkable 3km out, back on the Perast road.

From Kotor there's a choice of destinations and routes. A direct main road leads to Budva – skip this and you miss nothing. Far better to take the road up to CETINJE, a fascinating town reached by one of the most spectacular journeys in the country. But first **TIVAT** – which but for the '79 quake would probably by now be as developed as, say, Poreč. Even today this stretch of the Montenegrin coast is beginning to be littered with hotels and autokamps, stretched out along the pebbly beaches on either side of town. Tivat itself is a spacious place decorated with palm trees, and its central park, rather like Herceg-Novi, bursting with exotic blooms. Elegant houses of the C17th surround, but the single building of interest is the pretty little **Chapel of Sv Antun** of 1373, ornately adorned with the arms of Kotor's leading families. The town's development looks like it's getting back on its feet with some speed: the offshore island of PREVLAKA is given over to a hotel complex, and adjacent SV MARKO is home to the *Club Mediterranée* organisation. Most of the beaches too are pretty crowded. *Pržno* is about the best – reach it by irregular bus or hitching.

CETINJE

The trip from Kotor is the bus journey that scales the slopes of **Mt Lovčen** and heads for Cetinje, one of the most magnificent routes in Europe and not on any account to be missed. Looking at the mountain it seems impossible that a road could exist, an apprehension that persists when you're actually on the bus snaking your way up. It's a slow crawl, the road winding through dozens of hairpins as the air thins and cools. Below the gulf spreads out in picture-book clarity, Kotor just a blip at the foot of the mountainside – a superb view that's worth the assault on the nerves as the bus inches its way round rockfalls and incautious motorists. At about 3000ft the road runs through the **Lovčen pass** and suddenly you're in the Karst. Local legend has it that at Creation God was flying over the Balkans with a huge sack of stones; the devil crept up behind and slit the sack open, and what fell out was Montenegro. An appropriate image: the Karst is a lunar landscape of crags and boulders, a barren colander that swallows rain and melting snow, repaying the land with thin, patchy vegetation.

CETINJE sits on top of this apple-crumble terrain, surrounded by the frozen crests of limestone peaks. Until 1945 it was Montenegro's political and cultural capital – isolated and easily defended it could hold its own against the Turks – and formed the court for a fascinating succession of theocratic rulers. Travelling in the 1930s Lovatt Edwards described the town as 'sleepy and undistinguished, a city of pensioners', and it's true that the glories are all gone – most of the streets lined by low, unpretentious pastel-fronted houses. But in the centre you'll find leftovers of a more eventful past: palaces, now museums, remain as reminders of the time when the small town had its brief moment of importance.

Most engaging and most visited of these palaces is the **Biljarda**, named after a billiard table brought here from Kotor at great effort and expense by Cetinje's most famous son **Petar Njegoš II**. A squat, two-storeyed structure, the Biljarda is neither extravagant nor particularly imposing – which is probably how Petar II, who built it in 1836, wanted it. Petar was in every respect a remarkable man, as interesting as he is unknown

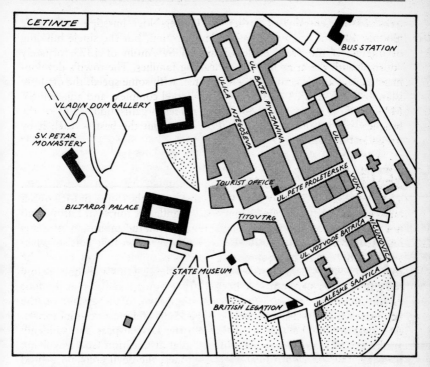

outside Yugoslavia: 6 foot 8 inches tall and stunningly good-looking, he was not only a successful secular ruler but a bishop, diplomat, notorious hounder of the Turks, poet of distinction and a crack shot to boot. The story always told of him, mainly because it was witnessed by an English noble, Sir Gardiner Wilkinson, is that he would frequently call for a lemon to be thrown into the air and shoot it down before it hit the ground – 'a singular accomplishment for a bishop' mused Sir Gardiner. Tutored by the Serb poet Milutinović, Petar greatly admired the French Romantics and in his short life – he died when he was 48 – produced several major works of his own. Most important of these was an epic drama entitled *The Mountain Wreath*, which is considered the greatest of all Yugoslav epic poems. He also spoke French, German, Russian and Latin, and read their literature, philosophy and jurisprudence in the original. Some of his reading material remains in the **Library**, preserved in the Biljarda along with rooms furnished in the style of his court. He achieved all this at a time when civilised Europe considered Montenegro no more than an obscure mountain outpost peopled by a race of barbaric warriors.

Two other sections of the Biljarda, are worth a look: the **Ethnographic Collection** with its dashing Montenegrin costumes – and the **Museum of**

the National Liberation. The Montenegrins played a vital part in the anti-Fascist war. After Tito's call to arms in July 1941 they rose against the occupying Italian forces with a unity unmatched by any other region: when an order was issued demanding the surrender of all arms, 50,000 heavily armed Montenegrins handed in two rifles – one didn't work and the other had been 'borrowed' from an Italian soldier. The Montenegrins were going to fight, and in the first few weeks they pushed the Italians out of all Montenegro except Cetinje and Podgorica (today's Titograd) – their revolutionary fervour such that they set about constituting soviets on the early Russian models. Montenegro was later partially re-occupied, but never during the whole course of the war was it completely defeated. The cost was horrifically high – proportionately Montenegro lost more of its people than anywhere else in the country. The museum illustrates this in a dispassionate, moving way; the walls are lined with row upon row of pictures of dead Partisans, some of the photographs taken from German archives and showing men, women and children at the moment of execution.

In a room next to the Biljarda a huge **relief map** of the region, constructed by Austrian soldiers in 1917, shows just how mountainous Montenegro really is, and as you walk around it's fairly apparent why no foreign power ever managed to conquer the country. Like the Italians and Germans after them, the Turks in over 300 years of near constant seige never managed to subdue the valleyed fastnesses. On three occasions, the last in 1785, they were able to force their way into Cetinje, but each time were expelled – and with heavy losses. Montenegrin males were taught to shoot when children, and their prowess with the sword – the *Yatgan* – was legendary: such was the state of their honour that they would, and frequently did, cut off the head of a colleague rather than let him fall into the hands of the Turks. In fact, during the fight with the Turks this lopping-off of heads became commonplace. Behind the Biljarda palace are the remains of a small tower; when Sir Gardiner Wilkinson was visiting he was shocked to see it decorated with Turkish skulls impaled on stakes and complained to Prince Petar, appalled that so civilised a man could permit such a practice. But when he continued his travels into Turkish-held Mostar he found his indignation misplaced: in front of the Vizier's palace was another round tower festooned in equally gruesome style – this time with the heads of Montenegrin soldiers.

The **Sv Petar Monastery** (Daily, 0700–1400, 1600–1900) behind the Biljarda was completed by the Bishop and Prince Danilo, founder of the Njegoš dynasty, in 1701. Built in chalk-coloured brick, it's an inarticulate structure, the double arcade of cloisters spoiled by a tacked-on roof and unbalanced by a multi-levelled tower. A small cruciform *chapel* contains the tombs of Njegoš notables, including Prince Danilo and the late Sv Petar, uncle of the celebrated poet king (who, incidentally, has his own lonely mausoleum on the peaks of Mt Lovčen). Dull stuff, but the **treasury** has some fine C15th and 16th icons and religious books, by far the most important of which is *The Octoich of the First Voice*, a gospel dating from 1493. Coming just 18 years after Caxton's *Histories of Troy* it's probably one of the oldest printed books in existence and certainly among the first ever printed in a Slav language.

A long brown-plastered building that looks more like a lesser C19th mansion than the home of Montenegro's last independent ruler, the **Palace of King Nikola I** is now the **State Museum** (Daily 0900–1900), its interior an approximation of how it would have appeared in his reign. Like Petar II, his predecessor, Nikola was an unusual man. During his 58–year reign he managed to use Montenegro's crucial position in the Balkans to trade off one superpower against another, and the bulk of his revenue was collected not in taxes but in handouts from the Russians and Austrians. Cetinje became a capital where no self-respecting country could afford not to have some sort of representation, and the Russians, French, Austrians, Italians and Turks all had Embassies or legations here. The former British Legation – in its elegance not unlike the Palace itself – still stands on Ulica Njegoševa. One thing that isn't mentioned in the museum is the fact that Nikola was also a pretty detestable creature, with all the ethics of a cornered sewer rat: throughout his wheeling and dealing reign he used official funds for personal gain while the Montenegrin people suffered intense poverty. When Russia gave grain to ease a famine among his starving people, Nikola sold it to the highest bidder; after 20,000 of his troops had died in the successful seven-month seige of Shkoder in Albania, he waited, then surrendered – using his foreknowledge to make a fortune on the Viennese stock exchange. His reign ended in 1916 when, amid accusations of treachery from Serbia, he allowed the Montenegrin army to be captured by the Austrians. He fled to France and there died in exile in 1921, outliving most of the men of his generation. There's a portrait in the museum showing Nikola smiling the smug smile of a survivor.

Finally, if you've time or inclination for yet another museum, the **Vladin Dom Gallery** (Daily 0900–1500) has an exhaustive and exhausting display of national and regional painting from the year dot to the present day – nothing remarkable other than some boastful C18th pictures of Montenegrin derring-do.

Rooms and food

If you're offered a **room** at the bus station, take it: the **Tourist Office** has only a few private places on its books and they're often all taken. The house at Baje Pivljanina 19, behind the office, seems to fill some mysterious accommodation function – rooms go for the usual price if you can find one. Because of this lack of beds it's best to arrive early so you can continue to Budva if need be. When I did the trip a couple of buses left Kotor before 7am, allowing you to see Cetinje and be in Budva by teatime – much the same is true of the reverse journey. For something to **eat** try the cheap and cheerful *restaurant* just up from the tourist office on the same side of the road.

The road down from **Cetinje to the coast** is only marginally less spectacular than the road up to it. After a few twists and turns the town disappears and the earth suddenly cuts away to reveal BUDVA, SVETI STEFAN and an eternity of blue sea 2000ft below.

DOWN THE COAST: BUDVA TO ULCINJ

In 1667 and again in 1979 **BUDVA** was devastated by earthquake: after the first it was entirely rebuilt by the Venetians, but the second proved fatal. Out of 187 buildings only 5 survived unscathed and today Budva's **old town**, a tiny walled citadel thrusting out to sea on its own peninsula, is a hollow shell of ruined buildings. A notice forbids entry to these none-too-secure streets, but it's really just there to protect the authorities – no one's going to stop you exploring. It's a ghostly place, bats and wild cats prowling amid piles of neatly stacked rubble and with only the rhythmic sighs of the sea to disturb the silence. Though some of the houses came out of the earthquake badly, others remained seemingly intact and belongings lie scattered about as if the occupants left in a hurry; shades of the *Marie Celeste*. In the early evening the old town is at its most atmospheric, the streets full of echoes of the disaster. Stepping back from the crumbling Venetian beauty to the hotels and their muzak momentarily disconcerts; walking through the old town is like swimming underwater.

Before the 1979 'quake, Budva was fast becoming a tourist resort, and today, in its new town of soulless concrete and glass hotels, the package industry has taken over completely. Previously, the old town must have provided a lively continuity with the past – a past which stretches back here further than anywhere else on the coast. In legend Budva was founded by Cadmus, son-in-law of Aphrodite and sower of the famous warrior teeth; in fact, records show that Budva was definitely an important Greek settlement as early as 500 BC. Four centuries of Venetian rule gave the town stability and protection from the Turkish raids that harrassed the rest of the coast, and from this background a fascinating character emerged. There can't have been many charlatans or imposters who managed to bluff their way to a throne with a name like **Šćepan the Small**. This diminutive character was selling herbs in Budva when a rumour went round that he was really a wandering Polish monk or, more grandly, the Russian Tsar Peter III, deposed in 1762, presumed murdered. Whether the Montenegrins of the day were gullible or Šćepan extremely personable we don't know, but he was installed as Prince, declaring that he was indeed Tsar Peter, but for convenience' sake his subjects could carry on calling him Šćepan the Small. As it turned out he was a gifted ruler, uniting the Montenegrin tribes in concerted attacks on the Turks to the south. And this was to prove his undoing; in 1774 the Vizier of Skadar, fearful of Montenegrin solidarity, bribed Šćepan's barber to slit his throat, and Šćepan the Small went to an early (and presumably short) grave.

For all its resurgent modernity Budva is still a good place to stay; it's fairly easy to find a **room** and worth considering as a base for exploring the rest of the coast. Besides, though there aren't any sights, the beaches are excellent and scenery superb. The modern town's only street of consequence runs at right angles to the sea from the hotels, and it's here you'll find the **Tourist Offices**, any one of which will be able to supply you with **private accommodation**. (*Montenegro Tourist*, near the hotels, opens till late and has rooms at reasonable prices.) **Eating** is geared to the tourist budget and correspondingly overpriced – try the *pizzeria* (follow the signs off the mainstreet) or the *fish restaurant* on the road to Sveti Stefan. To get to the **beaches** pass through the Hotel Avala and clamber along the slatted rocks until you strike sand. The less crowded beach is furthest from the hotels – you need to climb through a hole in the rocks to get there. Emptier still are the beaches on the island in the bay officially called SV NIKOLA but known locally as *Hawaii;* to reach it, take a boat taxi from the mainland beach.

The coast from **Budva down to the Albanian border** is probably the loveliest and least spoiled stretch in the whole country. The road runs below ranges of sharp summited mountains, green and blue under thin vegetation, occasionally burnt bright yellow with broom. By the roadside knarled and wizened olive trees twist and heave in huge groves, some planted in pre-Christian times and as much as 2500 years old. As you head south the crowds thin out and finding your own space on the beach becomes less of a fight. Getting a **private room**, though, isn't quite as easy; in peak periods you need to book early in the day to secure a place, a problem you won't encounter if you utilize the abundant **campsites** that line the coast road. Failing this it's possible to find an undisturbed spot where you can **sleep rough** almost anywhere along the road; just get off the bus midway between villages and start walking.

One place definitely not worth the halt is **BECICI**, a few kilometres around the bay from Budva. Originally it must have been a pleasant enough fishing village but is now a grim autocamp city which even the undoubted attractions of its long sandy beach can't redeem. Further down the coast **MILOČER** is Bečići's rich uncle, its prestige coming from the presence of the Yugoslav royal family's summer palace, now a luxury hotel. Belgrade's monied classes flock here in summer to enjoy the beach and ornamental gardens, and as a result prices are prohibitive – way over the odds for what Miločer has to offer. Just next to Miločer is the pride of Yugoslav tourism – the absurdly picturesque city of **Sveti Stefan**, photos of which you'll have seen adorning a 1001 posters. Joined to the mainland by a narrow causeway which arcs out into two perfectly formed sandy beaches, this former island town has also been converted into a luxury hotel. Between the wars all the inhabitants left to seek work further up the coast, and the small red-tiled stone houses built in the C15th and 16th became derelict and unusable. In the early 1950s it was decided to save the buildings, if not the town, by converting each of the houses into self-contained tourist suites. The plan worked and Sv Stefan is now one of Yugoslavia's biggest money-spinners, like Miločer its prices beyond most people's reach. You're allowed in on payment of a small fee to see how the other half lives and marvel at the town's rebirth, though if you've already been to old Budva, Dubrovnik or other places further up the coast I wouldn't bother to fork out for the privilege: as examples of medieval city centres they are far more striking and complete, and anyway Sveti Stefan's undeniable beauty is much better viewed from the shore.

PETROVAC-NA-MORU (Petrovac-on-sea) is a small hamlet comprising a few houses and a few more hotels dotted around a magnificent crescent-shaped sandy bay. There's an open-air cinema, a tourist office with private rooms – sparse in the high season – and precious little else: It's unashamedly and unfaultably a place where people go to swim and sunbathe and usually chocked with people doing just that. For a little seclusion hire a boat and sail round the headland or out to one of the tiny deserted islands in the bay.

SUTOMORE is similar – hotels and villas clustered along a sand and pebble beach. About a kilometre north, the remains of two **Turkish castles** sit etched into the rocks above the road. Known as *Haj* and *Nehaj* ('Fear' and 'Fear Not') the Turks built them as protection against Montenegrin raids on their trading caravans. The main thing about Sutomore today is that it's on the main Bar-Belgrade rail line, a recent connection that might have something to do with the town's rather drab feel. If you stop, take a look inside the C12th church of **Sv Tekla** – evidence of an unusual religious tolerance. At the far end of the nave there are two altars, one for the Catholic service and one for the Orthodox, both still in use today.

Much renewed and revamped since the earthquake, **BAR** is the working port of the Montenegro coast, its importance consolidated by the opening of the spectacular (if slow) rail route to Belgrade. An unengaging mishmash of modern building and oily docks, the only reason to be here is to pick up one of the **ferry links**: services leave for **Bari** in Italy three times a week and Bar is the last port of call for the *Jadrolinija* ferry before it moves on to Igoumenitsa and Corfu; tickets from Obala 13 Jula 4a. What activity there is in Bar's newly-built centre revolves round three spaceship-egg boxes that house the town's supermarkets. There's nothing in the way of antiquities, but catch a bus to the hospital, carry on walking and about 5 km outside town you'll come upon **Stari Bar**, the crumbling ruins of the original old town which was severely knocked about in a C19th scrap between the Montenegrins and the Turks. Little remains save a huge C16th viaduct.

ULCINJ

ULCINJ is the most southerly town on Yugoslavia's coast and immediately different from anything that precedes it. From Rijeka down to Bar the Venetian influence is universal but Ulcinj, only 18km from the Albanian border, has a marked oriental flavour: there are few Christian churches, the houses huddled round the bay in the cramped old town are Turkish, and until the earthquake of 1979 the town's six mosques were still in use. Why Venetian influences are excluded here dates back to 1571, when the town was taken over by a party of Algerian **corsairs** – survivors of the great naval battle of Lepanto – led by the Bey of Algiers, Ulaz-Ali. For the next three centuries it was home to a mixed bag of pirates, thieves and merchants: buccaneers who plundered shipping in the Adriatic and Mediterranean, burnt towns, took slaves and generally did as they pleased so long as they didn't turn their attentions to their nominal allies, the Turks. Gradually these corsairs – Algerians, Moroccans and Turks – adopted Albanian-style customs and formed a wholly Muslim town. An interesting legacy of their slave dealings is that a tiny proportion of Ulcinj's population – no more than about six families – is black, descendants of slaves brought over from Africa in the C16th. The pirating days came to an end in 1878 when the Montenegrin army that reduced Stari Bar to rubble did virtually the same to Ulcinj. From then on, despite various international treaties, the town belonged to Montenegro.

The C19th bombardment, however, concentrated mainly on the fortified **citadel** high up on the cliffs overlooking the bay, and the narrow patternless streets of the old town were left largely intact. These cramp into a valley that trickles down to the bay, their dilapidation camouflaged under abundant flowers and greenery. The dusty, lived-in high street is the focus of activity, especially on Fridays when the peasants from the surrounding area arrive for the **market** – a colourful affair with donkeys, vegetables and crudely-coloured linen taking over the square for the day. Many of the peasants still wear traditional costume, and though the use of the veil is now outlawed, women still pull a scarf or handkerchief across their faces, a vestige of the tradition.

Apart from its intriguing Muslim past the lure of Ulcinj is in its extensive and unspoiled **beaches**. It's possible to swim from the steel-grey bay of Ulcinj itself, but the best area is about 4km south of town, known as the *Velika Plaža* (Great Beach). To reach this you can walk, starting from the path near the Hotel Albatross, following the goat tracks and finally climbing down the rocks at the end of the promontory. This is a bit hairy, but far less mundane than the alternative, catching a bus from the high street or bus station. The fine grey sands of the Velika Plaža run right down to the Albanian border, and although there are the usual hotels and chalets strewn along the nearer reaches, the beach is so long – 12km – that it's easy to find a secluded spot. These sands, incidentally, are mildly radio-active, a property that lures arthritis sufferers here for a cure – hence the bizzarre sight of them burrowing and scrabbling round in the stuff like a bunch of drug-crazed moles. There shouldn't be any problem finding your own spot if you want to take all your clothes off, but if there is, catch a ferry from about half way down the beach (near the mouth of the river) to the small sandy island of ADA, where there are sections officially reserved for nude bathing. If you come out for the day, be warned, however, that most of the restaurants dotted along Velika are rip-off joints and you'll really do best to bring your own food.

Arriving or leaving Velika Plaža by bus (from behind the Hotel Lido) you see the decaying remnants of an age-old fishing technique – Albanian **Kalimere fishing**, where large nets are lowered by claws into the shallow lakes. This was made illegal in Yugoslavia in 1967, and at the top end of the lake behind the bus stop the deserted apparatus rots away like decomposing stick insects.

Practicalities

All accommodation problems in Ulcinj will be solved by the **Tourist Office** on the seafront: they have **rooms** and a supply of **apartments**. Both are in town, but you can also find rooms near the Velika Plaža; ask at the campsite on the road to the Hotel Lido. Because of its length the beach itself is ideal for sleeping rough – just don't go too close to the Albanian border. As for **food**, providing you don't mind spending a little more than usual you're spoilt for choice. There are all manner of fish and seafood restaurants on and around the seafront to pick from – *Sidro* is excellent and not expensive.

INLAND MONTENEGRO

Conclusively mountainous, the magnificent Montenegrin interior is one of the least accessible areas of Yugoslavia; much of the country is cut off by heavy snows through the winter, and huge drifts linger well into the spring months. This lack of easy contact with the 'outside world' has left it in a backward condition, with sheep farming and a few crops providing a frugal livelihood for the people who weather the harsh winters. It's here you'll find a degree zero economy that directives from Belgrade can do little to change – I remember seeing a shepherd gathering a few scraggy sheep by the roadside while a woman spun coarse wool into threads on a distaff. The willingness of bus drivers to cross near-impossible mountain tracks means you can take in some of the most spectacular routes like the **Rugovo** and **Tara** gorges on slow bus trips, but to explore more deeply you'll have to resort to walking, using a tent as base; tourist facilities disappear in all but the larger towns as soon as you leave the coast – and a discreetly placed tent won't arouse any curiosity.

Montenegro's main interior highway runs eastward from Petrovac, rising over the coastal ridge of mountains before dipping down to **LAKE SKADAR**, the country's largest lake, shared half and half with Albania. Enclosed by bare-topped Karst mountains, its blue water is patched with the essential colours of vegetation, shifting islands of green algae and lilies. There's something magical, almost eerie, about the lake. Through the thin heat-haze that shimmers above it, the mountains recede mysteriously in innumerable shades of grey and in the distance the suitably named *Prokleti Gora* ('Accursed Mountains') of Albania can just be made out. A strangeness reaches even the plants of the lake; a local delicacy is the *kasaronja*, a sort of water chestnut, that steadfastly refuses to bear fruit in times of drought, despite unlimited supplies of water in the lake itself.

North of Skadar a lowish and featureless plain runs to **TITOGRAD**, modern capital of Montenegro. Formerly known as Podgorica, the town was bombed to oblivion during the war by the Allies – the Italians and Germans had established a command there – and the rapid rebuilding that followed was a gesture of the new nation's pride as much as anything else. This hasty redevelopment has left a characterless agglomeration of high-rise flats, distinguishable only by their flat pastel colours; the bus and train stations are a kilometre out of town, and if you don't make the trip to the centre, you haven't missed much.

Titograd forms the pivot for two impressive mountain routes. **Heading north** the road climbs slowly on a thin ledge beside the river Morača, a few square wooden houses spotted on the valley sides, seemingly primitive but all connected to the electricity grid. Bringing the benefits of industrialisation to such places must be one of Yugoslavia's greatest expenses. As the valley begins to narrow you find the **MONASTERY OF MORAČA** squatting by the roadside like a gatehouse to the valley beyond. Morača's white and undecorated shape follows the neat rule that height plus width equals length – proportions that give the church its deceptively simple harmony. It is stylistically part of the Raška school, though the frescoes aren't as extensive or as impressive as those of its near contemporaries Mileševa or Sopočani. The few original works that date from the founding of the church in 1253 are mostly in the side chapels, and show scenes from the life of Sv Iljas (St Elija), gently coloured and with the flowing yet monumental style of the court painters, a style that was to find its greatest expression at Sopočani. Unless you're prepared to get off the bus and hope that the next one along will stop – and this depends totally on the benevolence of the driver – then you'll have to be content with a glimpse of Morača as you pass. Frustrating, but there are better – and more accessible – monasteries. Beyond, the Morača valley gradually pinches in and the river falls below in the deep gorge. The road passes through rock-hewn tunnels, black and featureless, and for a second as you enter it seems you're about to descend into oblivion. At the head of the valley the road snakes up the mountainside and all Montenegro lies below you – then suddenly vanishes as you turn a corner into the upland plain. By now the air is rarefied and even in summer has a knife-edge chill that threatens the bitter cold of winter, but the landscape is green, even rich, softening the shock of the wind and glimpses of barren-crested mountains.

If you **head west** rather than north from Titograd, the road reaches Nikšič via the Zeta valley. On the way the C18th **Monastery of Ostrog** can be seen from the road, perched high in the rock and sheltering the remains of one St Basilius the Miracle Worker. Though you can clamber up to this place of pilgrimage, it's a long walk from the bus route. To look at, **NIKŠIČ** seems a much-enlarged Cetinje, a flat town cupped on a plateau and rimmed by mountains. But the similarity ends there: a few dull ruins, some forgettable museums and Yugoslavia's best-selling beer is all the town has to offer, and there's nowhere cheap to stay. From here, but only in summer, it's possible to make the long haul up to **ŽABLJAK**, a town at the foot of Mt Durmitor and the springboard for the summer skiing in the nearby **Durmitor National Park**. Durmitor's forested slopes and the lakes behind have been made accessible to Belgrade, Skopje and Titograd by a local airport, and the park is popular; accommodation (when you can find it) is expensive. Along the main route comes the second of Montenegro's spectacular gorges, the **Tara** – even deeper than Rugovo (see below) though not quite as dramatic or nerve-wracking; the bus journey linking Žabljak with the Titograd road at Mujkovac runs via the gorge.

THE RUGOVO GORGE

From IVANGRAD there's a choice of route's leading to PRIJEPOLE or NOVI PAZAR. But it's the road to PEĆ via the **RUGOVO GORGE** that really stands out. From the 5200ft Čakor pass, the windswept ceiling of Montenegro, this route winds down from Swiss-like Alpine pasture into Kosovo and a vertically-sided canyon that is, quite simply, terrifying. Road and bus cling precariously to the side, while far below the river Pećska Bistrica rushes viciously through its narrow valley, the sides plunging straight and sheer, streams of water and shattered trees falling to the foment below, the summits too high above to be seen.

It was through this gorge that the second **Serbian army** retreated in the winter of 1915, long before there was even a road. Heavily defeated by the Austrians and Germans they had decided to march over the mountains in the expectation of reaching promised British and French supplies on the coast; the weather was atrocious and food non-existent – what little the Montenegrins had they were forbidden to sell to the troops as their king, Nikolas II of Cetinje, had made a secret and treacherous deal with the Austrians. Of the 250,000 troops who began the march 100,000 fell by the wayside from disease, malnutrition, exposure and the sheer exhaustion at having already fought a three-year war of attrition. When the survivors reached the coast the essential Allied help wasn't there and they were forced to continue their long march down to the town of Durazzo on the Albanian coast. Eventually Britain and France agreed to re-equip the Serbs on the island of Corfu, but those too far gone for medical aid were sent to die on nearby Vid – still known as the 'Island of Death'. En route a further tragedy took place that's a microcosm of the disparateness and the suffering of the south Slav peoples: when the boats left for Corfu, the sea was filled with bobbing loaves of bread, flotsam from a supply ship torpedoed earlier that day. Most of the young, starving Serbians had never seen the sea before, knowing only the shallow streams of their native country. They leapt out of the boats to wade across to the food and sank like stones. Their companions from the north and south who knew the Danube or the Macedonian lakes tried to hold them back, and in the scuffles the boats capsized and hundreds drowned.

TRAVEL DETAILS

Buses
From Kotor to Cetinje (2 daily; 4hrs); Budva 6; 45 mins); Titograd (4; 5 hrs); Zagreb (1; 16hrs); Dubrovnik (4; 2hrs); Peć (1; 7hrs); Ulcinj (3; 2hrs).

Trains
From Bar to Titograd (3 daily; 45 mins); Belgrade (6; 8hrs).

Chapter five
BOSNIA-HERCEGOVINA

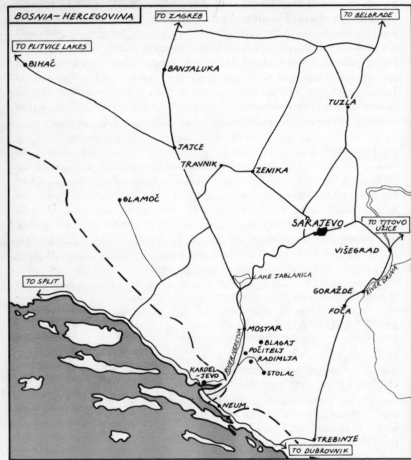

BOSNIA–HERCEGOVINA

TO ZAGREB

TO BELGRADE

TO PLITVICE LAKES

• BIHAĆ

• BANJALUKA

TUZLA

JAJCE

TRAVNIK •

ZENIKA

• GLAMOČ

SARAJEVO

TO TITOVO UŽICE

VIŠEGRAD

LAKE JABLANICA

TO SPLIT

GORAŽDE

FOČA

RIVER DRINA

MOSTAR
• BLAGAJ
• POČITELJ
• RADIMLJA
• STOLAC

RIVER NERETVA

KARDEL -JEVO

• NEUM

TREBINJE

TO DUBROVNIK

Forming much of the heartland of western Yugoslavia, **Bosnia-Hercego-vina** was the republic that most absorbed the Ottoman empire and it still retains a dominant Islamic religion and culture. Over a third of the population are Muslim, descendants of Serbs allowed a degree of freedom if they adopted the faith of their Turkish invaders. And though active worship is now on the decline, the threads of the Turkish past can be seen everywhere – in the mosques of towns and villages, in the costumes and especially in the food. If you've just arrived from the coast, the difference can be arresting.

Virtually land-locked, Bosnia-Hercegovina's countryside is agricultural and varied. To the north, **Bosnia** has lush mountain pasture interspersed with fertile plains; **Hercegovina**, founded in the C13th by Hercog (Duke) Stefan, comprises wide stretches of gaunt Karst gashed by deep gorges – dramatic travelling. The great draw is undoubtedly the capital, **Sarajevo**, a deeply atmospheric city where the region's three historical ingredients – nationalism, Turkish and Austrian occupation – underscore a buoyant individualism. It's the target for any trip here. From Sarajevo towns spread out along river valleys in three corridors: north to Croatia via **Jajce**, a compact fortress town of the Middle Ages; southwest to the coast through Turkish **Mostar**, now busily touristed; and east into Serbia through the **Drina valley**, centre for hair-raising raft trips.

SARAJEVO

'Mosques, minarets and fezes – holding the gorgeous East in fee while the river cools the air, splashing through the town and the bridge on which whatisname was assassinated.' So wrote Lawrence Durrell, summing up a city it's really impossible to compress into a few impressions. Running alongside the river Miljaka, **SARAJEVO** spreads out like a gesture between the mist-topped mountains: in the west giant hard-faced skyscrapers of post-war prosperity, progressing eastwards through the candy-coloured buildings of one foreign occupier, the Austrians, to the elegance and decay of another, the Turks. Here, more than anywhere else in Yugoslavia, Islam is evident, an active and integrated culture that generates an exciting oriental feel. Around the **Baščar-šija**, Sarajevo's old Turkish Bazaar, are graceful monuments to four centuries of eastern domination, like the stately **Gazi Husref Beg Mosque**, and all over town the untended graveyards of the faithful sprout like chalk outcrops, simpler memorials to absorbed invaders.

After the assassination of Franz Ferdinand, Sarajevo is now probably most famous as venue for the 1984 Winter Olympics, a prestige difficult to overestimate for Yugoslavia. As the ubiquitous stickers of *Vučko* the Olympic mascot slowly peel from windows and walls the wrangles continue: was it right to build new skiing facilities in Sarajevo, a town with no skiing tradition? Why not in Slovenia? As everyone paid for the Olympics in extra taxes on food, bus tickets and the like, how come only Sarajevo reaped the benefits? The usual arguments, but talk to anyone here and they'll tell you with dewey-eyed pride of how every hotel was full, how every telephone briefly and mysteriously worked. Whether Sarajevo can continue to build on this burst of glory isn't clear, but one thing is certain: with its mix of styles and peoples, buildings and customs, and its infamous place in European history, Sarajevo is the most fascinating city in Yugoslavia.

Arriving – and living

Arrive at the **bus and train station** and you're too far from the centre to walk in – take a number 1 tram, the main town circular, and get off either at the Princip Bridge (6th stop) or a little further at the Baščaršija, heart of the old town; tickets from the orange station booth or most kiosks in town – punch them as you enter.

You need at least a couple of days to see Sarajevo and you'll probably want somewhere cheap to stay. Private rooms, unfortunately, are in short supply, out of centre and expensive: bookings, for the energetic or hopeful, from *Unis Tourist*, Vase Miskina 16 (Monday-Friday 0700–2000, Saturday 0700–1600, closed Sunday) or the dour **Turist Biro**, Jugoslavenska Narodne Armije 50 (Monday-Saturday 0800–2000, Sunday 0800–1200). As ever the **Student Accommodation** is cheaper and better, though only open in July and August. Reserve beds via the tourist bureaux above, or go there directly: Studenski Dom *Stoyanovic*, Radičeva 4d is the most central and hence most popular – from the stations tram 1, 4th stop. Walk back down Vojvode Stepe and it's the third turning on the right. The *Student Centre* at Aleja Branka Bujica 2 (left off Proleterske Brigade, bus 24 from station) is further out, but has limitless supplies of rooms. Because the **Youth Hostel** at Zadrugina 17 is only a few minutes' walk from the stations, it fills fast in the summer: from the stations, go straight out of the forecourt, across the grass roundabout and down Kranjčeviča then first left up Tešanjska, first right and keep snaking up the hillside; opening hours 1400–0900, but with an uncertain 2200 curfew. For the **campsite**, take tram 3 or 4 to the end of the line at **Ilidža**, a Habsburg watering hole turned pleasure park; if you're driving it's just off the Mostar road.

Eating is problem-free: Sarajevo's *bureks* are easily the best in the country, particularly the spinach (*špinat*) variety. As an alternative try the intestine-shaped pastries filled with spiced meat and/or potato, sold by weight in the Baščaršija. All around here are cheap *kebab places* that'll fill you up, with yogurt to finish, for a few dinars. More substantial fare in the Bosnian-Turkish style is to be had from *Aščinica* at both 17 and 55 Baščaršija (the strip running down from the *sebilj* metal fountain); for cheap, but more ordinary sit-down eats try the *Dubrovnik Pizzeria* on Halači, straight down Baščaršija towards the river, or any of the self-service restaurants like *Bosna*, Marsala Tita 36, and *Herzegovina* near the cathedral. *Turska kava*, Turkish coffee can be had at any *kafana*, but make sure they brew it full strength.

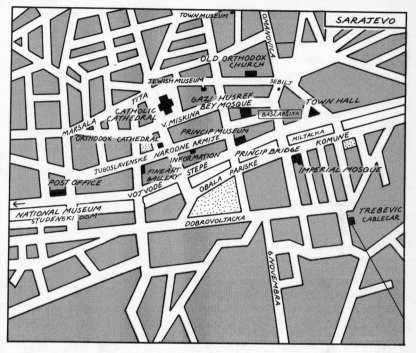

The Baščaršija and around

The **old centre** forms the eastern part of the city: the four broad streets of Maršala Tita, Vase Miskina, JNA and Vojvode Stepe run parallel to the river, zeroing in on the Turkish quarter each with its share of Austro-Hungarian pomposity, a few of the façades still brightly painted, but most fading to ornate ordinariness. Four hundred years before the Habsburgs arrived the Turks set up the administrative centre of their western possessions here, calling it *Saraj Ovasi* ('the palace in the fields') and giving the town its name. Ottoman presence was absorbed quickly, and, in a way, turned to the Bosnians' advantage. Heretics called Bogomils (see page 137), mostly local nobles, adopted the invaders' faith and became important in the running of the city, so much so that even the powers of the Sultans were second to their domestic control. The Vizier of Bosnia was allowed to spend but one night in the town each month – next day he'd be escorted to the city walls and politely ejected. Today you enter the market centre of the Turkish town abruptly: the original **Baščaršija** was flattened in a misplaced fit of post-war zeal and what's replaced it has a decidedly sanitised feel, crowded wooden chalets supplying tawdry scarves and sandals, tin and copper ware. Even so it's a noisy, smoky, hectic place, and everyone conspires to its pretence of genuineness. Just above the rose-gardened Baščaršija mosque **Kazandziluk** is one of the most animated market streets, with a constant tapping of tinsmiths beating out pots and plates. Prices aren't that cheap here, so bargain as strenuously as you can – not a process much admired by the shop owners.

Helping the Baščaršija get away with it all are the old stone warehouses and *hans* that survived the clean-up, some, like the Husref **Beg Bezistan** echoing their former use as indoor stores. But the star turn of the Baščaršija is the **Gazi Husref Beg Mosque**, built in 1530, possibly by a pupil of the great Turkish architect Sinan. It's the most exquisite mosque in the Balkans, with the elements of Turkish civilisation that are most fresh, elegant and sensuous – the wide tree-lined forecourt with its fountain, the brisk lines of the porch, and inside a crisp geometry of cube and dome, all expansive lightness and minature colour. At one side is Husref Beg's *turbe*, with an epitaph as delicate as the mosque itself: 'Husref Beg was overtaken by darkness in a state which was not sleep.' Nearby a clock tower shows the time in Arabic, or rather the hours of prayer – all through the year 12 on the clock had to coincide with sunset, the time of evening prayer, a feat so beyond the clock-makers that a man was employed to move the hands round each day. At midday you can still see the *muezzin* climb the minaret and sing (or rather yell above the noise of the traffic) the *ezan*, the nasal whine of the call to prayer: 'God is great and there is but one God. . . .'

Islamic tolerance of other faiths in Sarajevo was a tradition, and a few minutes' walk from the mosque you find the evidence in a **Synagogue**, place of worship for Sarajevo's Sephardic Jews, who settled here after expulsion from the Iberian peninsula in 1492. Now a **museum** (Tuesday-Friday 0900–1400, Sunday 0900–1300), it assembles a few pointers to the Jews' past, and, hanging like a black pendulum, the *Book of the Dead*, a massive list of those exterminated by the Nazis. Out of 14,000 Jews in Bosnia-Hercegovina only 2600 were to survive the war, and many left for Israel afterwards; so closed the sad episode of the Sephardic community.

Turn right onto Maršala Tita and you find the Orthodox **Church of Sv Archangela Michala**, closeted behind a wall that hid infidel worship from the eyes of Muslim neighbours. Of ancient origin, the church was damaged by fires that struck the city and the blunt exterior dates from the 1730s. Inside it's all darkness and sorcery, an atmosphere charged with the mysteries of Byzantium. On his feast day the hand of the patron saint is taken from its reliquary and dipped in water, which gains the property of healing the sick: vials are filled with the holy fluid and distributed to be drunk by the congregation. The wooden iconostasis contains icons from the C15th on, but a better collection of treasures is held in the **museum** next door (Monday-Saturday 0800–1800) – Bibles, silverware and a beautiful *INRI* icon near the entrance. Nineteenth-century taste bastardised Byzantine style, resulting in the lifeless formality of the **Orthodox Cathedral** on Trg Oslobodenja, built in the final days of Turkish rule with donations from rich Serbs, the Russian royal family and the Sultan himself – though his liberalism didn't spread to the local Muslims, whose tolerance ran out when they found the cathedral spire overshadowed the minaret of Husref Beg's Mosque. On the day of its dedication they rose to destroy it, being restrained only by the Turkish police. Subsequently, a more reasonable solution was found – the minaret was raised by a few feet and pride restored.

When the Austrians began their unpopular administration of the town late in the C19th they built a **town hall**, at the end of Vojvode Stepe in kitsch pseudo-Moorish style, thinking it would fit in with the Turkish buildings of the Baščaršija. As a reminder of continuing foreign control under a different name, you can imagine how well *that* went down with the locals. Today it's the University library; if you look inside to see how Austrian architects imagined a Moorish palace, be inconspicuous – I wasn't and was promptly thrown out. Across the river the **Imperial Mosque** looks cool and magnificent, and faces the town hall with, as Rebecca West put it, 'the air of a cat that watches a dog make a fool of itself'.

East of the town hall the streets climb to **Vratnik**, originally a fortified citadel, later a poor suburb choked with crumbling Turkish houses along winding alleys. Local law forbade new houses blocking the view of the old, and the result was a scramble of buildings, each peeping over the shoulders of its neighbour. A gut-busting haul to the citadel provides the best view of Sarajevo, from skyscrapers to old town, the Miljaćka running a blue ruled line as accompaniment. 'What a city!' wrote Ivo Andrić (see p. 236) 'a city passing away and dying to rise reborn and transfigured.' From high in Vratnik, such effusions seem well-justified.

Assassination

The assassination of the **Archduke Franz Ferdinand** in 1914 is one of those school-book facts most people store away for future 'explanation' of complex events; if the assassination wasn't the reason for the First World War it was at least its cause, goes the thinking. But no event in the tortured saga of the Balkans is ever that simple, and Ferdinand's death is one of the most complex – and the most bizarre.

In the 1870s Russia took advantage of weakening Turkish domination to fight and defeat them. At the Congress of Berlin a year later Serbia's independence was recognised, – and Bosnia handed over to Austria for enforced administration, a deeply unpopular move that stirred Bosnian Nationalist fervour. Secret societies and underground groups spread, and when in 1908 Austria annexed Bosnia, hatred began to boil. After 500 years under the Turks, Bosnians took domination by Vienna with vicious disgust.

Franz Ferdinand was heir to the Habsburg throne, and an arrogant, widely mistrusted bigot. When wind reached Vienna of Bosnian disquiet he organised a showcase display of Austrian military might on the Serbian border to coincide with the most important day in the Serb calendar, 28 June – the anniversary of the Kosovo defeat by the Turks and traditionally a day of mourning. On this of all days the Serb people and Bosnian Nationalists needed no reminder of their new dictators, and for the Austrian heir to drive through the streets of Sarajevo was to say the least foolish. To do so without any military force or local police protection virtually suicidal – when Emperor Franz Josef had visited the town a few years earlier every known anti-Austrian was placed under house arrest and double rows of troops lined the streets. Franz Ferdinand had 70,000 men a few miles away, but not one was with him on 28 June, and as he drove down what's now Vojvode Stepe towards the town hall, six Bosnian Nationalists were waiting to nail him. Two were schoolboys, the others in their early 20s, and none were proficient with the crude bombs they carried or could hit a brick wall with a pistol: one, Čabrinović, threw his bomb, missed and attempted suicide; the Archduke and his wife, Sophie Čoteć, arrived at the town hall shaken but unhurt.

Obviously Franz Ferdinand should never have come to Sarajevo; obviously the trip should have been abandoned. Yet inexplicably and inexorably he progressed toward his fate. An aide suggested diverting the procession away from the dangerous crowded Franz Josef Strasse (now JNA street) and continuing back down Vojvode Stepe to the hotel at Ilidža. This was agreed, but no one informed the chauffeurs. So when Franz Ferdinand's car turned by the bridge into Franz Josef Strasse an angry aide told the driver he'd taken a wrong turn. The car stopped and a slight young Bosnian called **Gavrilo Princip** stepped out and shot Ferdinand through the heart. Sophie Čoteć leant forward to hold her husband and a second bullet killed her immediately.

There isn't space here to go into the theories of intrigue that have grown out of the assassination: at first glance Franz Ferdinand's unprotected final hours seem almost the offering of a sacrifice, one that could bring Austria into a long-wanted war with Serbia, but the chance aspect of so much of the day's events refute such conspiracy. When Europe had shaken itself after hearing the news, events moved quickly. A month later Austria declared war on Serbia, even though no connection between the Serbian government and the assassins was ever found; Russia refused to countenance Austrian expansion; Germany supported Austria as a pretext for gaining Russian territory and attacking France. The Great War began.

On the corner of the assassination spot the **Princip Museum** (Monday-Friday 0900–1700, Sunday 0900–1300) has photos of Princip and his co-plotters. Three were hanged; Princip and Čabrinović, though were under 21 and with eleven other Bosnians were sent to Austrian gaols, where only nine survived the war, their diseased prison cells bringing slow, tubercular death. Today they're remembered as heroes, liberators of Bosnia, and lie buried in a little-visited **Mausoleum** on Kralja Tomislava.

The exact spot where Princip pulled the trigger is marked by a slightly comical set of footprints, but as you stand here and look out at what is really just another ordinary street corner, the weight of history, of being at the place where the straining muscles of Europe began to tear apart, hits you very hard indeed.

Sarajevo's other museums – and the Bogomils

National Museum of Bosnia-Hercogovina Vojvode Putnika 7, trams 1, 2, 3 and 5 from centre (Tuesday-Saturday 0900–1300, 1600–1900, Sunday 0900–1300). Local archaeological, ethnographic and natural history collections – of which the costumes and period rooms of the ethnographic section are most fun. Its main feature, though, is a series of *Stećci*, or Bogomil funerary monuments. The **Bogomils** (the name means 'beloved of God') were a mysterious bunch: an heretical sect, possibly of Bulgarian origin, they flourished throughout Bosnia and in parts of Macedonia from the C10th on. Not much is known about their beliefs, except what was written by their enemies who accused them of the standard devil-worship and unnatural vices – the word *bugger* is a distortion of *Bulgar*, then the usual term for a Bogomil heretic. It seems they believed the devil to be creator of the material world and so denied all things physical, rejecting possessions, the established churches, much of the Old Testament and the physical presence of Christ. Obviously this brought persecution by both Catholic and Orthodox faiths, and when the Turks arrived at the end of the C14th they shrewdly offered the Bogomils protection and freedom of worship – so long as they nominally considered themselves Muslim rather than Christian. As the decree from Rome at the time was that all Bogomils were to be burned, the Bosnian heretics not surprisingly turned their backs on organised Christianity – and the Turks consolidated their position in the Balkans. Eventually the Bogomils were absorbed into Islam, though not before leaving their *stećci* dotted around Bosnia-Hercegovina as funeral monuments – oddly solid memorials for a faith that revolted against the physical. The collection here has some of the best stones, of varying shapes and sizes but usually carved with crude stylised figures. Their Old Cyrillic inscriptions have a peculiar mix of sadness and dry humour:

Here lies Dragac. When I wished to be I ceased to be.

Here lies Orislav Kopijević. I have been pierced, I have been slashed,

I have been skinned, but I did not die of it. I just closed my eyes on the day of Christ's nativity and my lord, the duke, buried me and set up this memorial.

I beseech you touch me not. You will be as I am, but I cannot be as you are.

At RADMILJA (near Mostar, see p. 147) you can see a collection of these *stećci* still in situ.

In the museum's library – though not always on display – is another interesting relic of Sarajevo's mixed religious past: the rare and beautiful *Sarajevo Haggada*, an illuminated Hebrew Codex brought from Spain by the city's Sephardic Jews.

Museum of the Revolution   Vojvode Putnika 9. (Times as National Museum but open Mondays, closed Fridays) War museums are ten a penny in Yugoslavia, but this one struggles up from the ranks of the ordinary. To comprehend the detailed displays of events from 1878 on, buy the English guidebook: interesting photos, documents and a fearsome collection of arms.

Town Museum   Remzije Omanovića 31 (Monday-Saturday 0900–1700) The history of the town as revealed by its applied art and handicrafts. Once again the costumes are the best exhibit, though the pseudo-Moorish building also has its charms.

Gallery of Fine art.   (Tuesday-Saturday 1000–1300, 1600–2000, Sunday 1000–1300) Changing exhibitions on the ground floor and an above-average collection of Bosnian-Herzegovian art on the first, with highspots, portraits by Roman Petrović and Pero Popović.

Svrzo House,   Jovan Krsic 5; **Despić House,** Ognjena Price 2. Both were closed when I was here, and neither seemed in a hurry to open. The Svrzo House is a spacious building of unbaked brick and wood surrounded by a high wall and typical of a Bosnian Muslim house of the C19th; in contrast the Despić House belonged to wealthy Serb merchants and is a little grander. Venture in if you can.

Olympic Museum.   Nikola Tesla 7 (Daily 1000–1930) Very static array of posters, photos, ephemera and souvenirs of the 1984 Winter Olympics. Basically a prestige gesture.

Facts and things
American Centre   Omladinska 1 (Monday-Friday 0900–1630, Saturday 1000–1300). Newspapers, library, weekly films, US propaganda.
Cable car   (see map: Monday-Friday 1000–2000, Saturdays, Sundays and holidays 0800–2000) Whisks you up from the fuggy city to the sharp pine air of Mt Trebević. Great views.
Car Hire   *Avis*, Obala Pariske Komune 8. *Unis Tourist*, JNA 4.

Emergencies   Police, Augusta Cesarca 18 (tel. 92); Hospital, Moše Pijade 23 (tel. 94)

JAT   Vase Miskina 2. Sarajevo's airport is 12 km out, linked by regular JAT bus from JNA 24.

Maps   If you want to explore in detail the tourist bureaux will sell you an excellent map, more comprehensive than the one we've been able to print. The JNA 50 bureau has stocks.

Markets   Great fruit and veg. at the Wednesday market opposite the town hall – try the *borovnica* – wild bilberries. More general produce from the daily market on Maršala Tita; both good for cheap eating.

Post Office   Obala Vojvode Stepe 8.

Radio Sarajevo   English broadcasts every day at 1132, VHF 91.7, 95.3 or 98.9MHz.

Skiing   The 1984 Winter Olympics left Sarajevo with extensive facilities, which it's now trying to fill with tourists. *Mount Jahorina* is the best equipped, with slalom, giant slalom, downhill and cross-country courses; *Mount Bjelašnica* also has slalom facilities and moderately expensive pensions. Details, bookings, equipment hire from the Tourist Bureau; snow from November to April.

Train tickets *Unis Tourist* (Vase Miskina 16) make internal/international reservations, including sleeping cars.

THE NORTH-WEST

The main route north and west of Sarajevo runs through some of the most inviting countryside in Bosnia: verdant, copse-patched and fertile, every small field seems to double as someone's back garden. Cupped in a valley, **TRAVNIK** is the first town you reach, a jumble of houses surrounded by greenery, giving it the look of an untended garden suburb; indeed *Travnik* means 'place of grass'. It's a centre for local farmers, whose horses and carts roll in for the Thursday **market;** For this, the day to be here, traditional costume is worn and the whole thing progresses to picturesque effect. But if you miss it there are still a few threadbare leftovers from Turkish times to explore. Outside the Orient Hotel on Maršala Tita stand two **turbe**, the mausoleums of the Viziers of Travnik. When the Turkish governors were thrown out of Sarajevo, Travnik became the base from which they ruled the rest of Bosnia, and with an iron grip: in the right-hand *turbe* lies Djelaludjin Pasha, much hated in his day for the bleeding the people dry with taxes and ruthlessly removing opponents – he once beheaded 300 dissenters in a single day. The locals still use his name – *Djelali* – as a term of severe abuse. To the east of town the **Many Coloured Mosque** is the largest the Turks built, though no longer colourful nor particularly mosque-like, only the minaret gives it away. On the hillside above, the **Fortress** is firmly locked awaiting restoration, and I couldn't find a safe wall to jump over. To get near you need to cross a high flimsy-looking bridge – something bystanders will attempt to dissuade you from doing. Grit your teeth and cross as the view is fine.

If you keep on walking past the mosque out of town rather than turn up the hill you reach the ruined **Medressa**, a Muslim school built in 1892 when the railway ploughed through the old one. A swift kick to the door secures entry to the building, deserted years ago but with columns and walls still brightly painted, and unperturbed by the weeds that have taken hold. Plans are afoot to remodel it into a hotel, so have a look now while there's still something of the original left.

Travnik's slender claim to recent fame is **Ivo Andrić**, the writer who won the Nobel Prize for literature in 1961. He was born here and much of his writing concerns Bosnia and Bosnian history – which is probably why most people have never heard of him. *The Bridge on the Drina* is considered his best work, but a number of his other books have been translated, including *A Travnik Chronicle*, published in English as the *Bosnian Story* (see p. 236). Getting into his birthplace, the **Ivo Andrić Museum**, may prove a run-around: first try the door at S. Turudije, if it's locked go to the town museum just below the Borac store off Maršala Tita and agitate for the key. The rewards are a collection of his books and MSS, along with photos of the Nobel prize ceremony. Enthusiasts only.

Unless you're heading up to VLASIĆ (see below) there's not much point in utilising Travnik's private **rooms**. If you need to, book them from the **Turist Biro** which should by now have moved to the bus station; if it hasn't, try Maršala Tita 124 (Monday-Saturday 0700–1900, Sunday 0800–1100). Roughly twice a day buses leave Travnik for the **Ski resort** of **VLASIĆ**; a new road has meant growth but it's still cheap – an excellent if smaller alternative to Sarajevo: prices, ski-hire and chalet bookings from Travnik Turist Biro. While you're there try the **cheese** that's known as *Vlasić Sir;* made from the milk of sheep grazing on the mountains' rich alpine pastures, it has a delicious, delicate flavour.

JAJCE

Steeped in history ancient and modern, Jajce (pronounced Ya-it-say) is about the most attractive small town in Bosnia-Hercegovina. Tourist brochures always show the same photo of it: waterfalls of the Pliva spilling down to the Vrbas river, a sandcastle hill topped with a fortress standing behind. But when you arrive the town looks nothing like this, and to enter Jajce at the Pliva Gate, part of the old walls that rim the town's oval mound, is a disappointment – you need to zigzag through the Bosnian-Oriental houses that fight for a place below the fortress to see the town at its best. Now an empty ruin, the **fortress** was once stronghold of the kings of Bosnia: built by the warrior-noble Hrvoke Vukić, it became capital of his successors Stjepan Tomaš and Stjepan Tomašević, on whom it fell to defend Bosnia against the Turks. This proved a lost battle – most of the people adopted Islam in preference to only recently arrived Christianity, and the Christian kings needed outside support to prop up their authority. When the Sultan started to attack Bosnia he was generally welcomed without resistance, and Tomašević meekly agreed to give himself up if his life was spared: this he did and was promptly executed outside the town. So Bosnia fell to the Turks.

The crypt Hrvoke Vukić had built is one of a couple of subterranean attractions you need the help of the **Turist Biro** to explore; they're at Maršala Tita (open Monday-Saturday 0700–2100, Sunday 0800–1300) and also hand out private **rooms**, which fill quickly in July and August. For a consideration they'll open the **Catacombs** in the old town: Vukić, seems to have left this, his crypt, unfinished; perhaps it was raided by the Turks, or perhaps the king had unpopular connections with the Bogomils – some of their symbols are carved on the walls. Whatever was going on down here though needed to keep itself hidden among damp black stones, and it's good to get back out into daylight. A short way

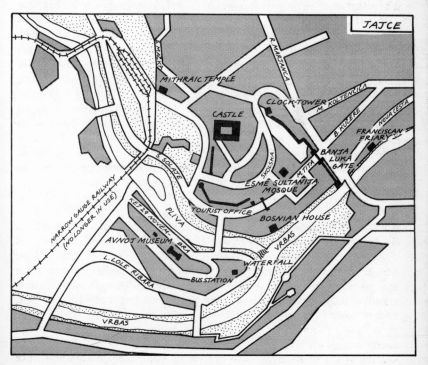

out of town (a Turist Biro person takes you there), the **Mithraic Temple** also has its mysteries. Mithraism was imported to Europe from India and Iran by Roman legionaries, and the carved C4 *altarpiece* clearly depicts the elements of a religion that for a while competed with Christianity – in fact paralleled its mystical elements. Mithras is shown drawing back the head of the sacrificial bull to let flow the blood that forms the earth and its crops, the semen issued in its death throes becoming living creatures. On either side are torch bearers, one with torch uplifted, symbolising spring and renewal, the other with torch extinguished – winter and death. The bull's slaughter parodied the crucifixion, and other ceremonies that would have been performed here mirrored the practices of baptism and Eucharist. In the end Christianity spread and Mithraism died out – not least because a religion that preaches constant victory and sacrificial death is more likely to be popular with a small group of soldiers rather than the mass of peasant farmers.

In later years Jajce acquitted itself well in resisting invaders. When Bosnia was handed over to the Austrians in 1878 it fought tooth and nail to keep them out, and in the last war it became a **Partisan HQ**, the chiefs of staff holding here the second, 1943, session of their parliament, the *Anti-Fascist Council for the National Liberation of Yugoslavia.* (AVNOJ). Delegates came from all over the country, often travelling for weeks through occupied territory, to declare King Peter and his exiled government divested of authority and raise Tito to the position of Marshal of Yugoslavia. It's for this that Jajce is, to Jugoslavs at least, famed and naturally there's a **museum** to the event – the actual hall where the meeting was held, decked out as it was then with the Partizans' slogan *Smrt Fasizmu – Sloboda Narodu* (Death to Fascism, Liberty to the People) above the stage. Another **museum** (both are open 0800–1200, 1400–1900 daily between March and October) has photos and mementos of the event, including a couple of Fitzroy Maclean, head of the British Mission, parachuted in near Jajce to liaise with Tito and report back to Churchill on the Balkan power balance.

Back to the old town, and two final buildings of interest. The **Church of St Luke** once held the body of the saint himself, bought from the Turks who seized it from its original grave in Epirus. When Jajce was about to fall to the Turks the local Franciscan Friars hurriedly carried it off to safety in Venice, where they hit on a problem: the Vatican already had a saint's head, Padua his (headless) body and in a church in Rome his arm had for some years been curing the sick. After a trial the Papal Legate declared the Jajce Luke to be the genuine item, but the Paduans went on venerating their alternative corpse all the same. Such is the power of faith. Little is left of the church today save a neat campanile, one of the town's landmarks. The Franciscans returned in the C19th and built a monastery and gaudily repellent church east of the centre: there's a museum (0900–1100, 1400–1800) cluttered with the ribs and bones of Jajce's ruined churches, and what's left of the unfortunate Stjepan Tomašević, whose grave was discovered in 1892.

Jajce's **market day** is Wednesday – something you don't really need telling as by 7a.m. the place is swarming with horses and carts all heading to the square on S. Solaje. Here you'll find home-woven clothes that combine incredible toughness with delicate decoration, hand-wrought metalwork and home-made cheese; and, reminding you that poverty isn't far behind the prettiness, beggars crouch by the roadside plaintively wailing for a few dinar. Markets like this are rapidly declining to the tourist bland-outs you find at Mostar; despite the sad edge, don't miss it.

Lastly, a couple of places to **eat**. *Bosanska Kuća*, just left of the Pliva Gate does Bosnian specialities of spiced meats at affordable prices, and *Pizza Fortuna* on a balcony in the shopping centre has the usual Yugoslav versions of Italian food.

If you're into **camping**, there's a site 8km out of Jajce on the Bihać road at the **PLIVA LAKES** – a really beautiful place to stay, even allowing for the heavy summer influx of tourists, with its dark wooded mountains and deep emerald lakes. The road there takes you past antiquated water-mills, tiny wooden boxes strutting above the river like storks and used until recently to grind corn; they seem almost too delicate to have stood the years of use they've evidently had.

HEADING NORTH-WEST

From Jajce the road follows the Vrbas Gorge, the river a green so vivid it seems the colour has run down from the forested hills that surround. At the end of the valley **BANJA LUKA**, Bosnia-Hercegovina's second largest city, doesn't have much going for it: flat and faceless, it was extensively rebuilt after an earthquake in 1969. The new town is better than many other recent developments though, and if you do wind up here there's an **Art Gallery** (Tuesday-Sunday 1000–1900), Trg 27 Mart 2, housed in the town's old railway museum, and a glossy **Regional Museum** (Monday-Friday 0900–1300/1700–1900, Saturday and Sunday 0900–1300). If you can get in, the **Ferhad Pasha Mosque** is a self-important sort of building: it was badly damaged in the earthquake, and has been restored with some lavishly coloured arabesques – worth seeing. Behind the Mosque there's not much left of the C15th **Castle**, bombarded by the Partisans after German troops held out there in the last days of the war: what remained was destroyed in 1969, and all you'll find today is a restaurant and a view of the river. To stay the night in Banja Luka you can get **private rooms** through the **Turist Biro** at Trg Palih Boraca 2, the main square in town (from the bus station take a red no. 10 to the centre); Monday-Friday 0800–2000, Saturday 0700–1400. Or in July and August you might try the **Studentski Dom** on Marx and Engels Trg, (bus no. 10 then 17); best check at the Turist Biro first as rooms here can prove more expensive than their private accommodation. For **night-life** just join the tidal *korso* that sweeps down Maršala Tita.

From Banja Luka it's an easy leap up to ZAGREB or east to the PLITVICE LAKES, the latter route taking you through BIHAĆ, whose once-Gothic church was transformed into a mosque in the C19th: a fitting hybrid for Bosnia.

THE ROAD TO MOSTAR

The main road from Sarajevo down to the coast follows the **Neretva valley**, a gorge of wooded slopes thinning out to bare Karst as you head westwards. Road and rail edge the same riverside route, which near Lake Jablanica passes a steel bridge collapsed in the rushing waters. It's the scene of a wartime incident that has become part of Yugoslav folklore. In the winter of 1943 the Germans led a successful offensive against the Partisans in Bosnia, forcing thousands of troops and 4000 wounded towards the impassable Neretva valley. Tito immediately had all the Neretva bridges blown; the Germans, knowing the impossibility of crossing the turbulent swollen river, built up troops in south-west Bosnia to ensnare the Partisans as they made for Montenegro. But on the night of 6 March Tito ordered a wooden footbridge to be strung across the crippled steel bridge, and succeeded in getting both wounded and Partisans safely across. The Germans were left waiting for a retreat that never arrived. It was probably the single most effective withdrawal in Yugoslavia's war, 'A fight to save the wounded', Tito called it, 'and the most humane battle in the history of warfare.' The destroyed bridge remains, a testament to his cunning stratagem.

MOSTAR

As you approach **MOSTAR** the mountain tops turn silver and the land becomes parched. Summers here are the hottest in the country, and the town itself lies by the river like burnt embers of bone under the sun. Tourists, who come by coach-load from the coast, spend an afternoon in the town and having snapped its one attraction and walked through the market disappear. Which is fair enough, really: an interesting enough place, Mostar isn't going to be the base for anyone's holiday.

The town developed under the Turks who used it as a seat of government for Hercegovina: mosques, public baths and *caravanserai* were built, and bang in the middle of town, the thing most people come to see, the **old bridge**. The name *Mostar* in fact comes from the word for a bridge keeper and this is one of the most elegant spans anywhere, throwing a steep arch over the hurried river below. 'Like a rainbow rising up to the Milky Way, leaping from sheer rock to sheer rock', whimsied one Evlija Ćelebija, passing through in the 17th century. Built in 1566, there's the inevitable apocryphal tale to its making: after his first bridge had collapsed the architect was told by the Sultan to build one that would stand or lose his head; when the scaffolding was about to be removed the terrified architect ran off and hid in a nearby village, and though the bridge held he never returned – just in case. When you consider that the only mortar used was a composite of eggs and goats' hair, his lack of confidence hardly seems surprising. Hang around the bridge long enough and one of the local lads will take position as if to dive, wait for a hundred or so fingers to hover above shutter releases and then demand a 100 dinars apiece to do the deed – at which the crowd disperses. If you want to see less mercenary performances of bravery/stupidity, come on 4 June when the diving championships are on.

The bridge runs over to the **Kujundziluk** or bazaar, originally the market street of the Turkish town. You can still buy crude copper ornaments and jewellery here, but it's a charmless place, a series of tourist shop windows rather than a street of artisans – the only visible sign of Turkish influence an occasional fez donned by charlatan shop-keepers. Put all this behind you and walk on: **Mehmed Pasha's Mosque** has something of the true Turkish heritage, its little cobbled courtyard, bubbling fountain and greenery showing their love for things gently sensual. In the middle is a C17th tomb, elaborate by the standards of Islam, which makes no pretence about death: corpses are brought to the mosque to be washed and wrapped in white cloth, then placed in simple graves, the head turned toward Mecca. *Nišans*, the sugary white gravestones, were simple affairs, a turban representing a man, a sword a Janissary, each decorated with a text from the Koran. Disturbance of tombs is forbidden, and all over Bosnia-Hercegovina *nišans* continue to tumble in untended patches. Mehmet Pasha's mosque itself is much like any other, high-domed and patchily decorated, though if you scale its minaret there's a fine view of Mostar old and new; and it's not every day you get to climb a minaret. The other mosque you're steered to is the **Karadzozbeg Mosque** off Maršala Tita; larger, grander and less intimate, with a 600–year-old Koran as prize possession. If you're into Turkish domestic architecture the **Biščevica Ćosak** stands on Biščevica 14 (erratic, but officially 0800–1900 daily), a little too eager to please, dolled up with an excess of carving and decoration in a picture-book idea of what a Turkish house ought to look like.

Turkish buildings don't have the monopoly in Mostar. Climb to the top of the hill and the **New Orthodox Church** stands high above the town, built in front of the older church in the 1870s. Cavernous and empty, it's a deeply atmospheric place, seemingly built and immediately left to rot, like a ballroom built for a single ball. And, finally, two unadventerous museums: a **Liberation Museum**, Maršala Tita 130 (Monday-Saturday 0900–1300 and 1600–1800), its standard display enlivened with photos of the Neretva bridge incident, and a miscellaneous **Town Museum** next door (open on request from Liberation museum, though you may need to wait for a group).

A few details

The best way to see Mostar is in passing but if you need to stop there are three **accommodation** alternatives. The *E Hotel* is temptingly near the bus/train stations at Maršala Tita 51 but its rooms are nearly double the price you'll pay if you walk into town and find *Apro Tourist* (Monday-Saturday 0700–1700) at the end of Kujundziluk, who do free maps as well as the cheapest private rooms in town; if they've run out, try *Neretva Tourist* in the Neretva Hotel (Monday-Friday 0700–1400, 0900–1200; Saturday 0900–1200). Cheapest rooms in July and August are at the *Studenski Dom* at 84a Radićeva (bus 2 or 3 from the stations or walk straight down Hercegovačke Brigade until Avenija 14 Februar, then ask; also bookable through *Olympic Tours* on Moša Pijade). Light **lunches** are to be had at the *Lovac Bife*, Bracé Fejića 21, **meals** at *Mimosa* on Trg 1 Maj (turn left off Brace Fejica after no. 65) Avoid the overrated restaurant on Kujundziluk – a tourist rip-off. Spirited evening **drinking** goes on on the terrace of the *Hotel Bristol* and in the *Bife* on Trg 14 Februar.

DOWN TO THE SEA: THE NERETVA VALLEY

Ten kilometres south of Mostar, **BLAGAJ** stands below the ruins of a castle built by Herceg Stefan – he of Hercegovina fame. Nearby, the river Buna resurges through the rock, and runs past the **Tekija**, one of the few surviving Yugoslav monasteries built by the **Dervishes**, an ascetic though fairly liberal bunch of Muslims who founded separate orders in the 15th and 16th centuries. The Tekija shows the Islamic style and tradition; broad-domed *hammam*, arabesque carving, and the *turbe* of an Islamic St George, **Sari Saltuk**. According to legend this pious dervish fell madly in love with Herceg Stefan's daughter Milica, so that when the local dragon (who lived in the cave near the Tekija) dragged her to his lair Sari Saltuk leapt forward and killed it, rescuing Milica (who duly became his wife). The Tekija reputedly built on the site of his conquest, probably bears no similarity to that you see today, which is recent rebuilding of a C19th design.

Like Sveti Stefan in Montenegro, **POČITELJ** is one of those towns the Yugoslavs have contrived with an eye to tourism: rising in a natural amphitheatre above the Neretva, its levels of stone houses have been given The Treatment and converted into artists' studios. Picturesque though it is, if you're passing through on the bus, there's no great reason to stop off. Just beyond Počitelj, however, a road turns towards Stolac, and about half way along at **RADIMLJA** is the most accessible site of the **Bogomil Stećci** found all over Bosnia-Hercegovina (see p. 138). The Radimlja monuments come in various shapes, some cuniform, some like trunk-shaped sarcophagi, but all in the local white stone and often carved with a figure whose right arm is outstretched and exaggerated in a mysterious gesture; other scenes show hunting and dancing.

As you leave the Neretva Gorge the valley broadens to a brown plain untidy with dilapidated roadside houses. On the narrow stretch that is Bosnia-Hercegovina's coastline **NEUM** deserves a mention as the only resort – an exclusively modern ghetto of workers' hotels. To the north, KARDELJEVO is the only port – and the place to head if you're making for the Pelješac peninsula and Korčula.

THE DRINA VALLEY

From Sarajevo, FOČA is a good place to start exploring: most spectacularly through **raft trips** down the Drina Valley (see below), though to the west there is also the **Sutjeska National Park**, 67 square miles of unspoiled, untouristed meadows and forest around the Zelengora and Maglić mountains. In these hills one of the fiercest and most crucial struggles of the last war took place, the 1943 **Battle of Sutjeska**, which saw some 127,000 occupying troops surround 20,000 partisans – nearly a quarter of them suffering from typhus. In the bombardment, Tito himself was wounded, becoming the only commander-in-chief of Allied forces to sustain an injury in combat. The Partisans were in serious danger of being wiped out, but with their superior knowledge of the country and skill at movement by night managed to find a gap in the surrounding enemy wall. The price was high – a division left behind to hold enemy fire was annihilated, and the immobile sick and wounded were massacred. Altogether 7,300 Partisans died in the engagement; their memorial stands at TJENTIŠTE, along with a mausoleum and museum.

FOČA is rapidly becoming a dreary modern town, though its small Turkish quarter and market (above the high street) have enough residual character to explore while you're waiting for a bus on to Višegrad. Down by the river the **Aladža Mosque** is a small, elegant C16th century structure of delicately balanced line and proportion and refined arabesque decoration. The tireless Turkish traveller of the Balkans, Evliya Ćelebi, left his eulogistic comment carved in the decoration: 'I have travelled much and visited many cities, but a land such as this I have never seen . . . written by the slave of God, Evliya, in the year 1074.' Sadly the mosque is rarely open – to see its colourful interior you'll have to content yourself with peering through shuttered windows.

By **raft trips** down the Drina the tourist people really mean raft, simply logs tied together and piloted by experienced *triftar*, whose skills are traditionally passed down from father to son. Since the dam below Višegrad tamed the lower stretches of the Drina it's not as dangerous as you might think – more of a gentle drift down to Višegrad overnighting at a Goražde hotel en route. Trips run from the beginning of July to the end of August, leaving Foča at noon each Saturday; details from the *Zelengora Hotel* or *Unis Tourist* nearby. Really living dangerously, a longer alternative is the run down from DJURDJEVICA TARA in Montenegro via the river Tara; a four-day journey described by the tourist board as 'intended for courageous people'. Details from the tourist office at Djurdjevica Tara or most local travel agents.

From Foča the Drina valley is more scenic than spectacular, though it has its moments as the road rises high above the river, flashing through rock-hewn tunnels. Slowly the steep valley sides widen and at the end of the gorge **VIŠEGRAD** spreads along the broadened valley, mountain ranges running down in random scribbles to the river. As at Mostar there's just one thing to see, and you see it straight away – the **bridge**. Built by the Turks in the C16th, it's as tidy as a draughtsman's drawing, strong yet graceful on its ten arches. Ivo Andrić's book about it – *The Bridge on the Drina* – is just as famous, though his subject is really the story of Bosnian families from the time of the building of the bridge to the First World War. Višegrad itself is a small, uneventful but likeable town, a useful stop-off with cheap **private rooms** – available from *Panos Tourist* at Maršala Tita 24 (Monday-Friday 0700–1900, Saturday 0800–1400, Sunday 0800–1200) – and a good restaurant, *Ušće*, at the jetty (follow signpost from the end of high street). When you arrive by bus get off in the centre; when you leave book your ticket from the station, which is a short way out of town. The choice of routes is to Serbia and TITOVO UŽICE, on the main Dubrovnik Belgrade road that rises steeply from the town to cross the Zlatibor mountains, or to SARAJEVO via ROGATICA – both half-day journeys.

TRAVEL DETAILS

Buses
From Sarajevo to Belgrade (5 daily; 8hrs), Zagreb (4; 8hrs); Travnik (5 a day; 2½hrs); Jajce (5; 3½hrs); Banja Luka (5; 4½hrs); Mostar (4; 2½hrs); Kardeljevo (8; 3½hrs); Foča (3; 2hrs); Visegrad (4; 2½hrs).

Trains
From Sarajevo to Mostar (4 daily; 2¾hrs); Kardeljevo (5; 3hrs).

Chapter six
SERBIA

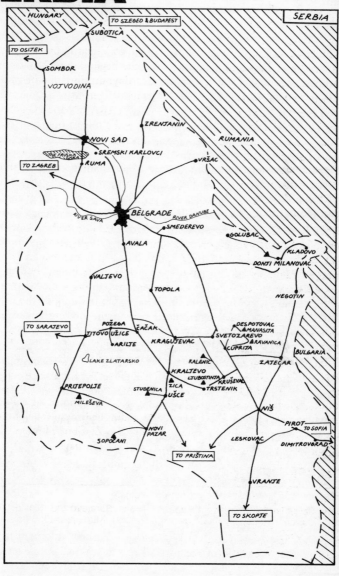

Though the largest, easily the most diverse, and arguably the most beautiful of the Yugoslav republics, **Serbia** is also one of the most neglected, and if people come here at all, most only spend a couple of nights in Belgrade before heading south for the better-publicised charms of Greece or the perennially well-patronised Adriatic coast. This is a shame, as Serbia's attractions can easily match those of the rest of Yugoslavia – and because it is so undervisited, it's also one of the cheapest regions of the whole country.

Serbia sports few picturesque towns – **Belgrade** is drab by anyone's standards and most other places similarly bland and modern – but it brags far greater assets in the **medieval monasteries** which populate the hills and valleys of its wonderfully green and rolling heartland, the best possible illustration of an age that Serbs, even today, look back on with pride. Getting to them can be difficult – they're normally tucked away in deliberately remote and inaccessible spots – but it's generally worth the struggle, both for the buildings themselves and some superb scenery. Among the finest are **Studenica** and the monastic churches at **Sopoćani** and **Mileševa**, with their marvellous C13th frescoes, painted by master-painters from Constantinople, centre of the Orthodox Christian world.

The **Vojvodina**, to the north, is Hungarian-influenced, and an autonomous province, its grand old capital **Novi Sad** worth a stop-over if you're pushing on up to Hungary or simply stopping in Belgrade; Albanian **Kosovo**, Serbia's other autonomous province, also with its fair share of monasteries and Serbian history, has its own chapter.

BELGRADE (BEOGRAD)

BELGRADE (Beograd) means literally 'White City', a striking misnomer for what must be one of the greyest of European capitals. Occupying a strategic point on the junction of the Danube and Sava rivers, it was the property of a warlike succession of Celts, Romans, Huns and Avars until the Turks wrenched it from the Hungarians in 1521, from when it formed the northernmost point of their empire. The Kalemegdan fortress – from which the modern city has grown – sweeps around a wooded bluff overlooking the wayward swerve of the Danube, quiet now, but for years the frontier between East and West, and at the very crux of Balkan squabbles and struggles for influence.

Towns as strategically important as this are rarely beautiful, and Belgrade is no exception: a couple of Muslim shrines and a dilapidated mosque are the only traces of 350 years of Turkish rule, whilst heavy shelling in the last war left virtually no street unscathed. A few museums, the Kalemegdan park and the raw vigour of its streets make it worth two or three nights, but it's a city that's soon exhausted, and even the most fanatically loyal Belgrader wouldn't advise you to stay any longer.

Orientation

Belgrade spreads untidily for miles, but most things of interest are either in the centre or within easy reach of it. **Accommodation**, however, can be more problematic. There are few alternatives and most expect you to pay for the privilege of staying in the capital. The peculiarly rude *Lasta Turist Biro* (Monday-Saturday 0700–1900) opposite the railway station have **rooms**, though you can usually haggle for one independently with the hordes of people hanging about outside. *Pansion Centar*, just a few doors along at Trg Bratstva i Jedinstva 17, has dorm beds for just a little more, and though often booked solid by groups is worth a try. If it's full you'll have to resign yourself to the much less central **Youth Hostel Mladost** out on Bulevar JNA – a 15–minute journey on tram 9 from the station and then 2 minutes' walk down Kapetan Zavisica. Cheapest **hotel** is the *Trim*, Kneza Višeslava 72, bus 53 from Kneza Miloša or bus 23 from Takovska. Those **camping** have a choice of three sites, best of which is *Košutnjak*, Kneza Višeslava 17, south of the centre in the Topčider Park: again bus 53. The *National* in Novi Beograd costs slightly less – bus 74 from the Tašjmadan Park.

The **Tourist Information Centre** (Daily 0800–2000), in the subway under Terazije, has free maps, copies of *Beogradscope* – a bi-monthly 'What's On' booklet – and information on just about every aspect of the city. Belgrade is served by a comprehensive and efficient system of **buses and trams:** you can either pay a flat fare or (much cheaper) buy a ticket of 12 strips in advance from one of the plentiful tobacco kiosks. The city-centre is divided into 5 zones and you use two strips for one zone, three strips for two zones and so on; if you want to skirt all these complexities or expect to be doing a lot of travelling on public transport, one-day unlimited travel tickets are available.

The city

The wide swathe of **Terazije** slices through the central and commercial hub of Belgrade; ask a taxi driver to take you to the city centre and he'll drop you here. Hardly elegant, it's none the less the place where wealthy Belgraders come to do their shopping. The art nouveau Hotel Moskva presides over all, its large terrace and fountain acting as focal point for such as remains of the evening *korso*, while underneath, a profusion of underground walkways – left-overs from the city's half-finished metro and filled with shops and bars – mirror the life that goes on up top.

Terazije leads straight into Maršala Tita – more shops mostly – or left onto Trg Marxsa i Engelsa, which opens out on to the domed bulk of the **Skupština** or National Assembly Building and, beyond that, the uncompromising monochrome Battenburg of the National Bank. Behind the bank is the **Church of Sv Marko**, a high, very solid, and rather bare neo-Byzantine structure that was built between the wars on the model of the monastery church of Gračanica in Kosovo (see p. 186). Its size makes

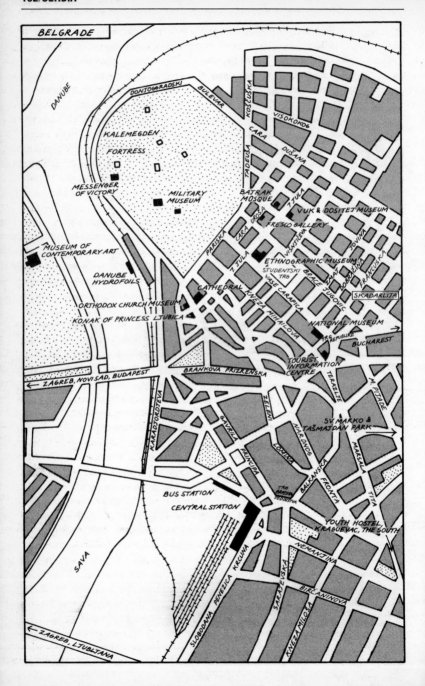

BELGRADE

DANUBE

DONJOGGRADSKI

BULEVAR

KOSCUSKA

VISOKOKOG

CARA

DUŠANA

TADEUŠA

KALEMEGDEN
FORTRESS

BATRAK
MOSQUE

7 JULA

UROŠA

VUK & DOSITET MUSEUM

FRESCO GALLERY

MESSENGER
OF VICTORY

MILITARY
MUSEUM

PARISKA

CARA

7 JULA

WISNTLENA

HOVINA

ETHNOGRAPHIC MUSEUM

MUSEUM OF
CONTEMPORARY ART

STUDENTSKI
TRG

VASE ČARAPICA

BRAČE JUGOVIC

IMAT

DOBRAČINA

FRANCUSKA

DANUBE
HYDROFOILS

CATHEDRAL

SKADARLIJA

ORTHODOX CHURCH MUSEUM

KNEZA MIHAILOVA

NATIONAL MUSEUM

KONAK OF PRINCESS LJUBICA

TRG
REPUBLIKE

BUCHAREST

TOURIST
INFORMATION
CENTRE

BRANKOVA PRIZRENSKA

TERAZIJE

M. PIJADE

ZAGREB, NOVI SAD, BUDAPEST

KARADORDEVA

ZELENI

GAVRILA

NARDNOG

SV. MARKO &
TAŠMAJDAN PARK

PRINCIPA

LOMINA

BALKANSKA

MARŠALA TITA

BUS STATION

FRONTA

CENTRAL STATION

TRG
BRATSVA
JEDINSTVA

YOUTH HOSTEL,
KRAGUEVAC, THE SOUTH

SAVA

SLOBODANA PENEZICA KRCUNA

NENANTINA

SARAJEVSKA

BIRCANINOVA

ZAGREB, LJUBLJANA

KNEZA MILOŠA

it a more impressive building than the city's Cathedral, but otherwise there's little enough to see – no one ever visited Belgrade for its churches.

In the other direction, Terazije runs down to **Trg Republike**, a mixed-up square flanked by glassy modern blocks and grubby classic remnants from more monumental architectural times. The equestrian statue is to Prince Michael Obrenović, hailing him as liberator from the Turks: he points meaningfully south, to the lands still to be extricated from the infidel. Behind him looms the **National Museum** (Tuesday/Wednesday/ Friday 1000–1700, Thursday 1000–1900, Saturday 0900–1700, Sunday 1000–1400), founded in 1844, installed here in 1946 and labelled by some as one of the foremost museums in Europe – though that's a claim that you should take with a liberal pinch of salt.

The *ground floor* holds a fairly ordinary, though extensive, collection of prehistoric and Greek and Roman antiquities – finds from various parts of Serbia and Macedonia. Things to watch out for are Greek gold jewellery from Ohrid, a good set of Roman figurines and some delicate Roman jewellery. Up a staircase littered with modern Yugoslav sculpture and you're on the *first floor*, devoted to medieval and later Serbian art: mainly fragments of monastic frescoes and an exhaustive series of C17th and 18th icons. The *top floor*, probably the most interesting, displays European painting from the 15th to 20th century: a thin scattering of Venetians, mediocre Dutch and Flemish works, and more promising C19th and 20th rooms, where most of the more major European figures have their say – Renoir, Degas, Pissarro and Utrillo are quite well represented.

Just off Trg Republike, the **Skadarlija** area was reputedly the Bohemian quarter of old Belgrade, though now it seems little more than a tourist hangout, a little too brightly painted to be real. No doubt the *Tri Sesira* ('Three Hats') café did once harbour artists and poets, but that was a long time ago and today it's mainly full of travellers in search of a quaint Balkan Montmartre, and some of the more aspiring Belgrade trendies. Most of the bars and restaurants, too, are prohibitively expensive. You may, though, be able to find one that's not, and should certainly sample the mouthwatering snacks on sale all the way down the street – try the rolls filled with goulash and/or *kajmak*, on sale by the fountain, or paper cones filled with deep-fried sardines.

From Trg Republike follow V. Carapića down past Studentski Trg and the University and you come to the **Kalemegdan Park**: the fortress whose development is in essence a microcosm of Serbian history, so mixed and multiple have its occupiers been. To Rebecca West, Kalemegdan 'meant life to those who held it, death to those who lost it', and high up here it's easy to understand what she meant: across the sloughy waters of the Danube the ruthlessly flat Pannonian plain stretches north, deep into Hungary; behind, the gentle hills of central Serbia roll south, forging into the mountainous backbone of the Balkan peninsula. Clearly, the army that commanded this river junction held the key to the Balkans and, perched high on this exposed corner, would take some shifting.

The first fortress was built by the Celts, expanded on by the Romans, and rebuilt in the Middle Ages by Stefan Lazarević – one of the last Serbian leaders, who clung to power in the face of unyielding Turkish expansion. The medieval town of Belgrade grew slowly within the castle walls, but with the coming of the Turks the whole place fell into neglect. Most of what you see now is the result of a short-lived Austrian occupation in the early part of the C18th. Then, and into the next century, European travellers regarded Kalemegdan as the beginning of their travels in the orient, its mosques and minarets signalling to them as they crossed over from the Austrian side of the river. A. W. Kinglake saw in the fortress a final, brooding frontier, the very end of Europe before the 'splendour and havoc of the east', and James Fraser, writing a few years earlier, felt crossing the river was 'like quitting the living for the dead'. Now Kalemegdan enjoys a happier function as the main haven of peace and quiet in central Belgrade, basking in the sun and relishing a shady twittering peace. And the fort itself remains a scarred and explorable testimony to Belgrade's historic ups and downs.

Mestrović's **Messenger of Victory** was originally supposed to stand in the city centre but was put up here after protests from more puritanical Belgraders about the figure's full-frontal nudity – it is quite obviously male. Now it looks over to the soaring post-war development of Novi (New) Beograd, something of a symbol for the city and depicted on almost all the tourist handouts. The falcon symbolises Slav freedom and the sword the defence of peace – notions made all the more poignant by the subsequent horrors Belgrade underwent in the last war. Just below here, four graves are reminders of that later era, among them that of Moše Pijade – one of the party's leading Marxist theoreticians, and Ive Lole Ribar, Tito's right-hand man in the Partisan struggle; the importance of these two figures is manifest in streets named after them in every Yugoslav city.

Don't leave the park without seeing the **Military Museum** (Tuesday-Sunday 1000–1700), housed in the labyrinthine interior of the fortress itself. It's a marvellous museum, well laid out and easy to follow despite largely Serbo-Croat labelling, at once a strong reminder of the past and a hopeful epitaph to it. Billed as a visual narration of Yugoslavia's wars – another way of saying a history of Yugoslavia itself – it is a story of occupation and resistance under Turks, Austrians and, later, the Nazis. The outbreak of the first world war is vividly illustrated by mugshots of Princip and his cohorts, and one of the luckless Franz Ferdinand shortly before his assassination. But the main focus of the museum is the war of liberation, with stark black and white photographs that help to bring home the brutality of those years. In one a young Partisan boy, Filip Filipović, raises his arms in a final gesture of defiance before being hanged by the Germans – a much reproduced photo that became *the* symbol of Partisan heroism. The museum comes to a climax with the flags of each Partisan brigade set above piles of captured enemy weapons. After the crimes you have just seen, it's a fitting conclusion.

Back outside the park stands the C19th **Cathedral**, a fairly undistinguished neo-Baroque edifice that went up in 1830 after the Turks relaxed their ban on church-building. In a way it's a centre for Serb patriotism: the relics of Prince Lazar were brought here soon after its completion and are still venerated today, and in the graveyard lies Vuk Karadzić, the scholar who phoneticised the Serbian alphabet and recorded and collected their previously oral folk poems. There's a **museum** devoted to him and the so-called 'father of modern Serbian literature', Dositej Obradović, at Gospodar Jevremova 21 (Tuesday-Saturday 0900–1300/1600–1900, Sunday 0900–1300).

Opposite the Cathedral is one of the few surviving Turkish buildings in Belgrade, most of which either burnt down or were destroyed after Serbian independence. **The Café?** used to be called 'The Café at the Cathedral' but after complaints of impiety from the priesthood opposite had to change its name to an enigmatic alternative that attracted more custom than ever and helped fuel the bar's reputation as no. 1 haunt of Belgrade Bohemians. These days it's still a good place to drink.

Just around the corner is the **Konak of Princess Ljubica**, wife of C19th Serbian leader Miloš Obrenović, whose jealousy for her husband became so legendary that it was said she hounded the women of her husband's court literally to death if they were unfortunate enough to catch his eye. The house she lived and raised her family in is today hers in name only, its interior a reconstruction of typical rooms of the upper classes at the time with their blending of the eastern influence of Turkey and the formal rigidity of western salons. Oriental touches – the Turkish Bath and window seats – and the Ottoman sense of spaciousness and light prevent any stuffiness.

Belgrade's other museums

Fresco Gallery, Cara Uroša 20 (Tuesday-Wednesday 1000–1700, Thursday 1000–1900, Friday 1000–1700, Saturday 0900–1700, Sunday 1000–1400) Excellent and convincing replicas of medieval frescoes from the more important Serbian and Macedonian monasteries: a good introduction – and incentive for visits – with all of the principal frescoes in one place helping to put things in perspective. Among the copies on display are the stirring and monumental *Dormition of the Virgin* from Sopoćani – probably the finest of all Serbian frescoes; the rich blue *Crucifixion* from the Virgin's Church at Studenica: and the buxom peasant *Virgin* from Peć, oddly enough framed by a cast of Radovan's exuberant west door from Trogir's Catholic Cathedral. You can also get a good close-up at what's left of Mileševa's *Deposition* (in the monastery it's too high to study in any detail) and the famous *White Angel* from the same church, which unfortunately seems to lose something in reproduction. Don't forget to ask for the multilingual guidebook.

Ethnographic Museum, Studentski Trg 13 (Tuesday-Sunday 1000–1700) Massive collection of national Yugoslav costumes and jewellery brought together principally to illustrate that, even under the Turks, creativity continued to flourish amongst the South Slavs.

National Museum of the Revolution, Trg Marxsa i Engelsa 11 (Tuesday-Sunday 1000–1700) Now the party are well installed in spacious offices across the Sava, the former HQ of the Communist Party's central committee has been given over to a permanent record of the revolution, with photos, documents and bits and pieces relating to the Yugoslav struggle – the blueprint for countless exhibitions like it throughout the country. An informative experience, though frustratingly labelled exclusively in Serbo-Croat.

Museum of Contempory Art, Novi Beograd (Daily 1000–1700, closed Tuesdays: bus 16 or 36 from the steps below Brankova) A disappointment. Well-arranged in a spacious modern gallery, these two collections of paintings – 1900–45 and 1945 to the present day – are a generally dull and derivative bunch. Yugoslav interpretation of major European trends such as Cubism, Constructivism and Modernism is apparent in the work of Tone Kralj, Ignat Job and Sava Sumanović, as is the perspective of the politically committed art of the 1930s which was to develop into the limp propaganda of the 1950s. But the later works of the 1960s and after chase just about every pop and post-pop fashion; depressingly directionless. From all this one or two paintings stand out – the skilled and sensitive self-portraits of the statesman Moše Pijade, the surrealist work of Milena Pavlović-Barilli, and the dark, hypnotic Primitive paintings of Ivan Generalić – though it's a comment on the disparate and ultimately self-cancelling diversity of C20th Yugoslav art that so large a gallery should have so little of worth.

Jewish Historical Museum, 7 Jula 1a (first floor) (Opening times uncertain). Detailing the history of the Jews in Belgrade and Yugoslavia as a whole, the Jewish Museum's most interesting and saddening sections inevitably concern the war years, when 67,000 of the country's 82,000 Jews were murdered by the Nazis and their collaborators. Many of the photos here show the concentration camps of central Europe – well known but none the less horrifying; a further section proudly recounts the activity of Jewish fighters in the war, with many pictures of Moše Pijade, most senior of the Jewish Partisans and most vilified by Nazi propaganda. A moving museum with good English information.

Museum 25 Maj, Botičeva 8 (Tuesday-Sunday 0900–1600. Bus 42 from Trg Republike) Ethnic items from most corners of the globe: 25 May was Tito's adopted birthday and this museum was opened in 1962 to house presents he had received from most of the world's leaders. A little way up the hill is **Tito's Mausoleum** (Daily 0900–1600), where his tombstone stands in a cool hall surrounded by flowers and a very stiff guard of honour. As you might expect, it attracts a steady stream of Yugoslavs, though reactions seem more restrained than, say, those at Lenin's tomb. Adopt the appropriate air of reverence and follow the arrows.

Museum of the Serbian Orthodox Church, 7 Jula 5 (Tuesday-Saturday 0900–1200, Sunday 1100–1300 Situated through a maze of first-floor corridors in the home of the Patriarchate of the Serbian Orthodox Church, this is a mixed selection of icons, devotional objects, robes and vestments. Labelling in Cyrillic and a disappointing lack of medieval items, most of which were destroyed by the rampaging Turks, make it a museum for only the most devoted or interested.

Forestry and Hunting Museum, Kalemegdan (Daily 1000–1700, closed Tuesday) Yugoslavia's forests and mountains are full of wildlife – wild boar, wolves, bears and the like still abound – and displayed here are trophies bagged by hunters and stuffed versions of animals so scarce you nowadays find them only in zoos. The formidable array of weaponry on show goes some way to explaining why.

Where to eat, where to drink ...
Belgrade is littered with **cheap restaurants**. Apart from the snacks in Skadarlija, and the stand-up joints behind the station, self-service restaurants are the best value option, and of these *Kasina* in Terazije is most reliable. Roughly opposite, the *Atina* does a selection of dirt-cheap pizzas (and incorporates a self-serve restaurant) as does the *London Restaurant*, on the corner of M. Tita and K. Milosa, along with more typically Slav food and a regular disco downstairs. *Konarac* in K. Mihailova is a young, animated and often crowded **bar** with restaurant attached; nearby, in Vuk Karadžiča, *Proleče* has probably the best and most reasonable collection of Serbian dishes in town. Around the corner *Galeria* is a small, smoky bar with questionably pricey drinks; far better to use the *Café?* in 7 Jula: drink prices haven't risen with the bar's notoriety and it remains about the best and most intimate place to drink (and eat) in central Belgrade. It's also worth sticking your head round the door of the *Hotel Moskva* lounge, where evenings are a near-pastiche of fin-de-siècle elegance, complete with obsequious waiters and string quartet.

Musically Belgrade is pretty dead: big-name bands occasionally visit but generally prefer more fashionable venues in the north of the country.

The *Student Cultural Centre* on M. Tita sometimes organises gigs as well as showing films and staging the occasional exhibition; a noticeboard inside details what's going on. The city hosts sporadic **festivals** throughout the year, among them a May pop festival and November jazz festival. Details of all events are published in the bi-monthly *Beogradscope*, available from the tourist office.

Listings
American Centre Čika Ljubina 19, just off K. Mihailova. Library, exhibitions and one of the few places in town to get your hands on an English-language newspaper.

Books *Prosveta*, Bulevar Revolucije 20, has a small stock of Penguins, a rarity in Belgrade and virtually non-existent in the rest of the country. There are loose selections of second-hand English books at *Serpska Knizevna Zadruga*, on M.Tita, and the *Antikvarijat* bookshop on the corner of K. Mihailova and Cure Jaksica.

Bus station Behind the railway station. Can be horribly confusing at first but it's really quite organised once you've worked out the timetables and destinations, which are all in Cyrillic. With your ticket you'll be given a small metal disc – don't lose it, as it gets you on to the forecourt where the buses leave.

British Council K.Mihailova 45. Library with English-language books and newspapers. To join you have to give proof of permanent residence.

Car rental *Avis* (Obilicev Vanac 25), *Hertz*. (Sava Centar, Milentija Popovica 9), *Unis* (Cara Uroša 10).

Car repair Austin, Rover, Renault, Peugeot at Laze Simica 17 (tel. 650 022); Audis and Volkswagens at Vojislava Ilica 145 (tel. 489 799); Citroëns at Dimitrija Tucovica 155 (tel. 411 730); Ford at Omladinski Brigada 31, Novi Beograd (tel. 692 524); Volvo at Svetozara Markovica 12 (tel. 320 901).

Chemist (24 hours) Corner of Maršala Tita and Kneza Miloša.

Embassies Australia (Čika Ljubina 13; tel. 624 655), Canada (Proleterskih Brigada 69, tel. 434 524), UK (Generalna Ždanova 46; tel. 645 055), USA (Kneza Miloša 50; tel. 645 655), Netherlands (Simina 29; tel. 626 699), Norway (Kablarska 30; tel. 651 626), Denmark (Sekspirova 5; tel. 667 826), Sweden (Pariska 7; tel. 626 422).

Emergencies Police: Ulica 29 Novembra, near the bus terminus (tel. 92); Ambulance: tel. 94; Lost Property: tel. 624.

Football *Red Star Belgrade*, the Liverpool of Yugoslav soccer, play at the Red Star Stadium (Banjicki Venac 1) though their long reign at the top has recently been interrupted by another Belgrade team, the *Jugoslovenske Narodne Armije* – Yugoslav People's Army – who play at the JNA Stadium at Humska 1.

Hosptials   The Boris Kidrić Health Centre, Pasterova 1 (tel. 683 755); for teeth the dental polyclinic at Ivana Milutinovica 15 (tel. 443 491).

Hydrofoils   Leave for points down the Danube twice a day, currently at 6 a.m. and 3 p.m. Information and tickets from the harbour office at Karadjordjeva 8. For a full account of the trip see p. 000.

JAT   International office at M. Tita 18 (tel. 642 773); domestic enquiries to Bulevar Revolucije 17 (tel. 343 433). Belgrade Airport is 18 km west of town: JAT buses run every 15 minutes from the Bulevar Revolucije office and the railway station.

Markets   The main flea market has been moved some 16 km out of town and because of petrol shortages is now almost extinct. The principal market in the centre of town is the long-established *Zeleni Venac*, a riot of meat, fish, produce and all good things.

Motoring Information   The Motorists Association of Yugoslavia, (**AMSJ**) Ruzveltova 18 (tel. 440 185).

Newspapers   English-language papers appear sporadically in the kiosk outside the *Hotel Moskva* and the *Prosveta* bookshop virtually next door.

Post office   For general postal services and poste restante the main post office is at Takovska 2. For international calls go to the post office in Zmaj Jovina, open 24 hours.

Radio Belgrade   Broadcasts daily in English at 12.02. VHF 88.9 and 95.3 MHz.

Railway station   Trg Bratstva i Jedinstva. Queues for tickets can be a nightmare, so buy yours in advance from Putnik, (Terazije 27) or a similar travel agency. Sleeping here can be difficult without a valid ticket.

Supermarkets   A giant one underground about midway down M. Tita. For late-night food and drink, the shops under Moše Pijade are open until 10 p.m.

Swimming   Loads of municipal pools. Good one at *Sportski Centar 25 Maj*, Tadeusa Koscuskog 63. You can also bathe on the beach on Veliko Ratno Ostrvo – the island at the mouth of the two rivers.

Taxis   Can be hailed or found in long lines outside the railway station, on Terazije, Trg Republike or other central spaces. Or telephone 765 666.

DOWN THE DANUBE

Hydrofoils leave from just below Kalemegdan for destinations down the **Danube,** a river not so much blue as a muddy brown, wallowing along and forming the border between Yugoslavia and Romania. Once a perilously fast stretch of water, since the building of the Djerdjap dam further downstream this part of the Danube has become in effect a placid slender lake, at times as much as a mile wide, its silty waters forming long wooded islands and fertile banks of green.

First stop is usually **SMEDEREVO,** where the last despot of medieval Serbia, George Branković, holed up when the Turks had occupied most of the rest of the country and he had been forced to cede Belgrade to the equally expansionist Hungarians. His fortress sprawls along the south bank of the river, a last retreat, once hemmed in by hostile Turks and Magyars and now framed by a modern patchwork of cranes and tower blocks. George was safe enough walled up here – the Turks did capture the castle in 1439 but oddly enough let him have it back again – and he ruled until his death in 1456; Smederevo fell three years later and remained in Turkish hands until the C19th. Further downstream is the **Castle of Golubac,** a far more romantic sight than Smederevo, clinging to a craggy outcrop and guarding the entrance to the narrower stretches of the Danube. Built by the Hungarians, it was subsequently commandeered by the Turks but abandoned in the C18th when their frontiers altered.

Eventually you arrive at **DONJI MILANOVAC,** a new town entirely rebuilt after it disappeared under the lake formed by the dam. Though itself without interest, it's here that you disembark for the excavations at **LEPENSKI VIR** – reached from the town by bus. The first remains of an early settlement were uncovered in this area in 1965 during an exploratory dig before work began on the dam. A year later the greater part of it was excavated and in 1967 the monumental stone sculptures for which Lepenski Vir became famous were found. The site itself – before it was flooded – seemed to have been a logical place for people to live: up on a raised shelf away from the capricious waters of the Danube ('Vir' means 'whirlpool') and with a ready supply of fish in the river and wildlife in the forest. Some seventy houses were uncovered in all, and in 1970 the finds were transferred to a plateau a little further up, which was roofed over and converted to a small **museum;** this is where you can see most of the major objects now. The stone sculptures are remarkable, mainly life-size heads, intricately and individually carved, dating back as far as 6000 BC – the oldest Mesolithic sculptures to be found anywhere in Europe. In fact the whole place gives a potent sense of a well-formed civilisation, with planned settlements and an art and culture of its own. Originally assumed a fishing village, experts have since mooted ideas that Lepenski Vir was some kind of religious centre: the bones of fish and deer that were found could be the remains of sacrifices and the heads depictions of primitive gods. This remains a matter for debate, and most anthropologists maintain that the heads represent actual inhabitants of the village.

From Donji Milanovac the Danube pushes sluggishly through the sheer **Kazan Gorge** to TEKIJA, where there's a bus up to the **Djerdjap Dam,** a Yugoslav-Romanian venture meant to tame the angry waters of the Iron Gates of the Danube and replace those exciting rapids as a tourist attraction. Before, the river cut through here with ruthless speed, its syrupy waters swirling and eddying dangerously, forcing barges and ships to navigate a narrow channel close to the right bank – where the water was still so fast they had to be towed by steam train. Now, thanks to the dam, the water is quiet, the river wide and serene, and there's not a hint of white water anywhere.

You can visit the hydroelectric station on the Yugoslav side (produce your passport and don't take photos), in the company of a guide, plentiful statistics and a short film outlining the history of the project: a true lesson in socialist struggle and achievement. Outside the complex stands the **Tablet of Trajan,** recently moved from its position high on the riverbank upstream. Dating from AD 102, this celebrates the completion of a road along the narrow Danube defile by the Emperor Trajan; a road that common Roman concensus had agreed impossible, having abandoned it some 80 years earlier. According to the tablet, the Emperor was considerably more determined than his compatriots, and he 'defeated both the mountain and the river' to finish the work.

Buses run on down to **KLADOVO,** a dull, grey sort of place with little apart from its caviar to bring you this far downstream. From here you can take buses into what must be one of the most remote and undiscovered parts of Serbia – the east.

EASTERN SERBIA

NEGOTIN, the first town of any note beyond Kladovo, is a small, secluded, provincial place, and only really animated at its Autumn Fair (21st–23rd September) when peasants from surrounding villages pile into town to trade, barter and generally have a good time. The people in this corner of the country are **Vlachs:** migratory gypsies who claim descent from the Romans, speak Romanian, and can be found in little isolated pockets all over the Balkans. They're an independent people, with their own mythology and ancient pagan beliefs: west of here, in the village of DUBOKA at Whitsun, women are said to fall into painful trances and communicate with the dead; to the north – in Romania itself – is Transylvania, homeland of the Vlachs and traditionally a country of vampires, witches and demons. . . .

Continuing south, it's not long before you reach **ZAJEČAR,** larger and livelier than Negotin but with almost as little to see; that is, apart from an excellent small **museum** devoted to objects discovered at the Roman citadel of **GAMZIGRAD** – about 13 km west of the town and easily reachable by bus. The fortress was mysteriously abandoned by the Romans, rebuilt in Byzantine times and then lost for close on 1000 years before its ruins were discovered by two enterprising C19th travellers. Now, despite being almost entirely rubble, it is possible to make out the rough shape of the fort and its individual halls and apartments; really, you could spend hours stumbling around amongst the mossy stones.

From Zaječar the road forges south west, and it's only a couple of hours down to the sprawling commercial mess of NIŠ.

THE VOJVODINA: NOVI SAD AND THE FRUŠKA GORA

The land that stretches north of Belgrade across the Pannonian Plain to the Hungarian border is known as **THE VOJVODINA** – like Kosovo an autonomous province within the Serbian republic. The name means 'the Duchy' as for years the region was part of the Austrian Empire. Keen to create a defensive front here after the retreat of the Turks in the C17th, the marshland was drained and settlers encouraged; among the first to arrive were 40,000 Serb families, fleeing the south in fear of Turkish resurgence. They were allowed freedom of Orthodox worship, establishing a new Patriarchate in the town of Sremski Karlovici, and soon migrants from all over central Europe came to farm the rich land. Their descendants remain, and more than anywhere else in Yugoslavia the Vojvodina contains a disparate mix of peoples: in addition to the sizeable Hungarian minority there are Romanians, Ruthenians (Ukrainian Russian), Slovaks, Croats, Gypsies, even Greeks. Everyone speaks Serbo-Croat, but in a laudable attempt to preserve cultural diversity children can go to schools where lessons are taught in their own ethnic language. Providing elementary and secondary education in Hungarian, Slovakian, Ruthenian and Romanian costs a great deal of money but, as the Yugoslavs point out, a fortune can't buy tradition, though it may just save it.

This jumble of people lives in one of the most uniform areas of the country. Mile after mile the flat, fertile plains roll north, endless expanses of wheat, corn, sunflower and soya bean flashing by with hypnotic regularity – the rich land of the Vojvodina has the capacity to provide enough crops to feed the whole country. Oddly the vastness and similarity of the landscape never grind down to monotony: pastel-painted towns and villages dash colour on the horizon, and in the middle of it all an island of low hills, the **Fruška Gora,** provides the single interuption to the level skyline. It's this area and the nearby town of **Novi Sad** that are the highlights of the Vojvodina; the other private little towns, though pretty enough, aren't really of much interest.

Novi Sad

Grand capital of the Vojvodina, **NOVI SAD** is the best base for excursions into the Fruška Gora, and worth a day or so in itself – a small but likeable old centre and the massive fortress being the main treats. Arrive at the bus or train station and you're some way out of the centre. A number 8 bus from the train station forecourt takes you in, and a few minutes' walk away the **Tourist Office** (at Dunavska 27, closed Sundays) will furnish you with a map and advice on accommodation. Private **rooms** are mostly on the outskirts of town and evaporate quickly at weekends, especially in summer, but there's a reasonably priced **campsite** on the *Ribarsko Ostrvo* ('Fisherman's Island'). When I was here the **Studenski Dom** hadn't got its act together to provide the usual service; when it does it could well be the cheapest alternative. For cheap **food** try the *Express Restaurants* next to the Hotel Vojvodina or near the cathedral. If you want to dine in style the *Chinese* on Dunavska isn't wildly expensive, but you pay for the view at the *Petrovradin Fortress restaurant*. Still in Petrovaradin there's an above average pizzeria, *Sremac*, Matije Gupica (the 'high street') 19.

For the last few years a **hydrofoil** has linked Novi Sad and Belgrade, but the unpopular length of the journey (half a day) has led to a cutback in services and the company is facing closure. If it's still running, tickets can be bought from the jetty just north of the Petrovaradin bridge.

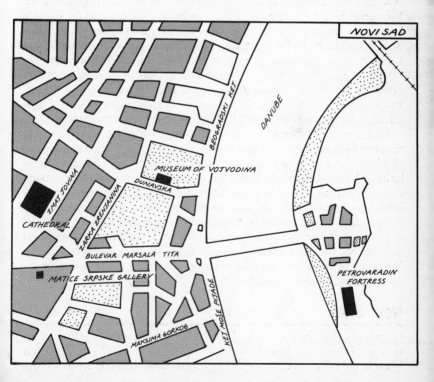

Novi Sad developed in tandem with the massive **Petrovaradin Fortress** on the Danube's south bank. There had been fortifications here ever since the Romans built an encampment on the hill to keep the Avars at bay, but the fortress took its present shape in the C18th when the Austrians turned it into a barrier against Turkish expansionism: shaken by the siege of Vienna in 1683 they took advantage of a lull in fighting to build an invincible last defence on the Danube to keep the Turks out of central Europe. Designed by the French military architect Sebastian Vauban, it was a truly vast enterprise, and took a hundred years to build. It has four independent subterranean levels with a total of 16km of tunnels; if the garrison were attacked 30,000 men could shelter underground and cover every inch of the surrounding land by firing through 18,000 loopholes – of which officers were normally acquainted with just a small section. The convicts forced to build it called it the 'Castle of Death' – as many as seventy a day died of overwork and disease.

The irony is that Petrovaradin became unnecessary even as it was being built. After a final bash in 1717 the Turks pulled south to consolidate their hold on Serbia, the threat subsided and Belgrade took over Petrovaradin's strategic importance. No assault was ever made on the impregnable fortress, and the only time shots were fired was in 1848 when the Hungarian garrison revolted and bombarded the city for several months. When they were eventually tricked into surrender, two-thirds of the town had been flattened, which accounts for the lack of earlier building today. The fortress eventually became a gaol, its most celebrated occupant being the youthful Tito, briefly imprisoned when as a young NCO in the Austrian army he was charged with propagating socialist ideas. The trip through the maze of passages is fascinating and shouldn't be missed: tours aren't regular so you may have to wait and tag along with a group.

Above ground the best thing is the view, Novi Sad's onion-bulbed skyline corralled by the modern town and the broad, silent Danube, making its way south in the foreground. Enjoying the protection of the fortress, Novi Sad flourished in the late 18th and early 19th centuries. Serbs and others travelled north to escape the Turks and the civilised capital somehow earned itself the title of the 'Serbian Athens'. The 1848 bombardment only temporarily upset things and today there's no better example of a flourishing bourgeois provincial town: its broad streets are sided by C19th houses, small parks and tidy squares, and an air of pleased prosperity abounds. Hub of the city is **Trg Slobode,** a spacious square with the town's brick-clad **Catholic cathedral** – an unadventurous piece of pseudo-Gothicism – slipped in on the east side. The streets off Trg Slobode are closed to traffic and a well-attended *korso* flows down to Novi Sad's most popular hangout, **Dunavska,** where summer evenings see free concerts and film shows, and, if you can squeeze in, lively performances of local folk dance.

One of Novi Sad's two worthwhile museums, the **Gallerija Matica Srpska,** celebrates an early upsurge of the arts in the Vojvodian. There's much work by Paja Jovanović, 98 years old when he died in 1957, the romanticised idealism developed in youth unaffected by the modern movement. His historical paintings are pretty dire, but there are some fine portraits of proud Edwardians. Look out too for the works of Stefan Meksić, whose *autoportraits* chillingly focus on themes of drink and death (Trg Proleterski Brigada 1, 0800–1500 Wednesdays and Fridays, 0800–1900 Tuesdays and Thursdays, 0900–1500 Saturdays, 0900–1300 Sundays, closed Mondays).

The other museum the **Vojvodjanski Musej** (Dunavska 35; daily 0800–1500, closed Mondays) has a good collection of burial artefacts found in ancient settlements along the Danube and Sava rivers, plus a worthy ethnographic section.

The Fruška Gora

Just about anywhere in Novi Sad you can look south to the low rolling hills of the **Fruška Gora** – pretty tame compared to the mountains elsewhere in Yugoslavia though no less likeable for all that. Tightly

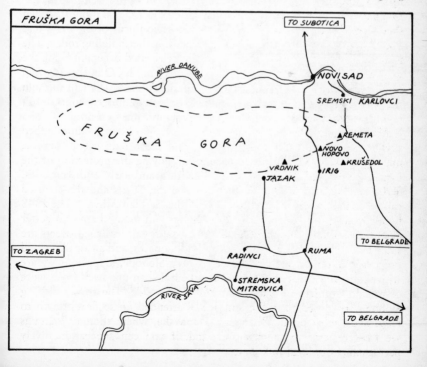

wooded, the hills have upland plains of wheat and vines, and on summer evenings a heavy, heady air hangs over the land, its dusty crimson sunsets somehow out of place this far north.

This is ideal walking country – which is just as well as there's no other way of getting about without your own transport. You can only get a bus from Novi Sad (direction Šabac or Sremska Mitrovica) as far as IRIŠKI VANAC, site of an impressive monument to the Partisans who fought from these hills. The monasteries south of here form handy stepping stones for wanderings: there are over twenty dotted around, built when the Turks clamped down on Orthodox worship after taking the nearby Patriarchate of Sremski Karlovici. The best three are close enough for a long day's walking: HOPOVO, KRUŠEDOL and VRDNIK.

HOPOVO, off the main road before the village of IRIG, is the most Byzantine in style, frescoed with the C17th works of an unknown monk-artist from Mt Athos, and decorated outside with a graceful twelve-sided dome supported by slender colonettes. A buzzing and verdant farmyard backwater 8 km away, **KRUŠEDOL** monastery church dates from the C16th, though most of its frescoes are from the mid–18th, as the Turks burned the original building. The interior's a little too rich, like an over-tattooed body; the best frescoes are the oldest, C16th survivors in the style of the Russian school. The war years saw Krušedol used by the Ustaše as a prison in which Partisans and their supporters were tortured and murdered. Bodies were roughly buried around the monastery, and afterwards a tiny paper note was found hidden in the hair of one of the victims, a woman:

> Jelica, my love my strength, forgive mother, I am separated from you, Mother gives you three thousand kisses on your little chin, God go with you, my child, dear living sweet heart, Mother is waiting for them to shoot her.

Krušedol has its ghosts.

Further west, **VRDNIK** was built in the 16th century, though the church dates from 1811. It was here that the relics of the great leader Tsar Lazar were brought from the monastery of Ravanica in the migration of 1683, out of fear that the Turks would desecrate them. Lazar's black wizened body was moved again during the war to keep it from the hands of the Ustaše, and it now lies in Belgrade's Orthodox cathedral. The monks' quarters today contain a hospital, but you can still see the church.

Between the Fruška Gora and Novi Sad, **SREMSKI KARLOVICI** is a refined little town with a cluster of Baroque building around a small square. If there's time the **Cathedral** sports a large rich iconostasis, all gilt and floral scrolls, the **New Patriarchate** nearby vying with it for sumptuousness. Just out of town a **Peace Chapel** commemorates the short-lived Peace of Karlowitz between the Austrians and Turks in 1699

– a curious building, its bell-topped rotunda echoing the shape of the negotiating table, and the windows cut like Union Jacks, in deference to Britain, one of the guarantors of the treaty's terms.

HEADING NORTH: TOWARDS SUBOTICA

Heading north across the **Pannonian Plain** the Hungarian influence becomes more and more apparent. Horse-drawn *fiacres* are the popular transport and the little villages preserve a Habsburg dictate: houses face the main street end-on with a single 'gossiping window', the idea being that doorways on the street were hot-spots of seditious chatter, and therefore banned. It's also in this region that you'll find what's left of Yugoslavia's **Communal Farms**, part of a project which ran briefly throughout the country in the 1940s and 50s. They were created immediately after the war, when land was taken away from the big property owners and shared out among the peasants and small farmers, who were then urged (if not forced) into collectives. This didn't work: early bad harvests and opposition from the peasants to working in such large units forced Belgrade to rethink. The traditionally less-developed areas like Macedonia and Bosnia, already struggling with the problems of centralised production in a region carved with natural barriers, were allowed to revert to smaller units where new technology and farming methods could be introduced gradually. Only in the flat arable fields of the Vojvodina, which actually benefited from the use of such methods, did communal farming take any hold.

SUBOTICA, 37km from the frontier, is a large town with little to recommend it. Throughout its history it has been shifted from one side of the border to the other with the result that the majority here speak Hungarian as their first language. The Habsburg influence is here too, in the famous and frivolous **Town Hall** of 1903, a lumpish and graceless building, its rhythmless curves and awkward angles splashed with once-gaudy colours, and inside a sea of toilet-green tiles and floral decoration. Not my cup of tea at all, but if you like such things it's possible to explore, visiting an above-average **Ethnograpic Museum** as you go. (Saturday and Sunday 0900–1300, Tuesday, Wednesday and Friday 0900–1500, Thursday 1000–1800). Best by default of Subotica's other buildings is the **Palata Likovnog Susreta** opposite the train station. Though small it manages to combine elephantine clumsiness with the ostentatious decoration of its larger neighbour; the kindest thing to be said of it is that it's not bland.

Subotica isn't a place to spend more than a couple of hours, and if you're heading north to Hungary I wouldn't break the journey. If you do wind up here the **tourist office** at Nusiceva 2 (tel. 024 274 342; turn left off Kidričeva by Putnik office) boasts some of the cheapest **rooms** in the country. The catch is they're usually full – phone ahead to enquire. Cheap **food** is supplied by a couple of *express restaurants* in the streets around the town hall in Trg Slobode; both do a good cheap Hungarian goulash. A **campsite** is also on hand, 8km further north, in the small resort of **PALIĆ**, whose lake is neither large nor exotic, but provides good swimming and the hire of all manner of watercraft; frequent buses run from Subotica.

SOUTH FROM BELGRADE: THROUGH THE ŠUMADIJA

Soon out of Belgrade bleak towerblocks give way to a green and brown countryside of mint-choc pasture and arable land, dotted with orange roofs. Twenty kilometres from the city you pass the wooded pyramid of **AVALA**, a favourite picnic spot of Belgraders, topped with a giant radio mast and Mestrović's *Tomb of the Unknown Soldier*, which sits on high, looking down on the rich, rolling Serbian hills. A monumental memorial to the First World War, in hulking grey marble and decorated with imposing caryatids, it can't help but seem a futile gesture, and not a little ironic – it was finished in 1938 and Italy and Germany both donated wreaths.

Beyond Avala the road cuts through the **Šumadija** or wooded land, stretching out either side in quiet forested folds and flanked far to the west by the distant hills of western Serbia and Bosnia. It's an almost English landscape, but wilder, less cultivated, not quite so neatly arranged. Here the early C19th risings against the Turks took place, the first instigated by the great Serbian leader, **Karageorge** – 'Black Goerge' – a pig farmer turned peasant commander who united wayward bands of rebels, planned forays into Turkish-held territory, and drafted the constitution of an independent Serbian state. Though still seen by the Serbs as the original founder of their liberty, Karageorge was a moody, unpredictable man and in 1813, when faced with an Ottoman army of unbeatable proportions, he deserted his men and fled across the Danube to the safety of the Fruška Gora. No one ever found out why, but it's as well to remember that he finally met his death at the hands of his fellow-countrymen, shot down on his return from exile by the new darling of the Serbs, Miloš Obrenović, who considered him too dangerous to have around.

TOPOLA was Karageorge's campaign headquarters, today an undistinguished little town but, as Milovan Djilas writes, 'one of the most powerful and venerated shrines in the Serbian national consciousness'. The relics of his short period of power crown the hill of Oplenac just above: principally, the fortified Balkan-style **konak** where he lived (now a small museum) and the **Karageorge Mausoleum**, a C20th Byzantine-style church that's plainly an attempt to prove the Karageorge dynasty as good as any other, linking its greatness to the magnificence of medieval Serbia under the Nemanjas. The great man's bones are installed in the south apse, traditionally the resting place of the medieval Serbian kings; and the mosaics that cover the interior are gaudy copies of frescoes from the Serbian monasteries – superbly worked, but ultimately leaving an effect of sterile ostentation. Downstairs are tombs built to receive the representatives of an unending dynasty, most of them empty: Oplenac is like a luxury hotel which boasts every possible comfort but lacks the guests – 'a sad monument to *folie de grandeur*' as Anne Kindersley sums it up. Open daily, your ticket will get you into both church and *konak*.

From Topola it's a short trip down to **KRAGUEVAC**, one-time capital of Karageorge's great rival, Milos Obrenović, but now the home of Zastava cars and a dusty modern town with little to tempt you to stay. During the last war it was the scene of one of the German's most vicious atrocities: 7000 people were shot here by the Nazis as a reprisal for Partisan activities in the area (100 males for each German soldier killed in an ambush); and to make up the numbers children from the local school were marched out as well. On the outskirts of town is a memorial park and museum, but more than anything the memory lives on in the people here: there's a paranoia of foreigners that you won't find anywhere else in Yugoslavia, and it's the only town in the country that accepts no responsibility for the safety of German tourists.

The cheap and very central *Hotel Sloboda*, just off the high street down Ulica Lenjinova, makes Kraguevac a useful place to **stop over** if you want to see the nearby monasteries – RAVANICA, MANASIJA and KALENIĆ. You'll need a full day for each one – and even then will have to set out early if you want to be back by evening. Before the monasteries, however, two towns. An hour and a half's bumpy ride through lush, curvaceous farmland leads to **SVETOZAREVO**, again almost entirely modern and with only a gallery of naive art to tease you off the bus. Another half an hour, across the thick fast gravy-flow of the Morava river and you're in **ĆUPRIJA**, a useful springboard for two of the Morava school monasteries – Ravanica and Manasija.

THE MORAVA SCHOOL MONASTERIES

RAVANICA stands at the bottom of a wooded corner just beyond the village of SENJ, a 10–minute bus ride from Ćuprija. It was founded by Prince Lazar and finished some time in the 1380s, first of the so-called **Morava School** monasteries which rose as the last fling of the dying Serbian empire. After his death at the battle of Kosovo in 1389, Lazar's body was brought back here and the monastery became centre of the cult that mushroomed around him: according to the heroic poems, Lazar lay decapitated for forty years on Kosovo field, until one day his head and body fused together again and he announced where he wished to be laid to rest:

> He preferred his splendid Ravanica,
> At the foot of the high mountain Kuchaj,
> For Lazar built there to God a temple,
> While he lived and ruled amongst his people,
> Built a church for his own soul's salvation,
> Built with his own bread and his own treasure,
> Not with the tears of widows and orphans.

The greater part of the battlements has been destroyed, but the ruins still ring the **monastery buildings**, enclosing a peace hard to reconcile with the squawking, motorised village down the road. The **church** stands out, a stocky five-domed honeycomb of different shades of brown, moulded with the characteristic patterning of the Morava School. Inside, the frescoes in the narthex date from an C18th rebuilding after the monastery had been plundered by the Turks; the abbot responsible for this – Stefan – is shown on the west wall. In the nave the medieval frescoes are disappointingly shabby, and those that are left dull and pock-marked. Apparently the Turks can't be wholly blamed for this – the plaster is said to have been badly prepared and so the colours faded quickly. Best are the *Cycle of Miracles* on the south wall and the *Entry into Jerusalem*, curving round the southern apse. On the opposite wall the badly-mutilated figure of Lazar stands next to his wife Milica: rather than let them fall into the hands of the plundering Turks, his mummified remains were removed to safety in the Vojvodina in 1683, and since the war they've been in Belgrade.

Squeezed into the narrow Resava valley, **MANASIJA** was once the artistic centre of Despot Stefan's kingdom and a seat of learning. As you approach the monastery the massive outer walls give it a doughty fortress-like solidity – and it needed this defence. Even when building began Stefan knew the days of his Serbian kingdom were numbered: with the defeat of his father Lazar at Kozovo a few years earlier, it was only a matter of time before the Turks reached the north. But no sense of uncertainty mars Manasija's marble church – from the outside solid and simple with just a frill beneath the eaves for ornament, inside some of the splendour of the medieval court is revealed. Decorated by master painters from Salonica and Athos, the church's **frescoes** show the furthest refinement of Serbian realism, the virtuoso use of colour – particularly blue – and delicacy of detail creating beautifully expressive portraits. Only a third of Manasija's original frescoes remain, but in their treatment of biblical themes all reflect a world urbane, rich and courtly. The aristocratic *Warrior Saints* of the north wall (perhaps the finest of the paintings) could just as well be holding books of poetry as swords, and the guests in the *Parable of the Wedding Feast* in the northern apse are Byzantine nobles eating the finest food from opulent dishes. Badly damaged, Stefan's *Portrait as Donor* looks out from the west wall, and he's buried here in a church that records the final flourish of a world soon to disappear in the years of Turkish rule.

Of the Morava monasteries, Manasija is unfortunately the most difficult to get to: best take a direct bus from Ćuprija to DESPOTOVAC – the nearest village – and walk from there; services aren't fast or frequent enough to take the other route and stop off at Ravanica on the way. Lastly, make sure a bus exists to take you back before you leave – there's nowhere to stay near Manasija save an expensive hotel.

The monastery of **KALENIĆ** is the culmination of the Morava School: finished around 1413 by a Serbian noble known as Bogdan, and wrapped in an exuberant, almost candy-striped skin, this is the style at its decorative, expressive best – adorned with lions, gryphons and birds in relief and chessboard geometric designs that rise to a high, central cupola. Inside, the **frescoes** are, on the whole, well preserved; the painters worked to a rigid plan which – since a thorough 1950s restoration – you can still make out. The *Marriage at Cana* in the south apse is one of the most striking, really an exquisitely arranged tableau of a medieval Serbian wedding, complete with the dress and custom of the period: if you look closely you can see the groom about to prick the finger of the bride, a blood-mixing pledge that was part of Serbian marriage ritual. You may notice, too, that each figure is eating with a knife and fork – evidence, Serbs say, of the high degree of refinement in Serbian society before stagnation as part of the Ottoman empire.

Kalenić is situated midway between Kraguevac, Kruševac and Kraljevo, and there are sporadic connections with nearby villages from all of those towns. I took a bus from Kraguevac to OPARIĆ, from where you can either wait for another bus or try your luck hitching.

THROUGH CENTRAL SERBIA: KRUŠEVAC, LJUBOSTINJA AND THE MONASTERY OF ŽIČA

The journey down to **KRUŠEVAC** is a dull slow trip, and the town itself has the spacious characterlessness of so many of its neighbours. Though there's little evidence of it now, this was Prince Lazar's capital when he lost the Battle of Kosovo, and his fort is now a small park, littered with rubble and stretches of wall and turret. The **church** in the middle dates from the 1380s, a fussy, well-kept specimen of the Morava School, with delicate tracery, rose windows and a polychrome exterior; checks, crosses and wierd dragon-like creatures predominate. The profusion of roofs and cupolas seems faintly excessive but they're a pleasant change after the dreary grey blocks of the rest of the town centre. Any frescoes have been totally lost, however, and the interior is small, charred black and uninteresting.

Among the exhibits in the nearby **National Museum** (Daily 0800–1800) is the gown that Prince Lazar is suppose to have died in on Kosovo field (though that's a bit hard to swallow) and a number of other artefacts relating to Lazar and the Serbian empire. Here too is a model of Mestrović's *St Vitus' Day Temple* – the real thing was going to stand on Kosovo field as a belated commemoration of those who died in the battle, but was never built. If the model is anything to go by it's probably just as well. If you have to stay in Kruševac – and there's little to hold you except bus connections – the D class *Hotel Evropa* has cheap rooms, but is nearly always packed out with student groups. I'd recommend you push straight on.

The main road forges west towards Kraljevo, following the wide floodplain of the Morava river. **TRSTENIK** is about half an hour away, a small town worth a stop for the monastery of Ljubostinja, which lies a couple of miles to the north. It's well signposted from the town, which drags along the road and fizzles out just before the monastery – an easy walk, but if you don't feel up to it one of seven buses a day will ferry you there. **LJUBOSTINJA** seems very much a working monastery, a small palatial estate where bees make honey and the nuns their own wine – stacks of empty bottles could make you think they like a drink here but in fact they're all for filling. It was founded in 1395 by Prince Lazar's widow, Princess Milica, who retired here with other gentlewomen to mourn her husband's death and the eclipse of medieval Serbia, which by this time really was on the way out. The **church** is a whitewashed patchwork of pastelly pinks and greys, inside warm and welcoming, displaying not so much Orthodox mystery as a light, bright homeliness. Few frescoes survive, but you can just make out the portraits of Lazar and Milica on the west wall of the narthex and – in better condition – those of their sons, Stefan and Vuk.

KRALJEVO is half an hour further on, an industrial town much destroyed in the last war and largely rebuilt to a new plan. It's a self-satisfied little place, mainly residential, centred on a shopping precinct which culminates in the inevitable over-stated war memorial and an arena-cum-square where the evening *korso* becomes a spectator sport. People use Kraljevo as a base for some of the monasteries but there are much better places to spend the night; only the monastery of ŽIČA – about 4km outside town – is best seen from here. There are buses every hour (direction: Matruška Banja) and once you've seen the monastery there's nothing to keep you from moving on.

The cupolas of **ŽIČA** crown the brow of the hill, painted a rusty red in imitation of those on Mount Athos. As one of the Raška School it's a far more monumental complex than the Morava monasteries; indeed, it was once among the grandest of all the Serbian monasteries. Here St Sava – patron saint of the Serbian people – founded the first Serbian Patriarchate when he returned from his self-imposed solitude on Athos to sort out the wrangles of his less capable brothers. Local tradition has it that he was led to this site by a golden thread, which is what the name of the monastery means. Žiča was the kingpin of his masterplan to establish the great and holy kingdom of Serbia as a force to be reckoned with in Europe: he crowned his brother Stefan here and in 1220 gave the monastery a charter that made it the owner of land as far away as Lake Skadar. If medieval Serbia reached a graceful conclusion in the monasteries of the Morava valley, Žiča was one of the places that its glories began.

However, its history is more interesting than the place itself. The church is a high, bare building, the result of an extensive 1950s restoration that corrected the damage and misuse of several centuries but left it just a little soulless. Even restored, the **frescoes** are in a sorry state of repair: most of the originals were lost to plundering Bulgarians in 1290 and all that survives are patches around the cupola and the *Crucifixion* in the south transept – difficult to see as the transepts have been sectioned off as choir stalls. The other remaining frescoes are C14th, best the rather stiff, stylised *Dormition of the Virgin* on the west wall.

STUDENICA

From **KRALJEVO** the road weaves its way around the sleek, wooded spurs of the Ibar valley. On the left watch out for the castle of **MAGLIĆ**, peering proudly down from a flattened peak on the east bank of the river, the C14th palace of a Serbian archbishop whose prime concern was to protect himself from marauders. This he did well, and the fortress must have presented a daunting prospect to any would-be invader. If you're travelling by car it's worth stopping off and climbing up – that's if you can make it across the river, which often runs too fast to wade. If you have problems there's a railway bridge 3km downstream.

The road continues down to USĆE, where a smaller and more exciting route branches off for the **MONASTERY OF STUDENICA**, twisting and winding its way up a valley furred with green forest. After about half an hour you reach the monastery, with the river of the same name frothing and foaming its tortuous course far below. The terrain here verges on the mountainous, with thickets of pines and high pastures faintly reminiscent of Alpine foothills or the French Massif Central. The monastery sits primly amongst all this, deliberately remote and inaccessible, first and greatest of Serbian monasteries and originally established at the end of the C12th by Stefan Nemanja, founding father of the Nemanja dynasty. Since then it has been chief among Serbian holy places and shrines – when the Archbishop of Canterbury visited Yugoslavia 20 years ago it was here he came to preach. At one time the complex had nine churches, of which three are left, standing in an oval paddock framed by the monastery's secular buildings. These give Studenica the feel of a workplace as well as religious retreat, firmly placed in the present with a thriving community of monks who both expect and welcome visitors. One hotel – out of sight beyond the monastery – and a couple of restaurants are enough to cope with a steady but never excessive stream of tourists, and though no one at the monastery speaks English you could try asking for Brother Jovan, who speaks German.

Centre of the monastic complex is the **Church of Our Lady**, built in the Raška School style in the closing decades of the C12th and borrowing from both Romanesque and Byzantine sources. The Romanesque sculpture – vine leaves, figures and strange animals that decorate the doors and windows – is reminiscent of many churches you can see on the coast. The clumsy exonarthex was added by Radoslav, a later Nemanjic ruler who spoilt the smooth polished serenity of the original marble structure with this plain and rather savage extension. In a marble tomb in the inner sanctum of the church lies Stefan Nemanja, below a fresco which shows him being presented to Christ and the Virgin – with Nemanja, the southern corner of churches became the traditional resting place of Serbian rulers. In marked contrast to the simplicity of Nemanja's tomb, his son Stefan-the-First-Crowned rests in an over-ornate C19th Viennese casket. He's a popular figure and gifts from local people litter the lid of the coffin; articles are placed underneath to soak up healing power.

Of the original **frescoes** – which were completed in 1209 – few remain, but those that do represent the first flowering of Serbian fresco painting: calm, monumental, and with a new and growing emphasis on the human form. The *Crucifixion* on the west wall of the nave is remarkably well preserved: Christ hangs against a background of deep blue, flanked by the bowed figures of the Virgin and St John, all is in rich blues, golds and deep maroons. It's a formal painting – Christ's body is gracefully draped, His hair hangs in ringlets, and blood falls symmetrically from His wounds – but also an emotional one, and it's hard to come away unmoved.

The tiny **King's Church** next door was built in 1314 by King Milutin, a royal edifice which while nothing special architecturally also has some revealing **frescoes**. On the north wall *The Birth of the Virgin* displays a humanism and narrative detail typical of Serbian painting at its height: on the left a woman holds a tray of surgical instruments; to the right the figure of Destiny fans the new-born babe; in the foreground a woman tests the water with the back of her hand before bathing the baby. By now, painters had become more interested in things like realism, invention and technique than straightforward symbolism.

It's a good idea to stay at Studenica and lap up some of its peace – the **hotel** isn't wildly expensive. **Buses** leave throughout the day for USĆE, from where there are frequent connections north to KRALJEVO and south to NOVI PAZAR.

NOVI PAZAR AND THE MONASTERY OF SOPOĆANI

En route to Novi Pazar you pass first through **RAŠKA** – really more industrial estate than town and stretching languidly along the river for several miles. Though there's nothing to stop for it's a major bus junction, and if you're heading south and don't want to go to Novi Pazar, this is the place to change.

After Raška you enter the **Sandžak**, a remote Muslim region of low mountains and few driveable roads that remained a solitary island of Turkish rule and a buffer between the states of Serbia and Montenegro until the late C19th ('Sandžak' was the Turkish label for its administrative provinces). **NOVI PAZAR** is its capital, a town that was an important stopping-off point on the caravan routes from Dubrovnik to Salonica and Constantinople until the annexation of Bosnia by Austria-Hungary cut it off from the coast. Now it's in the grip of total transformation: concrete towerblocks have ripped the heart out of its old centre, and the main square is an eccentric mess of department store and Turkish *han*, backed cynically by the neo-orientalism of the massive new Hotel Vrbak complex.

Never mind: the main street is a slender finger pointing east, retaining its Turkish houses and noisy bazaar atmosphere, thick with shouts and smells. What remains of the old Turkish quarter extends above here, a muddle of ramshackle houses heaped up behind and around the old fort – a relic from the town's Ottoman overseers and now a quiet, shady park where women sit by paths with children and beg. At the end of the main street is the **Altum Alem Mosque**, a C16th structure that's clearly seen better days; bash hard on the door (no. 79) and you should be let in. Inside, the mosque is small and intimate, not especially inspiring but with a gaily coloured *mihrab*. More evidence of the influence of Islam is on view at the **town museum** (Daily 0700–1500), just off the main square, though it seems that Novi Pazar was an important centre long before the Turks arrived. On a grassy mound about 3km north of town – you can walk it if you're energetic – is the **Church of Sv Petar**, where Stefan Nemanja held an early council that outlawed the Bogomil heresy in Serbia. In fact, the church is very much a pre-Nemanjic foundation, the nucleus dating from the C9th and the site probably a great deal earlier: in the 1950s the grave of the C5th Illyrian prince was discovered here, together with royal burial accoutrements that have since found their way to Belgrade. Now there's nothing but some badly chipped frescoes and a potent sense of antiquity; to get in, pick up the key from the house nearby.

Cheap **restaurants** and snack places abound in Novi Pazar, so you shouldn't have any trouble finding economic eats. Unhappily, the same can't be said of a **room**: the *Hotel Vrbak* seems to have stitched up the accommodation market almost entirely, and the town boasts no other hotel and no private rooms. Your best bet is the *pension* at the top end of 29th November, where they'll do you a bed for a third of the price of the Vrbak – just follow the *korso* to the end and it's right in front of you. Alternatives are the *Motel Ras* on the road to the Sopoćani monastery (buses every hour), or the *Tourist Dom* at the monastery itself for roughly the same price (buses every three hours). Both places do food so you needn't feel tied to Novi Pazar at all.

The Sopoćani Monastery

No one comes to Novi Pazar without seeing the **MONASTERY OF SOPOĆANI**, about 16km west of town on a road that cuts deep into the remote heart of the Sandžak; around halfway, just before the road forks right, are the remains of RAS, ancient capital of the Nemanjic kings and recently excavated. King Uroš I built the church at Sopoćani as his mausoleum: a Raška School foundation that stands out strong and white against the green woolly hills that surround it. Until fifty years ago it was little more than a ruin, and its frescoes had seen two centuries' exposure to the elements. Remarkably many survived and the church was rebuilt, since when it has remained – despite its fame – something of a retreat, a resting place where a few elderly nuns work out their days in an atmosphere of real tranquillity.

Stepping through the grassy exonarthex into the **church** proper, you realise how Uroš planned this as much a cathedral to his own family as to God: the frescoes are a celebration – or elevation – of the Nemanjic dynasty. Take a look at the fresco representing the death of his mother, Anna Dandolo, which gets the treatment normally reserved for depictions of the Virgin; look too at the east wall, where the C13th council of Stefan Nemanja has been added to the seven ecumenical councils. None of this prepares you for what follows: the frescoes in the nave are very different in both style and intent.

The work of master painters from Constantinople, the **nave frescoes** form a dynamic, inspired whole, suffused with love and faith: the elegant arrangement of *The Dormition of the Virgin* echoes the rhythmic parade of bishops in the apse; and its sad, handsome figures reflect the strong, stooping Christ on the north wall reaching down to haul up souls from Purgatory. The Dormition, in its traditional position on the west wall, dominates everything: Christ serenely central over his mother's bier holding a swaddled babe – the soul of the Virgin about to ascend to Heaven – while the Apostles stand silently by, very human, very dignified, posed in eloquent, almost musical relation to each other. Colours are muted green and gold, maroons mellowing to powdered pink, and only the women wailing from the balcony behind add a discordant note. In their grandeur, their emotion and originality, these paintings are hardly bettered anywhere in Byzantine art. How Serbian culture may have developed left to its own devices it's impossible to say, but looking at these frescoes it's tempting to imagine what could have been an explosion of creativity not unlike the Italian Renaissance, had not the Turks turned up and stifled it all.

WESTERN SERBIA: THE ROAD TO MILEŠEVA

The road west from Kraljevo takes you up to **ČAČAK**, a cheerless modern town, and from there down into the Djetinja valley through a steep grey gorge dappled green with occasional trees. On the far bank, a number of C17th **monasteries** shelter beneath precipitous heights, simple sober buildings from a time when believers were forced to hide themselves and their faith away in the remotest places; inaccessible by road, if you want to reach them you have to shout across for the ferryman.

Before long you're in POZEGA, where a road branches south for the village of **ARILJE**, whose creamy, cupola'd church is the only remnant of a monastery founded by King Dragutin in 1295. Dragutin was possibly the most incompetent of all Serbian monarchs: a Catholic zealot of the most fanatical kind, his overthrow of his father, Uroš I, and subsequent attempts to establish the Catholic church in Serbia led to his forfeiture of vast tracts of the empire and forced abdication in favour of his brother Milutin. This church is a rare reminder of his short reign: inside, the frescoes are less than perfect, but portraits of Dragutin, Milutin and his wife Katelina stand out – rich, royal representatives, studded with jewellery and finery, hardly aware of the tiny figure of Christ behind them.

Back on the main road, it's another short hop to **TITOVO UŽICE**, where in the autumn of 1941 the **Užice Republic** was declared – the first free Partisan state, which lasted just 67 days until the town was forcibly taken back by a German strike force 10,000 strong. From here Tito ran the war effort (a provisional government was set up), factories produced munitions and the party presses turned out newspapers and propaganda daily. Its eventual evacuation – a chaotic, hurried affair – was the first and one of the greatest Partisan defeats: casualties were grotesque, and the unit that defended the town fell to the last man, spurring Tito to offer his resignation as party leader.

The town today is a go-ahead sort of place that yearly becomes a bigger dot on the map. Its main square, Partizan Trg, is dominated by an austere greatcoated Tito, while all around award-winning architecture sneers at the Nazis' short-lived victory. Despite the location – scattered in a spacious well in the lush Serbian hills – it's not especially attractive, but it does make a good journey-breaker if you're heading west into Bosnia; if you want **to stay** the *Hotel Palas* has cheap doubles – 5 minutes' walk from the bus station.

After a spectacular trip across the high mountain pastures of **Zlatibor** – a favourite among Yugoslav health resorts – you descend to **PRIJEPOLJE**, scenically situated where the Lim valley has shallowed out to a broad bowl, and the best, or at least the nearest, base for the MONASTERY OF MILEŠEVA, where you can see one of the most important Raška School churches.

MILEŠEVA was founded around 1234 by Vladislav, grandson of Stefan Nemanja, but though planned as his own mausoleum it became much better known as the last resting place of his uncle St Sava, around whom flowered a cult that attracted Christians and Muslims alike: a precedent that so worried the Turkish authorities that they had his bones taken to Belgrade and burnt – devout Serbs still tell how on that day St Sava's body rose above the pyre and hovered in the stormy sky. Narthex and nave have together formed the main body of the **church** since the collapse of the dividing wall, though they're still known respectively as the blue and gold parts of the church – labels that refer to the predominant colours used in the frescoes. The collapsing wall left half a monkish portrait of Stefan Nemanja, heading a parade of the Nemanjic dynasty, from St Sava to Vladislav who, as donor, clutches a model of his church. On the south wall of the nave the famous fresco of the *Angel at the Tomb* gazes coolly down, serene yet strong, his eyes gently accusing. It's bound to ring a bell – the image first became widely known when it was projected across the Atlantic as part of the first USA-UK satellite link-up, and for a while it was one of the emblems of the United Nations. Just above – and rather difficult to see – is a lovely *Deposition*, with a shadowy, limp Christ tended by the Virgin and Mary Magdalen, and next to that a demure Virgin in an *Annunciation* scene: both repay aching necks.

The monastery itself is a shadow of the community it was: only two monks remain and, in a region predominantly Muslim this is one of the poorest of Serbian monasteries. Visible from here, high on a crag and I'm assured accessible, is a **castle** of disputed origin – the local story is that it's the idle brag of a rich woman who didn't know what to do with her money. More likely it was an outpost of medieval Bosnian kings.

To **get to Mileševa** you can either take a bus (four a day from Prijepolje bus station) or walk (about 45 minutes). You may find yourself having to stay the night in Prijepolje: if so, the *Hotel Mileševa* – almost next door to the bus station – has affordable double rooms.

NIŠ – AND SOUTH-EAST SERBIA

NIŠ is probably the last large town in Yugoslavia that anyone would want to visit: the grubby buildings of the centre play variations on the colours of its river, the Nišava, and the surrounding heavy industry has left a thick layer of dirt and depression over the town. What life there is mills around **Trg Oslobodjena**, a grim square of seedy 1960s development with a ghetto of hotels at one end and the uninteresting remnants of a large Turkish fortress at the other. There's nothing for you here, but as Niš is the main junction of the E5 *autoput* you may arrive with time to spare between connections. If you do, the **Crveni Krst Concentration Camp** (12 Februar Bulevar, on the same road as bus station walking away from town; Monday-Saturday 0900–1600, Sunday 1000–1400) is the most powerful and interesting of several morbid monuments to be found a few minutes out of the centre. Built as an army depot the camp is a sombre grey memorial to the bravery of its inmates: Partisans, Communists, gypsies and Jews rounded up prior to their torture and execution or deportation to the death camps of the north. On 12 February 1942 a suicidal escape attempt left fifty prisoners machine gunned on the walls – the bullet holes are still visible – but also with a hundred managing to scale the walls in one of the biggest breakouts of the war. Today there's little in the buildings save old photographs of prisoners, their smiling jaunty expressions horribly at odds with the pall of misery that still hangs over the place.

Altogether 30,000 people passed through Crveni Krst and many met their deaths at **Bubanj**, a hill to the south-west of town. It was here that the Nazis committed one of their worst atrocities in the final stages of the war: as the tide turned in favour of the Partisans mass executions were carried out to cover traces of the occupiers' crimes, with upwards of 1 000 people, mostly peasants, being shot each day. No one knows the exact total, but it's reckoned that at least 12,000 bodies lie on the crest of the wooded hill. An inelegant concrete **memorial** commemorates the dead, 'fists of defiance' rising brutally from the earth. It's clumsily done but the symbolism is moving, as is the inscription on the wall nearby:

From the blood of Communists and Patriots they grow

Fists of Revolution,
Fists of Rebellion,
Fists of Freedom.

They executed us
But they never killed us,
Never subjugated us

We trod on darkness
And made way to the sun.

Niš's other gloomy relic is on Brace Taškovica, a 24 bus ride from the centre – the **Čele Kula** or tower of skulls (Monday-Saturday 0900–1600, Sunday 1000–1400). It's the result of a typically Serbian gesture: surrounded by the Turkish army in 1809 one Sindelić and his men chose death before dishonour and ignited their gunpowder supplies, blowing to pieces most of the Turks – and all of the Serbians. To let the locals know who was boss, the Turkish Pasha later ordered the Serbian heads to be stuffed and mounted on the tower. After much souvenir hunting in the C19th only a few of the 15,000 skulls remain to return the tourist's stare, and though at the time they must have been a grisly statement of Turkish sovereignty, today the whole thing looks curiously like a fruitcake.

It's best not to get stuck in Niš overnight – there's no private accommodation and the hotels are wildly overpriced. If you need to stay, the **tourist offices** *Srbijaturist*, 12 Vozdova and *Putnik*, 2 Vozdova, will point you to rooms in the spa resort of NIŠKA BANJA, 10 km away.

Two routes run from Niš. Heading down the E5N takes you to the **Bulgarian border**, from whence you're within striking distance of Sofia. The road passes through the wilds of south-eastern Serbia, though they don't have much to offer. **PIROT** the first town of any size has had a tradition of carpet-making since Turkish times – haggle hard in the market and shops and you may pick up a bargain. East of Pirot the road falls into the Nišava canyon before reaching the border town of **DIMITROVGRAD**, best place to find out about occasional buses and less regular trains into Bulgaria.

To the south the E5N makes for SKOPJE and MACEDONIA, first crossing a dull plain to **LESKOVAC**, a textile town that describes itself as 'the Manchester of Serbia'. Conceivably, you might want to come this way to see the remains of the C6th Byzantine town of **CARACIN GRAD** (20km away) but you'll need your own transport, and if you make it rewards are slight – several extensive basilicas and some patchily preserved mosaics. From Leskovac the road slowly rises from the plain to follow the river Morava, the steep sides of its wooded valley intensely green. Where the valley broadens small settlements scatter their paprika roofs below the mountain crests, the road and rail routes tracing the course of the river. Below VLADICIN HAN the valley widens out, its sides flanked by ragged strips of cultivation – wheat, barley and grass merging into each other like a badly tended allotment. Most of what there is in **VRANJE** can be seen as the bus descends from the *autoput* – a broad arena of houses on the riverside, populated by oxen, ox carts and their drivers. There's a small Turkish quarter here with a large house that once accommodated the Pasha's harem, a note of the increasing

Turkishness found as you continue into Macedonia. **KUMANOVO** (see p. 212) has many mosques and a large Muslim population but little to detain you. Beyond mountains form the backdrop to an arid, bitty landscape, their heights topped with snow for much of the year – a grand and fitting prelude to SKOPJE (see p. 196).

TRAVEL DETAILS

Buses

From Belgrade to Novi Sad (hourly; 1½hrs); Subotica (hourly; 3hrs); Zagreb (hourly; 7hrs); Ljubljana (4 daily; 10hrs); Rijeka (3; 11hrs); Split (2; 13hrs); Dubrovnik (3; 14hrs); Sarajevo (5; 8hrs); Skopje (4; 9hrs); Kraguevac (hourly; 2½hrs); Kruševac (6; 3hrs); Kraljevo (hourly; 3hrs); Niš (8; 4½hrs); Titovo Užice (6; 4hrs); Novi Pazar (12; 6hrs); Priština (2; 8hrs).

From Kruševac to Kraguevac (2 daily; 2¼hrs); Titovo Užice (4; 4hrs); Niš (10; 3hrs).

From Novi Pazar to Priština (4 daily; 4hrs); Skopje (2; 6hrs).

From Novi Sad to Subotica (6 daily; 1½hrs); Zagreb (4; 7½hrs).

Trains

From Belgrade to Novi Sad (4 daily; 1¼hrs); Subotica (3; 3hrs); Niš (2; 4½hrs); Bar (6; 8hrs).

International Trains

From Belgrade to Budapest (3 daily; 6½hrs); Bucharest (1; 14hrs); Sofia (2; 10hrs); Istanbul (2; 25hrs); Athens (3; 24hrs); Prague (3; 19hrs); Moscow (1; 42hrs); Paris (1; 28hrs).

Chapter seven
KOSOVO

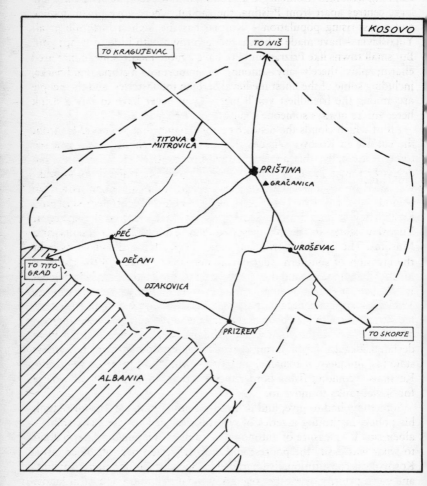

Although a province of Serbia, **Kosovo** is less explored, more politically unstable and immeasurably poorer than just about anywhere else in Yugoslavia. Around 80 per cent of the population are Albanian and, despite a history of considerable cultural repression, that's the official language, though nearly everyone speaks at least some Serbo-Croat. There's an Albanian newspaper and university, street signs are bilingual, and many of the older men still wear the beige felt skull-cap, or *plis*, which is the symbol of Albanian manhood. Few people know this portion of Yugoslavia: its landscape varies from the flat dullness of its central plain to the snow-capped heights of the mountains that skirt its borders, climbing west into Montenegro and south into Macedonia. There are few large centres apart from **Priština**, the capital, where government money and a fast-rising population – Kosovo has the highest birthrate in all Yugoslavia – have made a brash, modern town with little to tempt you. But small towns like **Prizren** and **Peć** have a more picturesque, minaretted charm; plus there's any amount of important historic landmarks, including some of the finest medieval **Serbian monasteries**, and the people are among the friendliest you'll meet – you never have to buy a drink here, you're always someone's guest.

All of which clouds the delicate **political issues** that are never far from the surface in Kosovo – issues that have largely shaped what you see today. Originally, this area was inhabited by the Serbs, but after the defeat of Prince Lazar here in 1389 they moved north and the vacuum was filled by Islamic settlers of Turkish and Albanian origin. After the second Balkan war in 1913, Albania became an independent state and Kosovo reverted to Serbian suzerainty – a backwater of the emergent Yugoslav state, its people despised and exploited as peasants and Muslims. The Second World War didn't help. Many Albanians thought the invasion of southern Yugoslavia and Albania heralded the dawn of an all-Albanian state, and they fought against the Partisans to help achieve it (though perhaps as many joined them). With Tito's victory in 1945 Kosovo again became part of Serbia, this time within a socialist federation of south Slav peoples. Nationalist undercurrents were immediately repressed, to the point where Albanian language and customs were declared illegal. Neighbouring Albania was by now a staunch Stalinist state (as, uniquely, it remains) and Tito – who had just broken with the Russians – couldn't risk a border incident that would provide an excuse for Soviet tanks to move in.

Something had to give, and in 1968 serious rioting led Tito to rethink his policy, instituting a series of reforms designed to give back some – albeit small – measure of autonomy, as well as stepping up financial aid to what was easily the poorest and most neglected part of the country. Kosovo was constitutionally upgraded to 'Socialist Autonomous Province' and given priority over other regions in the distribution of central funds: during the last two decades money from Belgrade has poured into Kosovo at a rate of 50 per cent higher than anywhere else in Yugoslavia.

Frankly, it's made little difference. The population here is poorer than the rest of the country, unemployment still absurdly high, and the gap between Kosovo and richer areas like, say, Slovenia, seems to be ever-widening. At best, extra money and concern have resulted in piecemeal and cosmetic improvements that have had little effect on the lives of ordinary people. Inevitably, this has led to fierce dissatisfaction, and in the spring of 1981 student demonstrations ignited concealed resentments that had been smouldering for some time, resulting in rioting that left 9 people dead and over 200 badly injured. The army sealed off the whole area and carted over 1,000 activists off to prison – 400 of whom are now serving terms of 15 years or more.

Feelings still run high – most of the young people I spoke to felt deeply and passionately Albanian, though since 1981 their voices have been stifled by the draconian powers handed out to the police here. Questions about Albanian nationalism are likely to be met with a stony silence: walls have ears in Kosovo at the moment, and everyone's reluctant to touch barbed subjects that can only get them into trouble. You get the feeling that the province has recently been stamped on a by a very large central government boot – and a deep core of resentment bubbles away underneath it all.

What about solutions? Opinions differ: one school of thought holds immediate economic considerations paramount, maintaining that economic problems must be solved before the stickier issues of Albanian nationalism can be dealt with. Another says that those problems are no nearer to being solved than they ever were, and that Kosovo has a right to recognition as a separate republic. Figures bear this out: Macedonians and Montenegrins both enjoy the status of republic so why can't the Albanians, who are numerically superior to both those groups? Belgrade – and virtually every Yugoslav outside Kosovo you care to ask – argue that if the Albanians had their own republic they'd have the right to secede from Yugoslavia altogether – perhaps even to join Albania – thereby setting a dangerous precedent for the federation as a whole. Albanians say they wouldn't do this – why should they? – most of them believe in the Yugoslav ideal, and want to remain part of it, just as long as they can secure the rights to which they believe they're entitled. Belgrade has little sympathy, and for the moment at least, seems content to coast along as before.

THE PLAIN OF KOSOVO

TITOVA MITROVICA is the first town you reach if you come down to Kosovo from the north – an ugly blanket of modern buildings through which peeps the occasional minaret. Further on spreads the Plain of Kosovo, in spring ablaze with red peonies that are said to blossom from the blood of the thousands of Serbs who died in battle here on 15 June 1389. This – the **Battle of Kosovo** – marks the end of medieval Serbia at the hands of the Ottoman Turks who swept across here to defeat a ramshackle Serbian force cobbled together under Prince Lazar. Serbia had already been in decline, but Kosovo was the turning-point, and from here the Turks flooded north, capitalising on an empire in complete disarray. In a little over fifty years they reached Belgrade, where they remained in control for five, generally oppressive, centuries.

Serbian epic poetry – oral songs collected and written down in the 19th century – weaves heroic tales of chivalry and honour around the circumstances of the battle, and it's partly through them that the sense of Serb nationhood remained strong throughout the Turk occupation. Before the battle, Prince Lazar was given two choices by God: should he choose an earthly kingdom he would win a great victory; should he plump for a heavenly one, he must build a church to God on Kosovo field and perish with his army. He chose the latter, and that's exactly what happened. As the poems point out:

> All was done with honour, all was holy,
> God's will was fulfilled upon Kosovo.

Lazar was decapitated and lay forty years here before being taken north and laid to rest in the monastery of Ravanica. The Turkish commander, Sultan Murad, also died (his mausoleum still stands) at the hands of a Serbian noble anxious to clear his own name of treachery. News of the battle took time to filter through to the rest of Europe and various rumours circled: at first it was thought the Serbs had won, and half the western world celebrated a victory over the infidel in a conflict that had become so clouded by Serb and Turk propaganda that no one knew the truth any more – comparisons with modern warfare are hard to resist. One thing is certain: the importance of Kosovo as *the* supremely important historic date for the Serbs makes the current provincial problems here even more intractable. Kosovo will remain part of Serbia just as long as it remains the most potent symbol of Serbian nationalism – which will probably be for ever.

PRIŠTINA

PRIŠTINA rises Las Vegas-like out of the plain, one half a shapeless muddle of red roofs, the other a sheer, soaring mass of new towerblocks. The city centre ranks with Skopje as among the most modern in Yugoslavia: the soul of the old Turkish city has been torn out and replaced with a series of white elephants built more to appease political pressure than to equip it for the modern age. Along the main street are skyscraping banks, the gleaming new Grand Hotel and a space-age university library. But the standing joke among Albanians is that the one thing all these buildings have in common is lack of what they're supposed to have: the banks have no money, the library has no books and the hotel rarely puts up any guests. An exaggeration perhaps, but one uncomfortably near the truth. Stroll around the **old town** and you'll immediately see why people are bitter. A miserable shambles of mud shacks and broken-down terraces, its cracked and subsiding façades look as if they've just (and only just) survived an earthquake. Children crawl through the streets in rags, beggars sit resigned to their fate and in the market lean peasants perch on crates to sell handfuls of spring onions. Vast injections of cash into Kosovo haven't changed these peoples' lives, and Priština is a sad indictment of Belgrade's lack of concern – and sensitivity – for Kosovo as a whole.

If you arrive by **bus** you'll find yourself on the outer fringes of town, behind an unpromising panorama of apartment blocks: from here it's either a bus or short taxi ride to the centre. **Trains** run only to KOSOVO POLJE, 8km west of the city (bus 7 to the city centre, number 1 to the bus station) and they're both infrequent and unreliable. If you want to stay in Priština be warned that **private rooms** are non-existent, and the down-at-heel *Hotel Union* offers the cheapest chance of a bed for the night; more comfortable and more expensive is the *Hotel Bozur* in the same street. For **food:** the Union has a *self-service restaurant* or there's any number of places in the old town that lay out tempting spreads in big steaming pots – no language problem, just point to what you want. Also, the wooden terraces that line the streets opposite the University house a promising variety of *bifes* and *grills*. **Information** is slightly harder to come by: there's no tourist office as such but you could try the *Putnik* or *Kosova Turist* offices – open Monday-Saturday.

But there's little enough to see here. Priština retains few links with the past and there's nothing to indicate its one-time status as capital of the Serbian kings. **Maršala Tita** is the main axis of the centre, carefully planted and the site of what is an unusually populous evening *korso*, famous for miles around and probably Priština's main excitement. The street bends aimlessly towards the old town, where you'll find the C15th **Imperial Mosque** – better inside than out – and a number of other, rather run-down mosques which seem to be kept permanently locked: the Muslim faith is on the decline in these parts, and it shows. A small **Museum**, devoted to the history and culture of the Kosovo region, has been closed for restoration for as long as anyone can remember. If it isn't still, I'll be surprised.

However, Priština does have one star turn, albeit not within its immediate boundaries. This is the **MONASTERY OF GRAČANICA**, 10 kilometres outside town, a short ride on a number 5 bus which you can catch from behind the Hotel Union. Of all the Serbian monasteries, Gračanica is perhaps the most externally impressive: a gentle succession of curving roofs build up pyramid-like to four small cupolas and a high, raised dome; herring-bone and cross-stitch patterns decorate the pale pinkish stone of the façade in a mixture of dazzling exuberance and almost geometric precision. It was built between 1315 and 1321 by King

Milutin, a rather unscrupulous, much-married womaniser – sometimes compared with Britain's Henry VIII – whose portrait, holding his church and clad in the stiff jewel-studded regalia of his office, occupies a pillar inside. His fourth wife Simonida is opposite, her eyes scratched out by centuries of peasants who powder and swallow the mixture of plaster and paint as a cure for weak eyesight – eyeless saints are common in Balkan churches. Simonida seems a timid, frail creature beneath her robes, and a sad one when you know her story. The daughter of the Byzantine emperor, she was sent to Serbia at the age of six to be Milutin's wife and a seal on a treaty between the two rulers. Milutin consummated the marriage too soon, left her utterly barren, and treated her with a mixture of brutality and devotion that was probably fitting for his station. She tried to run away and begged him to let her become a nun, all to no avail.

The lower reaches of the rest of the nave are all royalty: revelations of the courtly world that was medieval Serbia's golden age – for all his faults Milutin proved a successful and enlightened ruler, expanding the empire and instituting a legal system second to none. The frescoes that rise above, reveal the devout side of his court, with a mystical realism some have compared to Blake, others to El Greco, though the *Last Judgment* on the west wall is a macabre piece reminiscent of Bosch. In the side apses the comparison becomes clearer: *John the Baptist* in the north chapel is a severe figure, fiercely ascetic; in the southern apse *Elijah* sits in his cave, more interested in a life of contemplation than the food – a symbol of the Eucharist – offered by the raven.

PRIZREN

The **PRIZREN** bus takes around an hour and a half from Priština, cutting across the rolling Kosovo plain and then up into the hills, winding through green, wooded gorges. You're in the town almost without warning, dumped in the thick of dusty suburbs, about 10 minutes' walk from the centre. If Priština ranks as a bustling city, Prizren is a small, sleepy town; and where Priština is sadly dilapidated, Prizren is handsomely so; and it makes a much prettier base from which to explore Kosovo. **Accommodation** isn't hard to find: right in the centre are the *Hotel Theranda* – pricey but with cheapish four-bedded rooms – and the run-down and very reasonable *Hotel Turist* behind the church. Failing that, the **campsite** down by the river (10 minutes from the centre) lets out spartan *chalets* for a pittance. **Food**, as ever in this part of Yugoslavia, is no problem: everything's absurdly cheap and all the restaurants display what they've got in the window – Turkish style – so there's no difficulty choosing. Prizren has no official **tourist office**, but *Kosova Turist* and *Putnik* should be able to help with most queries: by the river in Moše Pijade and opposite the Hotel Theranda.

For 200 years Prizren was a seat of Serbian kings, a prosperous and wealthy city protected by Csar Dušan's monumental fortress high above the town. Few traces of glory remain however, wiped out by 400 years of Turkish rule, and today it's a muddled hotchpotch of brown roofs, slender minarets and the pepper-pot domes of Turkish baths, all sliced in two by the bubbling river Bistrica. Houses clamber up the hillside towards the fort that shadows the city, clutching the green in ragged tiers. If you'd just got used to Kosovo being bilingual, be prepared, for in Prizren most people speak Turkish as their first language, despite being for the most part Albanians and only eleven miles from the Albanian border. In fact, Turkish manners and customs have been retained here more than anywhere else outside Bosnia, something Albanian nationalists claim is self-perpetuating: it's easier to get a house, find a job, get things done, if you claim a Turkish rather than Albanian background. For a nation exploited and maltreated by the Turks for so long, Turkish customs seem to die hard.

Another Prizren peculiarity are its **Dervishes** who – though much depleted now – still meet for their annual rituals. In Britain dervishes tend to be associated with the fanatical Sudanese tribesmen who fought against Gordon at Khartoum; actually they're a peaceable sect, a mystic Moslem offshoot who preach universal love and recognise the teachings of both Christ and Muhammad – with the consequence that they're shunned by Christians and Muslims alike. They're probably best known for their frenetic ceremonies – here called *zirkas* – where they work themselves into a frenzied, trance-like state by howling, whirling or dancing – C19th travellers write of dervishes reaching such a mystical pitch that they could swallow white-hot coals, eat broken glass, and walk through fire without any ill effects. In Prizren the dervishes howl, chanting the names of God to an ethereal accompaniment of pipe and drum, until they reach a stage when they can stick pins into their cheeks without drawing blood or feeling pain. The point of it all is not so much to reach any particular state of enlightenment, but more to let out safely all bodily tensions. You can see the dervish ritual ceremony every 6 May in the Halveti Hall.

A short but lung-bursting trek takes you up to what's left of the **Fortress** which, in its time, must have been a considerable stronghold, guarding the craggy Bistrica pass which leads south through the Šar Planina mountains into Macedonia. If you follow the road – you can't get down to it from the fort – you reach the ruined **Monastery of the Holy Archangels**, 3km or so outside town: a remnant from the mid-C14th when Prizren was capital of Serbian king Stefan Dušan. Set in a clearing under the majestic grey rock of the Bistrica gorge, it enjoys a rare, almost spiritual peace – despite being plumb next to the main road and venue of impromptu football matches. Its massive complex of church. palace and chapels was substantially destroyed by the Turks under Sinan Pasha, who used the stones to build a **mosque** back in the town centre. An apocryphal tale tells how the Christians here thought this so outrageous they went all the way to Constantinople to complain to the Sultan, who sent them back to Sinan Pasha with a golden thread and an ultimatum – either he hanged himself or rebuilt the monastery. Somewhat fanatically, Sinan Pasha chose the former; the monastery remained in ruins and the mosque still stands by the river, a graceful domed structure that now houses a small museum of oriental manuscripts.

Wednesday – **market-day** – is the best time to be in Prizren, when the streets are choked with local villagers, many of the men in the traditional Albanian beige felt costume of hipster trousers, waistcoat and skull cap. Muslim women stroll in *dimije* – baggy trousers gathered at the ankle – and Catholic Albanian women don a gaily-coloured affair of white cotton and candy-stripes, with pleated aprons and a bustle at the back of the skirt. Just behind the market is the **Church of Bogdorica Ljeviška** (Our Lady Falling Asleep; Tuesday-Saturday 1000–1200/1400–1600), an early C14th structure built by King Milutin as a monument to the glory of his court and empire, with 5 cupolas, 3 apses and 5 aisles – perfect for processions and grand occasions. Inside, the church isn't looking its best: most of the frescoes have been lost and those that haven't are so pocked by Turkish plaster that the subjects look as if they are emerging from a snowstorm. On the west wall are the *Founders of the Nemanjic dynasty* – Stefan Nemanja, St Sava and Stefan-the-First-Crowned – appropriately regal representatives of a royal line that was in its prime when this church was built. The *Blessing of Christ* in the apse has the same sort of grace as the frescoes at Sopoćani, but otherwise you'll have to hunt around quite imaginatively to find anything all that fine. The painter was the Greek artist Astrapas – remembered with the architect on the east wall of the outer narthex in an inscription which details the contract drawn up between them and Milutin; for their pains they received a monthly salary of four buckets of flour, some salt and a bucket of ale. On the other side is another inscription, in Arabic this time, made by a travelling Turk deeply impressed by the church: 'The iris of my eye is the nest of your beauty.'

Finally, Prizren has two small museums of mild interest if you have a spare half-hour. There's an **Archaeological Museum**, housed in the old *hammam* behind the Ljeviska church – supposedly open daily 0900–1700 but times can be erratic – and the **Prizren League Museum**, which has a small collection of documents and artefacts relating to Albanian resistance to the Turks in the C19th. The other town *hammam* – near the Theranda Hotel – puts on sporadic exhibitions of fine art.

NORTH TO PEĆ: THE MONASTERY OF DEČANI

The road up to PEĆ meanders through the relentlessly flat plains of the **Metohija**, or 'churchlands', so named when Peć was centre of the Serbian church. Halfway, and you're in the dull little town of **DJAKOVICA**, home to the remnants of a sect of dervishes known as the *Bektashi*, who believe in the reincarnation of human souls into animals and wear bells on their feet to warn small creatures of their arrival.

Another half an hour and the village of **DEČANI** heralds the monastery of the same name, 2–3km west in a secluded enclosure where the plain begins to steepen into forested mountains that stretch far into Albania. The monastery was built between 1327 and 1335, the project of **Stefan Dečanski**, a Serbian king who afterwards took the name of this, his greatest creation. Probably the unluckiest, and certainly the most ineffectual of Serbian monarchs, Dečanski seems to have suffered the fate of all the characters of *King Lear* rolled into one. While still young he had tried to overthrow his father, King Milutin, who ordered his blinding and exile to Constaninople. By some trick of fate, or more likely just plain bribery, Stefan retained his sight and was later pardoned and allowed to return to Serbia; still feigning blindness he wasn't considered much of a threat. In the course of time Milutin died and Stefan discarded his bandages and assumed the throne – eager, well-intentioned, but equally unfit to rule. During his reign the empire foundered, the economy stagnated and Serbia's borders were threatened, with the result that he in turn was challenged by his son – Dušan – who had his father imprisoned and later strangled. It was an ignominious end, but for Serbia a fortuitous one. Under Dušan the golden age could resume.

Dečanski and Dušan crown the door through to the nave of the **church**, making their offerings to the enormous *Christ Pantocrator* above them. Dušan finished off his father's church which, at the time of his death was no more than semi-complete. It has the same fine chiselled quality of Studenica, its stripes of marble and stone weathered to a smooth, creamy lilac and beige. Western influences predominate: the architect, Fra Vita from Kotor, had clearly imbibed the styles of Italy and France, and sloped roofs decorated with blind arcading have replaced the cupolas of Gračanica and Prizren, doorways and windows are pilastered and reliefed. Unusually, Dečani suffered little under the Turks: it was to have been turned into a mosque, but the death of an *imam* from a piece of falling carving saw the plan abandoned. As a result the **frescoes** are so complete that going inside is like walking into an enormous pop-up book of the Middle Ages: the formal monumentalism of Studenica and Sopoćani has gone, replaced by complicated attempts at narrative rather than symbolism, multifarious cartoons that illustrate the calendar, the miracles and parables of Christ and the exotic, colourful world of Dušan's court.

Careful examination reveals a mass of familiar subject-matter, in colours that glow clear and precise. Byzantine bishops crowd the vaults – in their strict black and white formalism more reminiscent of the paintings of Mondrian than anything else – and the *Nemanjic family tree* in the narthex shines pristine turquoise and gold. Stefan Dečanski lies in the nave: for the locals – Christian *and* moslem – his coffin is a source of healing power and they come here for help, crawling underneath to absorb the blessing of the church's founder.

PEĆ

Whether you arrive by bus or train, first impressions of **PEĆ** will probably leave quite a lot to be desired: it seems dirty, perhaps a little seedy – a muddle of rickety low-slung terraces and once-sleek concrete. Don't let this put you off. Peć has a ramshackle, leafy sort of charm that grows – and is, in itself, an attraction of a kind. The tumbledown bazaar quarter can be exciting, especially on market-day, Saturday, and the town reclines beneath some of Kosovo's most breathtaking mountain scenery: the peaks that cower Peć are snow-capped all year round and the air here feels clean with an almost alpine freshness.

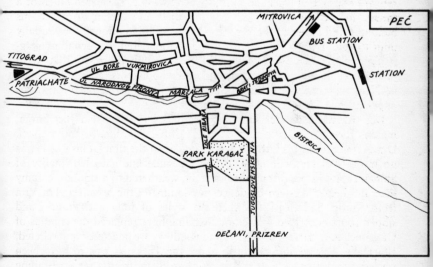

It's hard to believe now, but Peć was once a town of importance. In 1253 Archbishop Arsenius, anticipating trouble from restless Bulgars and Magyars to the north, moved the seat of the Serbian church here from Žiča, and the town became centre of a Patriarchate that extended west as far as the coast and north as far as Budapest. For his church he chose the safest of sites, well clear of the vicissitudes of history and invasion at the mouth of the narrow Rugovo Gorge, which in those days was almost impassable. Nowadays it's just a 20-minute walk through Peć's straggly suburbs to where the three churchs of the **Patriarchate** sit side by side in crumbly three-cupolaed union, linked by a long hall-like narthex put up in the C14th and decorated with homages to the Nemanjas. Arsenius's original **Church of the Holy Apostles** is the central, largest and most interesting, a dark mysterious place full of nooks and corners, with **frescoes** modelled on the church of Sion in Jerusalem (traditional venue of the Last Supper) and painted in the austere monumental style of the Raška School. Either side of the west door are a *Virgin and Child* and *St Nicholas* – giant solemn figures that give you a feeling of being watched even when you turn your back. The *Ascension* in the cupola is a swirling, visonary work, Christ sitting calmly on high above some terrified Apostles and a strong, earthy, peasant Virgin. The later frescoes are difficult to see in the light. High up in the west part of the church is a cine strip of *Christ's Passion* painted in the late C13th, each frame full of the drama of the moment. Strain your eyes and you pick out a number of familiar tableaux: a toady Judas cynically clutches Christ to kiss Him; a worried-looking Peter denies Him as the cock crows.

The two other churches of the Patriarchate were added by later arch-bishops in the first half of the C13th. **Sv Dimitrius** (on the left) is most rewarding, its frescoes freely arranged with a liberal choice of subject-matter that includes scenes from the life of the saint and a well-preserved *Birth of the Virgin*. The **Church of Our Lady of Odigitria** was finished around 1330: grand, open and well-lit it has none of the pitchy mystery of the other two. Nothing else remains of the original Patriarchate: the Bishop's Palace is gone, so are the outbuildings. Still, thirty or so nuns live on here in an enormous *konak*, working together in a small farming community that, by all appearances, looks to be thriving.

Some practical details. If you're heading west into Montenegro, Peć makes a good place to break your journey since it's relatively easy to find **somewhere to stay**. Of two hotels, the unpretentious and very central *Korzo* is the cheapest – along with a **campsite** and an excellent-value **Youth Hostel. Eating**, there's a *self-service restaurant* on the main street, any number of *grills* and *bifes*, and several cheap places dotted around the railway station. If you're looking for a bit more variety and can afford a bit of a splurge, the *Hotel Metohija* restaurant is really quite good, and not as expensive as you'd think. Should you need them, *Metohija Turist* in Maršala Tita have **information** and are open 0700–1900.

WEST TO TITOGRAD

Buses to TITOGRAD take one of two routes. The most direct and easily the most spectacular is immediately **west**, twisting a tortuous course up the **Rugovo gorge**, a startlingly deep, breathtakingly sheer chasm that leads west into Montenegro clutching a road to its side. The road hairpins and hesitates, sometimes lost in semi-darkness, sometimes emerging to face a horrific, almost bottomless drop, pulling out of what seems lemming-like suicide just when you think it's too late. The drivers swing the wheel with absurd confidence, climbing up above the summer snow-line to around 6000 feet, where you're faced with the stark wall of the mountains of Montenegro. On the subject of Montenegrin drivers, it's worth quoting Rebecca West's book:

The Montenegrins are a race of heroes, but since the Turks have gone they have nothing to be heroic about, and so they are heroic with their motor cars. A Montenegrin chauffeur looks on his car as a Cossack or cowboy looks on a horse, he wishes to do tricks with it that show his skill and courage, and he is proud of the wounds he gets in an accident as if they were scars of battle. It is a superb point of view, but not for the passengers.

If courage fails you, or you've already come this way, the other route takes you directly north up to ROZAJE, again across high mountains where the snow is thick throughout summer. I remember this as one of my more bizarre Yugoslav journeys: winding through misty, snowbound forests of firs and green mountain clearings strewn with grey, primeval boulders, holding a bawling Albanian baby and listening to Michael Jackson's 'Thriller' blasting down the bus.

TRAVEL DETAILS

Buses
From Priština to Peć (hourly; 1½hrs); Prizren (hourly; 1½hrs); Belgrade (2 daily; 8hrs); Skopje (5; 2½hrs) Novi Pazar (6; 2½hrs).
  From Prizren to Peć (hourly; 2hrs); Skopje (4 daily; 3hrs).

  From Peć to Titograd (4 daily; 8hrs); Skopje (5; 5hrs); Dečani (hourly; 45mins).

Trains
From Kosovo Polje to Peć (4 daily; 2½hrs); Skopje (3; 2½hrs).

Chapter eight
MACEDONIA

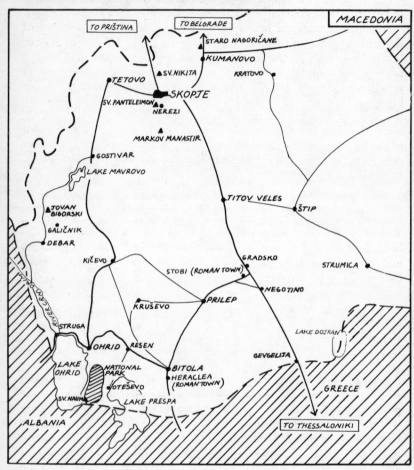

'Macedonia', they say, 'exists behind God's back,' an apt description. Tucked down in the south away from coast and capital, this has long been the poor relation among the republics, its sovereignty shunted around between Turkey, Greece and Bulgaria, its people long dependent on the lowest of incomes from farming. Neither is it much visited by tourists: all most people know of the region is the run down to Greece by road or rail, a journey that takes in some of the poorest and most backward agricultural areas and gives a distorted picture to those who don't stop off. For Macedonia, at its best, is magnificent. In the south **Ohrid** has a clutch of superb churches that date back to the C10th, and the lakes there and at nearby **Prespa** are a prime – though not overvisited – target. **Skopje,** the capital, along with **Bitola** and **Prilep** are the towns to head for; in fact the only main towns – Macedonia is a land of villages.

Summers here are the hottest in the country, and in July and August the lowland plains of tobacco field and opium poppy bake in an intense, brittle heat, with escape to the cool forested mountains and lakes a priority. Agricultural development is slowly pushing the region out of centuries of poverty, but the tourist industry has yet to take off in any big way. This can lead to problems in travelling – transport is sparse in the east and there are few private rooms or campsites. Hotels, however, often provide a cheap and viable alternative, and the region to the west of the E5 motorway – the most interesting part of the republic – is easy enough to get around. It's possible to make round trips here from Skopje to the lakes, and then to head on down for Greece.

Some history

From the decline of Alexander the Great's empire until the Second Balkan War of 1913, Macedonia covered parts of what are now Albania, Yugoslavia, Bulgaria and Greece. It was occupied by the Romans, Byzantines and most importantly the **Turks,** who colonised the region more thoroughly than anywhere else, their 500–year domination leaving reminders on nearly all the towns. With Ottoman defeat to Russia in 1878 there began a series of events that saw Macedonia carved up by a succession of powers: initially it was to become part of Bulgaria, but this was scotched by the Western Allies who left it entreated to Turkish rule. In response the Macedonians set up **IMRO,** a guerilla-style unit whose attacks eventually culminated in the **First Balkan War** of 1913. In a rare display of unity Serbia, Bulgaria and Greece joined forces to drive out the Turks, but at the height of triumph Bulgaria laid claim to sole possession of Macedonia – and began the **Second Balkan War.** Bulgaria was defeated and Macedonia divided: most went to Serbia, the south to Greece and a fraction to Bulgaria. IMRO, still intact, turned its attention to the new oppressor, Serbia, who responded with measures as harsh as any before – it became illegal to even mention the word 'Macedonia' on the streets.

With the outbreak of the Second World War Bulgaria joined the Axis and marched once more into Macedonia. A few IMRO members fought alongside the Bulgarians – seeing alignment with Bulgaria as a blow to Serbia – but many more joined Tito's Partisans, and in 1943 Macedonia was given republic status in the plans for the new Yugoslavia. After the war the Macedonian language, more like Bulgarian than Serbian, was officially allowed to be used for the first time in centuries. Problems remain, however, in that the southern area known as **Egej Macedonia** borders on an ethnically similar region in Greece. Yugoslav Macedonians see Macedonia as separated and deregionalised by this Greek presence – they still refer to their own republic as 'Free Macedonia'. Even now it's difficult for an Egej Macedonian to visit relations across the border, impossible if they have political connections. Not surprisingly this has caused some acrimony; when Greek Premier Papandreou promised 'change' a few years back visas were briefly granted – but now things seem to have returned to their old embittered norm.

SKOPJE

Hurrying down to Ohrid or Greece most people bypass **SKOPJE**, which is a mistake: no other town in Yugoslavia is anything like it. Encircled by a broad sweeping bowl of dark snow-capped mountains, it stretches out across a panorama of decaying minarets and modernistic slabs – a mix of ancient and modern, which resulted from the worst **earthquake** in recent Yugoslav history. The 'quake, on 26 June 1963, saw 1000 dead, 3000 injured, 100,000 homeless. Macedonia, poorest of the republics, reeled, turning to the world for aid and getting it on a grand scale: Russia sent a special clearing unit, America a complete military hospital, and as they worked side by side Tito declared the rebirth of the city a symbol of international unity and co-operation. Rebuilt, it boasts showpiece Western structures that can withstand force 10 on the Richter scale, and a consumerism more extreme than anywhere else in Yugoslavia. Sleek showrooms sell video recorders and state-of-the-art stereos, and kids on the street wear-up-to-the-minute fashions. Alongside, however, is still a traditional Islamic community, as you immediately realise wandering about the oriental bazaars and buildings of the old town. A vibrant meeting of cultures and a place confident of the future, in Skopje at least you feel the Yugoslav ideal succeeding.

Eating, drinking, sleeping

Arrive in Skopje by bus and you couldn't hope to be more central. The **station** is at the entrance to the old part of town or **Čaršija**, and a stone's throw from the **Tourist Information Centre** at Kej Dimitar Vlahov 1 (Monday-Friday 0700–1900, Saturday 0900–1500). There you can get a glossy leaflet on the town but no help with private rooms – there aren't any. Cheap **beds** are only available in July and August from the Studentski Doms either at the *K.J. Pitu Student Centre.* (I.L. Ribar 58), or the *Goce Delčev Centre* (Taftalidže 11); check with the tourist office first as venues change. At other times of the year it's a toss-up between the cramped **Youth Hostel** near the train station at Prolet 25, or finding an unofficial *sobe* by being as conspicuous as possible at the bus station. There's a **campsite** too, centrally placed near the stadium in Gradski Park.

Food is cheap at the *Pelister Self-service* on Maršala Tita 50, reliable at the *Hotel Tourist* in the same street, and interesting in the Čaršija where outdoor grills sell cheap meaty snacks, *tavec grau* (spiced beans) and *pasulj i vesulica* (baked beans with meat), both served in earthenware pots. Best places to **drink** are also in the Čaršija, and among the cafés that flank Ploštad Maršala Tita. Be warned though that Skopje closes early and most cafés start slinging out between 10 and 11; an exception is *Hotel Tourist bar*, which serves well into the early hours.

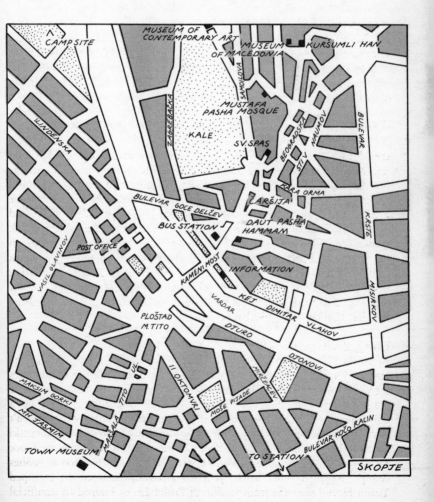

About town

Skopje divides neatly into old and new towns connected by the *Kameni Most* or stone bridge, an ancient structure of Roman foundation, though much remodelled subsequently. In the old days the Turks would tie Macedonians on to tables in the middle of this bridge, then charge from either side, slashing them with spears as they rode past. Fine sport. Today the bridge is a more mundane focus of life: on the near side **Ploštad Maršala Tita** marks the new centre – a broad café-lined square, much like any other but forming the sump for an impressive *korso* that rebounds across the bridge in the evenings, its destination the **Čaršija** or Bazaar. This is Skopje's old Turkish quarter, built (more accurately thrown together) in the years of Ottoman domination, and ironically the area least damaged in the earthquake. By night it's a ramble of low mottled buildings holding cafés and bars; by day some of the intimacy and a lot of the romance disappear – like the bazaar in Sarajevo the Čaršija has outlived its original purpose and is beginning to be preserved for tourists. A few years ago each of the narrow streets had its own trade or craft, carpenters, tailors, tinsmiths, even scribes did business on clearly defined territories; now it's mostly souvenir and jean shops, and the craftsmen only knock together sandals and shoddy leather goods – you need to look hard to find anything you can't buy in Leicester. For all this, the Čaršija keeps its noisy, earthy atmosphere, especially at weekends when the adjoining **Bit Pazaar** open market sprawls out its wares and all the tribes of Macedonia gather to sell their produce, from rough hand-woven fabrics to poor handfuls of crops. This, one of the largest markets in the country, has a variety of goods matched by the diversity of the people who come to sell them: Moslems, Albanians, village Macedonians and especially gypsies flock in from the surrounding countryside, a tradition unchanged by earthquakes or modernisation.

Just at the entrance to the Čaršija is the **Daut Pasha Hamman,** Turkish baths built by a C15th Grand Vizier and now home to an art gallery. (Monday-Friday, 0800–1700). Forget the paintings: humped and solid outside, cool and spacious in, it's the building that's the treat, its high, broad-domed interior decorated with almost edible facing, and silhouetted stars that beam down from stylised firmaments. Under the lower, lesser domes are a few medieval icons, sternly beautiful and ill-at-ease in this sensuous eastern building.

Skopje owed some of its wealth to being a stop-off on the Dubrovnik-Constantinople trade route, and in the **Kuršumli Han** (Monday-Friday, 0700–1500) above the Čaršija, merchants and their entourage of servants, horses and camels would spend a night on their travels – a sort of medieval motel. These *hans*, known further east as *caravanserai*, once littered the trade routes of the Islamic world, though only a few survive in Europe. The Kuršumli Han itself was severely damaged in the 1963 earthquake, but a thorough restoration has helped it regain much of its original stronghold appearance – a *han* needed to protect both merchant and the valuable goods he carried, hence the lack of windows on the ground floor. Inside the tidily arcaded courtyard a collection of statues fills the rooms but like the Daut Pasha Hamam it's the building, not the exhibition, that pleases.

Facing the *han* is the ruthlessly modern and uncompromisingly un-Turkish **Museum of Macedonia** (Monday-Saturday 1000–1800, Sunday 0900–1200), recently completed to house what survived of Skopje's several museums destroyed in 1963. Two of its three sections were open when I visited, and very good they were too – highlights include the concise *Macedonian archaeological collection* and (though it's nothing to do with Macedonia) an exhibition of fish-like stone heads from the 9000–year old settlement at Lepenski Vir (p. 160). Lack of cash was preventing the third, historical section from opening – but by now it should be on the way.

Behind the museum is the most imposing of Skopje's mosques: it's the decoration that distinguishes this, the **Mustapha Pasha,** with its C15th arabesque designs and stylised inscriptions of the four great Caliphs. Even before the earthquake many of Skopje's mosques had fallen into disrepair, and you get the feeling that the Islamic faith here is essentially a leftover of past times. Only a few of the mosques are in use, and the muezzins no longer call from the minarets – if you hear the call to prayer at all, chances are it'll be coming out of a loudspeaker. In the 17th and 18th centuries things were different, and so self-assured were the Ottoman powers they even permitted the building of a Christian church in the city – though with the proud proviso it shouldn't be any higher than their own mosques. Hence the little C17th **Church of Sv Spas** (Tuesday – Sunday 0800–1200, 1500–1800) is mostly underground, tucked away below the Mustapha Pasha mosque. Inside, its tiny, shadowy naos holds a masterpiece of peasant carving, a naively-decorated **iconostasis** whose biblical scenes snake around the screen, full of the detail of everyday life. Its carvers, the Filopić brothers, placed Biblical figures in Macedonian costume, and enacted their stories against a background of local peasant life – an honest and curiously moving act of faith. As a kind of signature, the brothers included themselves, working away with an apprentice on the right-hand side.

In Sv Spas's forecourt is the tomb of the much-celebrated local hero **Goce Delčev,** whose moustachioed portrait you'll find alongside Tito's in cafés and shops throughout the republic. Delčev is held in such high regard because of his place in the Macedonian separatist movement. He was among the early leaders of IMRO, the revolutionary Macedonian movement, though he opposed the rising against the Turks that IMRO engineered in 1903 – fears well founded, for Turkish suppression was immediate and savage. Delčev himself managed to escape but with a price on his head, and was murdered a few months later, attempting to return to his native Macedonia.

More or less opposite is the entrance to the **Kale**, site of Skopje's ancient citadel, whose few remains survived various fires and attacks from the C6th onwards, but couldn't withstand the drubbing of the earthquake. There's little to see nowadays save the odd crumbling gateway, but the view is the best you'll find – beyond the ramshackle minarets and the Čaršija, Skopje's skyline rolls out like downtown Dallas, its chocolate brown TV building and the concrete ski-slope arts centre angular interruptions beneath the dark mountains. From the Kale, Skopje's **Museum of Contemporary Art** (Tuesday-Saturday 1000–1900, Sunday 0900–1300) is a climb up the hillside and if it's a burning hot Macedonian day I wouldn't bother losing the sweat. Largely a collection of local art, it's weakly spiced with the work of a few modern masters – after the earthquake the museum's curator appealed to the world's most famous artists to donate a painting – though judging by what's here his enterprise seems to have been uncharitably rewarded. Only a *Head* by Picasso is of any note.

Back across the river, it's fair to say that once you've recoiled from the shock of the new, Skopje's centre isn't all that diverting. The single thing to see is the **Town Museum,** though how good this is I wasn't able to find out as the advertised opening times didn't relate to reality. But the building itself, fashioned in austerity-measure grey, tells its own story. It's the shattered remains of the old railway station, now a memorial to the disaster – the hands of the station clock frozen at 5.17, the time the earthquake destroyed the city. A sobering reminder, nudging you into uneasy speculation about what will be left standing after Skopje's *next* earthquake.

OUT OF SKOPJE; THE CHURCH OF SV PANTELEIMON AT NEREZI

The mountains around Skopje are dotted with fascinating but thoroughly inaccessible medieval monastries. Only one, **SV PANTELEIMON**, 6km away in the small village of NEREZI, has a decent road to it, and even then takes some reaching. Without your own transport there are two possibilities, easiest of which is the daily coach service from Ploštad Maršala Tita: this runs only in June, July and August and its future looks doubtful (ask at the tourist office) so you may have to fall back on taxis – take a 57 bus to the end of the line and catch one from there. Alternatively it's a couple of hours' exhausting walking up the mountainside, or chancing your luck hitching a lift with passing tourists.

It's worth making the effort: Sv Panteleimon sits neatly on a high bluff,

Skopje almost unreal miles below, submerged on summer days beneath a sweltering haze of heat and smoke. Of the monastery only the church survives, a tiny, homely affair built by the Byzantine Prince Alexis Comnenos in 1164, and a typical example of what's known as the Comnenian Macedonian period, a cross about a central domed square. But if the setting of Sv Panteleimon is breathtaking and the church itself harmonious, miniature and lovely, its **frescoes** are magnificent. Covered by overpainting until the early part of this century, their discovery revealed some of the finest Byzantine art of the 12th Century, startling in its fresh and realistic representation and breaking with the rigid stylisation of earlier Byzantine works. The most famous of the paintings, *The Virgin Embracing the Dead Christ*, is perhaps as sensitive, immediate and expressive a depiction of sorrow as anything in Byzantine art. The others share an easy precision and refined colouring: best perhaps the *Nativity of the Virgin* above the entrance to the naos – the women huddled, excited, questioning in a doorway – and the portrayals of the saints, particularly Sv Panteleimon himself, dapper and majestic by the iconostasis.

Unless you have your own vehicle or are into serious hiking it's near enough impossible to reach the other monasteries outlying Skopje. For the eager, **Sv Nikita** (near BRAŽDA 15 km to the north) and **Markov Manastir** (20km south) are the most interesting; contact Skopje's tourist office first to find out if and when they're open.

WESTERN MACEDONIA

Out of Skopje the road to Tetovo winds between rounded scrub-covered hills until all at once the mountains appear, their snow-tipped summits suspended mirage-like above the horizon. This is the Šar Planina range that separates Macedonia and Kosovo and at its foot **TETOVO** just about merits a stop if you're not reliant on buses. Much of it is familiar high-rise, but the suburbs have a village-style prettiness with gardened *konaks*, camouflaged in August and September by a cottage industry of tobacco drying. In the centre of town is the **Sarena Dzamija** (Coloured Mosque), covered with decorative panels outside and postcard views of Istanbul in. An odd mosque, but then some of Tetovo's Muslims were far from orthodox: as at Prizren there's a Dervish tradition, centred on the wood-built temple or **Tekija**, south-west of the centre and now a museum.

From Tetovo the road cuts through the **Vadar plain,** small villages hung like rock pools on the mountainsides, their Muslim influence always apparent in the white minarets that spike the greenery. GOSTIVAR is the first town you reach, an undistinguished place but the stop to decide on a route south. Most of the fast buses from Skopje to Ohrid take the eastern route through KIČEVO, but if you can co-ordinate connections the longer, slower journey via DEBAR is more rewarding.

To do this latter run you'll need to start early or you'll find yourself stuck for the night – which will probably mean camping – there's no practical accommodation beyond the campsites at **LAKE MAVROVO**, dammed in the 1950s to provide Macedonia with badly needed cheap power, and surrounded by its own National Park. Weekending Skopjians come out to camp here (there are two campsites, both of which fill fast in the summer), and for the big annual attraction of the **wedding ceremonies** at nearby **GALIČNIK**. If you're around on 12 July these are well worth getting to – transport is laid on from the **Tourist Office** on the western side of the lake. Galičnik's villagers were stock farmers, scratching a precarious existence from the thin mountain soils, and for many years the men were forced to travel to find work, often ending up abroad. By tradition the migrant workers returned home each July to see their families or marry en masse. Even today a Galičnik marriage is still a highly ritualised affair of tokens, symbols and traditions that include chaining the bride to the hearth and a post-consummation announcement by the groom that he found the bride to be a virgin. Ancient customs aren't usually all that emancipated.

Though the monastery of **SV JOVAN BIGORSKI** (St John the Baptist) is just a short distance from the Debar road, you'll need to rely on the humour of the bus driver to pick you up after a visit: a dangerous but usually effective technique of stopping the bus is to stand square in the middle of the road and make an unequivocal 'stop' gesture. What you find is a monastery complex of broad wood and brick *konaks* from the C18th, traditionally founded 500 years earlier by Stefan Nemanja. Much the most interesting feature is the church's **iconostasis**, carved in the C19th by the Filopić brothers (of Skopje's Sv Spas' fame), though this larger, later piece is in many ways finer. Each of the panels depicts biblical themes, the framing pillars thick with human figures and small creatures scaling upwards. It's a vivacious, complex work, and not a little creepy, as if the wood were too unnaturally rigid to contain all the life it portrays.

DEBAR, a faded Albanian town hard by the border, marks the beginning of the dramatic run down to lake Ohrid, edging all the way alongside the river Crni Drim – 'Black Devil'. Lacing through the mountains, it's an exhilarating journey – and at the end of it all lies OHRID.

OHRID

Why **OHRID** isn't overloaded with tourists it's impossible to work out. It's a beautiful place, quiet, magnificent and one that stands up well to all the claims made for it. The old town, medieval centre of the Serbian Orthodox world sits threaded on a hillside, a maze of Turkish architecture studded with some of the finest and best-preserved churches in the country. Below, the lake gleams limpid and warm, with good beaches and bordering a National Park. By anyone's standards Ohrid is compelling – and you'd be mad to miss it.

Rimmed by mountains, **Lake Ohrid** has almost Aegean clarity, with crystal blue waters ideal for bathing. Since being designated a UNESCO Natural Treasure, elaborate and expensive projects to clean up the lake have been carried out, and even the usually intractable Albanians have been persuaded into following suit. The result is that on a good day the deep waters – at 900 metres among the deepest in Europe – are transparent to a depth of 21 metres, which must in itself be some sort of record. For the nearest **beaches** of any size you need to make for the hotels on the eastern side of the lake – the further you get from town the more secluded and generally better they are. Apart from the excellent sandy beach near the Sv Naum campsite, all are pebbly.

Practical points

In recent years the modern part of Ohrid has spread, but the old town is quite small – it's possible to walk around it in under an hour – and using the lake as a guide it's easy to find your way about, however tortuous the streets become. **Bulevar Boris Kidrič** is the main thoroughfare, running straight down to the harbour and neatly dissecting the town into old and new. The **bus station** is smack in the middle of the two on Partizanske, with the **Tourist Office** at No. 2 nearby. They'll help with private rooms: go for category 1 addresses as they're most central, though if you want something cheaper you might try STRUGA, 7km away to the northwest and gathering momentum as a tourist centre. Ohrid's rooms are of a high quality, something that can't be said for the **Youth Hostel,** which is in any case often full; for the committed it's on Goce Delčev and open from April to October. Alternatively there are four **campsites,** best of them *Sv Naum* at the southern end of the lake: reach it by taking the bus towards the Monastery of Sv Naum and ask to be let off at the *autokamp*. *Gradiste* along the same route has inexpensive rooms in bungalows and static caravans, bookable at the tourist office.

Places for cheap **eats** are pretty limited as there's nothing much between take-away snack bars and tourist-budget restaurants: a single exception is the *self-service* behind the Lentica restaurant. Way upmarket and quite excellent, the restaurant near Sv Naum monastery is among the best in Macedonia, and one of several that serves up the fabled Ohrid trout or *pastrmka*, a fish that's been around almost as long as the lake itself. It's found only here, in Lake Prespa and Lake Baikal in Siberia, and is best eaten *à la Ohrid* – stuffed with vegetables and paprika, and grilled on charcoal. Ohrid's other speciality is its **eels:** before the Drin was dammed they swam 3500 miles to the Sargasso Sea to spawn and die, the elvers continuing the cycle by returning to the lake. These days special lorries ferry the eels from river mouth to lake and back.

Finally, if you're here in late August there's the **Ohrid festival**, a series of folk dance performances and concerts with the Cathedral of Sv Sofije as an atmospheric venue. Tickets and programmes from the tourist office.

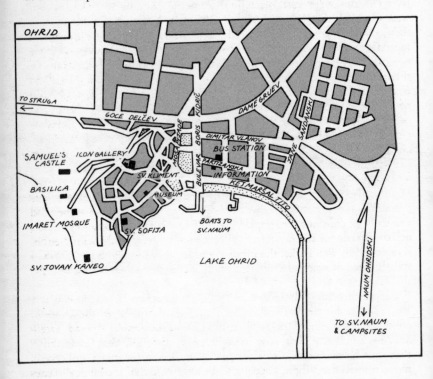

The old town and its churches

Clinging to a promontory at the north end of the lake, most of Ohrid's **old town** isn't really all that old – the wooden houses that overhang the narrow streets in a delicately coloured shambles of white walls and pale stone date from the C19th – but the story of the town, steeped in the history of the early Christian church, goes back a lot further. It owed its early growth to the Via Egnatia – the Roman road that linked the two great cities of Rome and Byzantium – and was settled by the migrating Slav tribes in the C6th, who gave the town its present name from their description *vo hrid* – on a cliff.

In the C9th the arrival of two monks saw the beginning of a scholarly and monastic tradition that was to last for 600 years. The monks, **Kliment** and **Naum**, were disciples of the missionary brothers Cyril and Methodius, and it's possible that the Cyrillic alphabet used by the brothers to translate the Bible into the Slav language was first fully worked out here. Certainly Kliment and Naum introduced Christianity to the Macedonian Slavs, making the town a base for missionary excursions throughout the Balkans and a home for monastic learning comparable to Mount Athos. Its territories were vast, stretching from the Danube to Salonica and westwards to the Adriatic, and the most brilliant church dignitaries, theologians and artists gathered here, instigating a near-frenzy of monastic building that gave the town over 300 churches – a supreme position that lasted until the arrival of the Turks in the C14th. Many of these churches have survived until today, though too often forgotten and neglected, encrusted into the hill like brown rotting teeth. The **Cathedral of Sv Sofije** (closed Mondays, times vary) is an exception: largest and oldest of Ohrid's existing churches, and one of the most majestic ecclesiastical buildings in the Balkans, Sv Sofije marks a highspot in early medieval church architecture. It's seen many alterations and additions since its foundation in the C9th – most damagingly transformation into a mosque – but what remains today has an austere splendour and above all a sense of light. The broad nave and aisles have none of the shadowy, lugubrious mystery you associate with the Serbo-Byzantine style, and the arches and vaulted roof continue the simple but firm feel of illuminated space. There's no iconostasis for the mysteries of the Communion to hide behind either – removed by the Turks, the *minbar* you see today was their addition, a stylish piece of oriental craftsmanship that holds its own in the ancient surroundings.

Despite structural alterations everything still focuses on the apse, where the **frescoes** are the earliest in the Byzantine tradition in the country, contemporaries of an C11th rebuilding. A monumental, stylised *Virgin and Child* fills the altar apse, towering over the *Apostles' Communion* that runs below, while a procession of angels, sharp-winged and severe, move toward the Virgin, kneeling in homage. Some of the biblical scenes depicted here went on to become motifs in Serbo-Byzantine painting; others like the *Scenes from the Life of Abraham* on the south wall, and the north wall's *Dream of St John the Divine* are unique. Look out too for the *Fiery Furnace* and *Jacob's Ladder* – illustrations that must have filled their early viewers with wonderment. In keeping with the Byzantine tradition there's a formal hierarchy to the frescoes, with ecclesiastical figures on the lower bands, Biblical scenes in the centre, and the Kingdom of Heaven surmounting all – an ordered spiritual world, defining the position of man and his Maker.

At the top of town on its own plateau, **Sv Kliment** (0800–1200, 1500–1700, closed Mondays) differs greatly from Sv Sophia both outside and in: a low wedge hugging the earth, the lines of the Macedonian-style church have been distorted by a C19th porch and it's hard to make out the original building that rises as a series of peaked brick fans. Built in 1295, it became a storehouse for Ohrid's treasures when the Turks entered the town, the most valuable of which were the relics of the saint himself, transferred for safekeeping from the church of Sv Panteleimon. The treasures have long since gone and once more the reason for visiting is the **frescoes**. Hidden under soot from centuries of incense and candles, a thorough cleaning in the 1950s revealed some spectacular late C13th works executed by the masters Mihail and Euthije. They mark a break from the static iconography determined by Byzantine Patrons, bringing new elements of folklore and medieval life into their interpretation of Biblical stories. It's as if the frescoes of Sv Sofije have suddenly come alive; the brilliantly coloured illustrations are full of vitality, movement and individuality, with a skilled handling of perspective that must have rivalled their Italian contemporaries. The *Garden of Gethsemane*, finest of the works, shows this to perfection: in a complex composition the disciples huddle as a sleeping group, each set apart by his posture and gesture. The *Lamentation* opposite has the same vigour, with the artists' observation of folk custom apparent – to the left four professional mourners chat among themselves, resting before the next bout of wailing. Really, there's more to both church and frescoes than can be said here. If you're seriously interested, pick up the informative booklet on sale in the church and continue across to the **Icon Gallery** (same hours), with works from the 12th to 19th centuries – though their age is discernible only by their condition, such was the little-changing style of icon-painting. Best of the rich ageing images are a stern C14th *Sv Kliment* and the *Evangelist Matthew*, both by Mihail and Euthije.

As you climb above the town, Ohrid's web of wandering streets and secret hillside alleys suddenly makes a lot more sense – and from the **Castle of Samuel** it seems almost ordered, the terraces of houses moving down in ranks to the lakeside. Save for the view and a few nervous lizards there's nothing within the ragged castle walls – they were systematically raided for building materials after the fall of the Emperor Samuel. Samuel, son of a Macedonian prince, retook most of Macedonia a few years after its capture by the Byzantine Empire in 968, and from the castle controlled his territories for 40 years. Sensing dangerous power taking root, the Byzantine Emperor Basil the Bulgar-Killer galvanised his forces to crush Samuel, and beat him in a decisive battle at Strumica. By Basil's vicious and salutory order, all Samuel's 14,000 men had their eyes put out, save one in every hundred who was left with the sight of one eye in order to lead the others back to Ohrid.

Following the path that runs down from the castle, you come upon the stumpy remains of an **early Christian Basilica**: carefully brush away the protecting sand and you'll find the original C5th mosaics. The church was excavated recently and it's reckoned that the size and rich materials would have made it one of the most important of the time; nowadays the local kids use it as a football pitch. Just below, and derelict from the outside, is the **Imaret Mosque,** where Kliment built his original monastery and school. Determined to erase the Slav tradition the invading Turks had it demolished and built a mosque on the site – the *turbe* nearby is of its benefactor, Sinan Yusuf Chelebi. Evidently they did a good job of razing the monastery, for modern excavations have revealed only the foundations and empty tomb of Sv Kliment, his bones hurriedly removed to prevent desecration.

Come to the end of the path and you're facing one of Yugoslavia's most famous postcard scenes. **Sv Jovan Kaneo,** a tiny cruciform church, which perfectly fulfils the unwritten rule that Byzantine churches should not only be beautiful but beautifully sited. Balanced on a cliff above the serene blueness of the lake the church meets both conditions, even though its interior has been stripped of decoration. Just below, a complement to Sv Kaneo's tinyness, the miniscule **Kaneo beach** is the best in town and – as you'd imagine – crowded throughout the summer.

Though you don't need an interest in churches or frescoes to soak up the feel of Ohrid, they add direction to your walks, and there are few other specific sights. The much-lauded **National Museum** didn't have a roof on when I was last here, though it's due to reopen 'sometime in the future'. Most of Ohrid's night-time action goes on around the cafés of the waterfront square, and it's fallen on the adjacent Moše Pijade to supply the souvenir shops mercifully absent in the old town. At the end of the street a plane tree landmarks the beginning of Goce Delčev, a scruffy gathering of handicraft and junk shops, which at least have the genuine item despite the multilingual signs.

The square is also the place to catch a boat to the **Church of Sv Naum,** an essential day trip from Ohrid. Boats leave daily at 8a.m., returning around 3p.m. (tickets from *Pallas Tourist*, 120 Moše Pijade) or you can haggle with one of the private operators. If you miss the boat there's a regular if cramped bus service from the station.

Founded by St Naum in the C10th the monastery reclines comfortably in its own wide paddock, looking out across the lake to the Albanian town of Podgradec. In a way the church is a bit of a fake: what you see today, a squat stone building with two raised cupolas, was assembled in fits and starts from the C16th to 19th, the porch a modern addition. Its frescoes are C19th imitations and there's piped muzak, but for all this the church and its grounds are almost soporifically beautiful, and only the most priggish purist could fail to enjoy them. As well as the impressive iconostasis, take a look at Sv Naum's tomb in a shallow side chapel where frescoes illustrate his life. One tells the story of a peasant on his way to market who was attacked by a bear. The bear killed his ox but Sv Naum, having a way with woodland creatures, intervened and commanded it to pull the cart – a homespun miracle if ever there was one. Naum is also held to be a sort of patron saint of the mentally ill, and if you're reading this near 3 July, try and make it for the **celebrations** on his saint day. Feasts are held in the grounds and pilgrims bring gifts to the church, carrying them three times round in supplication for a mentally afflicted friend or relation. Until quite recently the monks ran the monastery lodgings as an asylum: today they house holidaying tourists.

A discreet army camp behind the monastery reminds you that the border with Albania is only a couple of kilometres away, and a broad swathe cut in the forest marks the frontier of the countries. Albanians attempt to cross fairly frequently, though an agreement between the two countries allows for the repatriation of criminals, which the Albanian government more or less automatically invokes. The Yugoslavs use their discretion. Border guards on both sides are reputedly bored and trigger-happy – walking in the area isn't advised.

Around Ohrid
STRUGA, north and west of Ohrid town, provides private rooms at about half the Ohrid price, available from the **Tourist Office** on Proleterski Brigardski 2. An uneventful and unpretentious place, Struga falls either side of the river Drin as it briskly decants itself from the lake: the bulk of the population are Albanian and it's a cheerful, colourful little town, especially on Saturdays when the market arrives. When I was here the centre was being busily patched up and covered with concrete, and what looked like the first serious attempt at hotel building was edging in on town. If you do get here before the tourists, include the **National Museum** at Kej 8 Novembri in your wanderings – a dusty and faintly macabre collection of (stuffed) local animals gives you some idea of what to avoid in the surrounding mountains. Struga is also the venue for an international **poetry festival** at the end of August – worth checking out as some eminent poets come to recite their works.

KALIŠTA, a small indigenous Albanian village, is a 4km walk from Struga. Just past the Hotel Biser its **Church of Sva Bogorodica** has been badly renovated, but perched in the rocks above is a tiny **cell** once used by an ascetic order of monks: with the wind blowing in from the lake on winter nights the dank stone floors must have mortified the sternest flesh. To see the cell, ask one of the nuns around the church; donations are politely expected.

Only a few kilometres away from lake Ohrid, **LAKE PRESPA** is quite different. It's a wilder, elemental place, if anything even more magnificent – the pale mountains that run down to Greece plunge sheer and massive into its waters, and the whole area has a feel of rugged, rather frightening isolation. From Ohrid you can come here by bus, changing at RESEN for **OTOŠEVO,** most accessible of lakeside villages, but it's better to hike up through the **Galičica National Park** that straddles the mountain range between the two lakes – great views and easy walking through woods and alpine pasture. Otoševo's only problem is accommodation, with a choice between pricey hotel room and campsite – though you can quite easily (if illegally) camp in the woods all around. Across the lake is **PRETOR,** with the best sandy beaches and a campsite, and further round, **KURBINOVO,** whose church of **Sv Djordje** boasts unusual frescoes: Slav rather than Byzantine and totally unlike those of Sv Kliment or Sv Sophia. If you're driving it's worth noting that the **Greek frontier** here is closed to traffic.

BITOLA AND THE RUINS OF HERACLEA

BITOLA, Macedonia's second city, is worth visiting for two reasons: the remains and mosaics of its ancient city, *Heraclea Lynkestis*, and the chance to catch a train to Greece. The centre rises to a small-town prettiness of mustard-painted houses on geometric streets, their regularity upset by carelessly placed mosques, and evocative of the years before this century's upheavals when it was a secure and affluent place. The grand *konaks* of Maršala Tita still confront modern traffic with closed-shuttered propriety, though these days it's really a fairly typical Macedonian town around a fairly typical Macedonian market, a scaled-down version of Skopje's Čaršija with a neat *bezistan* or covered bazaar, both of which kick into action on Tuesdays. A town has existed here since the time of Philip of Macedon, and grew under the Roman occupation as capital of one of four districts into which Macedonia was divided and ruled. The **ruins of Heraclea Lynkestis** (turn left from the bus station onto Herekleja and head away from town until you see the sign) date mainly from this age. They're still being excavated and the archaeologists are confident of further exciting finds – so far they've unearthed an amphitheatre, two basilicas and an episcopal palace, but undoubtedly the best discoveries are the **mosaics.** The finest of these, in the Great Basilica, are from the early Christian period of the C5th: at first they seem simply decorative but a complex symbolism lies behind the designs – vines represent Christ growing from the spring of life, stags the constancy of faith, peacocks eternal life. Elsewhere scenes of hunting in paradise show the influence of earlier Hellenistic themes, all immaculately preserved. Enough remains of the town's foundations to give an idea of what it must have been like, and encircled dramatically by distant mountains it's an evocative and atmospheric place.

For a **room** in Bitola ask for cheapies at the central *Hotel Epinal*. There is a **Studentski Dom,** a fair walk out at Studentska 2 (head away from the bus station to town, turn left on Partizanska and ask) but no one there speaks English and the idea of foreign travellers staying struck them as very odd – but possible. The centre has the usual array of **cafés** and **restaurants;** try the **Bitola beer** – made from local soft water and very drinkable.

Bitola is only 18km from the **Greek border,** but getting to FLORINA and NORTHERN GREECE isn't as easy as you'd think. The nearest a local bus service gets is 5km from the border, from whence it's a question of walking or hitching. Trains do leave for FLORINA and THESSA-LONIKA infrequently (one a day, late afternoon) and at a speed that makes you think it'd be quicker to walk. A better idea all round is to go from the TITOV VELES junction to the north east, where you can pick up 'Express' trains.

NORTH FROM BITOLA: PRILEP AND TITOV VELES

North of Bitola the road bobs through the rather English landscapes of the Pelagonian Plain, fields of crops rashed with poppies, straggling behind low hedgerows. **PRILEP** is the most important of the towns here, gathered under a wild ragged outline of mountains, as dark and brooding as El Greco's Toledo. A workaday sort of place, it's the centre of Macedonia's tobacco industry, helping to supply the country's not inconsiderable need for nicotine. Six hundred years ago it was also the home of **Prince Marko,** son of King Vukašin, a Serb noble who fought at Kosovo. This much is fact, but a great tradition of epic poetry and folklore myth has attached itself to Marko and elevated him to the rank of medieval super-hero – a sort of Robin Hood, King Arthur and St George in one. He lived till the age of 300, having slaughtered innumerable Turks and other sundry villains, aided by his horse Sarač, a remarkable creature that not only had the gift of speech and could outrun all others, but also shared its master's prodigious appetite for wine. Like Arthur, historic reality reveals a more pragmatic character. Marko was defeated by the Turks and kept his princedom of Prilep only as the Sultan's vassal, ending his days fighting for the Turks *against* the Christians.

The forbidding **Castle** on top of the mountains is part of the legend, though it was in fact the second stronghold of the unfortunate King Samuel, who alternated his court between here and Ohrid in the C10th. It's difficult to give precise directions to the castle (roughly, turn left off Maršala Tita onto Markova and follow your nose up the hillside) but don't miss it – caught among the granite outcrops it's an eerie, desolate set of ruins, much more the home of a defeated king than a warrior prince. Dotted around are ancient **tombs** cut into the rock and several early Christian burial chambers – the mountain seems to have long held special significance for the people who lived on the fertile plain below.

Tucked in a narrow niche on the southern side of the mountain, the **Monastery of Sv Archangel** is rapidly crumbling away to complete destruction, and any future restoration will mean a total rebuilding from its rotting C14th timber foundations upwards. If you do get inside look for the *Tablet of the Thracian Rider* that's somehow intruded into the church. It shows a pre-Christian deity, possibly Rhesus, and goes some way to explaining the ambivalent nature of Marko's legend. The Roman legionaries of Thrace and southern Macedonia brought worship of the god into the area, and when Christianity drove the faith underground the memory of the warrior-god remained – and was sublimated onto the real character Marko.

The monastery is the biggest of fourteen **churches** in Prilep, most of which are in the old *Varoš* or suburbs that lie between the mountain and the new part of town. Most are normally kept closed but **Sv Dimitrije** (near where Markova becomes a track) is accessible, with remarkably well preserved and exquisite C13th frescoes in a church so square and simple it's like a gallery of medieval art. To get in, ask the caretaker in the hut nearby – he'll probably show you his own Primitive carvings.

Prilep isn't geared for tourists, and the only cheapish **rooms** are in the *Hotel Skopje*. If private rooms ever materialise the **Tourist Office** on Maršala Tita will be the first to know. To reach Maršala Tita and the centre from the bus station, turn right then left and head for the Hotel Lipa.

From here, the road north to Skopje passes through some of the best countryside in Macedonia – lowlands bowls of shimmering heat in the summer, the mountains sharp with crystal air. But there's not much to stop off for – the ruins of Stobi and Titov Veles are the only conceivable places of interest. To get to **STOBI,** catch a bus towards Titov Veles and ask to be put off at GRADSKO (make sure the driver will do this first) then walk 3km south to the site. Alternatively, go to NEGOTINO and catch a local service. Stobi is much older than Heraclea, founded in the Greek period and a venerable town by the time the Romans arrived – writing in 25BC the historian Livius describes it as 'an ancient city'. In the extensive ruins, that include an amphitheatre and a reconstructed hypocaust, it's possible to make out the shape of streets and buildings, though you need the help of the English-speaking guide to get the most from a visit.

TITOV VELES huddles on both sides of the Vardar, its Turkish houses rising on rambling and precarious tiers. It's an attractive and atmospheric place, especially at sunset as the light cuts across the valley, but really only worth interupting your travels if you want to pick up the (daily) train down to SALONICA or ATHENS.

EASTERN MACEDONIA

Eastern Macedonia hardly figures in Yugoslav tourist literature, and for good reason. What places of interest there are tend to be awkward to reach, and accommodation verges on the non-existent. In its remote rolling plateaux and uplands, though, the east is one of the places you're most likely to see costume and custom dating back centuries. To get something out of this you really need your own transport and some knowledge of Serbo-Croat, Macedonian or Greek, and travel details outlined here should be checked before you make a journey – bussing it in the east is a hit and miss affair.

First an exception. **KUMANOVO**, 35km east of Skopje, is painlessly reached and a good springboard for the **MONASTERY OF STARO NAGORIČANE**: 10km out of town along the Kratovo road (take any bus this way and get off where the road forks – the church is 4km along the left fork). Built from greying stone much bandaged over the years by brickwork and facing, Nagoričane gives the impression of a regal building fallen on hard times. It was founded in 1314 by King Milutin, who also commissioned its **frescoes** – executed by Mihail and Euthije, decorators of Sv Kliment in Ohrid and probably the most famous fresco artists of the day. Like the Ohrid works their compositions here are vital and elaborate – the best are *Scenes from the Passion* and the *Life of St George* – and continue the move begun in the C14th towards a narrative explanation of biblical themes. As well as the religious images there's a sympathetic portrait of King Milutin as donor, and his young wife. To get into the church you may need to ask for the key (*ključ*) from the houses nearby.

50km further east, **KRATOVO** sits in a hollow that looks as if it's been blasted out of the pale scrub-covered mountains around. Which indeed it has: the mountains here are volcanic and the basin is an extinct crater – hence the name. Though there's not much to show for it, Kratovo was for centuries the richest gold-mining town in the Balkans – initially under the Romans, later, after a boom in the C13th, under the Turks. By the C16th they yielded the Sultans a revenue of 70,000 ducats a year (the poet Zaifi impiously suggested his countrymen should make their pilgrimages to Kratovo rather than Mecca) but during the Austro-Turkish war the 'Golden Town' and its opulent buildings were flattened, and by the C19th the miners were so fed up of vicious Turkish exploitation that they upped and left, leaving Kratovo a ghost town. All you see today are a couple of raggy towers and high-arched Turkish bridges above the murky river Tabačka. Again no private rooms – the Hotel Breza provides the town's only bed for the night.

ŠTIP, only large town in the east, is like Prilep without the mountains – dull, modern and uninteresting. From here you can take the road to

Titov Veles across a primeval, anonymous landscape of high plateaux above the Vardar gorge. On one of these, the **Ovče Polje** or 'Sheep's Field', ritual sacrifices took place in fertility rites – analysed in one of the most brilliant passages of Rebecca West's *Black Lamb and Grey Falcon*, which sees the ceremony as a negation and distortion of the life force. The sacrifice of sheep and lambs, an attempt to restore to peasant women fertility no doubt lost by meagre diets and hard living, was still being practised before the war.

South of Štip lies **STRUMICA,** infamous in Macedonian history for being the place where Samuel's men were blinded in the C10th. It happened in a valley nearby, and the **Vodoča monastery** that overlooks the site was built as a reminder – its name comes from the words *vadi oči* – to put out the eyes.

On the frontier GEVGELIJA is the final train stop for Greece. Twenty km to its east is **LAKE DOJRAN**, a place marginally more interesting to read about than visit. Here the fisherpeople use captured cormorants to drive the fish into nets – a technique still found in China but long dead in most of Europe. It's dying out at Dojran too; nowadays more modern methods have taken over, and you'll be lucky to see the birds being used.

TRAVEL DETAILS

Buses
From Skopje to Belgrade (4 daily; 9 hrs); Priština (5; 2½hrs); Prizren (5; 4¼hrs); Peć (5; 5hrs); Tetovo (8; 1hr); Ohrid (5; 4hrs); Titov Veles (7; 1hr); Gevgelija (4; 4hrs); Niš (7; 4hrs).
From Ohrid to Bitola (10 daily; 1¾hr); Bitola to Prilep (10; 2hr); Prilep to Titov Veles (10; 2½hrs).

Trains
From Skopje to Niš (2 daily; 5hrs); Belgrade (2; 8½hrs).

International Trains
From Skopje to Thessaloniki (3 daily; 7½hrs); Athens (3 daily; 14 hours).
From Bitola to Florina (1 daily; 3hours).

Part three
CONTEXTS

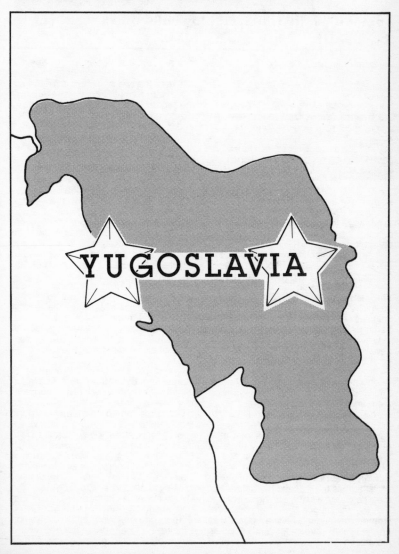

THE HISTORICAL FRAMEWORK

Balkan history is almost impenetrably complex – and that of Yugoslavia even more than most. The country as it exists today dates only from 1945, and well into this century the modern republics – Serbia, Croatia and Montenegro – were each independent states. What follows is necessarily a simplified (and brief) account, and it's intended primarily to provide a general framework for the more detailed accounts in the text and individual chapter introductions.

Beginnings: Illyrians, Romans and Slavs (BC-C5AD)

Although recorded history of the area now covered by Yugoslavia begins with the arrival of the Greeks in the C5 BC, recent archaeological finds have revealed settlements stretching back to the **Bronze Age** and beyond. Remains of one of man's earliest forerunners – *Homo Krapinesis* – have been found in Croatia, and discoveries at the Grapčeva Cave in Hvar along with stone forts in Istria show that a well organised form of society had reached the coastal areas by 4000 BC. Inland, ruins of a developed civilisation have been found at Lepenski Vir on the Danube – dating by general consensus to around 6000 BC and so one of the earliest permanent settlements in Europe.

From these isolated beginnings the tribes scattered over the country, gradually came together into two broad groupings: the **Illyrians** in the west, and the **Thracians** in the east. On the coast, around 700 BC, they were joined by colonies of **Greeks**, who had been trading along the Adriatic almost since they learnt to navigate. Their influence never spread far inland, but by the C3 BC it was extensive enough to provoke an Illyrian backlash – a confederation led by the semi-legendary King Agron, and later his widow Queen Teuta, driving them from all except Vis.

The Illyrians, however, had little time to consolidate these gains. To the east came progressive incursions of **Celtic** peoples, peacable at first but soon creating a territorial threat that led to battle; in the south spread the **Macedonian Empire** of Alexander the Great; whilst across the Adriatic the balance of the whole area was beginning to change with the campaigns and colonisations of **Rome**. The Yugoslav-Illyrian coast was an inevitable target for early Roman expansions, and using as their pretext defence against Illyrian piracy the C2 and C1 BC saw almost constant warfare between the two powers, culminating in 9 AD with formal Roman annexation of the region under the Emperor Tiberius.

Roman occupation lasted for a little under three centuries, its influence largely confined to the main coastal cities and provincial capitals (a pattern continued by later occupiers) but extending beyond these in the programmes of road building and tax collection. The fighting qualities of the Illyrians, which delayed Roman subjugation for so long, were turned to good effect in the Imperial legions. Discovery of large metal reserves made Dalmatia an extremely profitable area for the Romans, and the colony also provided several Emperors – Claudius, Diocletian and Maximilian among them.

Traces of the Roman presence are still visible throughout Yugoslavia, and there are three major sites: the Pula amphitheatre, the remnants of Salona and, most importantly, Diocletian's palace at Split. This for a time was the eastern base of the Roman Empire, after Diocletian's division of the territories in 285 – a division, into the two rival empires of **Rome** and **Byzantium**, that had significant shaping influence on the fragmentary development of Yugoslavia. The dividing line ran up from Budva through Montenegro to Belgrade – a line which you can still draw today to mark quite distinct regions. To the west, which followed Rome, the Latin alphabet is used and the people are predominantly Catholic; to the east, Byzantine-controlled into the Middle Ages, the Christian faith is Orthodox (as in Greece) and writing Cyrillic.

The disintegration of the Roman Empire in the C5 corresponded with a series of raids into Yugoslavia by Central

European tribes – the **Barbarians**. Goths and Huns both penetrated the country, but most powerful and wide-ranging were the **Avars** – who for a time controlled lands as far as Constantinople (Istanbul) – and the **Slavs**. The Slavs came originally from the Carpathian mountains (on the borders of what are now Romania and the Soviet Ukraine), from where they were driven by Avar – and Bulgar – raids. Unlike most of the other Barbarian tribes they had no real homeland to return to and settled with tenacity in Illyria-Yugoslavia. They had a particularly strong social structure, the *zadruga* – a system of extended families holding land and social responsibilities in common which survived Turkish occupation and could still be found in outlying areas until the last war – and they entered the Balkans in three highly individual groups. In the north settled the **Slovenes**; in the west, the **Croats**; and in the lands south of the Danube, the **Serbs**. These, along with a group of Romanised peasants known as **Vlachs** who occupied the mountains around Kosovo and northern Macedonia, either absorbed or displaced the Illyrians throughout the country, only a small coastal strip retaining their former Latinised character.

The Republics – and Turkish Occupation (C6–C19)

The three Slavic peoples – **Serbs, Croats** and **Slovenes** – originally shared a single common language and, to an extent, identity. Their distinct patterns of settlement, however, soon forged very different dialects, and the mountainous nature of their territories an isolated fragmentation. This, combined with the region's vulnerability, ensured their separate and highly individual development: at the beginning divided by the Catholic-Western and Orthodox-Byzantine spheres of influence, later as independent kingdoms and republics.

Perhaps the most unifying strand in medieval Yugoslav history – and indeed that of the Balkans as a whole – is the **Turkish Ottoman occupation**. Even this, however, affected the Republics in very different ways and degrees. The Turks held longest sway over Macedonia, parts of Serbia, Bosnia-Hercegovina and the fiercely independent mountain fastness of Montenegro: but save for a brief period in the C15–16, Croatia, Slovenia and Dalmatia all remained Christian and European under the rule of Austrians, Hungarians and, on the coast, Venetians. The unity, in fact, is more a result of the ending of Turkish rule than anything else. In 1877 the Turks were defeated by Russia and under the **Congress of Berlin**, held the following year, Serbia and Montenegro gained independence and the pressures towards some kind of Slav unity at last began to gather.

Croatia

The Croats were the first Yugoslav people to form an independent political unit, throwing off their allegiance to the Byzantine Emperor in 924 with the creation of a **Croatian kingdom** and royal dynasty by one **Tomislav**. This continued, unbroken, for two centuries, and Croatia developed into a well-organised medieval state, extending for a time to control of the Dalmatian coast. In 1089, however, the dynasty's last king, Kresmir, died without a successor and control passed to the neighbouring and related King Ladislas of Hungary.

Croatian history remained interwoven with that of **Hungary** for the next eight centuries, sharing its monarch, although being governed more or less autonomously by a *Ban* or Viceroy. It was a classic feudal state, the medieval Croatian nobles exercising influence at the Hungarian court, and remained so well into the C19. Control, however, shifted slightly with the Turkish advance into Europe – which in the C16 spread **Ottoman** power right across Croatia and into the Hungarian plains – but defeats at the siege of Vienna (1683) and again at the Battle of Zenta (1697) forced them into retreat, ceding Croatia-Slavonia to the **Habsburg** Prince Eugene of Savoy under the Treaty of Karlowitz.

Habsburg rule saw a return to power of the Croatian nobles, who played off Austrians and Hungarians in their factional struggles, but little change for the enserfed mass of the people. The period was marked by a series of violent **peasant revolts**, violently put down. The most famous – which figures prominently in socialist accounts of Yugoslavia's history – was led by the legendary **Matija Gubec** in 1573. This, however, like the others, presented no great difficulty to Habsburg power, Gubec being publicly executed along with some 6000 of his followers. It was only in 1848, with the revolutions in Austria-Hungary, that Croatian serfdom was finally abolished and an elementary bourgeois justice imposed.

After the defeat of Austria by Prussia in 1866, the Habsburg Empire was transformed into a **dual monarchy** – Croatia and Slovenia remaining part of Hungary, and Dalmatia going to Austria. This allowed Croatia to regain something of its old autonomy, though its *Bans* were still appointed by Budapest and, like Habsburg Slovenia, it slowly became a focus for aspirations towards southern Slav unity.

Dalmatia

Although now part of Croatia, Dalmatia's development has been very different – and through its tempting geographical position perhaps more complex than any other part of Yugoslavia. It was the region most extensively settled by the Greeks and Romans, and has been conquered and controlled in turn by Byzantines, Hungarians, Slavs from Croatia, Serbia and Bosnia, and (in part) by the Turks. Its most important and long-standing influence, though, was **Venetian**. Dubrovnik – or *Ragusa* – was one of the wealthiest Venetian city states, generally independent but closely linked to the great maritime empire in both its politics and trade. And all along the Dalmatian coast there are cities stridently Venetian in their architecture, built on the proceeds of similar contact.

Venetian power emerged in the C13 and lasted, somewhat shaky and decadent in its final stages, until subjugation to **Napoleonic France** in 1797. For Dalmatia this at first meant stretches of the coast ceded to Austrian rule but after Napoleon's subsequent defeat of Austria at Austerlitz, Dalmatia, with Istria and parts of Croatia, were incorporated into a single French-governed region known

rather fancifully as the **Illyrian Provinces**.

French occupation was brief – after Napoleon's defeat Dalmatia was re-assigned to Austria and Croatia-Slovenia to Hungary – but the experiment with unity, and an accompanied improvement in the economy, was a powerful stimulus to the subsequent movements for Slav unity. So too was Austrian oppression, which held on to the feudal society that had underpinned the Venetians' commercial success and moved hard to counter Dalmatian political aspirations towards a united Croatia.

Slovenia

Slovenia has affinities with both Croatian and Dalmatian history, though in comparison it's unusually straightforward. The Slovenes failed to set up their own medieval state, the Turks never reached this far north, and from the C8 until its incorporation into the Habsburg Empire in the C16 the region was ruled from **Germany**. Over the years there were various attempts to 'Germanise' the people but the Slovenes retained both their language and cultural identity. The former found fortuitous encouragement during the Protestant Reformation – the church authorities encouraging its use to the point of printing the Old Testament in Slovene – and they too had the first Slavic grammar and dictionary.

Napoleon's occupation here was a favourable influence, with **Ljubljana** becoming capital of the 'Provinces': an event which contributed significantly to C19 struggles for unity.

Bosnia-Hercegovina

In its early development Bosnia-Hercegovina is again quite close to that of Croatia. A territory of the early medieval **Hungarian Empire**, it emerged as an **independent kingdom** towards the end of the C12. Its founder, **King Kulin**, ruled from 1180 to 1204, an important period, which saw the emergence of **Bogomilism**, whose ascetic – and heretic – 'spiritually pure' lifestyle was adopted by the king and most of his nobles. Subject to hostility from both Catholic and Orthodox churches, the Bogomils were frequently persecuted from across their borders, and even subjected to a Hungarian-led crusade. The sect survived, however, and medieval Bosnia rose to considerable power in the last half of the C14 under the expansionist King **Stefan Tvrtko**. At his death in 1391 the kingdom included large parts of Serbia and Dalmatia – though much of this was in reality semi-autonomous, controlled from a series of isolated mountain castles by one of the Middle Ages' most ruthless and exploitative feudal nobilities.

This feudal savagery had unusual, if not perhaps surprising, effects with the **Turkish invasions** of the C15. Confronted by a religion which decreed that no believer should be enslaved to another, and (in theory at least) that no man should own more land than he can farm, thousands of Christian Bosnian peasants converted to **Islam**. So too, for equally pragmatic reasons, did much of the Bogomil nobility, who were offered freedom of worship for (nominally) considering themselves Muslim. As a result the transition to Turkish rule here was relatively straightforward. The king was replaced by a governor, and his aristocracy into a system of Muslim 'Begs' or *Beys*. To begin with this seems to have marked a general improvement in conditions, Ottoman rule being conservative and sometimes severe, but by contemporary standards fairly just. With the decay of the Ottoman Empire in the C18 and C19, however, the Bosnian ruling élite drifted back towards the corruption and tyranny of their Bogomil predecessors, and a particularly harsh tax collection system (imposed as in Serbia by the *Janissaries*) provoked a number of **Peasants' Revolts**. The most serious of these broke out in Hercegovina in 1874, spreading to Bosnia the following year, and its effects (and the conditions that had produced it) gained a certain notoriety in 'liberal' European circles. From the end of the C19, the '**Bosnian Question**' began to figure in Central European power politics. **Austro-Hungary** was given the right to administer the region – first through a neutrality pact with Russia, later, after Turkish defeat, under the Congress of Berlin. Conditions began to improve, with industry and mineral exploitation dragging the lands into the modern age, though the feudal land system remained virtually intact in the countryside. It was to be in the Bosnian capital, **Sarajevo**, that Slav nationalism finally burst on to the European stage – culminating, with the assassination of Archduke Franz Ferdinand, in the First World War.

Serbia

By far the greatest of the medieval king-dom-republics, Serbia emerged as an independent power at much the same time as Bosnia-Hercegovina. For five centuries after their arrival, the Slavs of Serbia had been involved in factional struggle between rival tribes – each led by a *Župan*, or chieftain – and had seen considerable threats of absorption, initially by the Bulgars, later as part of the Orthodox Byzantine Empire. At the end of the C12, however, these press-ures had receded, and a dominant *Župan* family emerged. This was the **Nemanjic dynasty**, founded in Eastern Serbia by **Stefan Nemanja** – a towering figure in Serbian history, who gathered about him a court as sophisticated as any in contemporary Europe and extended Serbian control over Montenegro and parts of what is now Albania.

The dynasty lasted over two centuries – a 'Golden Age' which plays a vital part in Serbian national consciousness, and which forged the Slavs' strongest links with the Orthodox Church. Stefan himself went into retirement at a monastery and his brother, the monk **Saint Sava**, estab-lished in 1219 the **Serbian Orthodox Church**. It was above all this religious identity which characterised the Serbs, and which survived the fall of the secular state after the death of the last great Serbian king, **Stefan Dušan** (1331–55), in whose time Serbia was probably the most powerful nation in the Balkans. Prior to Stefan's death, and the sudden Turkish advances, Serbia had spread to occupation of Macedonia, all of Bulgaria and the greater part of northern Greece. In 1355 the Serbian armies stood at the gates of Salonica, poised to extend to the east and perhaps to Constantinople itself. Nothing, however, came of this, as under Stefan's successors Serbia went into rapid and drastic decline. By 1389 **Lazar**, the last Serbian prince, was grouping the nation's forces for a last counter-attack and show of resistance to the Turks at the **Battle of Kosovo**. The result of this battle, in which he and most of the Serbian nobility were killed, was decisive. A few of the northern Serbian territories continued under isolated Christian rule, but in 1459 the last of these fell to Ottoman control – a state in which they were to remain for the next four centuries.

In keeping with Islamic tradition, the **Ottoman**-conquered lands were held to belong to God – which in practice meant the Sultan, his earthly designate – and were allocated to Muslim knights. Some of the Serbian Slavs converted, avoiding subjugation as serfs or *rayah*, but most did not and in the early years at least were not persecuted for their religion beyond the normal demands of feudal society. There was however heavy Serbian emigration – one of the most enduring effects of Turkish occupation – and Serbian communities were established in Dalmatia, Montenegro, Slavonia, Bosnia, and across the Danube in the then Hungarian-controlled lands of the Vojvodina.

It was the C17 which really signified the beginning of Ottoman decadence – in Serbia and throughout much of the Empire – and a particular resentment which surfaced was the growing recruitment and power of **Janissaries**. These were Muslim converts, taken forcibly as children from Christian families and trained into crack regiments of troops. At first they were simply an instrument of the Sultan's military will but in time they became a self-perpetuating élite, protecting their own position with unsurpassed savagery and exploiting the local peasantry through traditional feudal taxation. In opposition to them – and to the *Spajis*, Turkish cavalry units who played a similar role – there slowly emerged groups of Serbian rebel bands. These, known as the **Hajduks**, had existed as early as the C15, but in the later years of Ottoman rule they grew in force, conducting significant guerrilla campaigns from mountain and forest strongholds. As in Greece, where similar bands of *Klephts* harried the Turkish administrators, it was many years before they gathered into any kind of unity and national opposition to Ottoman rule, and when they did, in the **National Revolt** of 1804, they were at first easily put down.

The National Revolt, however, led by a former pig-farmer called **Petar Karageorge** ('Black George'), took root amongst the Serbs and found support among their Russian Orthodox co-religionists. The revolt broke out into a full scale **War of Independence** and Belgrade, Smederevo and other northern Serbian towns fell to Hajduk authority. Things were halted only by the wider events of European politics, Napoleon's invasion of Russia leading to the withdrawal of their troops in eastern Europe and leaving the Ottomans a free hand to crush remaining Serbian resistance. Karageorge was forced to flee across the Danube, and re-occupation savagely enforced.

A **second Serbian uprising**, led by **Miloš Obrenović**, a minor leader from Karageorge's Hajduk forces, was launched on Palm Sunday, April 1815, and once again found aid in Russia's South Slav aspirations. As the struggle continued, Russia threw its negotiating weight behind the Serbs and eventually, at the 1829 **Treaty of Adrianople**, the Ottomans relinquished control, retaining only a handful of military forts. Russia was given the right to protect Serbia's Orthodox Christians and Obrenović recognised as hereditary prince of an **autonomous Serbian state**. It was in a sense the first move towards a modern Yugoslav state, though up until the end of the C19 Serbia's status was kept under close control by the great powers of Europe. Internally, anyway, it was in no position to contemplate further expansion. Bitter factional disputes broke out between supporters of Obrenović and Karageorge, and out of the ten initial rulers of the new state four were deposed and three brutally murdered.

Montenegro

A part of the medieval **Serbian Empire**, Montenegro managed to carve out its own identity after the Serbian defeat at Kosovo and in the face of the Turkish conquest. Because of the mountainous nature of its terrain the Turks here were unable to gain any full control and Montenegrin rebels waged a ceaseless guerrilla campaign throughout the last years of the C14 and for most of the C15. Towards the end of this period **Ivan Crnović**, a Montenegrin Hajduk leader, welded together the anti-Turkish tribes to form a small **independent principality** with a capital at Cetinje, and this territory was ruled after his death by a series of Bishop-Kings. Of these, the most notable, and certainly the most culturally distinguished, was **Petar II** (1830–50), a legendary fighter and a fine poet, whose *Gorski Vijnac* ('Mountain

Wreath') is one of the great epic works of Yugoslavian literature.

The collapse of the Turks, and the 1878 **Congress of Berlin**, gave Montenegro vital access to the coast and official recognition of its independent **sovereignty**. In the years before the Balkan Wars it was perhaps the most peacable of all the Yugoslav territories, even experimenting with parliamentary democracy for a short period. Economically, however, it has always been one of the poorest Slavic regions and throughout the C19 there was substantial emigration – particularly to North America.

Macedonia

Macedonia's history – which has spawned the most complex political problems of all the republics – was until this century largely a question of two Imperial occupations, first under the **Byzantines** (who controlled the area, sporadically, from the C6 to C14), then under the **Ottoman Turks**, who remained here longer than in any other part of modern Yugoslavia, leaving only after the Balkan Wars of 1912–13.

Within these periods, the region also saw a brief phase of **Bulgar** rule – under **King Samuel** at the end of the C10 – and a longer one as part of **Stefan Dušan's Serbian Empire**. On these two turns of history, and on the Greeks' ancient links with the region under Philip of Macedon (and emotional links as part of Byzantium), rest the modern claims to the area, asserted by all three nations after the Ottomans had finally been driven out. To this confusion, with its various terrorist factions of the late C19, must be added the last century's rivalry between **Austria** and **Russia**, each of whom had vital trade routes and sea access through the area. It was as much through these conflicting and insoluble ambitions that Macedonia remained under official Turkish control for so long, the Great Powers having been unable to come to any deal with each other at the 1878 Congress of Berlin and **Ottoman rule** being extended, for three more decades, by default.

Towards Yugoslavia – the Balkan and First World Wars

The various strands of the Slavic kingdoms and republics begin to gradually interweave towards the end of the C19, and with the Russian defeat of the Ottomans and the momentous **Congress of Berlin** in 1878 start to take shape as a nation of South Slav peoples. As outlined above the Berlin treaty recognised the sovereignty of Montenegro, and it also gave formal independence to the by now well-established **Serbian kingdom**, with whom the **Montenegrins** were moving towards permanent union. Southern Slav tensions inevitably were to focus on **Macedonia**, with its continued Ottoman presence, and under the inspiration of King Peter I of Serbia a *League for the Liberation of the Balkans from Turkey* was formed, with the unique co-operation of Bulgaria and Greece with Serbia-Montenegro. The result, in 1912, was the short and successful **First Balkan War**, forcing the Turks to concede both Macedonia and the Albanian-dominated region of Kosovo to Serbia. Rather than consolidating their gains to the east, however, where Greece and Bulgaria both laid claims to parts of Thrace (and Greece to Constantinople), the allies fell out over control of Macedonia, Bulgaria eventually attacking both Greece and Serbia for sole possession of the Macedonian territories. This was the **Second Balkan War**, which ended within a single year – in 1913 – with the entry of Romania on the side of Greece, Serbia and Montenegro. Its result was a patched-up adjustment of frontiers at the **Treaty of Bucharest**, unsatisfactory to all sides, and not least to the divided Slavs of Macedonia. Serbia, though, came out a significantly consolidated Slav state, acquiring Western Macedonia and the greater parts of lakes Ohrid and Prespa. It was a triumph of a sort, and a spur to Slav nationalism in the north, where Hungary and above all Austria continued in power.

The position in the north, and on the coast, was again complex and fragmentary, but pan-Slav ideas and pressures were developing at a similar pace. In **Croatia** and **Slovenia**, which had become part of Hungary at the division of the Habsburg Empire, nationalists were divided between those who favoured an 'ethnically pure' Croat state – precursors of the Croatian Fascists of the Second World War – and the dominant advocates of unity with the south. This culminated in 1905 with the majority of the Croatian and Serbian political parties forming a Croat-Serbian Alliance. They were joined in their agitation by the **Dalmatian** delegates to the Austrian parliament, all of whom favoured Slav union.

As ever, things were more complicated in **Bosnia-Hercegovina**, part of the old Ottoman Empire but governed since the Congress of Berlin by Austria and formally annexed by it in 1908. Discontent, after this, became increasingly vociferous and Bosnian pan-Slavic movements mirrored similar activity elsewhere around the principle of union with Serbia. Austria, however, was determined to maintain its territories and began putting pressure on Serbia in order to crush the potential of – and aspirations towards – a pan-Slav state. On 28 June 1914 the **assassination in Sarajevo** of Archduke Franz Ferdinand, heir to the thrones of Austria and Hungary, gave them the excuse they had wanted. Although the Serbian government was unconnected with the incident (the assassin was a member of the 'Young Bosnian' nationalist movement – see p. 135), Austria issued it with an impossible and uncompromising ultimatum, and in July invaded. From the convolutions of Bosnian nationalism the **First World War** had begun.

The Serbian armies proved greater opposition than Austria had envisaged, forcing back the original offensive, but it was an unequal struggle and the Serbs' part in the war consisted mainly in helping to hold up the Salonica front. Away from the fighting the South Slav movement had its focus in the **Yugoslav Committee**, based first in Paris and later in London. Comprised mainly of nationalist politicians from Croatia and Serbia, the Committee ceaselessly lobbied the Allied Forces for the inclusion of a united South Slav state in any peace settlement. These hopes seemed initially dashed when by the secret Treaty of London in 1915 Italy was persuaded to join the war on the Allied side in return for a substantial slice of the Adriatic, including Istria and Trieste. In the end, however, the American president, Woodrow Wilson, came out in favour of independence for the Austro-Hungarian minorities. And so it was, that on 1 December 1918, the **Kingdom of Serbs, Croats and Slovenes** came into existence, its territories uniting these named republics along with **Montenegro** and **Bosnia-Hercegovina**.

Serbian Monarchy – and the Second World War

The new pan-Slav state – renamed **Yugoslavia** in 1928 – was faced with as many problems as it had solved. It came into existence, under western supervision, as a monarchy, headed by the Serbian prince **Alexander Karageorge**, and was subject from the beginning to claims of Serbian domination. These in fact had basis. The Serbs favoured a centralised state, and pressed hard towards this end when a coalition of the parties met to promulgate a constitution in 1921. Opposition came, above all, from Croatia, and from Stefan Radić's **Croat Peasant Party** – which refused to vote on any proposals and withdrew to Zagreb. The constitution as a result was even more centralist than it might have been, and its eight years of existence were constantly dogged by Croatian attempts to make it unworkable and have it overthrown.

Things came to an initial head when in 1928 Radić was assassinated by a Montenegrin with Serbian political sympathies. The following January King Alexander dissolved parliament and imposed a **Royal Dictatorship**. This was a disaster. Nothing was done to bring Croatians into any positions of power, and significant numbers of them joined a new, underground nationalist organisation – the proto-Fascist **Uštase** led by a lawyer called **Ante Pavelić**. The Uštase in 1934 assassinated King Alexander, who was succeeded on the throne by his son Prince Peter, at the time just ten years old. Authority passed to a regent – king Alexander's brother, **Prince Paul** – whose regime merely escalated anti-separatist repression.

These years, however, also saw the emergence of a new force in Yugoslav politics, the **Communist Party** which had the potential, at least, to cross regionalist divides. Established in 1920 on a wide base of revolutionary elements within the peasantry, and to an extent among the developing industrial working class, the Party had won a considerable number of seats in the early municipal elections, gaining control in both Serbian Belgrade and Croatian Zagreb. However, a short time before entering parliament, they found themselves, along with all communist organisations and trade unions, proscribed by the national government. Driven underground they regrouped, and worked to establish closer links with the Soviet Union. **Josip Broz** or **Tito** who had worked in Moscow with the Third International on his release from Yugoslav imprisonment, was the motivating force, and was in 1939 elected General Secretary of the Party.

The royalist government meanwhile had veered between alliance with its central European neighbours – forming the 'Little Entente' with Romania and Czechoslovakia – and increasing involvement with Nazi Germany, whom it saw as a protection against the 'Bolshevik threat'.

When the **Second World War** broke out, Yugoslavia initially proclaimed itself neutral, but by 1941 Prince Paul was formally aligning his government with the Italian-German Axis pact. It was a move which sparked immediate rebellion – Communist-supported, but led primarily by a group of Air Force officers who arrested the regent and put a young **Prince Peter** on the throne. Hitler's reaction was to bomb Belgrade – on 6 April 1941 – and to send his armies, with those of Mussolini's Italy, across the borders.

The Yugoslav forces opposed the **Axis invasion** but with little chance or hope of success. Within eleven days they had capitulated and the country once again was occupied and partitioned by foreign powers. **Germany** annexed most of Slovenia; **Italy** took Montenegro and the Adriatic coast; **Bulgaria** moved into much of Macedonia. In Croatia and Bosnia-Hercegovina, which with Serbia were allowed to remain individual puppet states, the Germans placed in power Ante Pavelić and the **Ustaše Fascists**: here, in a region which included 2 million Serbs, some of the worst persecution of the war was set in motion – Pavelić at its conclusion having slaughtered over 600,000 of their number.

Resistance: the Partisans and Četniks

Resistance groups were at first splintered among the country's various regions and political groups but within a few months two organisations stood out. These were the **Četniks** – pro-Serb, anti-communists led by Colonel **Draža Mihailović** and supported by King Peter's government in exile' in London – and the Communist **Partisans**, led by **Tito**. The Četniks' sporadic resistance soon ended in the face of savage German reprisals, and effective resistance passed to the Partisans. While Mihailović's inactivity quickly led to accommodation, and often open collaboration, with the Germans, Tito called for an all-out struggle regardless of the consequences. Despite horrific reprisals Tito's policy proved far more effective – with the result that many non-communists joined the Partisans. Mihailović, who himself was probably never guilty of collaboration, met with Tito on several occasions in 1940–1 but rejected all offers of joint resistance. It was a tragic decision, which almost inevitably precipitated fighting between the rival organisations: this broke out in November 1941 and a Četnik-Partisan **Civil War** was to last, in varying degree, until the country's liberation in October 1944.

Through 1942–3 Tito's Partisans constantly engaged the occupying forces. Twice they came close to annihilation – the first time being forced by the Germans to retreat from Croatia into the mountains of Bosnia and Montenegro, the second undertaking a legendary retreat, carrying their wounded across the Sutjeska valley – but these events only served to increase their national popularity and standing, attracting many to their ranks. In the areas that were liberated from effective Axis control they had the support and authority to set up a local *de facto* form of government – the **AVNOJ**, which was in effect a direct challenge to that of King Peter, still exiled in London.

In September 1943 a full-scale British military mission led by Brigadier **Fitzroy Maclean** was attached to Tito's HQ. With so many German divisions being tied up in Yugoslavia the Allies had to decide which resistance group to support: Maclean concluded that the Partisans were the only group worthy of help and as a result of the Tehran Conference the Allies withdrew all support from Mihailović and began to provide material aid to Tito. This established, the Partisans moved towards power, eluding a last

German attempt to liquidate Tito at his island headquarters of Vis, and as 1944 progressed playing a major part in forcing an Axis retreat from the central Balkans. With an eye to the future Tito met secretly with Churchill, and later concluded an agreement with the Russians, inviting Soviet troops onto Yugoslavian territory to take part in the **liberation**. This came about within months. On 22 October 1944 Partisan troops, together with Red Army units, entered Belgrade, and by the following spring Tito's Communists were in political and military control of the whole country – its territories much the same as before the war.

Even by the standards of Central Europe it had been an incredibly bitter and costly struggle. An estimated 1,700,000 Yugoslavs – nearly a tenth of the country's population – had been killed.

Tito's Yugoslavia

During the last months of liberation King Peter's emigré government had reached agreement with Tito, recognising his temporary authority as leader. Towards the end of 1945, however, the country moved towards democratic **elections**, the Communist Party, due to their official illegality, standing as the People's Front. As such they polled 90 per cent of the vote for the Federal Council. Royalist members who had taken part in Tito's provisional government resigned; the king remained in exile; Mihailović was executed; and a constitution modelled along Soviet lines was adopted.

Before long, large estates were confiscated, currency reform destroyed the financial base of the bourgeoisie and a Five Year Plan with emphasis on heavy industry was instituted. To finance the plan Yugoslavia's economy was closely linked with the **Cominform**, the soviet-controlled organisation of European Communist countries. However in June 1948 Yugoslavia's links with the Soviet Union were dramatically severed: Tito refused to bow to Soviet pressure over several major ideological issues and had begun to develop his own line in foreign policy. Yugoslavia was expelled from the Cominform and the Soviets made an unsuccessful appeal to Yugoslav party members to overthrow Tito. A period of

acute tension between the two countries followed, with the threat of Soviet invasion very real, yet Yugoslavia refused to respond to provocation – which included shelling of Yugoslav positions from Albania and Bulgaria – and from then on Tito began to evolve his own form of socialism.

A rigorous critique of Stalinism in the next two years led to a communism based on Yugoslavia's own specific needs. The ever-present nationalist question was dealt with by a **federal system** whereby each republic enjoyed autonomy in its internal affairs. This autonomy was tempered by the guiding role of the party and – increasingly – by Tito's own personal authority, but it was far more substantial than anything inside the Soviet bloc. Another major innovation was the introduction of the **Self-Management system** based on workers' councils in factories and producers' councils at regional level. It still exists: all factories, schools, hotels and the like are controlled not by the state but by the people who work in them – on the positive side this means diversification and a degree of competition; on the negative side it can lead to inefficiency and wasteful duplication.

Reforms in the 1950s continued into the '60s and Yugoslavia developed into the most liberal of all the established Communist states. Its innovations on the domestic front were mirrored in international relations with Tito championing the non-aligned movement worldwide.

Treading a delicate line between the superpowers gained Yugoslavia international credibility far in excess of its size or power.

Yugoslavia after Tito

Yugoslavia's success in moving away from the Soviet model and sorting out its nationalist problems had a great deal to do with the personal authority and charisma of Tito. When he died in 1980 many observers predicted the imminent collapse of the system. This hasn't happened: before his death Tito laid down the plans for a power-sharing leadership that would, politically at least, ensure the survival of the federation, and prevent, as he put it, the emergence of a Stalin after his Lenin: ultimate authority would change yearly from republic to republic. Now, five years on, there are creeping problems. A massive foreign debt, high unemployment and an inflation rate of 60 per cent plus have imposed severe strains on the system. Like other industrial nations caught in a world recession the problem is how to regenerate the industrial base: the temptation is to borrow, a policy that contains a number of pitfalls. If Yugoslavia **borrows from the West** it will be forced to make changes to the structure of its economy. But to make it more centralised and more 'efficient' – as the IMF would like – implies making political changes and moving closer to a mixed capitalist system. **Borrowing from the Soviet Union** has its own dilemmas. Quite apart from the establishment of a military presence in the Adriatic, a prerequisite of any Soviet offer, a loan would also neccessitate centralising the system. This form of centralisation would be quite different from the West's, and would imply a destruction of Self-Management and a return to the old Five Year Plan system.

Both sources of loan are therefore barbed with implications that are politically unacceptable, as each would effectively lead to the end of the present system. Nevertheless both have their adherents in the hierarchy, and it's this split which is broadly responsible for the fierce internal party debate now in progress. So far, the current Prime Minister **Milka Planinc** has looked to the

West for loans, but her programme of reform which went with the money has met with strong opposition from pro-Soviet elements in the party bureaucracy and those who see IMF money as an economic lever to edge the country closer to the West. At the other end of the scale there's criticism from the liberal reformers that the programme is not going far enough. Membership of the League of Communists is rapidly declining, and intellectuals are beginning to question whether the party is the correct vehicle for modernisation and change. This 'questioning' has recently gone too far for the authorities, who've begun to take a hard line on dissidents. A series of **political trials** in late 1984 meted out severe sentences to these intellectuals in an attempt to establish clear parameters to the debate.

The biggest fear for the authorities is that these political/economic differences get translated into regional disputes. As federal resources diminish, the temptation is for each Republic to feel it is not getting its fair share: Croatia has always been suspicious of Serbian power, and since 1970 a few nationalist groups have pushed for leaving the federation. A more worrying nationalistic problem is posed by **Kosovo**, where the Albanian majority have long demanded full Republic status. In 1981 their demands boiled over into full-bloodied riots which were suppressed only after tanks moved in. The Muslim Albanians have a strong case for full republic status, but the authorities cannot give it for fear the new republic will take advantage of the constitution which allows Republics to cede from the federation. The army's tanks may have muted the unrest but they haven't solved the problem: dissent in Kosovo has gone underground and central government intransigence has driven some activists closer to Albania.

The question for Kosovo, and for the country as a whole, is where to go from here: Planinc can only walk the tightrope for a time, and if her reforms aren't successful there will be plenty of party factions waiting to push her off. But, for the moment at least, Yugoslavia is still firmly unified, and, providing it can sort out its economic problems, seems destined to remain so for the years to come.

Factionalism and fighting: a political update

1988 and 1989 saw a dramatic worsening in relations between Serbs and ethnic Albanians in Kosovo. Long-standing differences were exacerbated by the rise of **Slobodan Milošević**, leader of the Serbian Party, whose dynamic personality and uncompromising political views rocketed him from comparative obscurity to the position of president of the Serbian Republic. Milošević, whose speeches have become increasingly anti-Albanian, argues that Serbia contains 40% of the country's population and a third of its land: yet in the federation of republics that constitutes Yugoslavia, is only one voice among eight – including the two autonomous provinces. Furthermore, with the six-hundredth anniversary of the Battle of Kosovo approaching, his speeches have stirred local sentiment by constantly playing on the myth of the Serbian Golden Age.

Milošević's popularity in championing the cause of the minority Serbs in Kosovo, combined with a hard-line approach to any minor civil disturbance by Albanians, led to an underground **hunger strike** by 1300 miners at the Trepca zinc mine near Priština in February 1989. After occupying the mine for eight days, the miners gave up their strike when several prominent Kosovo Communist party officials were removed from office. In the meantime, the Yugoslav president had sent in a large number of troops, realising that if any of the miners died (and many were close), Kosovo could well have seen a full-blooded rebellion.

The following weeks saw an unprecedented backlash against the Albanian community throughout the whole of Serbia. Massive **demonstrations**, often led by students, took place in Belgrade, and Novi Sad, capital of Serbia's other autonomous province, the Vojvodina, had the largest demonstration in its history. Milošević-inspired demonstrations also focused dissatisfaction with the worsening economic situation, dislodging the party leaderships in the Vojvodina and Montenegro. On 23 February the Serbian government passed amendments to the constitution effectively removing Kosovo's autonomy: Serbia gained control over its police, courts and civil defence, and moved a hundred tanks and 15,000 troops into the region to underline its control. **Riots** broke out in **Uroševac**, the police stormed the university at Priština and surrounded the Kosovo national assembly. A few days later the inevitable happened and demonstrations by ethnic Albanians turned into pitched battles with the police: two senior police officials were killed (one an ethnic Albanian, the other a Serb), and, officially, 29 other people were shot dead by police, though the true figures are probably much higher. From that date, Kosovo has effectively been under Serbian army occupation, and though the atmosphere has calmed, it seems likely that it could flare up at any moment.

The Kosovo question has crucial implications for the Yugoslav federation. With the hugely popular Milošević apparently pursuing the formation of a Greater Serbia, in direct opposition to the tenets of Titoism, the outlook for the country is bleak. Party officials in Croatia, Serbia's old enemy, were quick to voice support for the draconian anti-Albanian measures, but the feeling on the streets of Zagreb is of support for the ethnic community against what is seen as Serbian bullying: the Croat Communist Party newspaper, *Vjesnik* even likened Milošević's recently-published memoirs to *Mein Kampf*. Meanwhile Macedonia and Montenegro bear the brunt of the country's increasingly dire economic situation, while the richer republic of Slovenia seems to be steadily turning its back on the rest of country, looking economically, culturally and touristically towards the north. It does seem as if the old guard is on the way out – in spite of Milošević – and that most people think the only long-term economic solution is to shake up the country's inefficient and often corrupt system; there has lately been talk of joining EFTA, perhaps later even the EEC. But for the moment the future of Tito's great ideal of unification, and indeed of Yugoslav Communism itself, now seems fractured and deeply uncertain. As a Croatian journalist recently wrote, 'We have had two beautiful dreams imposed on us, Communism and Yugoslavia. Perhaps even one of them would have been too much'.

ARCHITECTURAL CHRONOLOGY

6000BC	Earliest settlements along the Danube.	Archaic village of **Lepenski Vir** – discovered in 1965 – oldest known Neolithic settlement in Europe.
C12BC	Illyrian and Thracian tribes inhabit the Balkans.	
C8–6BC	Coast colonised by Greek trading ports.	Few existing remains: small finds, jewellery and artifacts.
C4	Greek cities spring up along trade routes.	**Stobi** and **Heraclea** founded in 350 by Philip II of Macedonia. Trogir's *Relief of Kairos* shows Hellenistic decorative style.
229BC	**Roman conquest** of Balkan and Illyrian tribes begins.	**Pula's amphitheatre** built in grand imperial style – rich arcading and decoration. **Salona** (Solin) typical of early Roman towns.
AD285	Diocletian divides his empire into east and west.	**Diocletian's Palace** at Split: monumental and lavish complex of temples, apartments and garrison built as a retirement home for the emperor. **Hereclea** shows the zenith of Roman art: mosaics on early Christian themes combined with Hellenistic styles.
C6–7	**Slav migration**. Slav culture established in Balkans. First influence of Christianity through missionary teaching.	Slav tribes raid and destroy Roman towns and establish their own settlements. The **basilica of Bishop Euphrasius** in Poreč is the finest early Christian building on the coast – elaborate mosaics.
C9	Cyril and Methodius initiate conversion of Serbs to Eastern (Orthodox) church in Macedonia. Cultural influence of **Byzantium** spreads. **Serbian state** founded in defiance against Byzantine expansionism.	Earliest Byzantine churches at Cyril and Methodius' base, Ohrid, later destroyed by Turks. In **Zadar**, **Sv Donat** has elements of Byzantine and Carolingian style.
C10–11	Ohrid becomes centre of early Christianity and Byzantine influence.	Ohrid's **Sv Sophia** (1040) – has rich representational frescoes – the first two-dimensional religious art of the Christian era in the Balkans. **Sv Panteleimon** (1164) at Nerezi perfects the Byzantine fresco style.
Late C12	**Nemanja Dynasty**.	**Studenica** (1209) is the first great monastery church of the Raška style. Following the fall of Constantinople the greatest fresco artists of the period leave the city and work on the Raška churches, producing the highly decorated monasteries of **Sopoćani** (1265) and **Mileševa** (1234).
C13	Serbian Patriarchate established at Peć.	Building of churches at Peć begins; **Church of the Apostles** completed *c.*1250. The monastery churches of Gračanica (1314), Staro Nagoričane (1318).

C14–C14	Golden era of Serbian state. Domestic architecture flourishes under Serban kings.	**Stecci**. Bogomil memorial stones, scattered over Bosnia-Hercegovina. Main concentration at Radimlja near Mostar.
1389	Battle of Kosovo: beginning of Turkish hegemony in Balkans.	Spread of **Ottoman empire** into Balkans brings Turkish-style architecture. Serbs are pushed north, the Morava valley becoming the final site of monastery building, **Manasija** (1418) and **Kalenić** (1413) strongly defended against Turkish attack. Serbian lords build castles in defensive positions at **Smederovo** (1430) and elsewhere.
1420	**Venice** occupies the coast.	**Romanesque architecture** includes the cathedrals of **Rab** and **Zadar**. **Venetian-Gothic** buildings spread down the coast: the cathedrals of **Split** and **Trogir**; countless **campinili**.
Mid C16	**Dubrovnik** achieves *de facto* independence as city-state.	Italian architects (such as Michelozzi) employed to build Dubrovnik's places and churches: they work with local architects, notably Juraj Dalmatinac, who also designed **Šibenik cathedral** (begun 1431) and **Pag's old centre**.
C16–17	**Turkish presence** in Bosnia-Hercegovina strengthens.	**Gazi Husref Beg mosque** in Sarajevo (1531), bridges at **Višegrad** and **Mostar** are good examples of Turkish architecture.
1690	Serb migration into the Vojvodina.	**Vrdnik** and **Krušedo'** are among several Baroque-Byzantine monastery churches founded by migrant Serbs in the Fruška Gora.
1697	Prince Eugene of Savoy liberates parts of the north from the Turks; they become part of his **Habsburg Empire**.	The great fortresses of **Kalemegdan** and **Petrovaradin** are built to protect Austria from Turkish threat.
C18	Continued skirmishes between Turks and Serbs. Further movement of Serbs north.	Italian Francesco Robba designs Baroque churches and monuments in Ljubljana. His pupils are responsible for highly ornate buildings throughout Slovenia.
1877	End of Turkish hegemony: **Austria-Hungary** takes control of **Slovenia**, **Bosnia**, the north of **Croatia** and **Serbia**.	Austrian-style town houses built; civic architecture follows Classical or pseudo-Moorish themes. New road and rail systems open up the country.
1920	Establishment of monarchist Yugoslav state	
1945	Liberation from occupying Facist forces; beginning of Socialist Federation of Yugoslavia, led by Tito.	Repair to damage caused by Allied and Axis bombing; post-war housing shortage met by rapid building of high-rise blocks. Spate of monumental memorials to the war of liberation.

| 1963 | Earthquake in Skopje. | Much of modern town destroyed. International designs used for new centre include rail station, arts centre and post office. |
| 1980 | Death of Tito. | |

SERBIAN MONASTERIES AND THEIR FRESCOES

This is intended as a brief background to Eastern Orthodoxy, its architecture, frescoes and the styles of medieval Serbian church building. Throughout, Serbia refers to at least the area of the present-day republic; more often than not it includes today's Macedonia and sometimes the greater part of the Balkans themselves. Dates after churches refer to the completion of the frescoes; completion of the church could be anything up to a decade earlier.

Built by the medieval kings of the Nemanjic dynasty, which flourished from the late C12 until the early 1400s, and richly decorated with frescoes, Serbia's monastic churches represent some of the finest achievements of the Byzantine era. First and most astute of Serbian monarchs was **Stefan Nemanja**, who through a series of pacts and cunning allegiancies, broke free from the sway of Byzantium in 1190 and forged an independent Serbian state, initiating a **Golden Age** that Serbs look back on with pride. It was a civilised time – one story goes that when initialling a treaty with the Holy Roman Emperor Fredrick Barbarossa, Nemenja signed himself in a rich flowing hand while the Emperor could only manage an oafish thumbprint – with an explosion of Christian creativity that can be compared to the years leading up to the Italian Renaissance. Serbia developed a sophisticated oral literature and a national art and architecture, its kings producing a spate of small but richly decorated churches to house their bones for posterity. The peripatetic nature of the Serbian court led to a broad scattering of these monuments, and deliberately isolated monastic churches perch in supremely remote spots all over the country. When the Turks arrived in the C15 they either demolished them or turned them into mosques, covering the frescoes with plaster. Few survived intact, and it wasn't until this century that the churches were restored, the plaster chipped off their frescoes and the buildings once again turned over to monastic communities.

Serbia took its Christianity – **Eastern Orthodoxy** – from Constantinople: only the Orthodox Church could offer the Serbs a Patriarchate of their own and

anyway the country's ties with the east had always been stronger. The contemplative nature of Orthodox Christianity has always been important, shaping a monasticism more concerned with 'communion with God' than the pastoral nature of western monastic orders. Prayer and meditation could be undertaken either solitarily, which led to the oddly ascetic leanings of Orthodox monks – living in caves, wearing hairshirts, etc. – or communally, in a meditative monastic community. Centre of Orthodox monasticism is the Athos peninsula in northern Greece, where a number of monasteries make up an autonomous republic. The early Serbian rulers looked to here for inspiration and enlightenment, often retiring in old age to *Chilandar* – the Serbian Orthodox monastery which still exists today.

Orthodox churches differ from those in the west in a number of ways: naves and choir are replaced by a centralised circular or square plan, frequently domed (an intimation of Heaven) following the inspiration of the Emperor Justinian's C6 Cathedral of St Sophia in Constantinople. There are no seats – the congregation always stands – and the apse is separated from the main body of the church by an *iconostasis* – a heavy screen pierced by doors and richly decorated with the icons that form an integral part of Orthodox worship, acting as a sort of visual aid to the liturgy. Behind, the priest prepares bread and wine before the liturgy is sung.

But the most distinctive feature of the medieval Serbian church is its **frescoes** – attempts to encompass the entire heavenly kingdom as a background against which man could achieve ultimate union with God and so be cleansed of all sin. Frescoes were the medieval alternative to mosaics, which until then had been the principal form of church decoration. They had a number of advantages: not only were they considerably cheaper, but they lent themselves to a similarly monumental style and were almost as durable if executed properly. Painters would work quickly, usually in pairs, one grinding the pigments while another plastered the walls. First step was to apply several coats of lime plaster – usually four – and

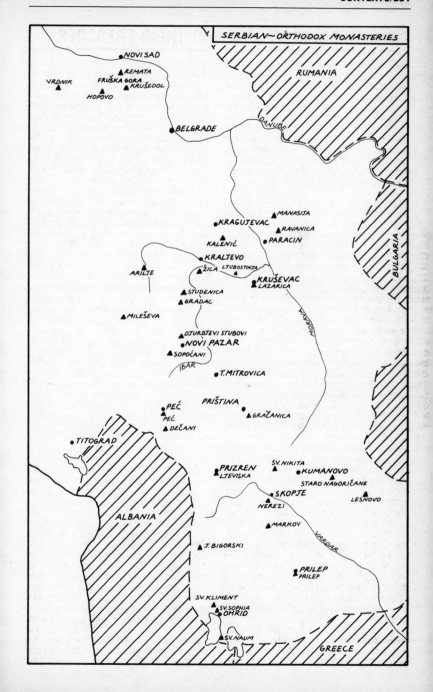

after the penultimate was dry, trace on a rough cartoon of the intended work. This was covered with a final coat and the diluted pigment painted straight on while the plaster was still wet and absorbent, so that the paint fused with wall itself rather than just remaining a surface layer; only later touching-up would have been done on dry plaster. Frescoes then, for all the preparation involved, were a quick and spontaneous medium, much less deliberate than mosaics. Finished, they were meant to be seen not as individual works but as part of the scheme for the church as a whole, and conventions had to be observed in their arrangement: *Christ Pantocrator* (Christ as Ruler of All) commonly gazes majestically from the central dome; the Virgin ascends to Heaven on the west wall of the nave; saints line the apse and, in Serbian churches at least, it was normal to paint a portrait of the dead king/donor being presented to the Virgin.

To the Byzantines, images were seen as paralleling the physical manifestation of God on Earth in Christ, so experiments in style were dangerous and rare. Nevertheless distinct stylistic developments, not only in Serbian architecture but in painting too, fall into three separate but related categories – the Raška, Serbo-Byzantine and Morava Schools. **Pre-Nemanjic foundations** went up in clutches in what is now Macedonia: **Sv Sophia** (1040) in Ohrid and **Sv Pantele-meion** (1164) in Nerezi near Skopje are the best surviving examples.

The **Raška School** style dates from the foundation of the Serbian state in the late C12th to the closing years of the 13th. Named after the capital of the early

rulers, it's more western, more estranged from Byzantium and consequently the most Serbian of the three; Nemanja's early kingdom was in many ways just as attached to Europe as it was to Constantinople. The influence of Roman-esque architecture is unmistakeable, with friezes of arcading and sculpted human, animal and vegetable decor-ation around doors and windows; the lunettes above portals often contain compositions – pietàs, nativities – in high relief. All churches were built of stone and a few, richer creations have façades of highly polished marble. Inside they're characterised by an absence of aisles, a central apse and raised dome, with deep side recesses that would later become transepts. Frescoes were kept deliberately simple, both in style and subject-matter, the technique monu-mental, focusing on well-known motifs from the Gospels – the *Last Supper*, the *Crucifixion* and particularly the *Dormition of the Virgin* were popular scenes. As time went on ancillary buildings – narthex and outer narthex – came to be adorned with 'profane' subjects – representations of kings and queens and historic events – but in the nave a strict iconography continued to be observed. Principal Raška School churches still standing include **Studenica** (1209), **Žiča** (1219), **Mile-ševa** (1237), **Sopoćani** (1265), **Peć** (1263), **Morača** (1252), **Gradac** (1275), and **Arilje** (1295).

As King Milutin extended Serbia into a fully-fledged empire so architecture took a new turn, resulting in the creations of the **Serbo-Byzantine School**, which flourished from the late C13 until Serbia was forced to yield to the Turks and flee

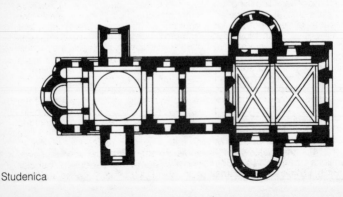

Studenica

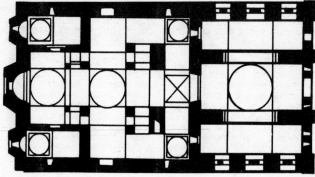

Gračanica

north. Under Milutin and his immediate successors Serbia was stronger than it had ever been, stretching its boundaries south and regaining the Byzantine strain it had to some extent lost; more than any other the Serbo-Byzantine School retains clear links with eastern tradition, turning the cruciform plan into a cross-in-square and topping churches with a profusion of domes and cupolas; important churches have four cupolas crowding around a central dome. The external sculpting so prevalent in the Raška churches is almost completely lacking here. Instead, façades were striped alternately with different coloured bricks and slats of stone, combining with the tiers of roofs and cupolas to produce a rich, exotic and more markedly oriental effect. The Gospels were still the chief source of inspiration for fresco artists, but were now combined with apocryphal stories, lives of saints, scenes from the church calendar and freer depictions of royalty – a new variety of material that led to less monumental scenes, breaking up church interiors into smaller, more varied panels. It became more important for paintings to tell a story than move the viewer, and the serene figures of Studenica and Sopoćani gradually gave way to livelier, expressive characters, captured in a landscape or standing in front of buildings – **Dečani** (1350) is probably the best example of this new narrative form. Major Serbo-Byzantine churches still standing include **Gračanica** (1320), **Bogdorica Ljeviska** in Prizren (1307), the **King's Church in Studenica** (1314), the later Archbishop's additions to **Peć** (1324/37), **Lesnovo** (1349), **Staro Nagoričane**

near Kumanovo (1318) and **Sv Kliment** in Ohrid (1295).

After the death of Stefan Dušan the Serbian empire slowly began to fall away, until the very existence of the Serbian state itself was threatened. The Turks swept relentlessly north through Macedonia, defeating the Serbs at Kosovo in 1389 and forcing them to take refuge in the hills of the Morava valley – safe, for the moment at least, from the clutches of the invaders. This signalled a fresh era in architecture – the **Morava School** – in which the Serbs continued, bloodied but unbowed, to build churches until the Turks were virtually on their doorstep. Church exteriors continued the candy-striped brickwork of the Serbo-Byzantine School but added touches from Raška, sculpting animal and vegetable motifs in low relief on doors and windows, and making first-time use of baked clay as well as stone. Buildings also kept their multiple domes, but were cut into a three-apsed trefoil plan that had arrived via Macedonia from Mount Athos. On the whole the churches of this period are simpler, less grandiose than their predecessors, almost as if in their quietness, they anticipate and symbolise the eclipse of the Serbian state. Frescoes too, were in some ways a meeting of previous styles, combining the inquisitive invention of the Serbo-Byzantine artists with the calm restrained technique of the Raška painters. Characteristics include accomplished drawing, imaginative use of colour and a spirited adaption of subject-matter; urbane *warrior saints* and *Christ's Miracles* became popular subjects, but in many cases painters

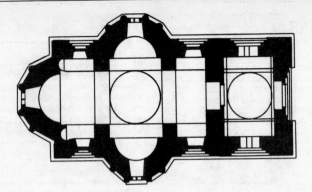

Kalenić

were content to produce placid evocations of their age. Principal Morava School churches include the **Lazarica** church at Kruševac (1370), **Ravanica** (1381), **Kalenić** (1413), **Manasija** (1418) and **Ljubostinja** (1405).

With Serbia firmly under the Ottomans, art and creativity stagnated. Morava School styles found their way to nearby Orthodox countries – Russia, Greece and especially Romania – and in the late C17 the monks and Christian artists and architects of the monasteries fled north of the Danube to the Habsburg Vojvodina, where they built new churches and monasteries – nostalgic communes that echoed those of Serbia's golden age; **Hopova**, **Krušedol** and **Vrdnik** are three examples. Later, while the rest of the country still suffered under the Turks, the Vojvodina became a flourishing centre for Serbian culture and arts, awakening a national consciousness that had been long considered dead.

BOOKS

Travel

Rebecca West, *Black Lamb and Grey Falcon* (Papermac £8.95) A remarkable piece of writing, erudite and all-embracing, and really the definitive work on Yugoslavia before the war. This is the sort of book you can dip into again and again, and it's only spoilt by some naively optimistic conclusions on a country that was, at the time (1937), a dictatorship. If the price is beyond you – though it really is worth every penny – *The Essential Rebecca West* (Penguin £4.95) includes a fairly representative chunk.

M. E. Durham, *Through the Lands of the Serbs* Mary Durham was one of the most intrepid of women explorers, and her (numerous) adventures through the Balkans make for captivating reading. Something of a folk hero in Albania, where streets are still named in her honour, her *High Albania*, published by Virago, contains a fair portion on Kosovo.

Sir Arthur Evans, *Through Bosnia and Hercogovina on Foot during the Insurrection* (Arno Press) An exciting and humorous account of a difficult and eventful trek by the youthful Evans as Turkish control crumbled. Buoyantly written, and good for Islamic background.

Sir J. Gardiner Wilkinson, *Dalmatia and Montenegro* Another stalwart C19th Brit braves what were then wild and unknown lands and unearths some interesting tales and facts.

Abbè Fortis, *Travels into Dalmatia* Bigoted but entertaining C18th Venetian on a voyage around the colonies.

Bernard Newman, *Tito's Yugoslavia* (Hale o/p) This avuncular and very English thriller writer once cycled through Yugoslavia and retraces his steps in a readable account of the country shortly after the war.

Evelyn Waugh, *Unconditional Surrender* (Penguin £1.95) Evelyn Waugh was sent to Yugoslavia as a liaison officer in the 1940s, and fictionalised his distaste for Partisan reprisals in this, the final volume of the *Sword of Honour* trilogy. If you can stand his politics, the acid style is brilliant.

Fitzroy Maclean, *Eastern Approaches* (Papermac £5.95) Fitzroy Maclean led the British mission to the Partisans during the war, and he's now held in some esteem throughout Yugoslavia. Basically an autobiography, this includes a racy account of the wartime struggle – compulsory reading for anyone remotely interested in the period or the country, or just Maclean himself. His *Disputed Barricades*, long out of print, is an excellent biography of Tito – and altogether a cogent resumé of C20th Yugoslav history.

History and politics

Fred Singleton, *A Short History of the Yugoslav Peoples* (CUP £6.50) Brand new, and the most complete history of the country you can buy.

Phyllis Auty, *Tito* (Penguin o/p) Probably the most complete – and impartial – biography of Tito by an English-speaking writer.

Milovan Djilas, *Tito* (Wiedenfield & Nicolson £7.95) By Yugoslavia's longest-running dissident and sensationally subtitled 'The Story from Inside', this is fascinating – especially after the adulation heaped upon Tito from other quarters. Djilas's rambling reminiscences present a fumbling military commander and scheming politician, motivated more by self-interest and a lust for power and luxury than anything else.

Art and architecture

T. G. Jackson, *Dalmatia, the Quarnero and Istria* First published in 1887 and unavailable now outside the better-stocked libraries, this is an illuminating three-volume guide to the art and, particularly, the architecture of the Adriatic coast.

Anne Kindersley, *The Mountains of Serbia* (John Murray £6.95) Highly personal but packed with information – a fine book if you want to read about the Serbian monasteries.

David Talbot Rice, *Art of the Byzantine Era* (Thames & Hudson £3.95) Informed and comprehensive appreciation of Byzantine icons and frescoes, with a chapter specifically devoted to Serbia. As a supplement see the Pelican guides to *Early Christian and Byzantine Art* and *Architecture* (both £9.95).

Literature

Yugoslav Short Stories (ed. S. Koljević; OUP 1966); *Introduction to Yugoslav Literature* (ed. B. Mikasinović; Twayne 1973); *New Writing in Yugoslavia* (ed. B. Johnson; Penguin 1970). These represent the most complete summation of C20th literary trends – if you can get hold of them.

Milne Holton (ed.), *The Big Horse and Other Stories of Modern Macedonia* (University of Missouri Press) Broad selection of contemporary Macedonian short stories, one of which is reprinted on p. 243.

Ivo Andrić, *The Bridge on the Drina* (Phoenix 1977) The most widely read work by Yugoslavia's only internationally known novelist. Others available in Britain include *Devil's Yard* (Greenwood 1975) and *The Pasha's Concubine and Other Tales* (Allen and Unwin 1969). For more on Andrić, and an extract from his *Bosnian Story*, see opposite.

Danilo Kiš, *Garden, Ashes* (Faber £3.95) Lyrical, sometimes turgid, novel by one of Serbia's most highly regarded contemporary writers.

YUGOSLAV FICTION

AN EXTRACT FROM 'BOSNIAN STORY'

Born in 1892, IVO ANDRIĆ is possibly Yugoslavia's best known author. Despite writing almost exclusively on his own country – particularly his native Bosnia – Andrić's insight into a people under foreign domination brought international critical praise, culminating in the Nobel Prize for Literature in 1961. The Bridge on the Drina, a fictionalised history of the town and people of Višegrad, established his reputation. A Travnik Chronicle, published in England in 1961 as Bosnian Story is perhaps the most accessible of his works, analysing the effects and intrigues in the Turkish controlled town. Ivo Andrić died in 1975.

At the beginning of the year 1807 extraordinary things began to happen at Travnik, such things as had never been known before.

No one in Travnik had ever supposed that the town was made for an ordinary life or for the trivial daily round – no one, not even the humblest true-believer in the backstreets. This basic feeling, that they were in some way different from the rest of the world, created and called to something better and higher, entered into every single human soul with the cold wind from the hillside, with the running waters of Šumeć, with the sweet-flavoured corn from the sunny fields about the town, and it never left them, even in sleep or poverty or in the hour of death itself.

This was true in the first instance of the Moslems who lived in the town. But even the lesser breeds of all three religions, scattered about the steep slopes or crammed together in a separate suburb, were filled with the same feeling, each man after his own fashion and according to his station in life. This was also true of their town itself which had something in its situation and plan which was peculiar, personal and proud.

Travnik was, in point of fact, a deep and narrow gorge, which successive generations had in the course of time built over and brought under cultivation, a fortified passageway in which men had settled down to live permanently, adapting themselves to it and it to themselves as the centuries went by. On both sides the hills divide steeply, crowding close together at a sharp bend in the valley, where there is barely room for the meagre river and the road beside it. The whole shape of the place is like a half-opened book, both pages of which are, as it were, illuminated with gardens, streets, houses, fields, graveyards and mosques.

No one has ever worked out the number of hours of sunshine of which Nature has docked this town, but undoubtedly the sun rises later here and sets earlier than in any other of the many towns and townlets of Bosnia. Even the people of Travnik do not deny this, but they add that while the sun does shine over their town, it shines as it does nowhere else.

In this narrow valley, in the bottom of which the Lašva flows and whose sides sparkle with springs, runlets and streams, a valley full of damp and draughts, there is hardly anywhere a straight road or a piece of level ground where a man can set his foot freely and without taking heed. Everywhere it is steep and uneven, tangled and intertwined, wound about and split up by private roads, fences, blind alleys, gardens and wicket gates, graveyards or places of worship.

Here, by the side of the water, that mysterious, unstable and powerful element, the generations of Travnik are born and die. Here they grow to manhood, sickly and pale, but tough and equal to anything life may bring. Here they live, with the Vizier's Residence ever before their eyes, proud, neat, fastidious and sly; here they work and thrive or sit idle and grow poor. Invariably canny and reserved, they never laugh aloud but they are not incapable of a smile; they talk little and prefer to talk scandal in whispers. And here, in waterlogged graveyards, they are buried when their time comes, each after his own faith and custom, and give place to a posterity like themselves.

Thus the generations change, transmitting one to another not only a peculiar personal heritage of body and mind, but a country and a religion; not only a hereditary sense of what is right and fitting and an ability to recognize and distinguish all the various paths, gateways and alleys of their intricate town but also an inborn aptitude for knowledge of the world and of men in general. All these qualities are the endowment of every Travnik baby as it comes into the world, but above all the quality of pride. *Pride is their second nature*, a living force which never leaves them but governs them and sets upon them a visible mark by which they may be known from the rest of mankind.

Their pride has nothing in common with the simple bumptiousness of prosperous peasants or of small country-townsmen who, when satisfied with themselves, swell visibly and are loud in self-congratulation. On the contrary, the pride of Travnik is all within; *it is more like a burdensome inheritance*, a painful duty towards oneself, one's family and one's town, or, strictly speaking, towards the exalted, lofty and unapproachable idea which the people of Travnik have of themselves and their city.

Still, every human emotion has its proper limits, and so has the feeling of one's own greatness. Certainly Travnik is the *seat of a Vizier* and its people are well-kept and well-bred, sensible and wise enough to talk with kings: but there came days when, even to them, their pride became a millstone about their neck and they could have wished to live instead, peaceful and carefree, in one of those obscure and ordinary market-towns which do not figure in the calculations of kings or in the quarrels of states and do not lie within the range of world events nor in the path of renowned and powerful men.

By now the times were such that there was no hope of anything at all agreeable and absolutely no expectation of positive good. For that reason the shrewd and self-reliant men of Travnik hoped that in fact nothing would happen and that life would go on, as far as possible, without change or surprises. What good could come of a time when kings were falling out, nations were giving each other bloody noses and whole countrysides were in flames? A new Vizier? He would be no better and no worse than the one before and his staff would be unknown

men, numerous, ravenous and possessed with God knows what new forms of covetousness. ('The best Vizier we ever had', they used to say, 'was the one who got as far as the frontier, then went back to Stamboul and never set foot in Bosnia.' Some stranger, a distinguished traveller, perhaps? – But we know what that means. They leave a little cash and a few presents in the town but after them comes retribution or, next day at least, a police inquiry and investigation. Who were they, what were they, where did they spend the night, who did they talk to? And in disentangling and clearing yourself, you lose ten times over any amount you may have made. Well then, a foreign spy? Or some confidential agent, of unknown authority and dubious intentions? The fact is you never can tell who is what, what he may have on him or whose outrider he may be.

In short, there's no luck to be had these days. Still, here's bread and here's one more day left to a man to eat and live through in peace in his finest of all the towns on earth, and God keep us from the public eye, from distinguished visitors and from great events.

Such, in these first years of the nineteenth century, were the inmost thoughts and wishes of the leading men of Travnik, but it goes without saying that they kept them to themselves: for in Travnik there lies between a wish or a thought and its visible or audible expression a long and devious road which is not easily traversed.

In recent times, at the end of the eighteenth and the beginning of the nineteenth century, there had been events and changes enough a great many in fact and in every direction. Events came pouring in from all sides, they clashed and eddied all over Europe and the great Ottoman Empire, and penetrated even into this little pocket of earth and collected there like floodwater or the silt of streams.

Ever since the Turks had withdrawn from Hungary, relations between Moslems and Christians had grown steadily worse and more involved and, in general, more bitter. The soldiers of the great Empire, the *Agas* and *Spahis*, who had been forced to leave their rich settlements in the fertile plains of Hungary and to return to their own poor, constricted country, were full of rage and illwill against everything Christian; at the same time they increased the number of mouths to be fed, while the number of hands to labour remained as before. On the other hand, these same wars of the eighteenth century which had driven the Turks out of the neighbouring Christian lands and sent them back to Bosnia had aroused bold hopes in the subject Christians and had opened up prospects hitherto undreamt of; and this too was bound to have its effect on the attitude of the *rayah* towards his imperial over-lord the Turk. Both sides – if one may talk of two sides at this stage of the struggle – both sides fought after their own manner and employed whatever tactics opportunity and the times might offer. The Turks resorted to repression and force, the Christians to passive resistance, guile and conspiracy, or readiness to conspire. The Turks fought in defence of their right to live and their own manner of life, the Christians for their own attainment of that same right. The Christians felt that the Turks were becoming steadily more oppressive and the Turks observed with bitterness that the Christians were beginning to give themselves airs and were no longer what they used to be. Out of this conflict of such opposite interests, beliefs, aspirations and hopes, there grew a painful tension which the long Turkish wars with Venice, Austria and Russia continually heightened and concentrated. In Bosnia the atmosphere grew heavier and darker, clashes became more frequent and life more difficult; everywhere there was less order and less assurance. The opening of the nineteenth century had brought the rising in Serbia as the visible sign of a new era and with it new tactics. The tension in Bosnia grew sharper and tighter still.

As time went on, the revolt in Serbia caused increasing anxiety, dissension, damage, expense and loss throughout Turkish Bosnia, and consequently to Travnik as well, though more to the Vizier, the authorities and the other Bosnian towns than to the Moslems of Travnik itself. They were not prepared to consider any war great or important enough to warrant their contributing their wealth, let alone their persons. Of 'Kara-

george's rising' the Travnik Turks spoke with a rather forced contempt, just as they always found some disparaging word for the forces which the Vizier sent against Serbia and which the irresolute and squabbling local commanders assembled, slowly and in disorder, in the neighbourhood of Travnik.

Napoleon's campaigns in Europe had long been a favourite subject of conversation in the town. At first men had talked of them as of distant events which might be explained and described but which had not, and could not have, any connection with their own daily lives. The arrival of the French army in Dalmatia suddenly brought this legendary 'Bonaparte' a good deal nearer to Bosnia and Travnik.

At the same time there came to Travnik a *new Vizier, Husrev Mehmed Pasha*, bringing with him a deep admiration for Napoleon and an interest in everything French, and that, as Travnik found, in a far higher degree than was fitting for an Osmanli and for a high official of the Turkish Empire.

All this disquieted and annoyed the Moslems of Travnik and they began to express their feelings about Napoleon and his exploits in short, non-committal sentences or simply by a lofty and contemptuous pursing of the lips. Even so, none of this could entirely remove and protect them from this same Bonaparte and from the events which with miraculous speed radiated from him all over Europe as a circular ripple radiates from its centre, and which, like fire or the plague, overtook alike the man who ran from them and the man who sat still at home. This invisible and unknown conqueror plunged Travnik into unrest, commotion and excitement, as he did so many other cities of the world. For years to come the stern, resounding name of Bonaparte was to fill this Bosnian valley, and whether they would or no the people of Travnik were often to mouth its knotty, angular syllables; it was long to echo in their ears and hover before their eyes. The 'Consular Age' had arrived.

© *Agencija Jugoslovenska Autoska 1961. (Translation Kenneth Johnstone.)*

ALBANIAN TALES FROM KOSOVO

Before 1945 the Albanian language was outlawed in Kosovo, and any literature was purely oral – tales, riddles, poems and proverbs told by villagers gathered together on winter evenings, and often accompanied by the one-string lahuta or two-string çifteli. Often stories would be moral messages, others recall with pride the old patriarchal society, but many are simply and deeply humorous and meant to entertain. As men and women never mixed together in company, they developed separate literatures: the tales that follow are men's stories, translated by John Hodgson from the collections of Anton Çetta, a folklorist who has worked for over 30 years to preserve in written form the declining oral tradition.

Your Wishes Are Granted

Once, in the old time of the king, three soldiers set out from the town of Prizren. When they reached Sopia bridge, heavy rain began to fall, and the soldiers took shelter under the bridge. When the rain stopped, the Pasha left the town to see what damage the rain had done to the crops, for it was harvest time. When he reached the bridge, he paused to look at the fields. He heard the soldiers talking, and stopped to listen. The soldiers were asking each other: 'What would you most like to have in this world?'

One said: 'I would not ask anything from God except to be able to go home for two hours to see my father and mother.'

'The only thing that I would want in this world would be to have the Pasha's daughter for my wife.'

The third said: 'I would ask God to have all my debts paid, so that I wouldn't owe anybody a penny.'

A few days later, the Pasha summoned the soldiers before him, and said to them: 'What did you each say under Sopia bridge that day of the heavy rain?'

At first the soldiers did not want to speak, but the Pasha forced them and in the end they told him exactly what they had said.

To the first soldier, who had only wanted to go home for two hours, the Pasha gave a month's leave.

To the second, who had wanted his daughter for his wife, the Pasha said: 'I'll call for her at once, and I wish you joy of her.'

He asked the third: 'What did you ask for?'

'I asked for enough to be able to pay my debts, so as not to owe anybody a penny.'

The Pasha said: 'Debts are with us until the day we die.'

And he took his sword and cut off the man's head.

Told by Selim Bucaj, from the village of Llodrovc.

The Poor Boy Who Cheated the Whole Village

In days long ago there was a poor boy who lived with his mother. They possessed nothing but a single cow. One day, he said to his mother: 'Let's kill the cow and ask the whole village to dinner, and give what's left of the meat to our neighbours. We have plenty of neighbours, and they always have animals to kill. And when they slaughter their cows, then they'll invite us to dinner and give us meat, and we'll live a little better than with our dry bread.'

So they slaughtered the cow, cooked a big dinner, and gave away the rest of the meat. A few days went by, and they waited for invitations, but none came. They waited for presents of meat. Nothing. They hadn't a bite in the house. So the boy took the hide of their dead cow and carried it to the city to sell. But nobody offered a single penny for it. He walked the city streets all day and towards dusk left the town and set off again home. But he was sorry to return empty-handed, and thought that he would stay in the town one more night, take the hide to market again the next day and perhaps sell it. And he wrapped himself up in the skin and lay down to sleep in a meadow outside the town. At dawn, the crows saw the hide and thought it was a dead animal. They swooped down upon it. The boy reached out one hand and grabbed a crow. He got up and, carrying the hide in one hand and the crow in another, went back to the city. He carried the two about all day, but still nobody would give him a single penny for his hide. Night fell, and the poor boy wanted somewhere to sleep. He knocked at some gates. A lady appeared and asked him: 'What do you want?'

'Can I sleep here? I'm not asking for a room or anything decent – just somewhere in the yard where the dog won't eat me.'

The woman invited him in, and allowed him to sleep on the porch.

So the boy wrapped himself in his hide again and lay down to sleep. But after a short time there came another knock at the gates. The woman appeared and opened the door. It was not the master of the house. The boy emerged from his hide and peered through a chink in the door. So this was the woman's lover. The man had brought a roast chicken, fruit, brandy, tobacco, and other things – an entire spread. The couple ate and ate and then went to bed. But just as they were settling down, the lady's husband knocked at the door. Her lover didn't know what to do – but the woman said: 'Quick, into the wardrobe.'

So he hid himself in the wardrobe, and the woman hid all the food in chests and cupboards around the room – some in one place and some in another. She went outside to open the gates, and at once rushed back and huddled under the blankets. The boy lay there wrapped in his hide, as if he had seen nothing. But the master of the house tripped over him as he passed through the porch, and said: 'What are you doing here?'

'I'm just a poor man. I've brought this skin to sell and I'm going round town with this crow, that knows how to tell fortunes.'

'But does this crow know anything?'

'He knows all the affairs of your household,' said the boy. 'He knows the past, the present, and the future.'

'Well, come in, and let's hear what he says.'

So they sat down on comfortable chairs, and the master of the house said: 'Tell my fortune.'

'This crow only speaks when you give him a sovereign.'

The gentleman gave him a sovereign, and the boy hit the crow on the head. 'Ngek,' went the bird.

'What does he say?'

'He says there's a roast chicken, some bread, and some other things in that chest over there.'

'What? We don't keep food in here. We have a kitchen.'

'That's what the crow says. Maybe he's lying, but I don't think so.'

Then the gentleman got up, and when he looked in the chest, there was the roast chicken, the roast meat, and the bread. He put them on the table, and the two ate together.

'All right,' said the gentleman again. 'Tell me something else.'

'He wants another sovereign.'

The man handed over another coin, and the boy said: 'In that cupboard over there, there's some brandy and tobacco.'

'That can't be,' said the master of the house. 'I only keep brandy in my tavern in town.'

'That's what the crow says, and I don't think he's lying.'

The master of the house went to look, found the brandy and tobacco, put them on the table, and the two drank together.

'All right, all right. Tell me something else.'

He handed over another sovereign. But the boy didn't hit the crow very hard, and the bird made no sound.

'What does he say?' asked the gentleman.

'One sovereign's not enough.'

The man put another sovereign on the table, but the boy still didn't hit the crow hard enough, and not a sound came.

'It must be something very important.'

The gentleman began to worry. He forked out still more sovereigns – one, two, three. . . . At the tenth, the boy decided to call a halt, and hit the crow. 'Ngek,' went the bird.

'What does he say?'

'He says there's a man in that wardrobe.'

The gentleman got up and opened the wardrobe, and found his wife's lover standing there.

'Who on earth are you?'

The man in the wardrobe simply shrugged his shoulders sheepishly and the master of the house shut the door on him, leaving him still inside.

'Sell me that crow,' he said to the boy in great consternation. 'I work alone down in my tavern, and I want that bird to tell me what's going on in my house. It seems to know everything.'

The boy wanted to sell the crow, but saw it was still dark. So he hesitated, and bargained until morning, and in the end asked for fifty sovereigns.

The gentleman thought this was a gift,

and handed over the money. So the boy left the house, threw the hide to the street dogs, and set off home. When he was near his village, the neighbours saw him.

'Did you sell the hide, then?'

'I certainly did,' said the boy, 'As soon as I arrived in town! And what a crush! I sold it for sixty sovereigns, and could have made more! But I thought they were joking when I asked them how much they'd give, but they said sixty, so I accepted the first offer. Some merchants have come from the coast, and they're looking all over for cowhides. If you get there quickly, you can ask up to two hundred!'

So the villagers upped and killed all their cows and oxen and collected great piles of hides and tons of meat. They loaded up the hides on carts and set off for town. When they arrived, nobody would give a penny for their skins.

'Why in heaven's name have you brought all these hides?' asked the townspeople.

'A boy from our village told us there were merchants from the coast looking for hides. He sold his for sixty sovereigns.'

'That was a lie.'

The villagers were furious, and swore they would kill the boy when they got home again.

But by chance, that night the boy said to his mother: 'Mother, I can't sleep very well in this bed over here. Let's change beds, just for one night.'

His mother agreed. In the middle of the night, the neighbours burst in with axes and attacked the old woman, leaving her dead. Shortly before dawn, the boy got up and placed his mother on the back of a donkey, took a basket of eggs, and set off again for town.

When he arrived in the city he took his mother's body and propped it up against a wall; he placed the basket of eggs beside her, and stretched out her hand, as if she were selling. He withdrew to the other side of the street and waited, watching. It was not long before a rich man came along and asked the old woman: 'How much are the eggs?'

The woman, of course, did not reply.

The rich man asked once again and, thinking the old woman was asleep, reached out and shook her, as if to wake her up. When he touched her, the body fell sideways, and the boy leapt from his hiding place: 'Aah! You've killed my mother!'

'Don't shout like that,' said the rich man. 'You'll bring everybody running!'

'Don't shout? I'll fetch the town guard and tell them you've killed my mother!'

'Wait!' said the rich man. 'I'll give you anything you want. Just don't tell anyone!'

'Only if you give me a hundred sovereigns and help me to bury the old lady.'

'Here you are,' said the rich man. 'Just leave me in peace.'

So he handed over a hundred sovereigns and they took the body to the mosque and buried it, the rich man paying the fee. The boy mounted his donkey and set off for his village. When he arrived home, the neighbours saw him, and said: 'What? Still alive?'

'I certainly am, and in fact you've all done me a good turn. You killed my mother, and I took the body to town. There were some merchants there from the coast, who asked me what I had on my donkey. I said "An old woman, a corpse," and they asked, "How much do you want for it?" I thought they were joking, so I said, "A hundred sovereigns," and at once they forked out the money. They took the body, loaded it on a cart, and set off, and told me to tell people I met that if anybody had any old people's corpses, they should bring them to town and ask anything they wanted for them. And believe me, I could have got three hundred for mine.'

So the villagers upped and got out their axes and set about killing all their old folk. They gathered the corpses, loaded them onto a cart, and took them to town.

At the entrance to the city, however, the town guard stopped them, and asked: 'What's going on with all these corpses? What's happened?'

'A boy told us that merchants from abroad have been looking for corpses. He sold his own mother for a hundred sovereigns.'

'And did you kill all these people?'

'Yes, we did.'

So the guardsmen leapt onto the villagers and put most of them in prison. But a few escaped and ran home. And when they found the boy who had cheated them they jumped upon him and tied him in a sack.

Now near the village there was a deep pothole. The villagers argued among themselves, and at last decided to throw him in this cave, and to let him die a horrible death. So two young men took hold of the sack, carried it to the pothole, and threw it in. But the sack stuck half way down, and wouldn't fall any further.

'We'll have to push it down,' said the two young men. 'Let's go and fetch a plank and give it a shove.'

And off they went. Meanwhile the boy in the sack began to sing a popular song of the mountains. A goatherd nearby heard him, and asked: 'What's all that noise for?'

'I'm singing.'

'Why?'

'In the village they told me I have to get married tonight, and I don't want to. "Get married, or else!" they said, and I said, "No!" And so they put me in this sack and left me here for an hour to think about it. "Think hard," they said. "If you want to get married we'll take you back home, and if you don't, we'll push you down the hole." But I still don't want to get married. And now they're going to kill me.'

'I'd really like very much to get married,' said the goatherd. 'Can I take your place?'

'If that's what you want, untie the sack,' said the boy.

At once the goatherd set to work on the knot. The boy climbed out, and the goatherd took his place. The sack was tied up again, and the boy took the herdsman's cape and staff and climbed up the mountain, whistling as he went.

When the two villagers came back they simply gave the sack a push without asking any questions, and down it went into the depths of the earth, goatherd and all. Then at dusk the boy reappeared in the village, cape over his shoulders, staff in hand, whistling cheerfully, and leading a great herd of a hundred goats. The villagers watched in bewilderment.

'You back again? Didn't we throw you down that pothole?'

'You did, and what a good turn it was. At the bottom there was an old fellow, two parts beard and one part man, who caught me in his arms and took me out of the sack and gave me something to eat. He had about two or three thousand goats. He asked me if I wanted to go back up, and I replied that I did; and then he asked me how many goats I wanted to take. I said, "Twenty," but he said, "No, no, take some more" and he forced me to accept a hundred. I didn't want to take them, but he was trying to make me take about a thousand. Goats down there grow like weeds up here.'

'So there must be some left,' said the villagers.

'What else do you think? Anybody who gets there early can bring back at least five hundred.'

So down they went, young and old, into the pothole. Only the women were left at home.

They did everything they could to get rid of that boy, but in the end he won. And he became a rich man, with plenty of land, and livestock, and all the good things of life.

Told by Ramadan Gjoka, from the village of Tërstenik.

THE TAILOR'S DUMMY

More a poet than writer of fiction, Vlada Uroševič was born in Skopje in 1934 and led a group of writers who discarded local and national themes for a greater involvement in the mainstream of European literature. This is one of his few short stories.

At midday the writer carried the dummy across the square. It was an ordinary tailor's dummy with a wooden base and no head. The beggars and town loafers abandoned their places in the shade and stared after him for a long time.

The writer had a hard time getting the dummy upstairs. 'Who're you carrying that thing for?' asked his neighbour, passing on his way out to the market. 'Nobody,' the writer panted, dragging the dummy along as one supports an unconscious man, holding it around the waist. The staircase was narrow, and the climbing became more and more difficult; the base of the dummy kept bumping against the bannisters. Finally the writer reached the door of his garret flat. He leaned the dummy against the wall and took the key from under the doormat.

'It's shameful,' said Lilla when she came to visit him that afternoon. 'Who said you could use my dresses like that?' The writer was standing in the middle of the room, surveying his work with satisfaction. The dummy was dressed in various odds and ends Lilla had left behind in his flat one day at the end of spring after she brought them back from the dry cleaner's. On the stump of the neck the dummy now had a plaster cast of the head of Aphrodite. Adorning the head was a large, black straw hat.

The writer was highly satisfied with what he had done. The head had been set slightly askew so the hat partly obscured the face, and the dummy looked out from under the brim as though it were trying to win affection. Lilla shrugged, made a grimace of disgust, and turned away. 'You might use your time more intelligently,' she said. 'You haven't written a thing for ages. Instead of writing you just act the fool.'

' "Go and find me if you can," ' the writer began reciting sadly, ' "a word as simple as a stone. . . ." '

Lilla was becoming impatient. 'I don't understand you,' she said. 'I don't understand this joke of yours with the tailor's dummy. I hope you aren't sleeping with it!'

'I need to be constantly surrounded by the characters I'm writing about,' he explained. 'I must live with my heroes. I'm writing a story, you know, about a man who falls in love with a tailor's dummy.'

'Charming,' said Lilla. She decided to take away the pieces of clothing that were hanging on the tailor's dummy, but in the end she changed her mind. Outside, the city was choking in orange-coloured dust, in the stench from the rubbish bins and the heavy smell from the shrunken river. She crossed to the door and went out onto the balcony. Down below, in the back yard, on the stark white concrete, some half-naked boys were sitting and cracking apricot pips. The other part of town, across the river, was the yellowish colour of faded postcards.

A tiny figure was walking along the street waving its arms and looking up. 'Here comes the painter,' said Lilla. 'We can't hide from him; he's seen me. Now he'll stay till midnight.'

The painter was delighted with the dummy. 'It's superb!' he shouted, gesticulating extravagantly. 'It reminds me of my student days. When I was at the Academy we never had any money for models, so we had to paint tailor's dummies. There are some dummies!'

The painter stayed a long time. The stars were hardly visible in the summer sky; they were smothered by the exhalations of the city, the moisture hanging in the air, the smoke. 'That's the constellation of Sagittarius,' mumbled the painter, pointing vaguely somewhere above the tops of the skyscrapers.

Then the three of them went out together. The painter was in raptures over the dummy and promised to paint it. He was sweating. The city was trapped beneath the stifling heat, and the baked air that had been sealed into the walls all day was only now escaping through the bricks. The people walked with difficulty along the streets; there was a sickly gleam in their eyes, and they were jumpy and irritable.

The following day, when Lilla went to visit the writer, she met his landlady on the staircase. 'I've had just about as much as I can take of all this!' shouted the landlady, flushed and panting. 'As much as I can take. First it's a girl, and now it's some kind of ghost and a tailor's dummy!' The landlady turned around as Lilla squeezed past her. 'Find somebody else!' she shouted. 'That man of yours is undressing a freak up there, an antique freak!'

'What's going on?' asked Lilla as she walked into the room.

The writer smiled bitterly. 'It's all so stupid,' he said. 'First thing this morning, in came the man to collect for the electricity. I was on the balcony. Suddenly he screamed and ran down the stairs. A little later the landlady suddenly appeared. I was just setting up the dummy when she came in.' The dummy was wearing a theatrical wig. The long red hair tumbled down in waves over its shoulders.

'How's the story getting on?' asked Lilla.

'I'm still mulling it over,' said the writer. 'It'll be an excellent story. D'you feel like going out?'

As they were saying goodbye, the writer asked Lilla for her sunglasses.

The following day Lilla found the dummy wearing her sunglasses. The dark glasses made a strong contrast with the white plaster head; it seemed as though from behind them the dummy was keeping an eye on everything that happened in the room. 'You're crazy,' said Lilla. 'I won't allow you to use my sunglasses like this.'

The writer tried to calm her. 'That's you,' he said, pointing to the dummy. 'When I'm writing about the dummy, I think about you. It's your twin.'

'Don't you mix me up in all this,' said Lilla. 'I don't want to be replaced by anybody – no matter who. I hope you don't take it to bed with you!'

'Don't be such a little goose,' smiled the writer. 'It's only a dummy.'

'You're beginning to frighten me,' said Lilla. 'I don't understand you any more.'

' "Go and find me if you can," ' the writer began reciting, ' "a word as simple as a stone. . . ." '

'All the same,' said Lilla, 'I don't like this game of yours with the dummy.'

'The story'll soon be ready,' said the writer soothingly. 'It'll be a splendid story. A young man who falls in love with a tailor's dummy. You'll see what a sensation it will be.'

'Are we going out tonight?' asked Lilla. 'There's a good Greek film showing at the open-air cinema.'

'All right,' said the writer. 'I just have a little more to add.' He stuck some cheap, shiny buckles into the dummy's hair, stepped back a few paces, and surveyed it with satisfaction. Then he jotted down something in his notebook. 'It gets more and more beautiful, don't you think?' he asked. Lilla was silent. She made a point of facing the other way.

In front of the open-air cinema they met the painter. He was eating peanuts. 'How's the story getting on?' he asked at once.

'Splendidly,' said the writer. 'I've worked out a new ending. It'll be a kind of absolute story.'

'Let's hurry,' said Lilla. 'It looks as if the tickets are nearly all sold.'

The writer said he was going to work for the following few days. Lilla did not come to visit him. Only when she finally got bored of going to the cinema alone did she climb up to his garret flat one evening. The dummy was standing in the middle of the room. The writer was lying on his bed. The light was not switched on.

'It's terribly stuffy in here,' said Lilla. 'You never air the place. Have you been out at all?'

'I've been busy writing,' he answered. 'The story's almost finished.'

Lilla made a wide detour around the dummy, stopped by the bed, and sat down. 'Now that the story's almost finished, will you clear that dummy out of here?' One could detect in her voice a scarcely concealed note of hatred toward that wooden figure dressed in her clothes.

'Don't be impatient,' said the writer. 'The dummy should be allowed to stay for a while. The young man in the story is very much in love with it.' The half darkness that filled the room was thick and sticky. There was a smell of unwashed clothes, of sweat. The fetid air hung in the limp rags.

'Are we going to go anywhere?' asked Lilla.

'Not this evening,' said the writer.

'Tomorrow?' asked Lilla.

'Yes, tomorrow,' said the writer with a sigh. 'I still have something left to write this evening.'

'All right,' said Lilla, rising. 'Wait for me tomorrow in the café on the quay.'

The first person Lilla met the next day was the painter. He told her he had seen the writer in the café on the quay. 'What happened to the dummy?' the painter shouted after her when they had already said goodbye.

'Nothing,' said Lilla. 'But something's going to happen soon.'

She climbed up the staircase, afraid that the landlady might spot her. She found the key under the doormat and opened the door. The dummy was standing in the middle of the room. Lilla walked up to it, slowly and cautiously, as though she were approaching a living being. She was overwhelmed with a sense of disgust and tore the wig from the plaster head. The bald plaster crown shimmered in the moonlight.

She quickly undressed the dummy. The brooches and buckles tumbled to the floor, where they cracked and shattered under her feet. Her hands trembled as she burnt the wig and the pieces of clothing in a small stove full of old papers. The room smelt of smoke.

She took the plaster head, opened the balcony door and leaned over the rail. The white blob of the head described a neat arc in the twilight; then there was a light explosion as the plaster shattered on the concrete paving of the yard. The cats fled from the rubbish bins, meowing with fright.

Lilla then threw the dummy itself from the balcony. The wood clattered loudly on the ground. A light was turned on outside, somewhere in the yard. An elderly voice could be heard shouting: 'Have you gone mad? I'm going to call the police!' Lilla quickly left the room, closed the door, and ran downstairs.

Excited voices could be heard in the yard. Doors were being opened. She thought she glimpsed several people gathering. She ran out into the street and kept running until she reached the corner. Then she walked slowly.

She had already recovered her calm by the time she came to the quay. She had seen the writer from a distance; he was sitting in front of the café, drinking beer.

'Hot, isn't it?' she said as she sat down.

'Terrible,' said the writer. 'Do you want a beer?'

'If it's cold,' said Lilla. 'I'm terribly thirsty.'

'I've finished the story, you know,' said the writer. 'It's ready at last. I wrote the end yesterday. D'you know how it finishes?'

Lilla drank her beer and simply raised her eyebrows curiously.

'The girl who loves him,' said the writer, 'goes to his place when he isn't there and destroys the dummy.'

Lilla lowered her unfinished glass.

'It's a strange story,' the writer went on. 'A kind of absolute story. This young man who falls in love with the dummy is writing a story. The story is about how a young man, who is in love with a dummy, writes a story. And he writes the story.' The expression on Lilla's face was cold. Under the neon light her face had a lifeless sheen as though it were made of plaster.

'Hurry up,' said the writer. 'Drink your beer. I want to go back to my place and read you the story.'

Lilla managed to speak only when they reached the staircase. 'What happens at the end of the story?' she asked.

'Oh,' said the writer as he unlocked the door, 'when the writer sees that she's destroyed his dummy, he strangles the girl. Funny, isn't it?'

Reprinted from *The Big Horse and Other Stories of Modern Macedonia*, edited with an Introduction by Milne Holton. By permission of the University of Missouri Press. © 1974 Curators of the University of Missouri.

ONWARDS FROM YUGOSLAVIA

Few countries border so many, and such a disparate mixture of countries as Yugoslavia. North and west are **ITALY** and AUSTRIA – the most obvious targets en route to Britain. **Venice** is just a short hop across the border from Ljubljana, and is the first of a rich chain of historic towns that arc across the north of the country towards Milan – **Padua**, **Vicenza**, **Verona** and **Mantua** all merit a stop. Further south, frequent ferries to **Ancona** offer a way into Tuscany; ferries to **Pescara** land you in the Abruzzi and not far from **Rome**; and those to **Bari** open up **Naples, Sicily** and the whole of the Italian south. The forthcoming *Rough Guide* covers the whole country. You may not want to linger in **AUSTRIA**, at present Europe's most expensive country, but it's worth at least considering stopping to sample the imperial elegance of **Vienna** and the medieval centre of **Graz**, just 50km across the border from Maribor; **Salzburg,** much touted and exceptionally beautiful, is also correspondingly pricey, and normally packed to bursting with tourists.

Cheaper – and for most Western visitors something of an unknown quantity – are the 'Eastern bloc' countries that ring Yugoslavia's north and eastern borders. **HUNGARY** is most accessible, the most liberal and most frequently visited, with its capital **Budapest** a cheap, convivial and cosmopolitan city you'd be silly to miss if you're in the north with time on your hands. Nationwide, the IBUSZ (tourist organisation) sort out rooms for around £3 a head and there are plenty of student hostels and a good range of campsites. You'll need to get a visa before you set off; these cost around £5, are valid for 30 days and are quickly and easily obtained from Hungarian consulates. **ROMANIA** veers from the craggy beauty of the Transylvanian Alps to relatively unexploited resorts on the Black Sea. Its capital, **Bucharest**, is connected by daily train from Belgrade – a 14–hour trip that must rank as one of Europe's slowest and most dismal train journeys. It's an interesting place, less bleak than its usual image (though the security police here are notoriously oppressive) but travelling cheap you'll find two inevitable problems. First you'll have to change a set amount of money each day. Second, Romania sports few bottom-rung hotels, private rooms are illegal and student hostels, where they exist, tend to be full to the gills throughout the summer months. Only getting in is easy – a three-month visa is available at frontier-crossings for a flat £10. More welcoming, and certainly worth a stopover if you're making for Istanbul, or (circuitously) northern Greece, is **BULGARIA**, and **Sofia** in particular – an attractive city, well loaded with the relics of Ottoman occupation, and linked to Belgrade by a twice-daily train. Forty-hour transit visas are issued on the spot at Bulgarian consulates for around £7; full entry permits can take anything up to a week to get and cost £10. For detailed accounts of all three countries see the *Rough Guide to Eastern Europe*, planned for 1986.

The unbending isolation of Enver Hoxha's regime in **ALBANIA** has produced what is by far the least visited nation in Europe. In fact it's impossible to visit individually, you can't get in at all if you're American and independent travel on from Yugoslavia is out of the question. Trips have to be organised in advance: in Britain with *Regent Tours* (13, Small Street, Bristol; tel. 211711), sole Albanian agents, who'll put you on a group visa. If you decide to go, remember that you can't get in if you have long hair or a shaggy beard, nor if you're carrying a copy of the Bible or Koran. You'll also be required to walk through a puddle of disinfectant as you walk across the frontier. Once there your tour will most likely take in the ex-Turkish outpost of **Shköder**, the Adriatic port-resort of **Durrës** and the capital **Tirana**, by all accounts the dullest of cities.

By far the largest proportion of people who visit Yugoslavia go on to **GREECE**. The main Jadrolinija ferry sails down as far as **Corfu** and **Igoumenitsa** (around 3 times weekly in summer) and trains run the tortuously slow haul from Belgrade to Thessaloniki and Athens 3 times daily; if you're in Macedonia a daily connection from Bitola to Florina makes short strides over the border quite feasible. **Thessaloniki** is Greece's livelier and less polluted second city and a good springboard for the various delights of northern

Greece: the islands of **Thasos** and **Samothraki**, the **Athos** peninsula and the monasteries of **the Meteora**; plus it's another viable journey-break before Turkey. From **Athens** ferries will transport you to just about any **Aegean Island** you care to mention. Whatever you plan, the revised edition of the *Rough Guide to Greece* seems an obvious investment.

LANGUAGE

Yugoslavia is harlequined with languages – Hungarian, Greek and Albanian all get a look-in – but the country's official language is **Serbo-Croat**, an amalgam of Serbian and Croatian dialects of a Slav tongue akin to Russian. Unless you're here for some time you're not going to make any great inroads into it; better to brush up instead what German, Italian and French you can muster, in roughly that order. German is widely spoken in the north and by returned *gastarbeiten* everywhere, Italian is universally understood along the coast, French was taught in schools in the 1950s: fish around and you should find a *lingua franca*. Outside the main tourist centres English is fitfully spoken, and what Serbo-Croat you pick up in one place won't necessarily help you out in the next – Slovenia and Macedonia both have their own languages, and though nearly everyone understands Serbo-Croat, regional pride dictates that the local alternative gets priority. But sally forth with the words and phrases listed below: even the barest knowledge makes for easier, and more rewarding, travelling. You'll find a detailed food glossary on p. 12, and to continue your studies *Teach Yourself Serbo-Croat* (Hodder & Stoughton £1.50) is a cheap if rather dated aid. *Colloquial Serbo-Croat* is forthcoming from RKP in 1986. Best of the phrase books available is *Travellers' Serbo-Croat for Yugoslavia* (Pan £1.25).

The Cyrillic alphabet – and pronunciation

Used more or less everywhere outside Croatia and Slovenia, the **Cyrillic alphabet** is easily learned despite its appearance. Get to know it as soon as possible, if only to read the signs on buses and train schedules.

А	а	a	as in farm
Б	б	b	as in but
Ц	ц	c	like the 'ts' in cats
Ч	ч	č	as in check
Ћ	ћ	ć	a little harder than the 't' in picture
Д	д	d	as Dylan
Џ	џ	dž	as in the 'j' of jaundice
Ђ	ђ	Đ, đ or Dj, dj	a softer dž; like the 'd' in verdure
Е	е	e	as in bed
Ф	ф	f	as in food
Г	г	g	as in got
Х	х	h	as in hat; or, before a consonant, like a softer 'ch' in the Scottish loch
И	и	i	like the 'ea' sound in pea
Ј	ј	j	'y' as in youth
К	к	k	as in kiss
Л	л	l	as in lost
Љ	љ	lj	like the 'lli' in colliery
М	м	m	as in map
Н	н	n	as in nut
Њ	њ	nj	like the 'ni' in opinion
О	о	o	always short, as in hot
П	п	p	as in pin
Р	р	r	as in rip, but sometimes rolled
С	с	c	like the 's' in super
Ш	ш	š	the 'sh' sound in shoot
Т	т	t	similar to the English 't'
У	у	u	as in the 'oo' in boot
В	в	v	'v' as in vat
З	з	z	'z' as in zip
Ж	ж	ž	like the 's' in pleasure

Each letter is pronounced, never silent – *kniga* (book) is pronounced *ker-nee-ga*.
Vowels are similarly sounded separately: e.g. *trinaest* (thirteen) – *tree-na-est*. The
combination **aj** is pronounced like the end of the English sigh; **ej** like the end of say;
oj like toy; **nj** like the ni in onion. **Stress** is important: a slight misplacing of the accent
renders the word unintelligible. We've marked the stress accent but remember two
rules: the last syllable of a word is never stressed – so in words of two syllables the
stress always falls on the first, eg, Zágreb.

Basics

Do you speak English/German/Italian/French?	Góvorite li éngleski/némački/italíjanski/fránsuski?
yes	da
no	ne
I don't understand	ne razúmem
I understand	razúmem
OK	u redu
please	molim (prosim in Slovenia)
thank you	hvala
two beers please	dva piva molim
hello	zdrávo
goodbye	zdrávo
or, more formally,	zbógom
good morning	dobro jutro
good afternoon/day	dobar dan
good evening	dobro veče
good night	laku noć (this is said only when leaving)
today	danas
yesterday	juče
tomorrow	sutra
day after tomorrow	prekósutra
in the morning	u jutro
in the afternoon	posle podne
in the evening	u veče

Questions

To ask for something in Serbo-Croat, use the third person singular of the verb to
have – *ima*. Eg 'Do you have any fish?' – '*Ima riba?*'; 'Is there a train to Belgrade?'
– '*Ima voz za Béograd?*' This construction stays the same whether the subject is
singular or plural. The answer you'll get will either be *ima* (yes) or *nema* (no), perhaps
the most irritating little word in the language.

I want	Želim
I want to go	Želim da idem
It's too expensive	to je préskupo
anything cheaper?	nešto jeftínije?
cheap	jéftino
expensive	skupo
I'm not paying for this	ne plačam za ovo
I want a room for one/two/three/four	Želim sobu za jedan/dvar/tri/četiri
where	gde
how	kako
when	Kad
why	žasto
good	dobro
bad	loš
here	ovde
there	tamo

Directions

Where is . . . ?	Gde je . . . ?
How far is it (to) . . . ?	Kolíko daléko (do) . . . ?

Where can I get a bus to . . . ?	Gde mogu da uzmem aútobus za . . . ?
bus/train/car/taxi/ferry/foot	aútobus/vos, vlak or treno/kola/trajekt pešice
How do I get to . . . ?	Kako mogu da dodgem do . . . ?
left	levo
right	desno
straight on	pravo
Is it near/far?	To je blizu/dalek
ticket	karta
bus stop/station	aútobus stánica
Is going to Belgrade?	Ide za Béograd?
I'm lost	Ja sam se izgubio

Some signs

Entrance	ulaz
exit	izlaz
toilet	toalét
men	muški
women	ženski
hot	vruče
cold	hladno
open	otvoréno
closed	zatvoréno
arrival	dólazak
departure	pólazak
police	mílicija
hospital	bólnica
no smoking	zabranjéno pušsenje
no entry	zabránjen ulaz

Numbers and dates

1	jedan	11	jedánaest	21	dvádeset jedan	155	sto petdéset pet
2	dva	12	dvánaest	30	trídeset	200	dve stótine
3	tri	13	trinaest	40	četrdéset	300	tri stótine
4	čétiri	14	četŕnaest	50	petdéset	400	čétiri stótine
5	pet	15	pétnaest	60	šezdéset	500	pet stótina
6	šest	16	šésnaest	70	sedamdéset	600	šest stótina
7	sedam	17	sedámnaest	80	osamdéset	700	sedam stótina
8	osam	18	osámnaest	90	devedéset	800	osam stótina
9	devet	19	devétnaest	100	sto	900	devet stótina
10	deset	20	dvádeset	101	sto jedan	1000	(jedan) hiljáda

In spoken Serbo-Croat the final deset or stotina is often dropped in simple numbers: eg 700 dinars becomes sedam dinar.

Sunday	nédelja
Monday	ponédeljak
Tuesday	útorak
Wednesday	sreda
Thursday	cetvŕtak
Friday	petak
Saturday	súbota

Days aren't capitalised.

INDEX

HELP US UPDATE

We've done our best to ensure that this, the first edition of **The Rough Guide to Yugoslavia,** is thoroughly up to date and accurate. However, things do change, and if you feel we've missed something out, got something wrong, or that more should be said about a particular place, do let us know. We'll be revising the book before long and would find it useful to hear from other travellers. For the best letters we'll send a copy of the new edition, or any other Rough Guide you prefer. Write to us at Rough Guides, RKP, 21 Ravensdon St, SE11 4AQ.

YUGOSLAVIA

With